D1090670

Role and Impact:

The Chicago Society of Artists

Louise Dunn Yochim

 ISBN No. 0-9602532-0-3

Book design by Jan Yourist with the photographic, research and general assistance of Barbara Lazarus Metz.

Cover design based on earliest known logo of the Chicago Society of Artists.

This book is partially supported by a grant from the Illinois Arts Council, a state agency.

DEDICATION

This volume is dedicated to all those artists, former and present members, through whose pioneering, resolute and professional efforts, the Chicago Society of Artists has nurtured and sustained its reputation as a highly esteemed and vital cultural group.

Acknowledgements

I am deeply indebted to:

Harold Haydon, Adjunct Professor of Fine Arts, Indiana University, Northwest; Professor Emeritus of Art, University of Chicago; Art Critic of the Chicago Sun-Times; author, painter, designer, for his notable contribution as member and past president of the Chicago Society of Artists and for his perceptive Foreword to this volume;

Clara MacGowan Cioban, Professor Emeritus of Art, Northwestern University, author, painter, printmaker, for her significant contribution as member and past president of the Chicago Society of Artists, and particularly for the guidance and wisdom reflected in her frequent letters to the Society, some of which are included in this volume;

The Board of Directors of the Chicago Society of Artists, Inc., and particularly to Frances Badger, Rowena Fry, Paula Gerard, Samuel Greenburg, Lucile Leighton, Evelyn Lewy and Elvie TenHoor for their assistance in recalling events, experiences and information of anecdotal nature relevant to the history of the Chicago Society of Artists;

Lillian Hall, painter, printmaker, treasurer of the Chicago Society of Artists for many years, whose meticulous record of membership dating back to 1940 was of inestimable value;

Maurice Yochim, Professor Emeritus of Art, Northeastern Illinois University, author, painter and sculptor, for his assistance in compiling the membership roster dating back to 1887.

Nelly Deachman Kerr, painter, teacher, commercial artist, past president of the All Illinois Society, lecturer on art, for her generous offer of research material concerning art in Illinois at the turn of the century;

Samuel Greenburg, painter, author, art consultant, Emeritus, Chicago Public Schools, for his keen critical and professional analysis of the content;

Markus Ziegler, linguist, for a judicious and incisive review of the volume and a layman's reaction to its content;

Annette Okner, Beatrice Schiller, Jan Yourist, painters and printmakers, for their dedicated service to the Society and yeoman efforts to raise funds for this publication;

Art Institute of Chicago for permission to use reproductions of paintings and sculpture done by members of the Chicago Society of Artists in the early thirties and forties, and exhibited in International, National, Regional and Chicago and Vicinity shows;

Towsley Secretarial Service for typing and Marion J. Idzik for photography;

Illinois Arts Council, Guarantors and Patrons, whose financial aid assured the realization of this publication.

Guarantors

Anonymous (2)

Patrons

Anonymous (4)
American Jewish Art Club
Artists Equity
Bettie Becker
Mr. and Mrs. C. Buhman
Gerri Butler
Janine Collier Charlton
Clara MacGowan Cioban
C. E. Cooper
Richard N. and Ida Padva Conte
Sadie Dreikurs
Margaret Driscoll
Dr. and Mrs. Jack Dunn
Dr. and Mrs. Maurice Dunn
Diane Duvigneaud
Barbara Fagan
Mr. and Mrs. Leonard Feinberg
Rowena Fry
Mr. and Mrs. Mark Gilbert
Garnet Gullborg
Marjorie Hartmann
Mr. and Mrs. Harold Haydon
Mr. and Mrs. Alvin Horwitz
Portia Karlsberg
Camille Andrene Kauffman
Mr. and Mrs. Norman Kleinbort
Stanley P. Kuta
Lucile Leighton
Evelyn B. Lewy
Professor Ely and Phoebe Liebow
Frances Hildes Loeb
Alice Mason
Mrs. Robert B. Mayer
Everett N. McDonnell Foundation
Frances McVey
Harry Mintz
Dr. Henry and Annette Okner
Dr. David and Iola Rappaport
Dr. Fred and Thilda Rappaport
Beatrice B. Schiller
Grace Spongberg
Jane W. Steiner
Elvie TenHoor
Marjorie M. TenHoor
Alex and Rachel Topp
Lionel Wathall
Carl and Aloise A. Zehner
Markus Ziegler

Foreword

It is characteristic of artists to band together, more often to promote a cause or to put up an exhibition than to defend themselves. It is equally characteristic for such associations of artists to disband quickly, once the immediate occasion is over. Given the basic qualities of creative artists—independence, devotion to their art, disdain for following the leader—artists tend to go it alone, even when that is contrary to their best interests.

All the more remarkable, therefore, is the long and uninterrupted life of the Chicago Society of Artists. As its history reveals, it has persisted through many changes of the cultural climate, and quite literally through generations of artists.

The Society has kept free of official associations, property ownership, and other embellishments of the establishment that harden the arteries of organizations, to hasten their demise as vital centers of creative endeavor. While other long-lived artist groups have crystallized into self-perpetuating dispensers of honors, and propertied academic institutions, the Chicago Society of Artists has maintained its identity in the realm of the spirit, more like a state of mind than an association for practical purposes.

Apart from exhibitions, its most tangible expression for many years has been the annual CSA calendar, yet even this eminently practical fund-raiser is a creative act, calling forth a new crop of block prints every year. It is typical of the Society's integrity that it refuses to let the calendar run beyond the edition that can be printed from the original blocks, despite the clear evidence that more could be sold with greater profit by mechanical reproduction.

Like any vital social organization, the Chicago Society of Artists changes with its membership. While it is different for each generation of artists, it owes its well-being for so many years to several constants. The loyalty it engenders probably is the most important constant element. Members stay members for a lifetime, contributing inestimably to the continuity of standards of excellence. Membership, and service to the Society are their own rewards, not dependent on personal gain.

Next come two interrelated constants. The members of the Society set their own standards for membership by jurying the works of applicants, and have regularly admitted young artists to membership, thereby assuring new blood and a contemporary spirit in the Society. While some other organizations have let partisan interests narrow their membership, or have set external qualifications, such as gallery representation and exhibition records, as criteria for admitting members, the Chicago Society of Artists has had confidence in the fairness and wisdom of members entrusted with administering the membership procedures.

Anyone who has participated in meetings to jury the work of prospective members must be impressed by the genuine interest and concern of CSA members as they pass judgment on their younger peers. Their concern is for fairness and openmindedness in deciding for and against candidates, and concern for the integrity and strength of the Society.

That sense of dedication to an organization, and even more to the profession of art, has sustained elected officers and volunteer workers through the years as they selflessly contribute to the ongoing life of the Society. In that spirit, Louise Dunn Yochim undertook the difficult and time-consuming task of compiling this history of the Chicago Society of Artists.

The importance of the arts in the life of the mind and spirit cannot be over-estimated. While this History serves its immediate purpose, and marks an historical moment, it has a broader significance as it weaves a part of the fabric of American art.

Harold Haydon

CSA Editorial Board

Preface

This book is designed primarily to chronicle the artistic achievements of the Chicago Society of Artists, documenting ninety-two years of its existence and professional performance, and to identify its aesthetic contribution to the cultural life of Chicago and the nation.

The content deals chiefly with factual data of historical consequence. It unfolds methodically but briefly the social, political, scientific and cultural events, as well as aesthetic movements which profoundly affected the artistic performanace of painters, sculptors, craftsmen-designers, authors, art critics, and art educators—former or current members of the Chicago Society of Artists.

Each artist's biographical data, credo, philosophical comments, anecdotal notes, sources of inspiration, influences related to his or her life and style of expression, are here given due recognition. Examples are reproduced to illustrate graphically each artist's approach to, and technique in his or her creative products. A roster of the Society's membership since 1887 is also included.

It is hoped that the reader will find the content of this manuscript a source of reading pleasure; but more important, a source of pertinent reference to the aesthetic heritage of American artists in general, from 1887 to date, and to the role that the Chicago Society of Artists in particular, has played in enriching this heritage for future generations.

Introduction

To fully appreciate the nature of art in any given period, or the creative vitality of a given group of artists, whether in the United States or abroad, it is desirable to examine a number of underlying factors, i.e., external forces, influences and movements which have been all-pervasive in the world of art, and which inspired or conditioned the aesthetic development of artists throughout each epoch in the history of mankind.

That is not to say that one needs to write a voluminous history of art for this purpose. A need exists, however, to formulate, in brief, a frame of reference, in which may be discerned a general pattern of influential elements, rooted in historical sources, and in an extraordinary repertory of modes, and tastes in art. More than that, the essence and character of the imaginative process must be examined in the light of other areas of creative endeavor. Indeed, in order to gain greater insight into, and fairly assess creative products, the creative process must be viewed against a background of the knowledge and thought of each successive period in history.

By focusing attention upon the historic circumstances of the times, i.e., the social, political, scientific and cultural influences, as well as the multifaceted art movements which profoundly affect the creative members of a society, while concomitantly shaping and cultivating their talents—it may then be possible to become cognizant of the process through which an artistic heritage has been forged. Thus may also be established a sense of continuity and relatedness to contemporary artistic trends. Insights gained from an analysis of pervasive influences have far-reaching implications. Implications, not only for each artist in the group, but also for groups of artists, pin-pointing the contribution that the latter have made collectively to the enrichment of the total cultural milieu within a given period of time.

In this context, then, and in the course of a limited span of time, from 1887 to date, it is the writer's aim to inscribe the achievements of the Chicago Society of Artists. For, when one reflects upon the fact that our nation is only two-hundred years old, and that the Chicago Society of Artists is ninety-two, it becomes essentially clear that this organization of professional artists is eligible to receive recognition for its contribution to the aesthetic growth of Chicago and the nation.

Some may reason that the existence of an organization for more than nine decades does not necessarily warrant exceptional treatment, other than perhaps for its endurance. Nonetheless, when numerous art volumes, museum and gallery catalogues are researched, it becomes convincingly evident that the works of an incredible number of Chicago Society of Artists' members were an integral part of most major regional, national and international art events. Moreover, a goodly number of these members also received highly-coveted awards, and other merited recognition for their artistic skills.

L. D. Y.

Contents

Role and Impact:
The Chicago Society of Artists

LILLIAN HALL and MILDRED WALTRIP (on ladder) working on a W.P.A. mural.

SECTION I

Cultural Changes Affecting America and American Art

Many trends and art movements have emerged abroad and in America since the Chicago Society of Artists came into being in 1887. Rapid waves of cultural change have swept this nation, leaving in the process a profound influence upon the nature of art and the life of the artist in America.

In the late nineteenth and early twentieth centuries, a series of major social, political and scientific events came about. Historians characterized the cultural climate here and abroad as that of materialism, colonialism, and social differences. The French Revolution, the Industrial Revolution, World War I, the Great Depression, social upheavals, political currents and cross-currents, the development and impact of science and technology, Sigmund Freud's exploration beneath the surface of man's consciousness, Albert Einstein's General Theory of Relativity, unifying ideas—connecting time with space, mass with energy and gravitation with the structure of space—all were influential factors and forces which were inevitably reflected in the ensuing multifaceted movements in the arts.

The concept of nature had long served as the primary source of inspiration in painting, sculpture and literature. During the eighteenth and nineteenth centuries, nature had been perceived as the principle that is fundamental to all forms and phenomena of the visual world.

The prevalent philosophy of art was firmly based upon the sublime harmony of nature. This was implicit in the works of such painters as Ryder, Homer and Inness; in the works of literary figures such as Walt Whitman and Henry James; and in the structures of architects Louis Sullivan and Frank Lloyd Wright.

Toward the end of the nineteenth century, however, a reversal in the artist's attitude occurred. Nature was no longer the sole source of inspiration nor the unifying element in art. The artist began to feel free to explore ideas, forms, shapes, texture, and color contrasts. He began to feel free to delineate anything that was within the realm of his interest and which could be realized through his own very personal style.

In 1905 a new and unparalleled art movement appeared on the scene in Paris. A group of young painters under the leadership of Henry Matisse held an exhibition of paintings at the third Salon d'Automne. The reaction to these paintings was startling, to say the least. So shockingly brilliant were these paintings in color, and so unusual in design, that critics everywhere referred to these artists as "fauves" (wild beasts).

There were also influences from non-European cultures upon the artist. African fetishes, Polynesian decorative woodcarvings, sculpture and textiles from ancient cultures of Central and South America introduced novel and unexpected form, color and texture combinations.

To the artist these unique and untried approaches to the designing of space suggested new ways of expressing ideas and feelings. These influences led to the development of diversified avenues to artistic expression and, in the process, brought into question and renounced the aesthetic and representational tradition of the Renaissance.

Meanwhile, in the United States in 1898, a group of American painters known as "The Ten" organized and held an exhibition of their works. This exhibit was intended as a protest against the almost exclusive patronage of European painters.

Ten years later, "The Eight" organized against the tyranny of authority in art in general and the still prevalent Europeanized studio art in particular. The diversity of aims and of style in this group, united though they were in their general objective, infused health and individuality into the evolving American tradition. Prendergast, Glackens and Lawson were considered the luminists. Henri and Luks worked in the Chase and Duveneck tradition with vigorous brush strokes. Henri's influence was also felt upon his contemporaries Sloan and George Bellows. With the latter painters, the objective became the interpretation of the American scene and the phenomenal realities of their social milieu. The entire group aligned itself with Sloan and Bellows. It was contemptuously called the "Ashcan School."

Members of this group were also responsible for bringing to the United States the International Exhibition of Modern Art, commonly referred to as the Armory Show. This exhibition was a definite landmark in the modern art movement on this side of the Atlantic.

A CHANGE IN THE ARTIST'S ATTITUDE

In the years immediately preceding 1914, various art movements in

France, England, Germany and Italy evolved in response to the tensions and upheavals of the time. The artist no longer had such patrons as the church, kings, and nobles to keep up a steady demand for his artistic products. The artist became resigned to isolation, and he proceded to work for himself or for a limited number of clients or collectors who enjoyed his work. It was then that he began to lean in the direction of the abstract and the non-objective. Being deprived of the traditional patronage, he consequently felt responsible, in some degree, to the few who would accept his increasingly nonrepresentational works. And this was the beginning of a new and independent attitude on the part of the artist. His independence subsequently gave birth to such movements as Cubism, Fauvism, Expressionism, Post-Impressionism, neo-Romanticism, Surrealism and Dadaism. From the close of the nineteenth century to the very recent past, art has been sustained by its own power—relying neither on nature nor man for its survival but upon art itself.

Unfortunately, the period of creative experimentation in the arts and the hope for social regeneration with which the twentieth century opened was brought to a tragic end during World War I. European society was shaken to its very foundation. What remained of traditional values became a sardonic mockery. Groups of artists, writers and musicians who had worked together disbanded. Although Paris continued to exert a strong magnetic power, drawing artists and writers to its Left Bank, nonetheless, the European artists and writers felt encumbered by a cultural crisis.

Interestingly enough, the shock of the war and the European crisis had a reverse affect upon the artists in the United States. Tendencies which were already prevalent here and in Latin American countries stimulated further interest in exploring the richness of indigenous cultures, i.e., their peoples, their native traditions, their creative products and the qualities of their emerging national cultures.

THE ARMORY SHOW

The Armory Show held in New York on February 15, 1913, at the 69th Regiment Armory was a revelation. No single art event, before or since, has had the inspirational and cogent impact upon American art, as did this exhibition. It presented an all-inclusive panorama of French as well as American painters. Among the former were Cezanne, Picasso, Matisse, Gauguin and Modigliani. These painters were later hailed as giants of all time.

Luks, Sloan, Bellows, Hopper, Marin, Demuth, Dove, Weber, Feininger, Stuart Davis were among American painters included in the Armory Show. The nation's artists were apparently stirred not only by the numerous canvases but also by the utterly new and innovative approaches to painting. Cubism, Futurism and Dadaism, more than any other art movements, fascinated the American painter. These expanded his artistic vision and gave a momentous impetus to subsequent abstraction.

In the United States, John Marin, Arthur Dove, Charles Demuth, Maurice Sterne, Preston Dickinson, Stuart Davis, Joseph Stella, Abraham Walkowitz, Max Weber, and Man Ray became known as the pioneer modernists. They brought a new spirit to the art of the nation, challenging the outworn Puritanism of established America.

With the aftermath of World War I came nationalism in American art. Artists Thomas Hart Benton, John Stuart Curry and Grant Wood became the major proponents of the American Scene movement.

In the Postwar era of "return to normalcy" and Prohibition (1919–1929), artists began to draw away from the public and all that they considered "commercial." Writers like Eliot, Pound, Cummings and Stevens, often expatriates, were considered obscure as were the painters Feininger, Ray, and Pascin, also expatriates. O'Keefe, Burchfield and Hopper painted objective records of local scenes.

From 1930–1940, the United States experienced a severe depression. Following the stock market crash in 1929, many younger artists like Shahn,Evergood and Pascin turned to political and social subjects. Mexican painters Orozco and Rivera painted murals in the United States, influencing a new mural movement. Mural painting was also widely encouraged by the Federal Art Project in 1933.

With the outbreak of World War II in 1939, many European artists including Chagall, Lipschitz, Tchelitchew, and Dali emigrated to America. Northwestern abstractionists Price, Tobey, Austin and Graves at this time received a great deal of recognition. This group was inspired by the Orient rather than by Europe. Abstract and surrealistic approaches to painting became increasingly popular.

THE INFLUENCE OF THE GREAT DEPRESSION ON THE ARTIST

A particularly dismal period in the annals of American history pervaded the late twenties and early thirties. These were known as the lean years, the years of the Great Depression. In October, 1929, the stock market crashed. Fortunes amassed through the creative efforts of men for many generations were wiped out overnight. Panic, suicides, economic, social and political upheaval traversed the land. Hunger marchers, agitators for revolt, vast armies of unemployed—all generated a mood of despondence, frustration and utter hopelessness.

In 1933 Franklin Delano Roosevelt was swept into office as thirty-second President of the United States. As president, he initiated a number of social and economic reforms. These brought some respite to the restless and to the needy of the land, slowly reversing the catastrophic and volatile tendencies to a more hopeful mood. Perhaps more than any other social innovations responsible for the brightened outlook were those sponsored by the Public Works Administration, which gradually provided employment for millions.

Among those who benefited greatly from the P. W. A. were local artists. Although they have been known to have a built-in tolerance for poverty and struggle, during the Depression artists were just as destitute as other mortals. True, seldom had there been a time in the lives of most artists when they did not have a serious concern about staying alive. But artists seldom applied for relief. They relied mainly upon their own resources for sustenance. Even in prosperous times, artists were not known to amass great fortunes. They lived for their art and their art alone. Nonetheless, times were different during the Depression; art was a luxury. Food, clothing and shelter were the leading and natural priorities of the day. As a consequence, the artist found himself in a desperate situation. The government sponsored projects came as a great salvation.

For the first time in American history, artists joined the ranks of the unemployed and thereby benefited from the proposed social and economic reforms sponsored by the federal government.

Also, for many artists this marked the first time they were being paid for their artistic contributions. Through government sponsored reforms, many opportunities for artistic production and growth emerged and much new talent was thus discovered in the United States. International, national and regional exhibitions of paintings and sculpture were organized. New York, California, Pennsylvania, Michigan and Illinois, among other states, staged extensive exhibitions. They reflected a diversity of artistic approaches and brought into national focus an abundance of newly discovered and highly merited talent.

The four stirring and notably outstanding events which occurred during the early 30's were the federally sponsored Public Works Art Project, the mural competition for A Century of Progress–World's Fair in Chicago (1933–1934), the National Exhibition of Paintings and Sculpture at the Art Institute of Chicago (1933), and the "Sixteen Cities" show at the Museum of Modern Art in New York in 1933.

THE FEDERAL ART PROGRAMS

The federally sponsored Public Works Art Project generated a great deal of excitement among artists and laymen alike. Government sponsorship of the arts was at this stage in American history a novel idea. But it was not a new idea in the history of other governments in the world. One needs only to be reminded of the Golden Age of Pericles and of the great building program of Athens which left an impressive record of the ancient Greek civilization to realize the extent to which governments have employed artists, artisans and craftsmen on civic projects. In Egypt, Greece, Italy and in many of the city and provincial governments of medieval and modern Europe, similar precedents had been established. In China and other Oriental countries and in ancient civilizations on the American continent, the employment of artists and architects by governments was a time honored procedure.

In our own time, the French government established an enviable record in encouraging its populace in the pursuit of the arts and in the advancement of interest in art education. Similarly, governments in Italy, Germany, Russia and other European countries used artists to enrich their environments and to meet the social and aesthetic needs of its milieu. Sweden, too, designed a deliberate art education curriculum, which led to the development of an outstanding industrial arts program there. In the 1920's also, the Republic of Mexico gave its support to a program of art which invited a group of its prominent artists to paint murals for public buildings, under the direction of the Ministry of Education. To this day these buildings remain as a tribute to the scope and imagination of Mexican artists. This mural program led to a very important art movement. It also spread the fame of Mexico and its artists, Rivera, Orozco, Siqueiros and others, far beyond the country's boundaries to every corner of the earth.

But in the United States for the first time, the government actually became a patron of the arts. Artists were able to afford the "sustaining luxury" of three meals a day, instead of one or two at best. Moreover, they had a place in which to execute their works. And, most important, they found an outlet for their creative products. Artists, young and old, were thus encouraged to produce their very best, since their artistic products were actually used, i.e., distributed to government institutions, hospitals, and schools for all to view, and for many to enjoy.

Many Chicago artists participated in and benefited from the Federal Art Project.

THE CENTURY OF PROGRESS MURALS

The second of four major events of artistic stature, which also occurred in 1933, was the Century of Progress World's Fair in Chicago. It, too, offered unique and challenging opportunities for the mature and the young artists of America. For aside from the commercial and cultural exhibits which were to be housed in the highly imaginative and fantastic architectural structures, there appeared to be a distinct need for murals to enchance the interiors. A mural competiton was therefore initiated entirely for this purpose. And in what seemed an unprecedented coalition, architects, artists, and designers worked jointly to accomplish what would emerge as one of the highest possible aesthetic results, realized through the collective talents of many. The mural competition offered a prestigious inducement for any artist to attempt. Through a commission such as this, one could gain some recognition and be handsomely rewarded for artistic efforts.

This was to be a gigantic event—dramatic, informative, entertaining, and reflective of a Century of Progress—an event which could possibly leave an indelible mark upon present and future generations. Indeed, it was to surpass in size, beauty and proportion all other World Fairs which had ever been staged before and to reflect American goals and style. Technology, science, industry and the arts were duly represented. All exhibitions were to be staged on the man-created island, off the shores of Chicago's front yard, Lake Michigan. Artists everywhere were eager to become part of this creative and exciting enterprise, for they saw in it a unique opportunity to make a sizeable contribution to its beauty and to the realization of personal dreams. They rose to the challenge.

Temporarily, artists forsook their easel paintings. Instead, they responded with buoyant enthusiasm to the laborious task of designing gigantic murals. As the buildings in which the international exhibits were to be housed were being prepared, artists strolled through the unfinished structures, familiarizing themselves with the nature, size

The CENTURY OF PROGRESS logo
(Courtesy of the Chicago Historical Society)

A FRANCES BADGER mural depicting the memory of days of 1893 and the Columbian Exposition, displayed at the Century of Progress, 1933.

and design of the buildings. With that view in mind, they made deliberate plans for murals which they hoped could be appropriately adapted to the exact specifications of the allotted wall space. These plans were then submitted to a jury of selection and designated for possible use in the interiors of the Century of Progress buildings.

Prior to the final stages in the development of murals, however, all selected entries, i.e., the meticulously detailed preliminary color renditions, were exhibited at the Increase Robinson Studio Gallery in Chicago. Artists from all over the country competed in this mural competition. But most of those who competed had never dreamed of having to make anything larger than three-by-four foot canvasses, particularly during the Great Depression years. Few artists could afford to buy art materials. Large canvasses, paints, brushes and frames for completed works were not easy to come by. But artists were courageous and hopeful for a better day. At this time they were more hopeful yet for a miracle—one that might lead to an important commission.

Among those who were finally selected for this prestigious and challenging undertaking were Chicago artists Frances Badger, Davenport Griffen, David McCosh, Richard Cristler, A. Raymond Katz, William S. Schwartz and Rudolph Weisenborn. Among selected New York artists were Bourdelle, Kunyoshi and Biddle.

The mural competition did much to generate further interest in mural painting in Chicago. It also created an ever increasing demand for murals. Restaurants, theatres, shops, industrial complexes, temples, churches and private homes used murals as an integral part of interior decor.

Chicago Society of Artists members were involved in the mural movement. Frances Badger was commissioned to do a number of private murals. Frances Badger, Peggy Burrows and Rowena Fry executed a mural consisting of nine panels for the American Marietta Corporation. In the more recent past (1955 to 1969), Andrene Kauffman did a series of nineteen ceramic murals and stained glass windows for the Third Unitarian Church of Chicago.

Panels depicting the SEVEN LIVELY ARTS painted for the Riccardo Restaurant. Top row, left to right–LITERATURE by RUDOLPH WEISENBORN, PAINTING by VINCENT D'AGOSTINO, DRAMA by IVAN ALBRIGHT, ARCHITECTURE by AARON BOHROD. Second Row, left to right–SCULPTURE by MALVIN ALBRIGHT, DANCE by RIC RICCARDO, and MUSIC by WILLIAM S. SCHWARTZ.

Malvin Albright, Ivan LeLorraine Albright, Aaron Bohrod, Vincent D'Agostino, Ric Riccardo, Rudolph Weisenborn and William S. Schwartz were invited to paint seven panels for the Riccardo restaurant. The murals, placed above the bar of the restaurant, depicted the "Seven Lively Arts." They were: "Literature" by Rudolph Weisenborn; "Painting" by Vincent D'Agostino; "Drama" by Ivan

LeLorraine Albright; "Architecture" by Aaron Bohrod; "Sculpture" by Malvin Albright; "Dance" by Ric Riccardo; "Music" by Willaim S. Schwartz. The two Albright brothers and Aaron Bohrod were members of the Chicago Society of Artists.

W. P. A. FEDERAL ART PROJECT

In August, 1935, the Federal Art Project of the Works Progress Administration was set up under the direction of Holger Cahill in Washington, D.C. Established as a part of a nationwide conservation program of the W. P. A., the Federal Art Project provided work relief to employable artists. Since its inception, more than 350 separate projects were put into operation in 44 states throughout the country. At its peak, 5,300 men and women were employed. Of this total, 49% were occupied in creative work in the fine arts, 29% in practical arts, 16% in art teaching and 6% in administration and clerical services. W. P. A. artists worked on a salary basis generally uniform throughout the country and worked under artists classified as supervisors. Some of the divisions were: Mural, Easel, Graphic Arts, Sculpture, Poster, Photographic, Index of American Designs, Art Gallery Tours and Lectures, Scenic Designing, Arts Service Unit, Art Teaching, Exhibitions, Creative Home Planning, Stained Glass, and Display Information.

In Chicago, the Illinois W. P. A. project was headed by Increase Robinson. The Painting Division was under the direction of Norman MacLeish; the Sculpture Division was headed by Sculptor Edouard Chassaing and assisted by Peterpaul Ott. All were members of the

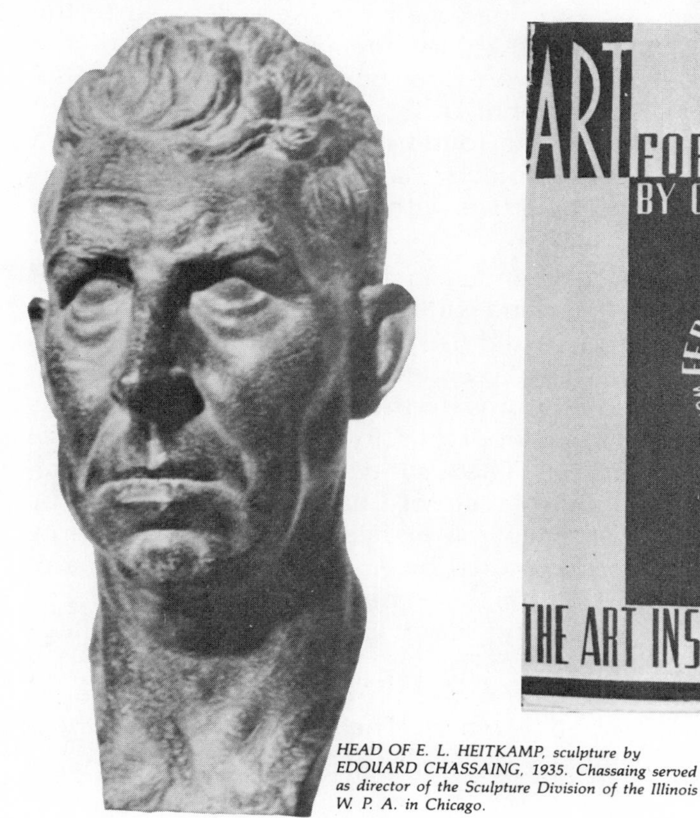

HEAD OF E. L. HEITKAMP, sculpture by EDOUARD CHASSAING, 1935. Chassaing served as director of the Sculpture Division of the Illinois W. P. A. in Chicago.

Catalogue cover of the FEDERAL ART PROJECT EXHIBITION held at the Art Institute of Chicago in 1938. This exhibition displayed the public works of Chicago artists.

Chicago Society of Artists. A design workshop was headed by John Walley. Les Margoff headed the unit which organized the monumental American Index of Design, now a treasure of the Metropolitan Museum of Art in New York.

Busily engaged in creating art and lecturing on art were Norman MacLeish, Rudolph Weisenborn, Julio DeDiego, Rifka Angel, Aaron Bohrod, Leon Garland, Todros Geller and many other members of the Chicago Society of Artists.

In Illinois there were about 180 painters, 60 sculptors and numerous other creative artists involved in the W. P. A. project. 710 of the 770 persons enrolled in the state were from Chicago.

During 1936, 6136 supported institutions had received 268,462 items on allocation from the Federal Art Project. These included: 500 completed murals, 1462 pieces of sculpture, 7695 easel paintings, 1511 prints, 105 posters, 130,092 photos, 4395 arts and crafts objects, 15,973 maps and diagrams, 322 stage sets, 155 dioramas and models for visual education and 4253 lantern slides. These figures represent only 45% of the works produced under the project.

In February 1937 primarily works by sculptors but also works by other artists of the W. P. A. Federal Art Project were exhibited in the Federal Art Gallery, One East 38th Street, New York City.

In October 1938, the works of Chicago Artists of the Federal Art Project were exhibited at the Art Institute of Chicago. In November 1939, an exhibition of Painting and Sculpture designed for Federal Buildings was held at the Corcoran Gallery of Art, Washington, D.C.

Many members of the Chicago Society of Artists were included in all of the above mentioned exhibitions.

At the Art Institute of Chicago nine galleries were devoted to the W. P. A. works under the title, "Art for the Public." Some of the paintings, prints and sculpture were previously shown at the 1937 Paris Exposition and in Washington, D. C.

As unemployment eased, artists found other means of earning a livelihood and left the W. P. A. projects. Aaron Bohrod and others accompanied the armed forces as artists with combat units. Many were drafted into service.

The W. P. A. Project officially ended in 1943. The ramifications of the W. P. A. art project were far and wide. The nation is still enjoying the murals, easel paintings, sculpture and bas-reliefs located in various public institutions, civic structures, hospitals, post offices, schools, libraries, zoos and museums. In the Chicago Water Bureau's collection office on the ground floor of City Hall, there is a mural called "Water" by Edgar Britton. The County Hospital has a fine collection of paintings, a fountain by sculptor Charles Umlauf, murals by Edwin Boyd Johnson, a ceramic mural by John Winters. Twenty murals in oil on canvas were executed by Andrene Kauffman, one of which is at Cook County Hospital. Max Kahn's "Illinois River" and Norman MacLeish's "Brick Factory" are at Chicago Teachers College South, where paintings by Frances Badger, Adrian Troy, Frederick Remahl and Hester Miller Muray are also on view. In the Hild Branch Library, Frances Coan painted a mural. The Spalding High School houses a collection of paintings by Frank Perri, Michael Ursulescu,

THE W.P.A. PROJECT GALLERY. Seated from left to right, LILLIAN HALL, assistant to the supervisor of the gallery; BEATRICE LEVY, supervisor of the gallery; and JOHN WALLEY.

William Jacobs, Scapiceli, and Stenvall. At the Chopin Elementary School there are paintings by Macena Barton, Francis Chapin, and Walter Crawiec and sculpture by John Fabion. At the Burbank and Hirsh high schools are murals by Andrene Kauffman; at the Nettlehorst and Carl VonLinne elementary schools there are murals by Ethel Spears. There are three murals done in egg-tempera by Henry Simon hanging in the school library of Wells High School. In the social room at this school there is also a collection of paintings by Todros Geller, William S. Schwartz and William Jacobs. Edgar Britton's and Rudolph Weisenborn's murals are in the lunchroom at Lane Technical High School. In the LaFayette Elementary School collection are included paintings by Aaron Bohrod, Tunis Ponsen, William S. Schwartz and David Bekker.

The Krannert Art Museum at the University of Illinois, under the direction of C.V. Donoven, has preserved 436 works by 159 W. P. A. artists. There are more than 400 graphics and 20 oils there. The collection includes a Bohrod, Stephan, two works by MacLeish, a Ralph Henrickson, an Edgar Britton, an Emil Armin and Nicola Ziroli.

Among the major muralists in Chicago, members of the Chicago Society of Artists were Ivan LeLorraine Albright, Frances Badger, Aaron Bohrod, Peggy Burrows, Rowena Fry, Davenport Griffen, Harold Haydon, A. Raymond Katz, Andrene Kauffman, Norman MacLeish, Ethel Spears, Charles Umlauf, Edgar Britton, Edward Millman, Grace Spongberg, Julio DeDiego, Lillian Hall, Natalie Henry, and Lucile Leighton.

Although the mural movement initiated by the Federal Government in the early days of W. P. A. provided some work for a few

MINING IN ILLINOIS, mural (10'x5½') for the Eldorado, Illinois Post Office, 1937 by WILLIAM S. SCHWARTZ.

established mural painters, the ramifications of the initial venture were far greater than was anticipated. For as the movement gained momentum, many artists found commercial outlets for their mural painting skills. Actually, the list of mural painters increased in direct proportion to public demand.

Interest was generated not only in private sectors, but in commerce and industry as well, and this provided many artists with a satisfactory means of earning a livelihood. Theatres, department stores, large and small neighborhood shops, interior decorating establishments, restaurants, bars, industrial complexes, shopping centers, religious institutions—all indicated an extraordinary interest in acquiring murals for specifically designated purposes, incorporating these into existing or newly designed decor.

A significant trend had been set, and the artist emerged as the appreciated beneficiary of that interesting phenomenon.

In more recent years, muralist William Walker, generally referred to as one of the fathers of the current mural movement in the United States, was responsible for stimulating further interest in mural painting in Chicago. He was involved with the "Wall of Respect" in 1967, a project sponsored by the Organization of Black American Culture. That "Wall" was given credit for being the stimulus that brought murals—in the sense of social communication—out of their post-Mexican Revolution, post-Depression dormancy. Chicago now has about 70 mural artists.

In his words William Walker explains: "I try to give a sense of

ETHEL SPEARS working on a W. P. A. mural.

'somebodyness' to people who are struggling to survive, and a sense that there is a solution to problems. I paint what mankind can be about, what he can overcome. I also try not to insult the intelligence of people."

Since the inception of the Chicago Society of Artists in 1887, a series of social, political, and scientific events have occurred. Each has left its mark upon the creative individual. The Armory Show held in New York in 1913, World War I, the Great Depression, the Federal Art Program, the W. P. A. Art Project, the Century of Progress Exhibitions in 1932 and 1933 and the mural movement in the United States—all were highly significant events which energized the arts and gave impetus to various art movements here and abroad.

ART · SCHOOL
THE · ART · INSTITUTE
OF · CHICAGO
CATALOG
OF · COURSES
OF · THE · DAY
EVENING
& · SATURDAY
SCHOOLS
SEASON · OF
1920 - 1921

An early logo of the School of the Art Institute of Chicago. (Photograph by Barbara Lazarus Metz)

2 Chicago: Its Cultural Beginnings

Increased interest in the arts in Chicago became apparent as early as 1890, when a city Art Commission was established. Its primary function was to approve all works of art before they became the property of the city. Notable acquisitions such as Lorado Taft's "The Fountain of the Great Lakes" and "The Fountain of Time" were two pieces of sculpture purchased by the city with the Art Commission's approval. At the request of the mayor, the Commission acted in various other capacities, whenever it seemed judicious for the city's aesthetic improvement.

The Architectural Club, another group, directed its energies toward a similar end. A Municipal Art League, organized in 1890, has done its share in motivating and arousing civic pride among Chicago's more than two-million inhabitants. The trustees of the Art Institute administered the Ferguson Monument Fund, designed to be used for the erection of statuary and monuments in Chicago.

The Art Institute of Chicago was incorporated May 24, 1879, for the "founding and maintenance of schools of art, and the cultivation and extension of the arts of design by any appropriate means." The museum building upon the lake front was first occupied in 1893. The Art Institute of Chicago, with its valuable collection of paintings, reproductions of bronzes and sculpture, architectural casts, and other objects of art, was later instrumental in bringing periodically changing exhibits for public enlightenment and enjoyment. Connected with it, the largest and most comprehensive art school in the country has since then nurtured young and aspiring artists and trained teachers of art.

The Field Museum of Natural History, another cultural institution, was established in 1894, largely by Marshall Field. Its interests were devoted mainly to anthropology and to natural history. The nucleus of its great collection was acquired from various exhibits of the Columbian Exposition held in Chicago in 1893. This collection of American ethnology was of exceptional richness and value and was constantly expanded by research expeditions.

The oldest choral society, the Apollo Music Club, dates back to 1871. Its choral groups, through its local and regional concerts, added infinite pleasure to many music-oriented audiences.

The Chicago Symphony Orchestra which was founded by Theodore Thomas in 1891 served the city with great distinction. It has recently become world renowned for its technical skill and sensitively rendered orchestral performances.

And finally the Chicago Society of Artists, which is the object of deliberate scrutiny in this manuscript, is the earliest known group of painters, sculptors and printmakers in the United States. It was established in 1887.

All of these organizations put forth great effort to sustain and nurture a climate conducive to creative interests, and they established a firm foundation for further expansion of aesthetic matters.

Other organizations were also noteworthy for their contributions. The Municipal Art League of Chicago, the Illinois Academy of Fine Arts, and later the Chicago New Century Committee were three active organizations whose sole purpose was to initiate activities which furthered artistic interests. Many years later, the All Illinois Art Society was formed. It, too, was geared toward similar goals. Community sponsored outdoor art fairs, to which the city's artists and public responded with great enthusiasm, launched a new and novel means of bringing art to the people.

THE MUNICIPAL ART LEAGUE OF CHICAGO

The objectives of the Municipal Art League of Chicago were as follows:

> The object of the League was to promote civic art, the fine arts, industrial arts, and to stimulate civic pride in the care and improvement of public and private property.
>
> The affiliated clubs were pledged to a special interest in the work of the artists of Chicago and Vicinity, and to encourage and promote in every possible way their annual exhibition.
>
> In 1901 the Municipal Art League voted to establish a Municipal Art Collection to consist of works by artists who are or have been active in artistic life of Chicago, the object being the encouragement of works of art worthy to be in a public gallery.

Included in this collection were Chicago Society of Artists members

Pauline Palmer, Oliver Dennett Grover, Adam Emory Albright, Charles W. Dahlgreen, Rudolph Ingerle, Edgar Rupprecht, Edgar S. Cameron, Harriet Krawiec, and Oskar Gross.

Officers and Directors of the Municipal Art League of Chicago were Paul Schulze, President; Mrs. Maude Merritt, Frederick C. Hibbard, Vice-Presidents; Mrs. Frances A. Barothy, Secretary; O. C. Brodhay, Treasurer.

Directors were Mrs. Frances A. Barothy, Gustave A. Brand, O. C. Brodhay, Mrs. Charles S. Clark, David R. Clarke, Frank V. Dudley, Mrs. LeRoy Herbst, Frederic C. Hibbard, Henry K. Holsman, Rudolph F. Ingerle, Miss Eleanor Jewett, Charles Fabens Kelley, Mrs. Frank G. Logan, Mrs. Maude Merritt, Mrs. Robert W. Millar, Robert E. Moore, Charles S. Peterson, Mrs. Albert J. Pohlman, Paul Schulze, Mrs. Summer Sollitt, and Frank F. Taylor. Most were prominent citizens and active participants in Chicago's cultural life for many years.

THE ILLINOIS ACADEMY OF FINE ARTS

In 1926 a group of civic-minded individuals and heads of various organizations gathered in Chicago to create the Illinois Academy of Fine Arts. Its purpose was "to promote the production and sales of the works of living artists of Illinois and for the encouragement of all of the fine arts."

J. F. Cornelius was its first president and represented the Uptown Civic Music Association; F. J. Reichman was vice-president and represented the Arts Club of Chicago; Mrs. Florence M. Cook was its secretary and Choral Director and she represented the Morgan Park Club of Chicago. The treasurer was C. Lynn Coy, president of the Chicago Society of Artists.

EXHIBITION AT ROMANY CLUB

The first exhibition of oils, water-colors, cartoons, etchings and drawings, miniatures, sculpture, and wood carvings by members of the Illinois Academy of Fine Arts was staged at the Romany Club, 36 Bellevue Place, Chicago, during the month of October 1927.

This exhibition marked the final event of the first year tour of the Academy, which was opened in 1926 at the State Museum in Springfield under the auspices of the State of Illinois. Forty members of the Chicago Society of Artists participated in the exhibition at the Romany Club. Oils were exhibited by Jean Crawford Adams, Emil Armin, Frances Badger, Fred Biesel, George Leigh Caldwell, Edgar Speis Cameron, Charles W. Dahlgreen, Gustaf Dalstrom, Elizabeth Englehard, Oscar B. Erickson, Ruth Van Sickle Ford, Frances M. Foy, Emile J. Grumieaux, V. M. S. Hannell, Rudolph Ingerle, Camille Andrene Kauffman, Walter Krawiec, Beatrice S. Levy, Louis A. Neebe, Minnie Harms Neebe, Gregory Orloff, Pauline Palmer, Josephine L. Reichmann, Torry Ross, Felix Russman, Frances Strain, Ida VanHorn, Laura Van Pappelendam, and Florence White Williams.

Water-colors were exhibited by Charles Biesel, Julia Sulzer Griffith, "Pop" Hart, Thomas M. Kempf, Ethel Spears, Elizabeth Colwell, and

SNOWBOUND, oil by LOUIS ALEXANDER NEEBE

Todros Geller with Sculpture by C. Lynn Coy, Emil Armin, Tud Kempf, and Wood Carvings by Thomas Kempf.

A TRAVELING EXHIBITION OF ILLINOIS ARTISTS' WORKS

A collection of paintings by Illinois artists, which the Illinois Academy of Fine Arts was planning to ship to Springfield for an exhibition at the Illinois State Museum, was shown briefly at Newcomb and Macklin's, 2 West Kinzie Street, Chicago. A jury composed of Beatrice Levy, Agnes Potter VanRyn, John T. Nolf, Edward T. Grigware, Emile J. Grumieaux, Rudolph Ingerle and Frederic Victor Poole selected some 300 paintings and prints from a total of 700 submitted. Tennessee Mitchell Anderson, Emory P. Seidel and Albien Polasek selected the sculptures.

The incomplete survey afforded during the brief showing indicated that the exhibition would have at least one desirable characteristic—variety. Whereas the first Illinois exhibition held two years earlier was selected by two distinct juries—one modern and one conservative—effort was made at the second exhibition to reconcile the two viewpoints in one jury. The effort apparently met with success.

STILL LIFE, oil by EMILE JACQUES GRUMIEAUX, 1932. Grumieaux served on the jury of the Traveling Exhibition of Illinois Artists' works.

The purpose of the traveling exhibition of Illinois artists's work through a number of downstate cities was primarily educational. Mrs. Mary E. Aleshire, director of the exhibitions of the Illinois Academy, expressed the view that the virtue of variety would be a valuable one if the exhibition was to offer something of interest to as wide a public as possible. That the artistic standard of the collection was high was demonstrated at the viewing at Newcomb and Macklin's. A partial list of contributing artists showed the presence of canvases by ranking painters and sculptors of Chicago and other cities in Illinois.

THE FIRST EXHIBITION AT ILLINOIS STATE MUSEUM, Springfield, Illinois

The second art exhibition by members of the Illinois Academy of Fine Arts was held in the galleries of the Illinois State Museum, Springfield, April 14 to June 24, 1928. The Board of Museum Advisors included some noted scholars. They were Charles Beach Atwell, Ph. D., Professor of Botany, Northwestern University, Evanston; Fay Cooper Cole, Ph. D., Professor of Anthropology, University of Chicago and Field Museum, Chicago; Lorado Taft, L. H.

D., Professor of Art, University of Illinois, University of Chicago and Art Institute of Chicago; and Henry Baldwin Ward, Ph.D., Professor of Zoology, University of Illinois, Urbana.

The major goal of the Illinois Academy of Fine Arts was to establish a permanent art gallery for the Illinois State Museum in order to provide the local art groups throughout the state an organization in which all could be adequately and fairly represented.

A few descriptive passages which reviewed the achievements of the Academy within one year were included. The catalogue states:

> It is true that youth with its fine and high enthusiasm dares to do what its elders think the impossible and the young Illinois Academy of Fine Arts was no exception to this time-worn rule.
>
> A traveling exhibition comprising more than 400 pieces of original paintings, sculpture and prints by Illinois artists was considered an undertaking of too great a magnitude by many, but then the year had closed and fifteen Illinois cities and towns had been visited with this mammoth exhibition, the impossible had been accomplished.
>
> The University of Illinois, the State Teachers' Colleges at Normal and Macomb, and the cities of Joliet, Eureka, Peoria, Rock Island, Moline, Freeport, Sterling, Rock Falls, Aurora, LaSalle and Chicago received the exhibition with enthusiasm.
>
> While for seventy-five years the State Museum at Springfield has shown exhibits depicting nature in Illinois, the Illinois Academy of Fine Arts was the first organization to hold an art exhibition under the auspices of the State. During the three months it remained at the State Museum, thousands of tourists and residents of central and southern Illinois visited the exhibition.
>
> This attendance furnished ample proof that works of art should be permanently shown in the State Museum. Because of the apathy of former years, many fine art collections that should have remained in Illinois have been bequeathed to other states. Illinois is now more than a century old and as a state should be preserving examples of her fine arts as well as of her nature, industrial and commercial products.

Among those whose works were included in the second Illinois State Museum exhibition were the following members of the Chicago Society of Artists:

Oils by Jean Crawford Adams, Adam E. Albright, Ivan LeLorraine Albright, Frances Badger, Macena Barton, Charles Biesel, Fred Biesel, Jaroslav Brozik, Claude Buck, Edithe J. Cassady, Francis Chapin, Ruth VanSickle Ford, Belle Goldschlager, Emile J. Grumieaux, Lenore Smith Jerrems, George Josimovich, Harriet B. Krawiec, Beatrice S. Levy, Louis Alexander Neebe, Minnie Harms Neebe, Gregory Orloff, Pauline Palmer, Tunis Ponsen, Mary B. Poull, Josephine L. Reichmann, Frederick Remahl, Increase Robinson, Charles Schroeder, Leopold Seyffert, Frances Strain, Morris Topchevsky, Laura Van Pappelendam, Louis Weiner and Florence White Williams.

Watercolors by Jaroslav Brozik, Rowena Fry, Emile J. Grumieaux, Thomas Hall, Josephine L. Reichmann.

Graphic Arts by Eugene Glaman, Beatrice Levy, Frances Badger, Frederick Remahl.

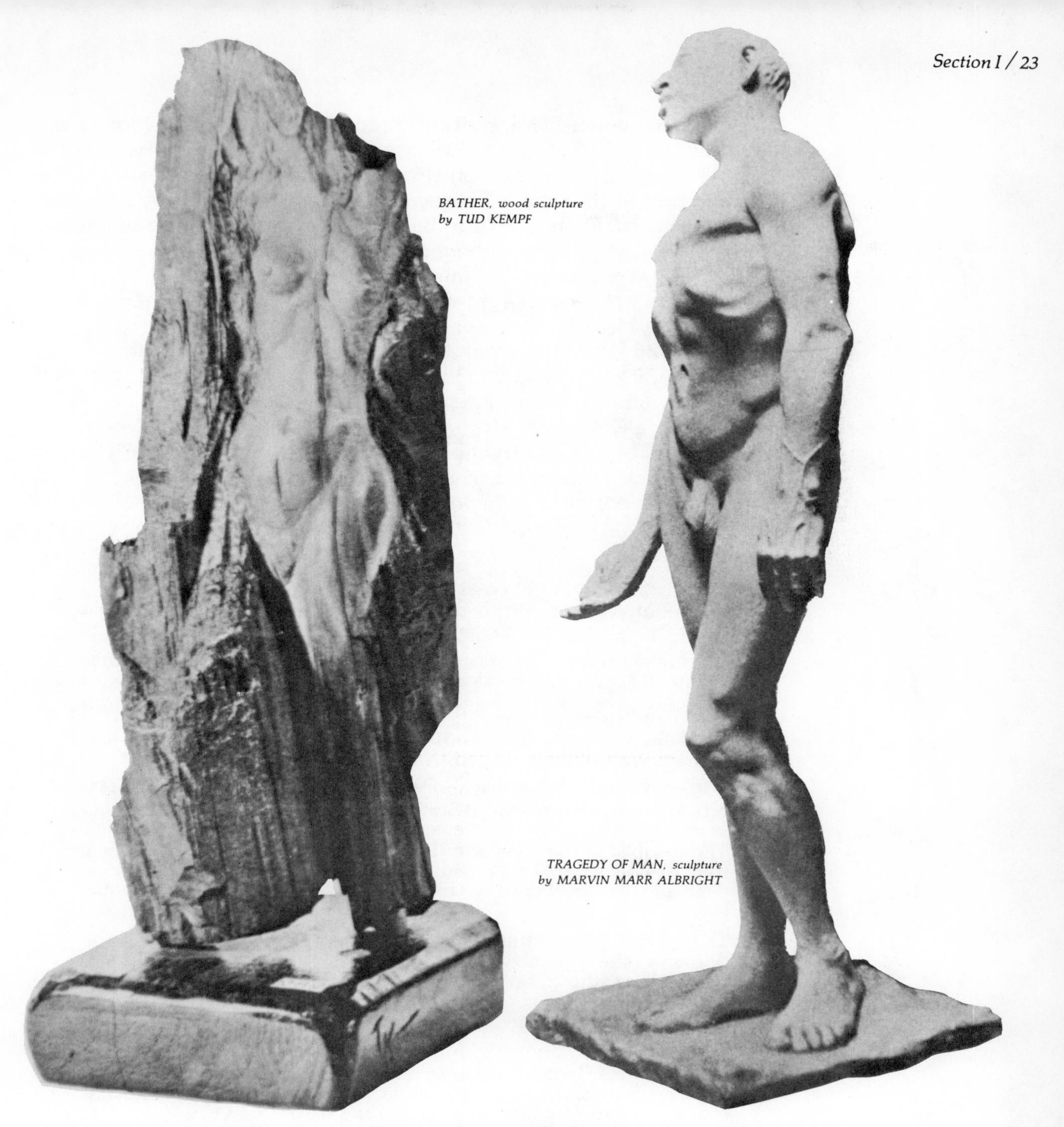

BATHER, wood sculpture
by TUD KEMPF

TRAGEDY OF MAN, sculpture
by MARVIN MARR ALBRIGHT

Sculpture by Malvin Marr Albright, Emil Armin, Tud Kempf and Albin Polasek.

EXHIBITION AT THE UNIVERSITY OF ILLINOIS

An exhibition of 100 paintings by members of the Illinois Academy of Fine Arts was also held in the galleries of the new Architects' Building at the University of Illinois under the supervision of the University Department of Art and Design.

Many of the best known artists of Illinois of both conservative and modernist tendencies were represented. Paintings which were awarded prizes in Chicago during the previous season were part of the show. The exhibit was a good review of what had been exhibited in Chicago during the year. This was the second exhibition by Academy members to be sponsored by the University and the first in the Architects' Building.

EXHIBITION AT NAVY PIER

Since 1926, the Municipal Art League of Chicago and the Illinois Academy of Fine Arts served in their respective capacities as benefactors of Chicago's cultural interests. Twelve years later, during Mayor Edward J. Kelly's administration, a Chicago New Century Committee was created. Under its direction, an exhibition by Chicago artists was sponsored and held in the Exhibition Hall of the Navy Pier. The officers of this committee included Mayor Edward J. Kelly, Honorary Chairman, and Chauncy McCormick, Chairman of Chicago's New Century Art Committee. Charles S. Peterson was appointed Chairman of the Navy Pier Exhibition Committee.

The Executive Committee consisted of artists and art critics Macena Barton, C. J. Bulliet, Paul Gilbert, Eleanor Jewett, Winnifred Pleimling and Adline Lobdell Pynchon. A General Committee was also appointed. It consisted of Chicago artists, most of whom were members of the Chicago Society of Artists. They were Jean Crawford Adams, Fred Biesel, W. M. Farrow, Todros Geller, Mrs. Albion Headburg, Mrs. C. B. King, Walter Krawiec, Sara D. Stake and Louis Weiner.

In the Foreword, Charles S. Peterson, Chairman of the Navy Pier Exhibition Committee stated:

> The exhibit on the Navy Pier last year met with so much approval that it was decided to repeat it this year, hoping, if the second year was as successful as the first, it would become an annual event.
>
> The exhibits shown this year, we believe, are of even higher quality than in the last shown, so it is evident the artists are doing their part. If now the public will show the same interest and give as much support to this year's exhibit as it did to the show last year, we shall be much encouraged in our efforts to make these exhibits annual.
>
> Some 600 artists are participating, all of them working in Chicago. The Committee has endeavored to make the exhibit as representative as possible, covering the entire field of art in all its phases. And instead of having all works sent in passed on by a jury, it has been left to each artist to select the two works that he or she considers his or her best.
>
> There are competent attendants on hand to give information, answer inquiries and quote prices. No commission is charged on any sales made, the entire amount going to the artist.
>
> The thanks of the Committee are due to Mayor Edward J. Kelly and his administration, particularly Corporation Counsel Barnet Hodes, for the free use of Navy Pier and much other assistance; to Mr. Chauncy McCormick, whose support has done so much to make the show possible; to the press for the generous publicity given us; to the exhibiting artists and to all who have given their help.

CROWD, oil by FRANCES STRAIN

Among other Chicago artists, Chicago's New Century Committee Art Exhibit Catalog included seventy-three members of the Chicago Society of Artists. Each artist was permitted to submit two works of art, and most did. The Society's artists included Howard Anderson, Emil Armin, Frances Badger, Laura Bannon, Macena Barton, Rosana Barton, David Bekker, Irene Bianucci, Charles Biesel, Fred Biesel, Mary S. Bornath, Fritzi Brod, Ethel Crouch Brown, Marjorie Carter, David B. Cheskin, Grant Dahlgreen, Gustaf Dalstrom, Elise Donaldson, Frances Foy, Rowena Fry, Karl Gasslander, Todros Geller, Paula Gerard, May H. Gilruth, Eugene Glaman, Bacia Mansfield Gordon, Samuel Greenburg, L. V. Grover, V. M. S. Hannell, Natalie Henry, Magda Heuermann, William Jacobs, Joshua Kaganove, A. Raymond Katz, Andrene Kauffman, Tud Kempf, Harriet Krawiec, Walter Krawiec, Beatrice S. Levy, Clara MacGowan, Frances H. McVey, Harry Mintz, Verne Mullen, Donald Mundt, Peterpaul Ott, Pauline Palmer, Winnifred Pleimling, Tunis Ponsen, Mary B. Poull, Frederick Remahl, Ceil Rosenberg, Torry Ross, Flora Schofield, H. A. Schultz, Grace Seelig, William Earl Singer, Ethel Spears, Grace Spongberg, Ivy N. Steele, Jane W. Steiner, Frances Strain, Julia Thecla, Morris Topchevksy, Carolyn D. Tyler, Oscar Van Young, A. S. Weiner, Louis Weiner, Louise Dunn Yochim and Maurice Yochim.

THE FIRST OUTDOOR ART FAIR

One of the earliest outdoor Art Fairs on record in Chicago was held in Grant Park during a weekend in August 1932. For the first time, artists brought their works out of their studios and displayed them in makeshift stalls or simply laid them on the grass in Grant Park.

The novelty of this event caused a great deal of excitement and

The Grant Park Art Fair sketched on the last day of the fair (August 18, 1932) by SAM GREENBURG. The sketch shows TODROS GELLER showing one of his nudes to C. J. BULLIET. Beside Geller is CATI MOUNT and looking around his shoulder is RAYMOND KATZ. RIFKA ANGEL and her shawl are in the foreground. Rear, left to right, starting extreme upper corner are WILLIAM JACOBS, JULIO DeDIEGO, FRANCIS CHAPIN, LOUIS WEINER, MINNIE HARMS NEEBE and EMIL ARMIN. This sketch appeared in the CHICAGO EVENING POST, August 30, 1932.

An overview of the GRANT PARK ART FAIR, 1932.

curiosity not only among the artists, but also among the gathered viewers who walked aimlessly through the installations. Comments ranged from the very ludicrous and naive expressions to the exhuberant and most appreciative. Viewers asked questions which often led to good-humored laughter, but seldom to any sudden rash of sales since this was the time of the Great Depression. But when an artist sold a painting or a sketch, large or small, everyone reveled in his or her good fortune. This enlivened and revived the hope that others too may possibly enjoy a similar stroke of luck.

Those artists who did not do well financially were disappointed, but they enjoyed the experience of being outdoors and chatting with fellow artists and attending viewers. In general, though, there was a feeling of comradeship. Certainly, the collective commiseration in prevalent "bad times" and the visible lack of "buying power" were elements of mutual concern to both artists and laymen alike. But the event was nevertheless fun—and a social success to boot.

Some incidents occured on that day which added to the excitement of the occasion—like Eleanor Roosevelt's sudden appearance on the scene! She purchased a small watercolor for one of her grandchildren. As she chatted with the artist, a curious but friendly crowd gathered around her. People shook her hand and smiled, seemingly delighted that they had the opportunity to meet her. Soon her chauffeur beckoned her exit and she disappeared as suddenly as she had arrived. But the fair had come to life! Her presence added a touch of

Some members of the Chicago Society of artists participating in the Grant Park Art Fair, 1932. From left to right JULIO DeDIEGO, SAM GREENBURG, TODROS GELLER, (unknown), LEON GARLAND, RAYMOND KATZ, LOUIS WEINER, AARON BOHROD and EMIL ARMIN.

whimsy and good-natured buoyancy to this event.

One woman was intrigued by one of Ivan LeLorraine Albright's paintings resting on the ground against a chair. When she asked the price, William Earl Singer, who was tending Ivan's exhibit in the latter's absence, asked if he could be of help to her. She said, "Yes, would you please tell me what the price of this painting is?" Mr. Singer replied, "Three dollars and ninety-five cents." The lady responded, "I have to ask my husband about it." The painting was priced two thousand dollars! As the lady attempted to leave, Mr. Singer pursued his attempt to sell by saying, "Why, lady, that is a very important painting by a very important artist." She obviously was not impressed by his comment and was about to walk away when Mr. Singer continued, "This painting will last forever. You can even send it to the laundry when it gets soiled." The laughter which echoed through the fair must have embarrassed the lady beyond description. She, too, disappeared in a great hurry!

Since 1932 there were many such art fairs held in Chicago. These have undoubtedly helped the local artist. And that not only because these events have stimulated sales but also because laymen's appreciation and interest in things artistic have grown correspondingly.

Art fairs were and still are a means of raising funds for scholarships to needy students, for special educational programs, for community social centers, for churches, temples, and for various urgently critical and humane causes. Exhibiting artists pay commissions received from sales of paintings, prints, drawings, sculpture, jewelry, weaving and other crafts. In this respect Chicago artists have been very coooperative. They have also been very generous with their donated contributions to auctions which provide an additional source of income for the institutions who sponsor the art fairs.

In more recent years, outstanding juried art fairs have been staged annually. Among these are those held at the Old Orchard Shopping Center, the Rosenstone Gallery of the Bernard Horwich Center, the 57th Street Art Fair and the Old Town Art Fair.

Chicago exerted a great deal of effort toward the development of artistic affairs in the city. Through the establishment of an Art Commission, major museums, organizations such as the Municipal Art League, the Illinois Academy of Fine Arts, the New Century Committee, the outdoor art fairs, and particularly through the efforts of many civic-minded and dedicated individuals, Chicago was headed in the right direction as far as the visual arts were concerned.

Many members of the Chicago Society of Artists were an integral part of the city's artistic endeavors. They have played a prominent role in the city's aesthetic development. The Society's established and highly respected reputation through the years not only on a local but also on a regional and national level has placed it in the forefront of all the major groups of artistic note.

Wilson Ralph C broker C1733	804
Winthrop Asphalt Shingle Co C4479	1021
Witter T L rep C582	815
Witwer Edward B law Rand 5246	815
Wolfsohn M E real est C3406	1509
Woman's Board of Missions of Interior C1388	1315
Worcester Lumber Co C3852	1409
Y M C A Gymnasium C6789	5th flo
Y M C A Library C6789	2nd flo
Y M C A Parlors C6789	2nd flo
Y M C A State Executive Committee C2254	8
Young Churchman Rand 1448	5
Zemon Construction Co contrs Rand 5297	4
Zuetell William real est C6551	11

ATHENÆUM BUILDING

59 E. Van Buren Street

The Athenæum Building is a seven-story building centrally located, well lighted, and has excellent elevator service both day and evening. The building is occupied principally by artists, musicians and other professional people. For further information apply to

WILLOUGHBY & COMPANY
Agents.
7 West Madison Street.
Tels. Central 418. Auto. 41-397.

Anderson Hugh B music tchr H6874	324
Anglo-French Art Co H7497	606
Armbrust J T artist H154	718
Athenaeum Restaurant A65-184	61 E Vanburen
Athenaeum Studio Wab 5522	318
Barry J J mngr H2564	63 E Vanburen
Bertsch Fred S artist H5889	703
Bieckett W H music tchr Wab 6123	306
Calvert G S physician H2056	406
Cooper O B artist H5889	703
Coopers Studio Wab 5878	500
Century School of Music & Oratory Wab 5522	310
Chicago Opera College music tchr	300
Chicago School of Watchmaking Wab 4822	604
Dixon F M artist Wab 8333	726
Duffell W E music tchr Wab 5522	3
Gamble Hinged Music Co pub H5924	67 E Vanbur
Hanson Chester N director Wab 5522	3
Hanson G M music tchr Wab 5522	3
Heberlein Conrad violin mkr	4
Human Science School	3
Jones Alma Miss music tchr H7578	4
King Jessie music tchr	4
Kuss Edward C vocal culture	4
Ladd M C School Wab 5522	3
Lowry A K music tchr	4
Malillac F Mme violin tchr H7578	4
McGregor A G lantern slides H8121	6
Meyers Stephen M Piano Co H3773	2
Middleton Matilda artist Wab 5520	7

The ATHENAEUM BUILDING where the Chicago Society of Artists had their headquarters on the top floor in 1891. (from the Chicago Central Business and Office Building Directory, 1916, page 24)

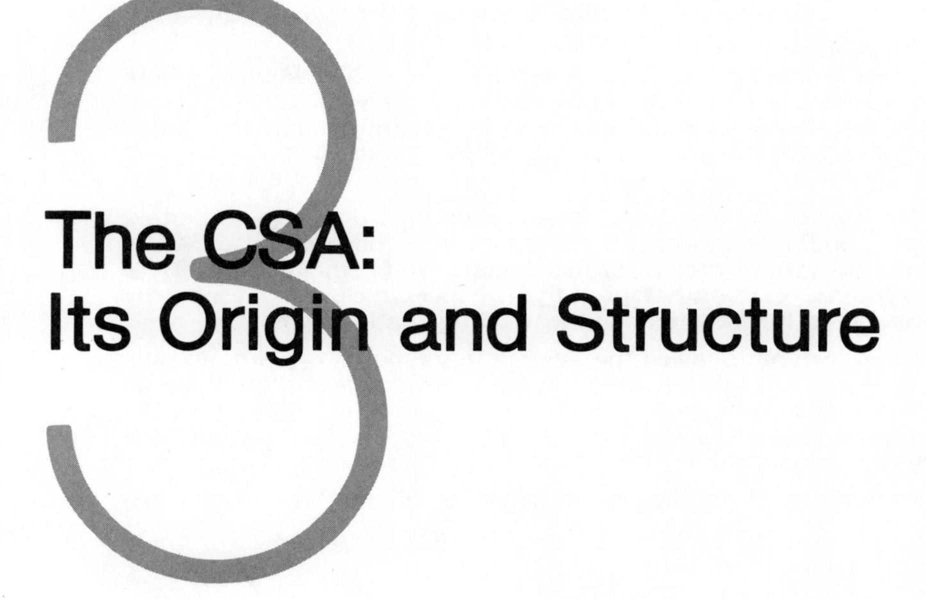

The CSA: Its Origin and Structure

Historical records apparently justify several underlying motives which impel professional artists to enter into a close-linked relationship. Foremost among these motives, undoubtedly, is an earnest desire on the part of each artist to grow culturally, spiritually and professionally along with an unswerving resolve to achieve the ultimate in self-expression. Not the least of these motives, however, may be an inherent eagerness on the part of each artistic 'soul' to share with his peers in a community of aesthetic interests. But, whatever the case may be, it is reasonable to assume that motives such as these and possibly some happy combination of other circumstances, may ultimately lead to the emergence of a Society of Artists.

The earliest source of information concerning the origin of the Chicago Society of Artists has been traced to **An Historical Sketch** through the courtesy of the Chicago Historical Society. The anecdotal nature of its content is worthy of note since it reveals in deatil the scope of the Society's activities, and credits those who were actively engaged in the promotion of its program at the end of the 19th century. It is quoted here verbatim.

AN HISTORICAL SKETCH

The Chicago Society of Artists was organized in the year 1887. Artists were invited at that time to meet in the studio of the late Mr. Spread, then in the Lakeside Building, to talk over the possibility and necessity of organizing a society, whose first object would be "The Advancement of Art in Chicago, and the cultivation of social relations among its members." The Artists had few opportunities to exhibit their pictures to the public or to associate with each other; so the Society originated. The small gatherings on Saturday evenings at Mr. Spread's studio soon grew to larger and more enthusiastic meetings making it apparent that larger club quarters were necessary to accommodate the increasing membership, and to widen the field of operation.

With Mr. Spread as the first president, the Chicago Society of Artists was incorporated under the laws of the state on April 17, 1889.

In the same year galleries were fitted up at 208 Wabash, where the work of the Society progressed so rapidly that the spacious walls there were soon too small for the exhibitions and the rooms inadequate for the accommodation of the guests at receptions and lectures.

The Directors, who were conservative regarding new undertakings, found, nevertheless, that to remain in these premises would delay the natural growth of the Society, and removed in 1891 to new rooms, on the top floor of the Athenaeum Building, especially constructed for galleries, clubs, meetings and lectures.

Good fortune followed the Society in its march onward, and the future looked brightest when the fire that occurred in the building in April, 1892, swept away in an hour and totally destroyed all the furniture, properties and everything the Society had accumulated since its organization.

At the time of the fire, an exhibition of Oil and Water Color Pic-

Catalogue cover of the 7th ANNUAL BLACK AND WHITE EXHIBITION in 1895.

THE
SEVENTH ANNUAL
BLACK AND WHITE
EXHIBITION
OF THE CHICAGO
SOCIETY OF ARTISTS

WILL BEGIN ON FRIDAY, MARCH 15, 1895
AT THE GALLERIES
274 MICHIGAN AVE., COR., PECK COURT
CONTINUE DAILY UNTIL SATURDAY, MARCH 30
THE GALLERIES WILL BE OPEN MARCH 15, 20 AND 27
UNTIL 11 O'CLOCK P. M.
THE PRESENCE OF YOURSELF
AND FRIENDS IS REQUESTED

Invitation to the 7th ANNUAL BLACK AND WHITE EXHIBITION in 1895.

tures and Sculpture was open to the public, and was universally declared to be the best ever held by local artists. This exhibition was totally destroyed. It seemed especially disheartening, for it was at this time Mr. Charles T. Yerkes first made his generous offer to give, through the Society, two prizes—one of $300.00, and another of $200.00, for the best two Oil Pictures painted by Chicago artists. This mishap did not affect Mr. Yerkes' interest, for he, immediately on hearing of the loss, again offered his prizes, to be given at such time as the Society was ready to hold another exhibit.

This the members prepared for, and in about a month after the fire held another exhibition in the galleries belonging to Mr. Stevens.

The 'Yerkes' prizes are still given annually, and Mr. Yerkes has done much to encourage art, a fact that will be remembered gratefully as a matter of history.

The 'Ferris' prize of $50.00 is given by Mr. W. J. Ferris, annually, for the best black-and-white picture.

The 'Mead' prize of $25.00 is given by Mr. Wilson L. Mead, for the second best black-and-white picture.

The prizes given by these two gentlemen have added much to the interest of the yearly black-and-white exhibition, and the interest such men show in the progress of art encouraged the members. When the Society shall have secured the good will of a few such men, the stability of the Chicago Society of Artists will be secured.

Now, the Society occupies the 'Blair' house, on the corner of Peck Court and Michigan Avenue.

The house is arranged as club rooms. Studios and living rooms are rented on the upper floors to its members.

During the season of 1894-95 the society had given Saturday night entertainments, which have been largely attended, namely: 'Memories of the Art Palace,' Professor Lorado Taft; stereoptican exhibit, Professor Morse, President of Chicago Lantern Slide Club; lecture, 'The Dutch Masters,' John H. Vanderpoel; reception, opening of the annual water color exhibit; gentlemen's night, 'high jinks,' ladies' bohemian night; 'Evolution of Landscape Painting,' illustrated, Charles Francis Browne; 'Reminiscences of American Art in the Sixties,' J. W. Pattison, of Jacksonville, Illinois; 'The Spirit of Realism in Art,' Professor S. S. Curry, Ph.D.

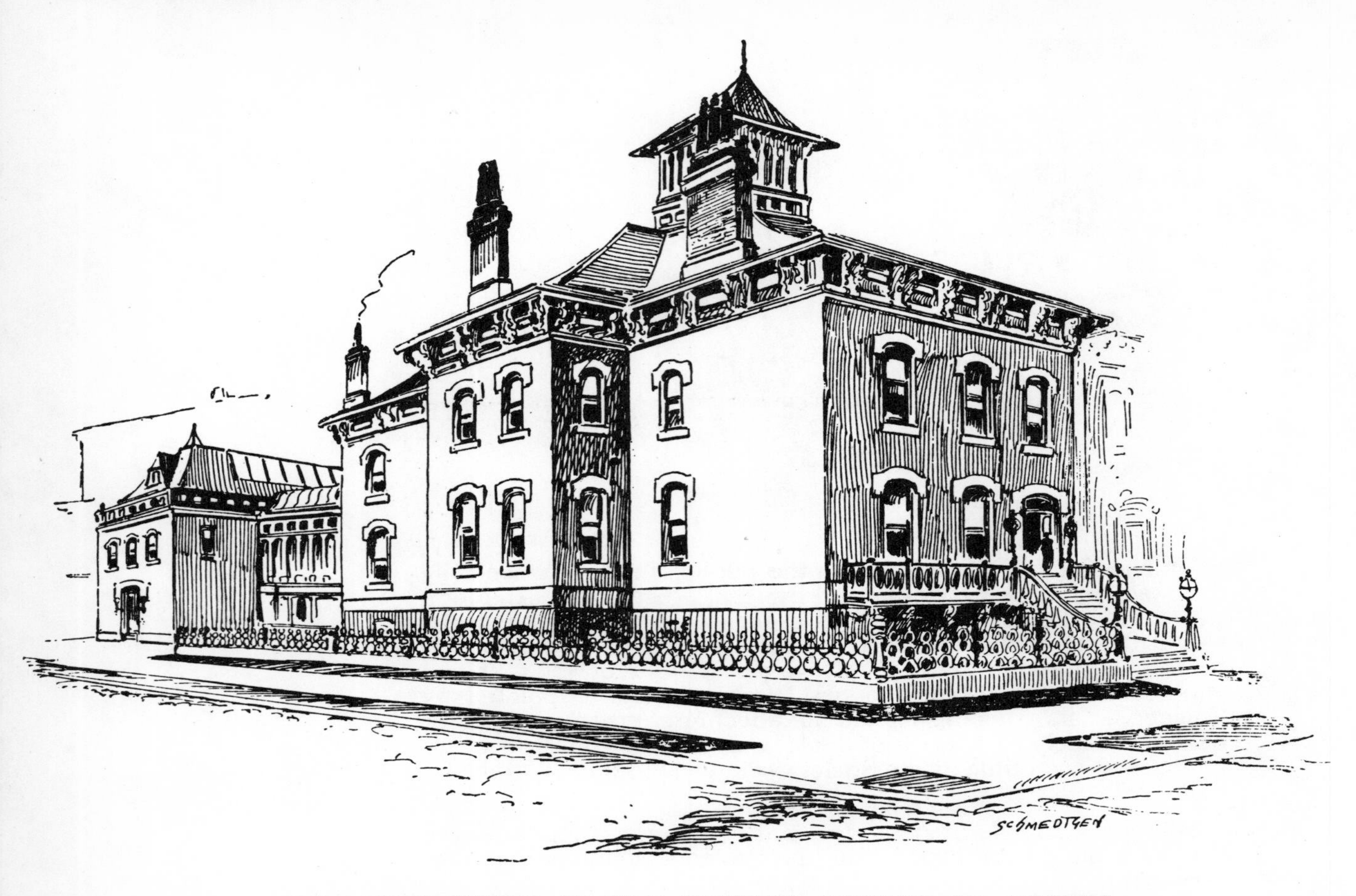

NEW CLUB HOUSE OF THE CHICAGO SOCIETY OF ARTISTS.

BLAIR HOUSE, the Chicago Society of Artists' headquarters in 1894. This illustration appeared in the May 5, 1894 issue of THE GRAPHIC.

The following gentlemen have promised to deliver addresses upon the subjects placed opposite their respective names:

John Vance Cheney—"Art Movement on the Pacific Coast."

Hamlin Garland—"Impressionism and Other Things."

Professor Halsey C. Ives—"An Art Pilgrimage."

General William Sooy Smith—"Reminiscences of Whistler's Early Days."

On Monday, March 20th the Chicago Ceramic Association will give a reception in the society's galleries in honor of the black-and-white exhibition."

Included in the schedule of events which the Chicago Society of Artists designed for its Saturday night entertainment, were a number of songs, the lyrics of which were apparently composed by some of its members. These were sung to the tunes of 'Hail Chicago,' 'Forty-Nine Bottles,' 'The Jolly Coppersmith,' 'Old Lang Syne' and 'Maryland.' Some of the songs were sentimental, others satirical in content, particularly one which referred to jurying procedures for annual exhibitions at the Art Institute of Chicago. Still other songs expressed judicious praise for the trustees, the President of the Institute and for the city itself for its support to art and industry. All of the songs projected a spirit of common devotion and aesthetic interest, binding together a group of professional artists in a warm relationship.

CHICAGO SOCIETY OF ARTISTS
274 MICHIGAN AVENUE
CHICAGO

March 1, 1895.

The Chicago Society of Artists has decided that in order to enlarge its sphere of usefulness and assist in its efforts to disseminate Art knowledge, an increase in the number of Annual Members is necessary.

In consequence, I am instructed by the Directors to invite you to become an Annual Member. A short history of the Society appears in the Catalogue and shows the distinctness of its purpose and the excellent results it has already accomplished.

The many advantages which the Society has to offer are fully set forth in the accompanying Catalogue.

I am your respectfully,

LOUIS J. MILLET,
Secretary.

APPLICATION FOR MEMBERSHIP

Chicago .... 189 ....

I hereby apply for membership in the *Chicago Society of Artists*, and subscribe to its articles of association and by-laws.

Name ....

Occupation ....

Place of Business ....

Residence ....

Kind of Membership ....

....
APPLICANT.

Regular Membership Initiation Fee . .	$25.00
Association " " "	15.00
Annual, payable yearly in advance, .	10.00
Annual Dues, payable quarterly in advance . .	24.00
Life Membership	100.00

An 1895 application for membership in the Chicago Society of Artists.

Again, through the courtesy of the Chicago Historical Society, and for the record, the songs are as follows:

TUNE: "THE JOLLY COOPERSMITH"

The artists in this great old town,
All love to sculp and paint;
We sculp most any way
And we paint most anything
Around these halls you'll see our stunts,
We make the right along,
And if you listen to us now
We will sing you a song.

CHORUS:

La, La, La, etc.

The trustees of this Institute,
Are mighty good to us;
We get most anything
And that without a fuss,
We wish them all a ripe old age,
So they'll be with us long;
And if they listen to us now
We'll sing to them this song.

CHORUS:

La, La, La, etc.

Three hundred pictures are upstairs,
And a lot of sculpture, too,
To pick this lot took three hard days
Some job, we're telling you;
If you should nurse a little grouch,
Perk up and try to see
The jury's done its level best,
And join the jamboree.

CHORUS:

La, La, La, etc.

In Prexy Hutchinson we've got
The best man in this Town
To fill the job, we think a lot
Of him and his renown;
Director Harshe he's the stuff
The man to have about
And Secretary Burkholder
We couldn't do without.

CHORUS:

La, La, La, etc.

TUNE: "FORTY-NINE BOTTLES"

Eleven hundred canvasses
Kites stacked against the wall
He brought them from the basement
To await the jury's call
But when the jury saw them
They cried "No good at all"
And they chucked a lot of pictures out
From hanging on the wall.

Now Mr. Buehr, he said "I think
Those trees are not well drawn"
"They look like feather dusters"
Said Egar Cameron
And Lucie Hartrath said "Oh dear,
Those cows we must reject"
"O chuck it out," said Norton, and
He lit a cigarette.

TUNE: "HAIL CHICAGO!"

Gem of cities of our nation, we to thee
our homage bring,
And with loving admiration, we
thy praises loudly sing,
Thou the proud and strong young giant
standing by the inland sea,
Fair art thou and self reliant, proudly
then we sing to thee.

CHORUS:

Hail Chicago! Hail Chicago!—first in
art and industry
Hail Chicago! Hail Chicago!—strong,
courageous, proud and free;
Never shall thy people falter, all the
world thy fame shall fill,
Naught thy loyalty can alter, nor thy
spirit of "I Will."

Come to the children of each nation,
from the lands across the sea,
Some of high and some low station,
seeking refuge here with thee,
With thy native sons and daughters, all
shall love and honor thee
Till like sound of mighty waters, this our
song of praise shall be:

CHORUS: Hail Chicago! etc.

TUNE: "AULD LANG SYNE"

When once again the year rolls round
And its time for our Annual Show
We're glad to gather in this hall
To greet the friends we know
We're pleased to see new faces here
And hope that from now on
They'll join our ranks and play our pranks
And help Art Right Along.

They say that this is the best show
They say that every year
But we must shout for our own work
Its best to boost, that's clear
We drink a toast to all of you
We drink it hearty and long
But owing to the Volstead Act
We cannot make it strong.

In 1889 the Society authorized its first contribution of $100.00 as a prize to be awarded to a painter, sculptor or printmaker for a meritorious work of art at the Annual Chicago Artists and Vicinity Exhibitions held at the Art Institute of Chicago. Pauline Rudolph, a Chicago painter, was the first recipient of the Society's prize. This established practice by the Chicago Society of Artists has been continued to the present day.

For twenty-five years, the Society functioned without any major changes or crises. In 1913, however, after the highly controversial Armory Exhibition in New York, a few of the members threatened to split into so-called "conservative" and "modern" groups. In its long history, strangely enough, this controversy was the only serious threat to the Society's existence. A group of artists who called themselves conservatives did finally separate. Most of the original group, which also included some of the conservative element, nevertheless remained to achieve a strong and cohesively functioning group of moderns. This group constituted the nucleus around which the present organizational structure was built.

Through the years the Chicago Society of Artists strived to retain its vitality. By means of a careful jury system, it resolutely maintained a consistency in the selection of its members—based only upon highly accepted professional standards. In this process also, the Chicago Society of Artists aligned itself with progressive art movements in the nation.

To date, the Chicago Society of Artists has earned the distinction of being the oldest continuously active art organization in the United States. Included in its membership are painters, sculptors, printmakers, art educators, artist-writers and art critics. Its members' works have been included in major regional, national and international exhibitions and have also been represented in numerous private, public and permanent museum collections. Paintings, murals, sculpture, stained glass windows and tapestries—works which adorn architectural structures and which enrich the interiors of countless school buildings, churches, synagogues, temples, hospitals, post-offices and various other civic and cultural institutions—are manifestations of enduring evidence which documents the Society's aesthetic contribution.

In contemplating further the Society's historic past, it becomes apparent that its charter members have left an indelible imprint upon the aesthetic life of Chicago and the nation. This fact has been clearly substantiated in numerous columns devoted to the Society's activities and reviewed by distinguished critics of Chicago newspapers. Inez Cunningham, Irwin St. John Tucker, J. Z. Jacobson, Sterling North, Meyer Levin, Samuel Putnam, Forbes Watson, Phil Nesbit, C. J. Bulliet, Eleanor Jewett, Frank Holland, Harold Haydon and others have all at one time or another, and often in concert, extolled the artistic achievements of individuals in the group and frequently applauded the highly professional status of the entire Society.

In the course of time, charter members have passed away. Others have moved to greener pastures or to warmer climates but still have retained their membership in the Society, contributing block-prints to its annual publication, "The Chicago Society of Artists Calendar," and paintings, prints or sculpture to its exhibitions.

Those who remained in Chicago and those who have joined the Society recently are pursuing their major interests with vigor, individually as well as within the context of the organization's structured activities. A goodly number of its members have been actively involved in the Chicago Society of Artists for nearly thirty years; others for even a longer period of time.

The vitality of the Chicago Society of Artists is, no doubt, inherent in the versatility and diversity of each of its members. A loosely structured program of activities allows for flexibility in the Society's functioning. It also accords a common purpose to the group as it provides a climate that is conducive to cohesiveness and creativity.

The Chicago Society of Artists' enduring qualities as an organization may be rightly attributed to the enterprising efforts of its Board of Directors. It is comprised of long-time members as well as the newly elected. The Board of Directors is voted into office by the entire membership. New Board members are added as vacancies occur. The complete group, however, meets at exhibition openings and at other events which are especially designed to enlist total membership participation in social and professional matters.

What has made this heterogeneous group of professional artists function in a harmonious relationship for as long as it has is not difficult to determine. Its carefully planned activities certainly played a major role in the Society's existence. For those have served to spur interaction among its older and younger members—the former providing an inspiring link, the latter an infusion of lively sparks in the unbroken chain of continuity.

Thomas Dewey once concisely stated "Wherever there is interaction, there is also continuity." Lively interaction may very well account for the Society's longevity and for its profound effectiveness in cultural matters.

THE NATURE OF THE GROUP: ITS STANDARDS OF TASTE

In any long range view of historic evidence, it becomes essentially clear that groups as much as individuals develop a sensitivity to aesthetic values which, in turn, evolve as standards of taste. Implicit in these standards, however, is not necessarily the imposition of the proverbial "straight jacket" upon the creative person, nor upon the creative process. Rather, it is that which may be seen in the light of universally accepted criteria, principles, or guidelines by which professionalism is indentified, sustained or evaluated.

Writers, poets, dramatists, critics, musicians, painters, sculptors and scientists are known to have a built-in tolerance for deviation from established criteria, if only for the sake of creativity. More often than not, they justify the validity of taking liberties or poetic license in the creative process. Nonetheless, those who are involved in productive endeavors are ever-mindful of the universally accepted qualities which place a higher premium upon one work of art above that of another on the evaluative scale of professional performance. Indeed, they are fully aware that were it not for this allowance or tolerance, new and novel discoveries in art, music or science—approaches, techniques, processes, methods, and most important individuality in self-expression—all would be stifled, adding neither zest to life nor progress to cultural development.

When standards of taste reflect the genuine spirit of a group and are not merely a semblance of homogeneous trends, they do bring intrinsic character to its creative entity.

The levels at which standards of taste are realized depend largely upon the resources that have been made available and the talents that have been conditioned and nurtured through the utilization of these resources.

The Chicago Society of Artists, because of its longevity, has been visibly affected by eclectic as well as cosmopolitan tendencies, revealing through its works an outward manifestation of an evolutionary process. The group is a composite of many elements from traditional academicism to surrealism and abstraction; no one style is dominant. In broad terms, it may be simply stated that there are present "pure" artists, the pioneer modern group, the American scene group, the social content group, abstract artists, surrealists and neo-romantics in the Society.

But the lines of demarcation between styles are not clearly defined. For the truly determining and operative factors in this group are individuality and originality in self-expression.

THE CHICAGO SOCIETY OF ARTISTS: ITS ROLE IN THE MODERN ART MOVEMENT

After the Armory Show, artists in Chicago, no less than those in New York, were stirred into action. Some of the artists began to ponder over their personal approaches to artistic expression, asserting their own positions firmly and rejecting the new and innovative elements appearing on the national and local scene. Others expressed their displeasure with frenzied furor, denouncing the traditional views, and looked with disdain upon those who pursued the conventional and academic style of painting. It was then that artists divided into two distinct camps and classified themselves either as "conservatives" or "modernists."

The Chicago Society of Artists aligned itself with the evolutionary growth of the modern art movement in the country. These artists became known as "the wild ones" as did their counterparts in Paris. Spurring this trend were also a number of New York artists who came to serve as Artists-In-Residence at the Art Institute of Chicago. Being protagonists of the modern art movement, they urged their students to broaden their visual horizons in pursuit of individual goals.

The movement was further propelled by the Bauhaus School of thought and its exponents of the new vision: Walter Gropius, Joseph Albers, Wassily Kandinsky, Paul Klee and Laslo Moholy-Nagy. Artists of the new Bauhaus founded on American soil at the Institute of Design in Chicago embraced the theory which strived for the closest connection between art, science and technology. The scope of artistic expression was widened through their leadership. Students began to explore the infinite possibilities of new media, processes, materials and

THE TAILOR, oil by LEON GARLAND (Courtesy of Mrs. Sadie Dreikurs)

methods heretofore unknown to them and to tread upon new terrain with confidence and lively interest.

Helpful in leading art students as well as young artists into the general direction of the modern art movement were a number of Chicago's professional artists. Two of these, members of the Chicago Society of Artists, were Artists-in-Residence at the Hull House. There Sadie Ellis Garland, a protege of Jane Addams, and Leon Garland, her husband, both painters and printmakers, taught students of all ages. There, too, Sadie Garland introduced group painting, a method she now employs in the treatment of psychotic patients. Leon taught batik and metal crafts. Both were former students of Lhote and Leger in Paris and were among early abstractionists—trail blazers in Chicago's artistic circles.

Samuel Greenburg, painter, printmaker, author, and also a student of Lhote, conducted private classes in his studio for many years. He was a major proponent of the modern idiom in painting.

Among others who were considered the early abstractionists and members of the Society were Paul Kelpe, Harold Hantke, Wilfred Smith, Tud Kempf, and Marguerite Hohenberg. A. Raymond Katz, muralist, head artist for Balaban and Katz, did extraordinary modern posters for the Chicago Opera. Mitchell Siporin, a muralist, and Edgar Miller, who designed stained glass windows for Diana Court and who won a national mural competition for the St. Louis Post Office, were both exponents of the modern art movement in Chicago.

Further impetus to the modern movement was given by drama critic

C. J. Bulliet (then with the Chicago Evening-Post). He came under the influence of his friend and artist Rudolph Weisenborn, an independent, highly controversial artist-teacher and firm believer in Cubism. Through him, C. J. Bulliet became thoroughly enchanted with the modern art movement and became Chicago's best known art critic for many years. In time, he wrote "Apples and Madonnas" in praise of contemporary art and "Art Masterpieces of 1933 and 1934," describing Art Institute exhibits of world masterpieces.

Fritzi Weisenborn, wife of Rudolph, in later years became the art critic for the Chicago Sun-Times. Although she shared her husband's feelings and preferences, nonetheless she was unbiased in her appraisals of other artists' works. More often than not, she reviewed exhibits in a candid and engaging manner, neither derisive nor partial to any particular idiom.

Still later, Frank Holland, art critic for the Sun-Times, and Inez Cunningham, art critic for the Herald-American, favored the more innovative contemporary artists. But they, too, impartially reviewed exhibitions of Chicago's artists despite the fact that their preferences leaned toward those whose traditional tendencies were somewhat modified.

Indirectly, but nonetheless playing a vital role in boosting the modern art movement in Chicago, was Oswald Brod, husband of Fritzi Brod (modern painter and member of the Chicago Society of Artists). "Ozzi" Brod was the chief buyer of art books for Kroch's and Brentano's. Local artists were able to fill their studio libraries with current books on modern art or any other art movement due to the reasonable discount rates Ozzi accorded to them.

By 1932 the tempo of the modern art movement increased perceptibly. In Chicago, small and large galleries suddenly emerged. These galleries catered primarily to artists whose works deviated from traditional or academic approaches to painting or sculpture.

Some of the galleries were owned or directed by members of the Chicago Society of Artists. For example, The Little Gallery, located in the Auditorium Tower and established in 1932, was directed by

THE DEAD SOLDIER, oil by NICOLA ZIROLI. Ziroli held an inaugural one-man exhibition at the Little Gallery.

Samuel Greenburg and A. Raymond Katz. The committed policy of this gallery was to exhibit modern art only. Among those who held their inaugural one-man shows in this gallery were Aaron Bohrod, Paul Kelpe, Eve Garrison and Nick Ziroli. Other one-man exhibitions held in The Little Gallery were those by Gertrude Abercrombie, Rainey Bennet, Julia Thecla, Tud and Thomas Kempf, A. Raymond Katz, Louis and Minnie Harms Neebe, Gregory Orloff, Emil Armin, Rivka Angel, David Bekker, Gus Dalstrom, Frances Foy and Samuel Greenburg.

The Increase Robinson Studio Gallery, located in the Diana Court, was a large and prestigious gallery of modern art. Increase Robinson, painter, and former president of the Chicago Society of Artists, was its owner and director. There Katherine Kuh delivered instructive discourses on modern art. Both of these women were profoundly influential in widening the scope of artistic vision and in developing a keen sense of appreciation for contemporary trends in art in Chicago and elsewhere.

Later, Kuh's ingeniously dramatic displays in the Art Institute's Gallery of Interpretation intensified her missionary efforts. There she unraveled the subtle and sublime mysteries of creativity, focusing upon the artist's intent, the structural basis of his works and the philosophy which enveloped the artistic production. She skillfully dissipated some illusions and created others in the process. Through her penetrating analyses of works of art, many viewers came away with a deeper sense of appreciation for artistic endeavors than they nurtured prior to this type of exposure. For these were indeed enlightening and visually aesthetic, well documented exhibits.

The significance of Katherine Kuh's contribution to the local art scene cannot be underestimated. The impact of her presentations was unmistakably impressive and visibly palatable. Through her efforts thousands of viewers, school children and adults, have been exposed to her interpretations of art. This audience constituted a tremendously potential group of appreciators so vital to the survival of the artist and his ego.

As director of the Renaissance Society Gallery of the University of Chicago, Frances Strain sponsored many and varied contemporary art exhibitions, reinforcing the growing interest in modern art in the city.

For many years, Jean Crawford Adams, director of the highly respected Arts Club, sponsored exhibitions of modern art from foreign lands. As a painter, Jean Crawford Adams was in the forefront of the modern art movement in Chicago. Her works were included in every major national and international exhibition held in the United States.

Marguerite Hohenberg, another member of the Chicago Society of Artists and one of the leading Chicago abstractionists, was also director of the Hohenberg Gallery on Oak Street. Primarily, works of abstract painters were exhibited in her gallery.

The Remahl Gallery on 57th Street catered to contemporary painters and sculptors.

In the more recent past, the Chicago Society of Artists acquired its own gallery named The Chicago Society of Artists Gallery on Orchard and Lincoln Streets. It was designed and constructed by Bob Bailey, one of many of the Society's dedicated members. The gallery was in-

BOB BAILEY in the Chicago Society of Artists Gallery. Bailey designed and constructed the gallery space.

tended to be used for the display of paintings and sculpture created by the Society's members only, either in one-man or group shows, and for the entire group's annual exhibitions. For several years the Chicago Society of Artists struggled to maintain it. But when the up-keep became too prohibitive and burdensome, the idea of gallery ownership lost its luster and was finally abandoned by the group.

One Chicago publisher for more than three decades has focused attention upon Chicago art and artists. As publisher, art patron and collector, L. M. Stein held a profound regard for artists whose stature he recognized and admired. He was without a doubt one of the most dedicated publishers of art books in the city, lauded by art critics and laymen here and elsewhere.

Under his personal and tasteful guidance were published a number of books. The first was **Art of Today:** Chicago, 1933, edited by J. Z. Jacobson. Other books followed. They were **The Ten Commandments, A Portfolio of Ten Prints in Full Color** by A. Raymond Katz; **Linoleum Cuts** by William Jacobs; **William S. Schwartz** by Manual Chapman; **Thirty-Five Saints and Emil Armin** by J. Z. Jacobson; **A Volume of 60 Woodcuts: From Land to Land** by Todros Geller; **Building Human Relationships Through Art** by Louise Dunn Yochim.

All of these books except the last chronicled the lives and works of Chicago painters, sculptors and printmakers. Since Mr. Stein's death in 1957, few if any publications concerned specifically with local artists and their achievements have been published.

A COUNTER-MOVEMENT: "SANITY IN ART"

Concurrent with the increasingly popular modern art movement in Chicago in 1933 was the counter-movement "Sanity in Art." It

KACHINAS, woodcut by TODROS GELLER, 1936 (Courtesy of the Chicago Society of Artists)

reflected a sincere expression of indignation and uncompromising contempt for prevailing trends in art. Principally, it was a protest against the existing and "arrogant" abuses of long established approaches to painting and sculpture. It was an earnest protest against the indiscriminate use of color, the utter disregard for subject matter, the gross distortions of nature, human form or other animate or inanimate objects, the disdainful regard for consciously structured canvases and finally—and most vehemently—against the lack of sensitivity on the part of modern artists to traditionally established and guiding principles of art.

The chief advocate and champion of the "Sanity of Art" movement was Mrs. Frank G. Logan, a patron of the arts and wife of the Art Institute's honorary president and donor of its main prize. She called for "Sanity in Art" and organized a national movement against "isms" and "depressed subjects." Her espoused cause had the unqualified support of Eleanor Jewett, art critic of the Chicago Tribune, who pleaded eloquently and pervasively to reverse the modern art movement. Miss Jewett gathered many followers along the way. Among these were naturally the conservative element among the artists, as well as among the laymen. Their joint efforts were intended to meet only one objective and that was to turn the tide from modernism back to established traditionalism or academicism.

The modernists, however, continued to be intransigent, firmly rooted in their belief that an artist's horizons must be expanded in order to regenerate his creative self and to bring to the surface new and novel interpretations of personal ideas.

Whether the conservative elements have, or have not, succeeded in advancing their points of view seems no longer a matter of interest. However, if one is to judge from the proliferation of artistic trends which have emerged in the last four decades, the exact opposite appears to have been achieved.

HEAVY THE OAR TO HIM WHO IS TIRED, HEAVY THE COAT, HEAVY THE SEA, by IVAN LeLORRAINE ALBRIGHT, exhibited in the Century of Progress Exhibition of Painting and Sculpture at the Art Institute of Chicago in 1933. (Courtesy of the Art Institute of Chicago)

4 The CSA: Contribution to International, National and Regional Exhibitions, 1933–51

A significant number of works by members of the Chicago Society of Artists constituted a viable aesthetic force in international, national and regional exhibitions. The record is unmistakably impressive, not only in terms of numbers and quality, but also in meaningful substance and in diversity of styles.

The following two chapters will be devoted entirely to the scrutiny of a series of noteworthy art events. The object is to establish the extent to which the members of the Chicago Society of Artists individually or collectively have contributed toward these events and, thereby, to the aesthetic growth of the city and the nation.

The careful chronicling of participants and their recurring representation in major exhibitions of national and international scope, described in ensuing accounts, may be of only passing interest to the layman. In fact, it may even be trying his patience! But to artists of the thirties and to those who will recall with a sense of nostalgia the excitement of each important event and each involved artist—this chronicling of artists and their works is a meaningful and memorable experience. The frequent appearance of some names will no doubt reflect a consistency in qualitative performance—a consistency which characterized the membership of the Chicago Society of Artists time and again.

An artist's stature is measured in direct proportion to the acceptance of his works by prestigious galleries and museums in this country and elsewhere. At least, that has been true in the past and holds equally true today. Exhibiting works of art alongside highly esteemed contemporaries enhances an artist's own stature as a professional. In the eyes of the layman and in the opinion of art critics and museum directors, that kind of acceptance generally commands utmost respect for the works of the artist. Whether one cares to submit to this premise or not is not a matter of debate. The fact remains that due recognition from authoritative sources has a profound affect upon the career of an artist.

The frequent representation of individual members of a group in important exhibitions reveals an impressive point, no doubt. Particularly, as this fact relates to the consistency and worthy achievement of each. But, it also reflects upon the professional standing of the group of which the artist is an active member.

The reader's indulgence is therefore invited, as he peruses the lists of names included in Chart I, and considers the purpose for which they are intended.

The first of the major artistic events to be recorded in this chapter occured in the early thirties. It was "A Century of Progress Exhibition of Paintings and Sculpture," held at the Art Institute of Chicago in 1933.

RAILROAD STATION, oil by DAVENPORT GRIFFEN, 1933

RECOLLECTION OF THE SOUTHWEST, bronze by THEODORE ROSZAK
(Courtesy of Maremont Collection)

INTERNATIONAL EXHIBITIONS

A Century of Progress Exhibition of Paintings and Sculpture, Art Institute Of Chicago, 1933

The organization and content of the exhibition held at the Art Institute of Chicago was carefully delineated in the Foreword to the catalogue written by Robert B. Harshe, Director. It is quoted here verbatim, because it clearly indicates the nature, structure and extent of "A Century of Art Exhibition of Painting and Sculpture."

> The exhibition of painting and sculpture celebrating 'A Century of Progress' has been assembled (with one exception, Whistler's "Portrait of His Mother") entirely from American sources. Private collectors and guardians of public collections have been so generous, that, with the significant examples already owned by the Institute, it has been possible to arrange a sequence of the masterpieces of painting, beginning with European works of the thirteenth century and coming to European and American examples of today.
>
> The theme of the 1933 Exposition, 'A Century of Progress,' has been broadly interpreted to mean, not only art of the last century, but a hundred years' progress in American collecting. In 1833 very few great works were on this side of the Atlantic; today the United States possesses treasures of amazing quality, inspiring not only to our artists, but to the rapidly growing public who are coming to feel the need of art in their daily lives. Particularly during the last twenty-five or thirty years many brilliant examples of painting have made their way westward, some going at once into

HARVEST OF THE SEA, oil by FLORA SCHOFIELD, 1933

museums, more finding their way into private hands. One of the chief aims of the present showing is to exhibit works which are rarely if ever seen by the public, emphasizing in this way the resources of the nation.

The exhibition contains oil paintings, watercolors, drawings and sculpture. The painting division is made up of three main parts. First: European paintings from the thirteenth through the eighteenth centuries. These works have been hung in historical sequence. Second: Nineteenth century painting, mostly French and American (and containing one gallery of early American examples), arranged in a series of galleries so as to throw into relief the great artistic personalities of the last hundred years. Third: Twentieth century painting, American and International, presenting the art of significant contemporaries.

In the section given to watercolor, drawings and pastels, there will be found a similar division. A small group of old master drawings will start the survey; then, works of Nineteenth century artists and last, examples by contemporaries. Over a hundred pieces of sculpture (all of the last hundred years) complete the exhibition.

> At the same time, in the Print Galleries, a survey of masterpieces in prints, closely paralleling the Exhibition of A Century of Progress is being held.

Thirty-nine members of the Chicago Society of Artists were represented in "A Century of Progress Exhibition." Oil paintings, watercolors, drawings, and sculpture were exhibited at this highly significant cultural event. (See Chart I).

International Watercolor Exhibition, Art Institute of Chicago, 1934

Among other painters from the United States there were thirty-one members of the Chicago Society of Artists who represented Contemporary American Painting in the International Watercolor Exhibition at the Art Institute of Chicago in 1934. Their works were hung alongside works of artists from Austria, France, Germany, Great Britain, Guatemala, Italy, Mexico, Poland, Russia, Spain and Switzerland. (See Chart I).

International Exhibition of Contemporary Prints, Art Institute of Chicago, 1934

Represented in the International Exhibition of Contemporary Prints were thirteen members of the Chicago Society of Artists. They were Ivan LeLorraine Albright, C. W. Anderson, Peggy Bacon, Francis Chapin, John H. Clifford, Elizabeth Colwell, Charles W. Dahlgreen, Julio DeDiego, Frances Foy, Beatrice S. Levy, Tunis Ponsen, Theodore J. Roszak, and Charles A. Wilimovsky.

Other exhibitors were artists from Austria, Belgium, Canada, Czechoslovakia, Denmark, France, Germany, Great Britain, Holland, Hungary, Italy, Mexico, Japan, Norway, Poland, Roumania, Spain and Switzerland. (See Chart I).

International Watercolor Exhibition, Art Institute of Chicago, 1935

An International Exhibition of watercolors, pastels, drawings and monotypes was held at the Art Institute of Chicago in 1935. Interestingly enough, the Jury of Selection consisted of two members of the Chicago Society of Artists, Edgar Miller and Jean Crawford Adams. The third, Louis Ritman, was not a member of the Society.

Represented in this exhibition were American Indian paintings and works from Austria, France, Germany, Great Britain, Holland, Hungary, Italy, Japan, Yugoslavia, Mexico, Persia, Roumania, Russia, Spain, Sweden, and the United States.

Among the exhibitors from other countries were some illustrious names such as: Miguel Covarrubias from Mexico; Pavel Tchelitchew from Russia; Fred Castellon from Spain. An impressive list also came from France: Jean Dufy, Raoul Dufy, Andre Lhote, Georges Rouault, Andre Dunoyer de Segonzac, Maurice Utrillo, Edouard Vuillard. From Germany: George Grosz, George Kolbe, Emil Nolde, Karl Schmidt-Rottluff, Karl Zerbe and others. From Italy: Gino Severini. From Japan: Fuji Nakamizo.

The largest representation in this exhibition was from the United States. Thirty-nine members of the Chicago Society of Artists were

THE LAST ACT, oil by
FREDERICK REMAHL

among others representing this country. Included were paintings, drawings and sculpture. (See Chart I).

International Watercolor Exhibition, Art Institute of Chicago, 1936

Members of the Chicago Society of Artists who were not included in the International Watercolor Exhibition in 1935 were represented by watercolors, drawings and prints in 1936. They were Frances Badger, Roff Beman, Fred Biesel, Fritzi Brod, Elizabeth Colwell, Davenport Griffen, Emile J. Grumieaux, Natalie Henry, Carl Hoeckner, Ann Michalov, Edgar Miller, Edward Millman, Harry Mintz, Frances Strain, Laura VanPappelendam and Nicola Ziroli. (See Chart I)

NATIONAL EXHIBITIONS

Delphic Studios, New York, 1935

During the month of May of 1935, the Chicago Society of Artists organized a traveling exhibition of oil paintings. The entire exhibition was first held at the Delphic Studios in New York. Later it was taken over by the American Federation of Arts. Under its sponsorship the exhibition was sent on tour. Fifty-five painters participated in this traveling show (See Chart I).

New Jersey State Musuem, Trenton, New Jersey, 1936

In 1936, the entire Chicago Society of Artists exhibit, again emanating from the Delphic Studios in New York, was installed in the New Jersey State Museum, Trenton, New Jersey. From here, under the auspices of the Federation of Arts, the exhibition traveled to Washington, D.C.; Delaware; Ohio; Bemidji, Minnesota; and finally Rockford, Illinois. In March of 1936 the Chicago Society of Artists' traveling exhibition culminated its tour (See Chart I)

Riverside Musuem, New York, 1939

During February, 1939, the Chicago Society of Artists held an exhibition of paintings and sculpture at the Riverside Museum in New York. The Society was featured as Chicago's "Outstanding Society of Modern Artists." Clara MacGowan, then president of the group and member of the Department of Art Education, National Education Society, wrote the Foreword to the Catalogue, which briefly explained the goals of the Chicago Society of Artists.

> The Chicago Society of Artists, organized in 1887, was the first Society of its kind in the city of Chicago. Its purpose has been to unite artists in fellowship and to combine their efforts in the advancement of art. During all this time the group has striven to maintain a high professional standard and to follow the individual artist's freedom to work as he wished.
>
> The work of the Society reflects in no small measure the physical nature and social life that is Chicago in all its diversity.
>
> Here, typically enough, the members represent different cultures

PASTORAL, oil by GEORGE MELVILLE SMITH

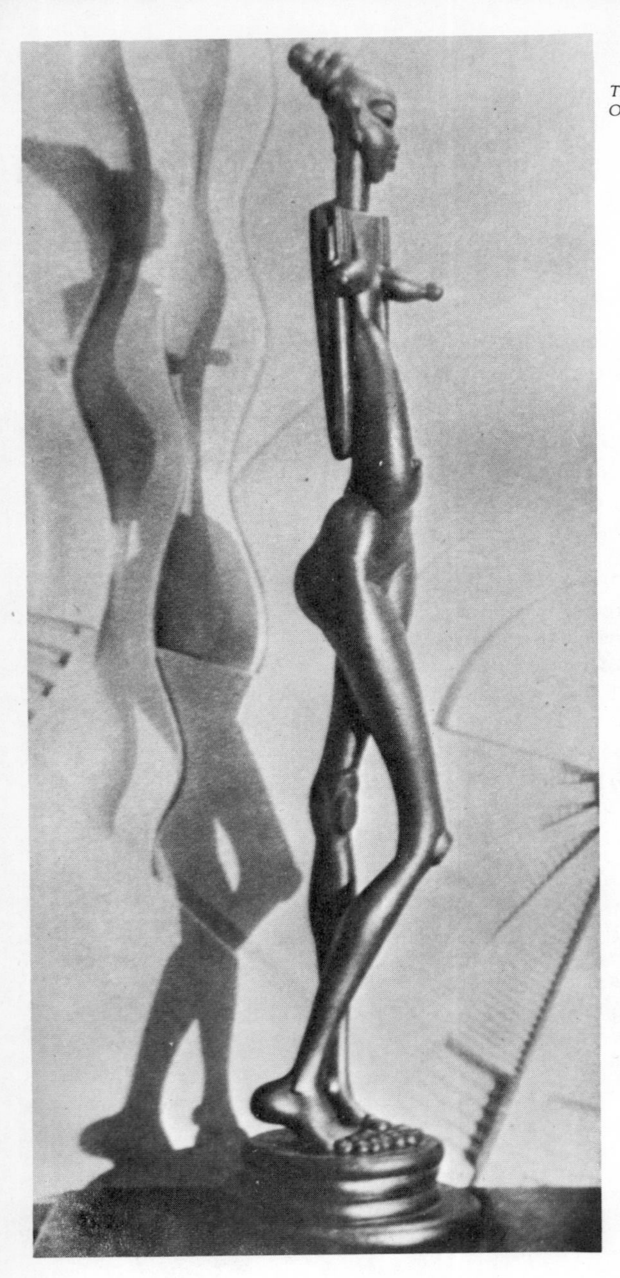

THE IDOL, sculpture by OLGA CHASSAING

CHRIST AND THE LITTLE CHILDREN, sculpture by CHARLES UMLAUF, 1943

and backgrounds. Many to whom this city is now home, spent their childhood in various parts of the world. These artists in expressing what is so native to them have enriched Chicago art in a very real sense. Certainly, that accounts for the fact that the total output of the Society is not limited to so-called 'regional art'.

Always progressive and advanced and nationally known as a modern group, the Chicago Society of Artists has been the vanguard of artistic development in Chicago and Middle West.

Fifty-seven members, which obviously constituted a large percentage of the total membership, participated in this exhibition of paintings and sculpture (See Chart I).

"American Art Today," The New York World's Fair, 1939

In 1939 an exhibition of American paintings, sculpture, drawings, and prints was held in New York in conjunction with the New York

World's Fair. That year a volume entitled **American Art Today** was published by the National Art Society. In it were included reproductions of each exhibitor's work. Holger Cahill wrote the introduction to the volume. Altogether it reflected an impressive record of artistic achievement in the United States, in which members of the Chicago Society of Artists played a significant role.

In his introduction Holger Cahill stated that this exhibition represented "a wide perspective of our country's creative expression in the fine arts. The 1,200 works included in the exhibition were selected from 25,000 entries submitted. There is no doubt that this represents the most extensive and most thorough winnowing of American Art which has ever taken place, a winnowing based on competent professional opinion. Artist committees in every section of the country have given their judgment on what they consider the most typical and representative American works in the fields of paintings, sculpture, drawings and prints."

Among those represented in this exhibition from the State of Illinois were fifty-five members of the Chicago Society of Artists.

Obviously, the total number of the Chicago Society of Artists represented in the American Art Today exhibition was an impressive one not only because of the aggregate representation in this exhibition, but, more important, because of the nature and quality of its content. All of this, of course, reflected credit upon the Society's artistic integrity. Moreover, these Chicago artists brought stature to their city (See Chart I).

American Painting and Sculpture, Art Institute of Chicago, 1941

Thirty-three members of the Chicago Society of Artists were included in the American Painting and Sculpture Exhibition held at the Art Institute of Chicago in 1941. Among the eight prize winners in this exhibition were three from the Chicago Society of Artists. They were Edwin Boyd Johnson, Sam Ostrovsky and Maurice Ritman.

John Corbino, painter, New York; Charles Hopkinson, painter, Boston; Robert Philipp, painter, New York, served as the New York and Chicago Jury for Painting.

The New York Jury for Sculpture were John B. Flannagan, sculptor, New York; Waylande Gregory, sculptor, Bound Brook, New Jersey; Wheeler Williams, sculptor, New York.

The Chicago Jury for Sculpture consisted of Carl Miles, sculptor, Bloomfield Hills, Michigan; Emmanuel Viviano, sculptor, Chicago; Warner Williams, sculptor, Chicago.

Daniel Catton Rich, Director of Fine Arts, Art Institute of Chicago, wrote a revealing account of the exhibition. His introduction "American Art, 1940" was written for the catalogue of the 51st Annual American Painting and Sculpture Exhibition. In a rather cursory manner he touched upon prevalent trends in American art. A few prophetic notes were vaguely implied. Sociological influences affecting most artists of that period were summarily inferred.

> The exhibition, the fifty-first annual of American paintings and sculpture, resumes the series interrupted by last season's showing, Half Century of American Art. Most of these works were done dur-

ing the past two years, and many of our leading artists were included. As in previous exhibitions of this kind, no attempt has been made to emphasize one style or one school. Rather the Institute has tried to show Chicago just what is happening to art in America.

What changes do we find in the 1940's exhibit? Most striking perhaps is the dearth of 'pure painting,' that is to say, little primary concern with elements of line, color texture and space. Even our most distinguished workers in this tradition have begun to interpret American subject matter rather than subjects from the studio; Eugene Speicher paints 'Farm News' and Alexander Brook visiting the South resumes with 'Georgia Jungle,' a haunting report of Negro life. Others like Henry Mattson, Franklin Watkins, Bernard Karfiol and Peppino Mangravite explore a poetic and romantic strain. Here they are joined by Fletcher Martin's dramatic episode of shipwreck 'Home From The Sea.'

There is a new interest in the Old Masters. Painters today are less apt to argue over Cezanne and Picasso than over Rembrandt, Titian and Goya. Ann Brockman's large canvas 'Evicted,' John Corbino's 'Harvest Festival,' and Fred Nagler's version of the 'Crucifixion' are three canvases in point. This does not mean that we are headed back to the scholarly anemia of the 90's. Our men are looking for vigor of design and new vision—not mere patina. Mural painting—largely under Federal patrongage—has been doing its part in teaching Americans (who are weak in this vein) how to compose figures into broad, integrated patterns.

Dogged, humorless proletarian art is on the wane. Where social sympathy appears as in Philip Evergood's compelling picture of a slum child it is apt to have strong emotion behind its message. The symbolism of Joseph Hirch's 'Hero' and Gregorio Prestopino's 'Fortress' (the latter almost prophetic of Europe's approaching famine) shows the painter's deep concern over contemporary problems. Other Americans like Reginald Marsh and John Sloan see life with an ironic eye while at the same time recognizing its verve and color.

There is less out-and-out regionalism. Grant Wood has forsaken Iowa for a sky dig at American legend, 'Fable' by Parson Weems continues the spirit of his earlier Midnight Ride of Paul Revere. Landscape no longer follows the vacation pattern of a generation ago. Millard Sheets' flowing, decorative California, Pleissner's lightstruck Florida, Zepeshy's cold Michigan, and above all Curry's panorama of Wisconsin interpret the mood and character of the region rather than its superficial atmosphere. Chicago entries show the city still a major theme, often conceived with rich overtones of color.

As before, the exhibition included the work of various independents who refuse to be classified. In the half-abstract 'Harvest' of Karl Knaths, the glowing 'Poppies' of Georgia O'Keefe, and the fantasy of Arthur Dove we find contrasting examples of American experiment. Surrealism, last of European art movements, may be detected in Castelon's strange 'Invitation' and Guglielmi's 'Mental Geography.'

In sculpture there is a double return to beginnings: hard stones and archaic forms. Where in the past much has been dinky or fancy, there are new aspirations towards the monumental and the organic. Such classicism as does appear in this vigorous groups of sculpture is of the calm, decorative variety.

Through the whole exhibit there is plenty of evidence that the artist of 1940 is part of our own baffled world. In better or worse (depending on whether you like art to take you away from what's going on or whether you prefer to have the present intensified),

STRAWBERRY PRINT, oil by FRANCES FOY, 1943.

> the artist has come out of his studio and thrown himself into life. His sharp eyes take in the ruin of cities, the death of the land, and whirlwind of war. Feeling these things deeply, he expresses them strongly.
>
> And, since the artist is a sensitive person, remember that his account—though at times exaggerated—may cut deeper than the America we applaud on the movie screen or follow day by day in the pages of our fiction magazines.

Of the thirty-three members of the Chicago Society of Artists included in the "American Painting and Sculpture" exhibition, twenty-six were painters and seven were sculptors. (See Chart I).

Contemporary American Painting, University of Illinois, Urbana, Ill., 1948–1951

In 1948, under the auspices of the College of Fine and Applied Arts of the University of Illinois in Urbana, the first Contemporary American Painting Exhibition was organized. It was an invitational show which later became an annual event. In 1949, Claude Bentley

MESSAGE FOR MERCY, oil by GERTRUDE ABERCROMBIE. This painting was included in the Contemporary American Painting Exhibition, at the University of Illinois in 1951.

and Felix Ruvolo, both members of the Chicago Society of Artists, were recipients of two of the ten awards for meritorious works of art. In 1950, nine members of the Society were included in the show. They were Claude Bentley, Francis Chapin, Julio DeDiego, Edward Millman, Harry Mintz, Felix Ruvolo, Mitchell Siporin, Emerson Woelffer and Zsissly. Gertrude Abercrombie, Rainey Bennett and Copeland Burg, as well as some of the participants of previous years, were included in the 1951 exhibition of Contemporary American Painting.

In the "Introduction" to the catalogue for the 1950 exhibition of Contemporary American Painting, Rexford Newcomb, Dean of the College of Fine and Applied Arts of the University of Illinois, expressed his views in the following partial quote:

> In this third annual exhibition of Contemporary American Painting, the University of Illinois presents an opportunity to consider the development of painting in this country at the Mid-century. The paintings in this exhibition were chosen with the basic purpose of securing technical excellence, diversity of approach, and varying emotional responses, as well as variety of subject matter and content.
>
> The Jury of Selection has surveyed the field of American painting with the intention of securing fine work not only from artists with established reputations but also from those painters who, though less well-known, give every indication of professional competence. We confidently believe this collection to be as representative an exhibition of the painting being done in America today as can be encompassed in any show of 147 canvases.

GARDEN IN THE WOODS, oil by COPELAND C. BURG, 1951

At the Mid-century we are prompted to look in two directions: backward over the ground we have traversed artistically since the turn of the century; forward in an attempt to fathom what the next fifty years may hold for us. We are inclined to ask whether or not what we see here represents true artistic progress or simply change. In thus considering the exhibition, it is well to remember that this is not a terminal result, something secure and fixed, but rather a sort of statistical average at an arrested moment in the witherward of American art expression.

Nor can we be sure that what we see is completly American, for not all the artists represented here have American backgrounds. Some are Americans only in the sense that they currently live and work in America. Not all these painters look at life alike, or at art alike. Some are concerned with the objective aspects of their environment. Others are concerned with subjective experiences and reactions. Some of them, as the painter Robert Henri once expressed it, 'see beyond the usual, become clairvoyant.' It is then that they reach into reality. 'Such,' says Henri, 'are the moments of...greatest happiness; such are the moments of...greatest wisdom. If one could but record the vision of these moments by some sort of sign! It was in this hope that the arts were invented.... (See Chart I).

CHART I

The CSA: Contribution to International, National and Regional Exhibitions, 1933–51

A. A Century of Progress Exhibition of Paintings and Sculpture—Art Institute of Chicago, 1933

B. International Watercolor Exhibition—Art Institute of Chicago, 1934

C. International Exhibition of Contemporary Prints—Art Institute of Chicago, 1934

D. International Watercolor Exhibition—Art Institute of Chicago, 1935

E. International Watercolor Exhibition—Art Institute of Chicago, 1936

F. Delphic Studios Exhibition—New York, 1935

G. New Jersey State Museum Exhibition—Trenton, New Jersey, 1936

H. Riverside Museum Exhibition—New York, 1939

I. "American Art Today" Exhibition—New York World's Fair, 1939

J. American Painting and Sculpture Exhibition, Art Institute of Chicago, 1941

K. Contemporary American Painting Exhibition, University of Illinois, 1959, 1951

	A	B	C	D	E	F	G	H	I	J	K
Abercrombie, G.				●		●	●	●	●		●
Adams, J. C.	●	●		●		●	●	●	●	●	
Albright, I.	●	●	●	●					●		
Albright, M.	●								●	●	●
Anderson, C. W.			●								
Angel, R.	●	●		●					●		
Armin, E.	●	●		●		●	●	●			
Arquin, F.	●			●		●	●	●			
Bacon, P.	●		●	●					●		
Badger, F.	●	●			●	●	●	●			
Bannon, L.				●							
Barton, M.	●	●						●			
Bekker, D.				●					●		
Beman, R.				●					●		
Beneduci, A.				●							
Benson, T. E.	●			●		●	●	●			
Bentley, C.											●
Berkman, B.						●	●	●	●		
Bianucci, I						●	●	●			
Biesel, F.	●				●	●	●	●	●		
Blackshear, K.		●				●	●	●			
Bohrod, A.	●	●		●					●	●	
Breinin, R.									●		
Britton, E.		●		●						●	
Brockman, A.										●	
Brod, F.					●	●	●	●			
Brown, E. C.						●	●	●			
Buck, C.	●										
Burg, C.										●	●
Cameron, E. S.	●										
Carter, M.						●	●	●			
Chapin, F.	●	●	●	●					●	●	●
Chassaing, O.								●			
Cheskin, D.						●	●	●			
Clifford, J. H.			●								
Colwell, E.			●		●	●	●	●			
Dahlgreen, C.			●						●		
Dalstrom, G.	●	●		●		●	●	●	●		
DeDiego, J.			●	●					●	●	●
Dehn, R.	●			●					●		
Donaldson, E.				●							
Douthat, M.				●							
Dyer, B.									●		
Englehard, E.						●	●	●		●	
Fabion, J.										●	
Ford, R. V.	●										
Foy, F.	●	●	●	●		●	●	●			
Fry, R.		●					●	●	●		
Geller, T.						●	●	●	●		
Giesbert, E.	●	●		●							
Gilruth, M.				●							
Glaman, E. F.									●		
Greenburg, S.				●		●	●	●	●		
	A	B	C	D	E	F	G	H	I	J	K

	A	B	C	D	E	F	G	H	I	J	K
Griffen, D.	●				●				●	●	
Griffith, J. S.						●	●	●			
Grover, J.						●	●	●			
Grumieaux, E.					●			●			
Hackett, M.	●	●		●						●	
Hall, T.						●	●	●			
Hannell, V.M.S.		●		●							
Havens, L.									●		
Haydon, H.									●		
Henry, N.				●							
Hevermann, M.						●	●	●			
Hoeckner, C.					●	●	●	●	●		
Jacobs, W.		●									
Jacobson, E.		●		●							
Jerrems, L. M.				●							
Johnson, E. B.		●		●		●	●	●	●	●	
Judson, S. S.	●								●		
Katz, A. R.		●				●	●	●			
Kauffman, C. A.	●	●		●		●	●	●			
Krawiec, W.	●										
Levy, B. S.	●		●			●	●	●	●		
Loeb, S.									●	●	
Lucioni. L.	●								●	●	
McDonald, G. L.						●	●	●			
MacGowan, C.						●	●	●			
MacLeish, N.						●	●	●	●		
Michalov, A.					●				●		
Miller, E.		●			●						
Millman, E.					●				●		●
Mintz, H.					●	●	●	●	●		●
Mundt, D.						●	●	●	●	●	
Norton, J. W.	●										
Orloff, G.						●	●	●			
Ostrovsky, S.	●								●	●	
Ott, P.						●	●	●	●		
Phillips, M.	●								●	●	
Ponsen, T.	●		●			●	●	●			
Poull, M. B.						●	●	●			
	A	B	C	D	E	F	G	H	I	J	K

	A	B	C	D	E	F	G	H	I	J	K
Reibel, B.						●	●	●			
Remahl, F.						●	●	●			
Ritman, M.										●	
Robinson, I.	●										
Rosenthal, B.								●		●	
Roszak, T.	●		●								
Rothstein, C.						●	●	●	●		
Ruvolo, F.										●	●
Schofield, F.	●	●				●	●	●			
Schreiber. G.		●		●					●	●	
Schultz, H.		●		●		●	●	●		●	
Schwartz, W. S.	●										
Seyffert, L.		●								●	
Shopen, K.	●			●					●		
Sinclair. G. V.		●	●							●	●
Singer. W. E.									●		
Siporin, M.									●		●
Smith, G. M.	●				●	●	●				
Spears, E.		●		●		●	●	●	●		
Spongberg, G.		●									
Stenvall, J.		●	●	●		●	●	●			
Strain, F.					●	●	●	●			
Swan, J.									●		
Thecla, J.		●		●							
Topchevsky, M.						●	●	●	●		
Torrey, F.									●		
Troy, A.									●		
Umlauf, C.								●	●		
Van Pappelendam, L.	●				●	●	●	●			
Van Young, O.						●	●	●			
Vavak, J.				●				●			
Viviano, E.				●				●	●	●	
Warner, H.									●		
Weiner, A. S.						●	●	●			
Weiner, L.						●	●	●			
Wilimovksy, C.	●		●			●	●	●	●		
Woelffer, E.					●	●	●	●	●		
Ziroli, N.					●	●	●	●	●		●
	A	B	C	D	E	F	G	H	I	J	K

THIRTY-SEVENTH ANNUAL
EXHIBITION
BY ARTISTS
OF CHICAGO
AND VICINITY
JANUARY 12 TO MARCH 5
NINETEEN HUNDRED THIRTY-THREE

THIRTY-SIXTH ANNUAL
EXHIBITION
BY ARTISTS
OF CHICAGO
AND VICINITY
JANUARY 28 TO MARCH 20
NINETEEN HUNDRED THIRTY-TWO

THIRTY-NINTH ANNUAL
EXHIBITION
BY ARTISTS
OF CHICAGO
AND VICINITY
JANUARY 31 TO MARCH 10
NINETEEN HUNDRED THIRTY-FIVE

THE ART INSTITUTE OF CHICAGO

THIRTY-FOURTH ANNUAL
EXHIBITION
BY ARTISTS
OF CHICAGO
AND VICINITY
JANUARY 30 TO MARCH 9
NINETEEN HUNDRED THIRTY

THE ART INSTITUTE OF CHICAGO

Some early catalogues of the Artists of Chicago and Vicinity Exhibitions held at the Art Institute of Chicago. (Photograph by Barbara Lazarus Metz)

5

The CSA: Contribution to "Artists of Chicago and Vicinity Exhibitions," A Sampling: 1936, 1942, 1949

For many years the Art Institute of Chicago has sponsored Artists of Chicago and Vicinity Exhibitions. These were annual events to which local artists looked forward with great anticipation. Those whose works were accepted by the Jury of Selection were naturally pleased. But those whose works were rejected were very unhappy, and they went about town casting a not-so-silent gloom. In the often lively discussions between "winners" and "losers," the jury got the brunt of it all—since they were the cause of many an artist's displeasure.

No less anticipatory was the selection of awards for meritorious achievement in art, offered by the Institute at these annual events. The presentation of awards took place at special receptions given in honor of the artists included in the exhibitions. Again there were some artists who contained their personal pleasure while others were deeply and visibly disappointed. The differing opinions among the artists resulted in a controversy which bluntly and openly questioned the final selections of the jury. No matter what the jury did, its action ultimately precipitated a good share of criticism by many disgruntled artists. But this was not the end of the issue. When the exhibits opened to the public, there was more than the jury to contend with!

At times, newspapers and art periodicals presented overly-critical reviews of the exhibitions. This angered those artists who were dis-

JENNY, oil by RUTH VAN SICKLE FORD, 1935. Awarded the Chicago Woman's Aid Prize of $100 in the 39th Annual Artists of Chicago and Vicinity Exhibition.

dainfully treated, and pleased those who were not. And, then there followed a deluge of letters to the "Voice of the People" columns, reflecting irreverent thoughts from angry artists, and their friends. Sometimes vehement protests were staged by groups of artists.

All in all, the Annual Artists of Chicago and Vicinity Exhibitions created provocative situations. In a sense this was good; good, for the Art Institute because there was an increased interest among the viewing public and correspondingly increased its attendance record. But there was also benefit to the artist since he reflected on his own successes or failures more intently. Moreover, the exhibitions and subsequent controversy and personal reflection generated the pursuit of artistic interests with renewed vigor and resolute ambition.

How well did the Chicago Society of Artists fare in the Artists of Chicago and Vicinity Exhibitions? The answer unquestionably is very well, not only as far as the number of artists represented in these annual events but equally as well in the number of awards meted out to the Society's members. In fact, from 1911 to 1951, fifty-seven members of the Chicago Society of Artists were awarded seventy-nine prizes for oils, watercolors, prints and sculpture at these annual exhibitions.

The award recipients are listed as follows: Leon H. Roecker, 1911; Charles W. Dahlgreen, 1919, 1934; Edgar S. Cameron, 1917; Carl Hoeckner, 1923; Beatrice Levy, 1923, Leopold Seyffert, 1924, 1925; Mary Stafford, 1925; Cora Bliss Taylor, 1925; Sidney Loeb, 1926, 1945; Rudolph F. Ingerle, 1927, 1928; Lenore Smith Jerrems, 1928, 1930; Oskar Gross, 1928; Davenport Griffen, 1928, 1930; Malvin Marr Albright, 1929; Olga Chassaing, 1929, 1933; Flora Schofield, 1929; Charles Wilimovsky, 1929; Francis Chapin, 1929, 1933, 1935; Gregory Prushek, 1930, 1932; Macena Barton, 1931; Frances Foy, 1931, 1943; Belle Goldschlager, 1931; Edwin Boyd Johnson, 1931; Jaroslav Brozik, 1932; Claude Buck, 1932; Laura VanPappelendam, 1932 1942; Agnes Potter VanRyn, 1932; Jean Crawford Adams, 1933; Aaron Bohrod, 1933, 1934, 1935, 1936, 1937, 1945, 1947; Robert Jay Wolff, 1933; Peterpaul Ott, 1934; Elise Donaldson, 1934; Edouard Chassaing, 1935; Ruth VanSickle Ford, 1935; Theodore Roszak, 1935; Gertrude Abercrombie, 1936; John Stenvall, 1936; Harry Mintz, 1937, 1945; Maurice Ritman, 1942; Felix Ruvolo, 1942; Oscar VanYoung, 1942; Salcia Bahnc, 1942; Copeland Burg, 1942, 1951; Charles Umlauf, 1943; Zsissley, 1943; Julio DeDiego, 1944; Edgar Miller, 1944; Don Mundt, 1944; Mario Ubaldi, 1944; Sylvia Shaw Judson, 1945; Rainey Bennett, 1945; Ivan LeLorraine Albright, 1945; Frank Vavruska, 1945; Mar Carter, 1951; Elizabeth Engelhard, 1951; Leopold Segedin, 1951.

Further evidence attesting to the vitality and stature of the Chicago Society of Artists as a group is clearly demonstrated in the prodigious number of members whose works were consistently accepted by highly professional Juries of Selection and included in the Artists of Chicago and Vicinity Exhibitions at the Art Institute of Chicago.

To list all the members whose works have been selected for inclusion in every exhibition would be repetitious, tedious and intolerably boresome. A few exhibits a number of years apart, however, need to be examined as a sampling if for no other reason than that participating members of the Society should be catalogued to provide the reader with visible evidence of their laudable record through the years. It is of consequence also to register for posterity the achievements of those proverbial giants in the group whose names appeared repeatedly in major exhibitions in this country and elsewhere. They constitute the core of artists who have laid a firm foundation for the Chicago Society of Artists, the strength of which has inspired others to pursue their aesthetic goals within the Society for ninety-two years. The Fortieth, Forty-Sixth, and Fifty-Third Annual Artists of Chicago and Vicinity Exhibitions have been selected for the purpose of noting the outstanding members of those exhibitions.

40TH ANNUAL EXHIBITION

The 40th Annual Artists of Chicago and Vicinity Exhibition was held at the Art Institute of Chicago in 1936. Apparently, the Society as a group had reached its productive peak that year since ninety-two

HOME SWEET HOME, oil by JOHN F. STENVALL, 1936. Awarded the Robert Rice Jenkins Memorial Prize of $50 at the 40th Annual Artists of Chicago and Vicinity Exhibition.

members of the Chicago Society of Artists were represented in this exhibition; this was the largest number of the Society's members whose works were included in a juried show at the Art Institute of Chicago since 1888. Few artists' groups in Chicago can boast as much!

For the Society this was an impressive achievement and a fitting tribute to its potency and vigor. More than that, it was a visual testimonial to the soundness and stature of the group. (See Chart II).

46TH ANNUAL EXHIBITION

Six years later, the Chicago Society of Artists apparently still maintained a remarkable degree of performance, keeping its professional status high and receiving due recognition for its creative endeavors. At the Forty-Sixth Annual Exhibition by Artists of Chicago and Vicinity in 1942, ten prizes were awarded. Six of these prizes were given for oil paintings by Salcia Bahnc, Oscar VanYoung, Copeland C. Burg, Laura VanPappelendam, Felix Ruvolo and Maurice Ritman—all members of the Chicago Society of Artists.

The Jury of Selection consisted of Alfred Faggi, Woodstock, New York; Ernest Fiene, New York; and Peppino Mangravite, New York—a highly professional jury, by most rigid standards.

Members of the Society were again represented in large numbers. Some of the usual names reappeared in the catalogue of this exhibition, but others, which were probably recent additions to the mem-

IN QUEST OF BEAUTY, oil by EDITHE JANE CASSADY, 1937. Exhibited in the 41st Annual Artists of Chicago and Vicinity Exhibition.

COMPOSITION, oil by SALCIA BAHNC, 1942. Awarded the Mr. and Mrs. Frank H. Armstrong Prize of $300 at the 46th Annual Artists of Chicago and Vicinity Exhibition.

HEAD, sculpture by MARR CARTER, 1951. Awarded the Mr. and Mrs. Joseph A. Golde Prize of $100 for sculpture at the 55th Annual Artists of Chicago and Vicinity Exhibition.

STILL LIFE, oil by MAURICE RITMAN, 1942. Awarded the Renaissance Prize of $100 at the 46th Annual Artists of Chicago and Vicinity Exhibition.

bership roster, were also listed. Included were sixty-eight painters and sculptors from the Chicago Society of Artists. (See Chart II).

53RD ANNUAL EXHIBITION

In 1949 at the 53rd Annual Chicago Artists and Vicinity Exhibition, the works of seventy-two members from the Chicago Society of Artists were included among other Chicago artists' paintings, prints and sculpture.

Daniel Cotton Rich, Director, said:

> Instead of an exhibit which has been submitted to a jury, this year's annual was assembled by a committee of three curators, Carl O. Schniewind, Curator of Prints and Drawings (who chose also graphic work), Katherine Kuh, Associate Curator of Painting and Sculpture and myself a Curator of Painting, who selected the rest. This method was adopted by the Institute for several reasons. In the last few years, despite different juries, the Chicago exhibitions had taken on a great sameness. Certain artists, it was found, were not sending in their work. We suspected that others had paintings or sculpture or prints in their studios which they did not consider of 'exhibition' size or significance though these sometimes proved to be their most sincere and original expression.
>
> The problem that faced the organizing committee was vast. Artists in Chicago live everywhere in our widely scattered city. Add to this that the 'vicinity' takes in a radius of one-hundred miles and

> you will readily see that we did a tremendous amount of traveling in the months in which the exhibit was assembled. It was obviously impossible to visit every studio in the area. Though hundreds of artists were consulted in their studios, thousands of others were seen in group exhibits, galleries, art centers and in special depots where artists' organizations brought together works by their members. Some two thousand additional paintings, sculpture and prints were assembled in the Art Institute. Surely never before were so many works produced by Chicagoans viewed for a single exhibition. The Committee is grateful for this cooperation which has made the showing possible.
>
> In our selection only one subject was kept in view; to tell the story of art in Chicago this year. No 'school' or 'style' was preferred; you will find the work of older and established artists along with the work of newcomers. It must be clearly stated that the Committee had nothing to do with awarding prizes. This was left to a capable jury of artists, all of them well known Americans, a painter, a sculptor and a printmaker.

Despite the fact that the selection of works of art for this exhibition was done by a committee of curators instead of by the usual Jury of Selection (painters, sculptors or museum directors), the result was no less favorable to the members of the Society. Obviously, the Committee's selection of works proved to be reassuring. The selection also was a clear manifestation of the Society's consistency in professional performance, so that regardless of the character or the structure of the Jury of Selection, the fact remains that sixty-six members of the Chicago Society of Artists' works were selected for this local, but significant, annual event. (See Chart II).

In that listing it is apparent that a number of new members joined the ranks of the Society and were included in the 53rd Annual Exhibition by Artists of Chicago and Vicinity at the Art Institute of Chicago.

CHART II

The CSA: Contribution to "Artists of Chicago and Vicinity Exhibitions," A Sampling

	1936	1942	1949
Abercrombie, G.	●	●	●
Adams, J. C.	●	●	
Albright, I. L.	●	●	●
Anderson, H.			●
Armin, E.			●
Arquin, F.	●	●	
Badger, F.	●		
Bahnc, S.		●	●
Barton, M.	●		●
Bekker, D.	●	●	●
Beman, P.	●		
Benson, T. E.	●	●	
Bentley, C.			●
Berdick, V.			●
Biesel, F.	●		
Bohrod, A.	●	●	
Britton, E.	●		
Brod, F.	●	●	●
Brown, E. C.	●		
Buck, C.		●	
Burg, C.		●	●
Burrows, P. P.			●
Cameron, E. S.	●		
Cassady, E. J.	●		●
Chapin, F.	●	●	●
Chassaing, E.	●		●
Dahlgreen, C. W.		●	
Dalstrom, G.	●		
DeDiego, J.	●	●	
Donaldson, E.	●	●	
Englehard, E.		●	●
Ewell, H. C.	●		
Fabion, J.		●	
Florsheim, R.		●	●
Ford, R. V.	●	●	●
Foy, F.	●		●
Frano, T.			●
Garland, L.	●	●	
Garland, S. E.	●		
Geller, T.	●		●
Gerard, J.		●	
Gerard, P.			●
Giesbert, E.	●	●	●
Glaman, E. F.			●
Gordon, B.			●
Greenburg, S.		●	●
Greene, M. Z.			●
Griffen, D.	●		
Griffin, N. K.			●
Gross, O.	●		
Grover, J.	●		
Grumieaux, E. J.	●	●	
Hackett, M.	●	●	●
Hannell, H.	●		
Hartmann, M.	●		
Haydon, H.	●		
Hoeckner, C.	●		
Hohenberg, M.	●		
Ingerle, F. R.	●		
Jacobs, W.	●	●	●
Jacobson, E.	●		

	1936	1942	1949
Johnson, E. B.	●	●	
Jones, E.		●	
Josimovich, G.	●	●	●
Judson, S. S.		●	●
Kaar, V.			●
Kaganove, J.	●	●	●
Katz, A. R.	●	●	
Kauffman, C. A.	●		
Kelpe, P.	●	●	
Kluczewski, F.		●	
Krawiec, H.		●	●
Krawiec, W.	●		●
Levy. B. S.	●	●	●
Loeb, S.	●		
MacDonald, G.		●	
MacGowan, C.	●		
MacLeish, N.	●	●	
Mason, M.	●		●
Millman, E.	●		
Mintz, H.	●	●	●
Mundt, D.	●	●	●
Nichols, D.	●		
Ostrovksy, S.		●	
Ott, P.	●		
Perri, F. S.		●	●
Pink, H.	●		
Pleimling, W.	●	●	●
Ponsen, T.	●		●
Pryor, Y.			●
Reibel, B.	●		
Remahl, F.		●	●
Ritman, M.		●	
Robinson, W.		●	

	1936	1942	1949
Ropp, H.	●		
Rosenberg, C.	●		
Rothstein, C.		●	
Rupprecht, E.	●		
Ruvolo, F.	●	●	
Saunders, T.	●		
Schatz, D.	●		
Schofield, F.	●	●	●
Schultz, H.	●	●	
Schwartz, W. S.	●	●	●
Shopen, K.	●	●	●
Sinclair. G. V.	●		●
Singer. W. E.	●	●	
Spongberg, G.	●		
Steele, I.	●		
Theckla, J.			●
Thomas, H.		●	
Troy, A.			●
Umlauf, C.	●		
VanPappelendam, L.	●	●	●
Van Young	●	●	
Vavak, J.	●	●	
Vavrushka, F.		●	●
Viviano, E.	●	●	
Warner, H.	●		
Weber, H.			●
Weiner, E.		●	●
Wilimovsky, C.	●		
Woelffer, E. S.		●	●
Yochim, L.	●	●	
Yochim, M.	●	●	
Ziroli, N.	●	●	
Zsissly	●	●	●

The DIANA COURT BUILDING where the Increase Robinson Studio Gallery was located. (Courtesy Hedrich-Blessing)

6 The CSA: Exhibitions in Local Galleries

In addition to participating in international, national, regional, and local shows sponsored by the Art Institute of Chicago and museums and galleries in New York and elsewhere, the Chicago Society of Artists held it own annual exhibitions. These were generally held in local galleries, hotels or rented headquarters which could readily facilitate the whole group.

AUTUMN EXHIBITION, Stevens Hotel, 1928

One of the earliest Chicago Society of Artists exhibitions on record was held in 1928 at the Stevens Hotel on South Michigan Avenue at Seventh Street. Prior to this date, participation in annual shows was open to non-members as well as to members of the Society. But this exhibition was different in that it was limited to members only. It was a juried exhibition. Therefore, it implied that not all members' works would automatically be accepted.

Some members may have chosen not to submit their works, and thus avoided being subjected to the whims of a jury. Others may have simply felt no desire to exhibit "at this point in time." And still others may have had their works rejected. Nonetheless, the limitation of entries to the Society's membership only was in itself indicative of a

THE BLACK MESA, oil by MINNIE HARMS NEEBE

sense of exclusiveness which was beginning to permeate the group as a whole. But whatever the reasons may have been, the fact remains that a new precedent had been set. This was a significant departure from the Society's previously established policy, and this policy remains in effect to this very day.

Presiding over this group in 1928 was Emile J. Grumieaux. Charles Edward Mullin was vice-president; Increase Robinson, secretary; Mary B. Poull, treasurer. Emil Armin was chairman of the Exhibition Committee.

Serving on the Jury of Selection for this show entitled "Autumn Exhibition" were H. Leon Roecker, John Norton, Agnes Potter VanRyn, Gerrit V. Sinclair, Felix Russman, Gustaf Dalstrom, and Jean Crawford Adams. The unusual feature of this particular Jury of Selection was that all jury members were members of the Chicago Society of Artists. They were put into the delicate position of jurying their own professional colleagues.

This modus operandi demanded of its Jury of Selection undaunted convictions and a high degree of objectivity. Rarely has the practice of selecting a jury from its own ranks been adopted by a closely knit group such as the Chicago Society of Artists. The ramification of that type of precedent could have had dire effects upon the stability of any organization. But, obviously, the membership held this group of jury members' professional integrity in high esteem, or it would not have chosen them to perform in this capacity.

As a result of this newly initiated practice in jurying, fifty-four painters, sculptors, and printmakers were selected for this exhibition. They were Jean Crawford Adams, Ivan LeLorraine Albright, Emil Armin, Frances Badger, Salcia Bahnc, Macena Barton, Charles Biesel, Kathleen Blackshear, Mary L. Bockius, Jaroslav Brozik, Elizabeth Colwell, Gustaf Dalstrom, Edward Diskor, Frances Foy, Todros Geller, Julia Sulzer Griffith, Edmond Giesbert, Emile J. Grumieaux, Charles E. Hallberg, Eleanor B. Hatch, Grace Hall Hemingway, May B. Hoelscher, George Josimovich, Camille Andrene Kauffman, Thomas Kempf, Walter Krawiec, William J. Krullaars, Beatrice S. Levy, (winner of gold medal), Charles Edward Mullin, Louis Alexander Neebe, Minnie Harms Neebe, Margrette Oatway, Gregory Orloff, Laura VanPappelendam, Mary B. Poull, Gregory Prusheck, Josephine L. Reichmann, Increase Robinson, H. Leon Roecker, Hubert Ropp, Torry Ross, Theodore J. Roszak, Olive Rush, Felix Russman, Agnes Potter VanRyn, Theodore Saunders, Eve Watson Schutze, Gerret V. Sinclair, George Melville Smith, Ethel Spears, Frances Strain, Elizabeth Taylor, Morris Topchevksy and Ida VanHorn.

Some of these artists stayed with the Chicago Society of Artists until their death.

INCREASE ROBINSON STUDIO GALLERY, Diana Court, 1930

"A Flower Show by Chicago Artists" was the theme of an exhibition held in the prestigious Increase Robinson Studio Gallery in Michigan Square, Diana Court, Michigan at Ohio Street, during the month of June in 1930.

Artists painted flowers in every possible medium and idiom and in unusually original settings. Some paintings were delicately rendered, others were powerful in color and bold in design, ranging the full gamut from realism to surrealism and abstraction. Reflected in this exhibition was the characteristic individuality of each participating artist, and correspondingly his unique approach to the theme imposed upon exhibitors by the gallery director, Increase Robinson.

Most members of the Chicago Society of Artists who appeared in the Stevens Hotel Exhibition also participated in this exhibition in 1930. But in addition, there were others listed who apparently joined the Society later. Among them were: Rifka Angel, Tressa Benson, Ethel Crouch Brown, Edithe Jane Cassady, Elise Donaldson, Milton Touthat, Emanuel Jacobson, A. Raymond Katz, Harriet B. Krawiec, Clara MacGowan, Yvonne Pryor, Romolo Roberti, Harold Schultz, Kenneth Shopen and Louis Weiner.

MICHIGAN SQUARE, Diana Court, 1935

As the Chicago Society of Artists expanded its activities, new members joined its ranks. Under the guidance of its officers Clara MacGowan, president; Ivan LeLorraine Albright, vice-president; Kathleen Blackshear, secretary; Harold Schultz, treasurer; the Society functioned

BRICKYARD ON THE HUDSON, oil by INCREASE ROBINSON

effectively in aesthetic matters and kept the group in the forefront of cultural happenings in Chicago.

With each successful annual event the number of member participants increased significantly. In the exhibition held in Michigan Square, Diana Court in November of 1935, seventy-four members were involved. Under the title of "Paintings and Graphic Arts," works were submitted by a number of newly admitted members. They were Malvin Marr Albright, Florence Arquin, Laura Bannon, Fred Biesel, Aaron Bohrod, Edgar Britton, Fritzi Brod, Francis Chapin, David Cheskin, Rowena Fry, Karl Gasslander, Jeanne Grover, Thomas Hall, V. M. S. Hannell, Henry R. Hantke, Eleanor B. Hatch, Edwin Boyd Johnson, William J. Krullaars, George Luks, Helen Mann, Edward Millman, Harry Mintz, Peterpaul Ott, Harry Pink, Tunis Ponsen, Maurice Ritman, Gilbert Roche, Flora Schofield, William Earl Singer, John F. Stenvall, Franklin VanCourt, Joseph Vavak, Emanuel Viviano, A. S. Weiner, Charles Wilimovksy, George Woodruff and Zsissly.

Gold medal winners at this exhibition were Joseph Vavak, Franklin VanCourt, and Francis Chapin. Edgar Britton, Harold Schultz and John F. Stenvall were recipients of Honorable Mentions.

FINDLAY GALLERIES, 338 S. Michigan, 1935

During World War II, Americans responded to the call of action in support of the war effort. Artists everywhere had either voluntarily joined the service or were duly drafted as artists with combat units. If they were beyond the age limit they served on the home front in rehabilitation centers in hospitals, working with patients in the Arts and Skills programs. Others worked on the W. P. A. project designing propaganda leaflets, posters and other informative materials to stimulate the sale of war bonds. Artists were among those who worked long hours in industry, producing ammunition, fire arms and various types of indispensable war equipment for the fighting troops and among those who worked to relieve the manpower shortage.

But the creative person's need to express his reactions to life never ceases. Often, after long hours of service to the needs of the nation, artists painted and sculpted late into the night to relieve their tensions from the sometimes strenuous, often boring daily routine.

Artists who remained on the home front were keenly aware of the grief and the misery which had befallen many. This sensitive awareness of the dismal and hopelessly distressing circumstances led

THE CHEF, oil by V.M.S. HANNELL, 1932

JOAN OF ARC IN MONTEBOURG,
oil by AARON BOHROD, 1945

artists to paint and sculpt subject matter that had been motivated by war, expressing sadness and moral indignation but always hoping for a happier day—a warless world. The impact of such paintings or sculptures was generally persuasive, and reactions drew strong emotions in the realization that war is ugly and inhumanity of man to man is unbelievable.

Many exhibitions of paintings and sculpture dealing with the subject of war were held throughout the land. In Chicago, members of the Chicago Society of Artists presented its 56th Annual Exhibition in July 1945. Eleanor Jewett, Art Critic of the Chicago Tribune reviewed the show.

> The 56th Annual Chicago Society of Artists Exhibition of paintings and sculpture is by all odds the most important July exhibit. It is beautifully installed at the Findlay Galleries, 338 South Michigan Avenue. The exhibition theme is 'The Artist Looks at the Home Front.' As one might imagine, the subject is open to various interpretations and the painters have taken full advantage of practically all of them.
>
> Hubert Ropp, who was president of the Society last year and conceived the idea for this show, offers one of the most poignant paintings in 'Waiting Room,' in which a harassed young sailor holding his sleeping baby while his tired wife dozes beside him on the hardwood bench. It is a typical 1945 portrait group, handled by Mr. Ropp with gentleness and imagination. Mr. Ropp, by the way, is dean of the Art Institute Art School.
>
> Scaled to a different note, but still as up to the minute as Mr. Ropp's canvas, is the decorative and amusing 'No. 89,' by May H. Gilruth. The artist gives us a line of women waiting their turn to buy in a meat market and 'No. 89,' is the number one weary shopper holds up to show her place in the hopeful throng. This ticketing of the buyers will be recognized at once by the many thousands who identify themselves in the same way at numberless

shops throughout the country.

There are several busy and prosperous war gardens in the show. Frances Badger with '1945' presents one of the most colorful and quaint. Miss Badger's unique manner of treating her themes invariably contributes a highlight to any exhibit of which her work is part. Tunis Ponsen offers 'Home Front Activity,' a war garden with a steel mill in the background. Ethel Spears shows still another type of garden, as beautifully and generously detailed as her paintings invariable are. Yet another type of garden is seen in Laura VanPappelendam's 'The Edward's House With a Victory Garden in the Front Yard,' which is taking the vegetable plot out of the vacant lot with a vengeance.

Emil Armin brings up another timely topic in 'Children Bringing Paper,' a delightful and quaint rendition of a popular theme. Orval Caldwell has a satisfactory account of the same activity in 'Paper Troopers.' 'What No Points?' by Aloise W. Aigner, illustrates one of those amazing moments which the food shopper again will recognize with a start.

The paintings which deal with the men in the armed forces are of as great importance as those devoted to gardens and markets. Among them is the extremely interesting and beautifully painted 'Convalescent Workshop,' by Rowena Fry, a group of sailors painting, weaving or just sitting staring into space. 'Between Trains,' by Elizabeth Engelhard, is another station scene characteristic of these hurried, out of joint travel days. Again we sense the discomfort of present railroad journeys in 'Furlough Travel,' by Paula Gerard, showing a sleepy group of service men on a crowded train.

On the work front there is the well handled 'U. S. O. Worker' by Nan Rice; 'Mending Service' by Frances McVey; 'Drafting' by Beatrice S. Levy; the strident, stirring, 'Smoke and Steel' by Winnifred Pleimling; 'The Hand of Industry' by Dorothy Stafford; and 'Maywood Industry' by Verne V. Mullen.

Clara MacGowan's 'Concerning Values' is a subtle piece of painting, interesting in technique, and Ethel Crouch Brown puts another pertinent home front activity into our thought with her 'Service Flag,' a painting of an old house wearing with honor its bright badge, a service flag with three stars on the window of its croupy chest.

Z.A.M., oil by DON MUNDT, 1944

CHICAGO
NO-JURY SOCIETY
OF ARTISTS
1926

The Catalogue Cover of the CHICAGO NO-JURY SOCIETY OF ARTISTS 1926 Exhibition. Cover design by EMIL ARMIN. (Photograph by Barbara Lazarus Metz)

7 The CSA in the "No-Jury" Movement

One more significant movement occurred in the early stages of Chicago's art consciousness. Members of the Chicago Society of Artists presumably played a dominant role in this movement.

As far back as 1925, a group of artists joined in protest against the policies and academicism of the Art Institute of Chicago. The organization consisted primarily of those artists who had legitimate complaints, that is, those who were duly incensed at the prevalent jury system and its intransigent views concerning modern art. Their indignation was directed mainly toward two factors: first, jurying methods employed in accepting or rejecting works of art, and second, the idea of any jury arbitrarily passing judgment upon professional performance, whether done in the conservative or in the modern idiom. These artists claimed that juries were generally biased. More often than not, they perpetuated their own personal tastes and prejudices. Time and again, highly imaginative works of art were rejected, only because the tastes of the jury were limited in scope. As a result of jury's "narrow" and limited views concerning innovative approaches to art, artists frequently came to be victims of circumstances. Occasionally even artists with established reputations succumbed to the whims of a "narrow-minded" jury. And, for that reason, some well known painters, sculptors and graphic artists flatly refused to submit their works to any juried exhibition.

In Chicago there were a number of artists who harbored feelings of disdain for any jury. Among those was Rudolph Weisenborn, a well-known painter and muralist and a highly esteemed teacher of painting. Although he was often invited to serve on juries of Selection at the Art Institute and elsewhere, his own paintings were not infrequently rejected by conservative jurors serving the same institutions.

Consequently, and to counteract the "unfair" or "shabby" treatment of Chicago artists, No-Jury exhibitions were assembled. Eventually, a No-Jury Society was formed in Chicago. The group was patterned after the Salon des Refuses in Paris, a vanguard organization which also rebelled against the tyranny of jurors and academicism.

In keeping with the philosophy of the No-Jury Society, each artist became the sole judge of the works he submitted to an exhibition, whether he classified himself as a modern or as a conservative.

THE GARFIELD PARK MUSEUM EXHIBITION, 1939

Many members of the Chicago Society of Artists were also active members of the Chicago No-Jury Society of Artists and participated in its annual exhibitions. For example, in the Fourteenth Annual Exhibition of the Chicago No-Jury Society of Artists held in 1939 at the Garfield Park Museum in Chicago, thirty-five members of the C. S. A. were included. Two members of the Society held important offices in this organization. Macena Barton was its president, and Fritzi Brod, its vice-president.

C. J. Bulliet, art critic of the Daily News, wrote the Foreword to the catalogue for this exhibition, in which he expressed succinctly the philosophy of the Chicago No-Jury Society of Artists. In it he stated:

> No-Jury's job is to keep burning the torch of art freedom in this peculiar era when tendencies, radical as well as conservative, are toward regimentation.
>
> Inner circles in most of our established art societies seek so to muster their powers and resources as to maintain a 'status quo.' Living is hard, opportunities are few in comparison with flush times when art was a great adventure, and creative artists took

FRITZI BROD, vice-president of the Chicago No-Jury Society of Artists, 1939. Brod is shown here with her exhibit at the Grant Park Art Fair, 1933.

BACK PORCH, oil by GUSTAF DAHLSTROM

long chances, gambling on brilliant results. Now artists consider carefully what they send to their official shows, and art organizations go into earnest huddles before daring to depart from something they have established as a 'norm.'

And yet, it is only by creative energy taking long chances and hoping for brilliant results that art can make progress—that art, indeed, can even hold its own. For art, like life, deteriorates when the will to progress atrophies.

No-Jury stands for fearlessness and spontaneity. It is an 'escape' for the established artist, just as it is an opportunity for the artist unknown.

The unknown artist, of course, has here the chance to emerge from obscurity. This trying year, No-Jury is grateful to the City of Chicago for donation of exhibiton space in its handsome Garfield Park Museum.

A PLACE FOR READING OR CONVERSATION, linocut by LAURA VanPAPPELANDAM, 1952

NO-JURY EXHIBITIONS, 1957 and 1958

Several other No-Jury exhibitions were held in later years. Some, such as the Garfield Park Museum Exhibition, were sponsored by the No-Jury Society of Artists. Other exhibitions were sponsored by the Art Institute of Chicago, all Chicago art organizations in cooperation with the Honorable Richard J. Daley, Mayor of Chicago. Financial support for these special events was sometimes through the city's budgetary allocations, but more frequently through the generosity of civic and culturally-minded citizens of Chicago.

Thousands of Chicago's painters, sculptors and printmakers responded enthusiastically to this type of exhibition. Chicago's Navy Pier was the natural choice for such events. The space area was ideal for its accommodation of the overwhelming flow of entries. Moreover, since there had been no limitations set on size, gigantic canvases and mammoth pieces of sculpture were included in these exhibitions. Had the area been smaller, it would have been impossible to display the works to advantage or to stage an event of such magnitude.

The initial impact upon each viewer as he entered the exhibition hall (this blocks-long area) was awe-inspiring, to say the least. To this writer, who assisted behind the scenes in the planning and staging of one of these exhibitions, it was gratifying to observe the highly emotional impact that the exhibition had upon thousands of viewers. Most impressive was the prolific nature of this exhibition—a tribute to the productivity of Chicago's artists.

Victor Perlmutter, painter and member of the Chicago Society of Artists, was directly responsible for several No-Jury exhibitions at the Navy Pier. As Director of these events, he achieved what might have seemed to others as an impossible task, not only in the way he expedited the numerous organizational details but also in the attractive installation of thousands of paintings and sculptures in the half-mile long exhibition hall.

Arnold Maremont, art collector and benefactor of many significant art events in Chicago and elsewhere, subsidized some of the No-Jury exhibitions.

In 1957, in the No-Jury exhibition held at the Navy Pier, one-hundred-sixteen members of the Chicago Society of Artists were represented.

Another exhibition of Chicago artists was staged in the Navy Pier in 1958. Again it was sponsored by the Art Institute of Chicago and Chicago art organizations in cooperation with the Honorable Richard J. Daley, Mayor of the City of Chicago. In the introduction to the catalogue, Arnold Maremont wrote the following:

> The tremendous success enjoyed by last year's No-Jury exhibition encouraged its sponsors to undertake the 1958 Chicago Artists Exhibition.
>
> The exhibition was open to all artists residing in Illinois within a radius of 100 miles of Chicago. No work was rejected, and all of the works submitted are on display. The exhibition is supported by the Art Institute and the leading art organizations of our city.
>
> Prizes totalling $7,450, contributed by the Art Institute, have been awarded by a distinguished jury of awards. The Art Institute will select its annual Chicago and Vicinity Exhibition from the works on display.
>
> This year, more than 2,100 artists were represented by one work each. The exhibition, in terms of participating artists, is probably the largest ever to be held in this country.
>
> A departure from last year's No-Jury show is the selection of an unlimited number of meritorious works by the jury. The works thus honored are designated by the color tabs on the frames and sculpture stands.
>
> The extraordinary response of Chicago artists to the invitation to exhibit dramatizes the great need of our artists to bring their work before the public and is conclusive proof of the need for a permanent municipal art gallery where Chicago artists may exhibit their works on a continuing basis.
>
> I wish to thank Mayor Richard J. Daley for his interest in this exhibition, and for his sympathetic understanding of the cultural needs of our city. I am grateful to the Art Institute, its Board of Trustees and staff, the distinguished group of ladies and gentlemen who served on our committees, and the participating artists and art organizations who have made possible this splendid demonstration of art in our city.

One hundred and ten members of the Chicago Society of Artists were represented in the 1958 No-Jury exhibiton at the Navy Pier.

BLOCK PRINT CALENDAR
BLOCK PRINT CALENDAR
RTISTS CALENDAR 1937
BLOCK PRINTS FOR
HICAGO
OCIETY
of ARTISTS
LOCK PRINT
ENDAR

An assortment of CALENDARS produced by the Chicago Society of Artists (Photograph by Barbara Lazarus Metz)

The CSA: Publications

No historical background delineating the activities of the Chicago Society of Artists may be considered complete without focusing some attention upon its uniquely enterprising efforts, in addition to its usual group exhibitions.

Since 1937, the Society has been involved in another artistic venture, namely the publication of its prestigious annual blockprint calendar. The idea of the calendar evolved under the leadership of its former president and Professor of Art at Northwestern University, Clara MacGowan, with Beatrice Levy acting as chairman of the calendar committee.

The purpose of the annual calendar was twofold: first, to extend the range of the Society's activities, and thus broaden the scope of its audience; second, to provide a means of financing the Society's catalogues for scheduled group exhibitions as well as any other yearly publications.

During the summer of 1936, the Society published "The Artists Calendar—1937," to which thirty members of the Society contributed fifty-four prints. The publication and distribution of this work was carried out by the Calendar Committee and the officers of the Society. The original signed prints of this calendar were shown at Mandel Brothers Gallery and the Evanston Art Center in the fall of 1936.

The members of the Chicago Society of Artists who have con-

HORSE AND BUGGY, linocut by BEATRICE S. LEVY, 1937, produced for the Society's first calendar (Courtesy of the Chicago Society of Artists.)

tributed to this first issue of the published calendar were Gertrude Abercrombie, Emil Armin, Florence Arquin, Kathleen Blackshear, Fritzi Brod, Gustaf Dalstrom, Julio DeDiego, Elise Donaldson, Frances Foy, Karl Gasslander, Todros Geller, Emile F. Grumieaux, V. M. S. Hannel, Henry R. Hantke, Carl Hoeckner, Andrene Kauffman, Beatrice S. Levy, Clara MacGowan, Harry Mintz, Gregory Orloff, Peterpaul Ott, Felix Russman, Flora Schofield, Ethel Spears, John F. Stenvall, Laura Van Pappelendam, A. S. Weiner and Louis Weiner.

As good fortune would have it, the calendar has continued to receive wide acceptance and enthusiastic support. Through the years, its distribution numbered in the thousands with an ever-increasing and earnest demand for more. Having reached extremely popular proportion in the United States, the block-print calendar has also been in

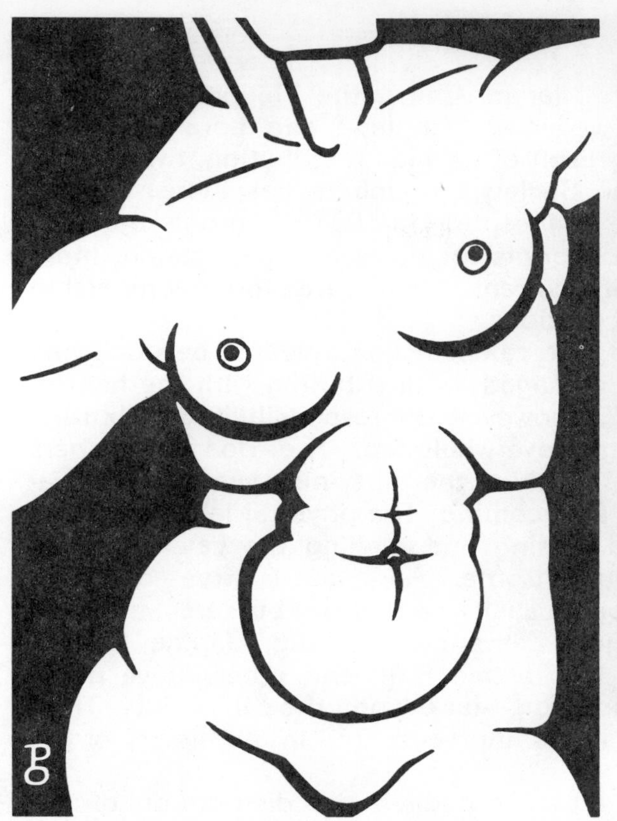

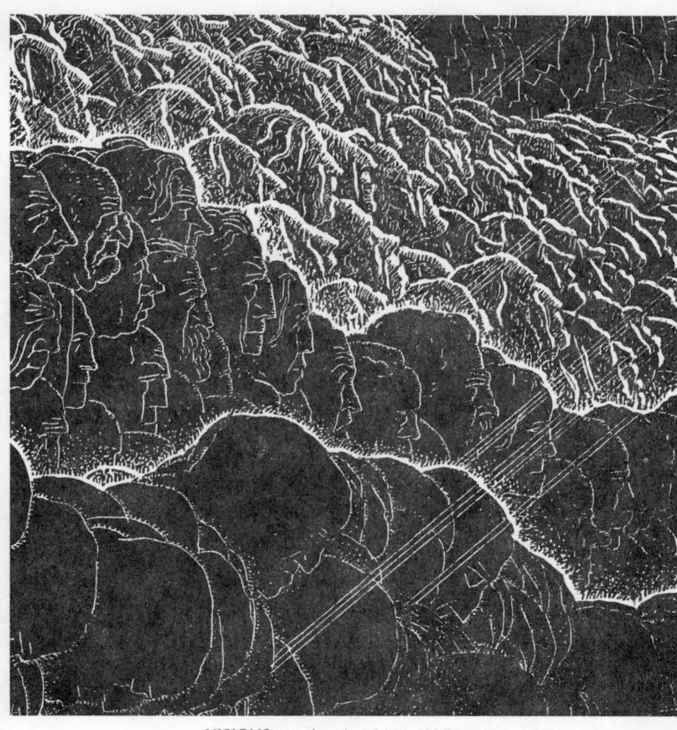

VISIONS woodcut by CARL HOECKNER, 1937, produced for the Society's first calendar (Courtesy of the Chicago Society of Artists)

TORSO II, linocut by PETER PAUL OTT, 1937, produced for the Society's first calendar (Courtesy of the Chicago Society of Artists)

FACTORIES, woodcut by GREGORY ORLOFF, 1937 (Courtesy of the Chicago Society of Artists)

demand in Canada, Mexico, Japan, China, the Philippines, Hawaii, Spain, France, Germany, Sweden and England, and more recently in Tanzania and Ghana. As a result of its wide distribution, the interest in printmaking among the Society's members has increased correspondingly. In fact, since its inception in 1937 when only thirty artists submitted original blockprints for the yearly publication, more than sixty-five artists of its current one-hundred-four membership have participated in recent editions.

Each year prior to 1973, the calendar continued to be published and somehow the Society managed its distribution with the help of dedicated members. In 1973, however, the responsibility and burden of distribution had become overwhelming. The Board Members threatened to discontinue publishing the thirty-nine year old publication unless more help was forthcoming. The physical labor and time involved in packaging, addressing and mailing the calendars was becoming increasingly burdensome. And, as is true of other organizaitons, a few members usually carried the burden.

Members Frances Badger, Catherine Cajandig, Janine Collier, Gustaf Dalstrom, Rowena Fry, Lillian Hall, and others have given generously of their time and effort—far beyond the call of duty. Their dedication to the organization is unprecedented in the history of the Society.

For many years, these artists expedited the distribution of the calendars with deliberate patience and imperturbable calmness. However, in 1971 with the demise of Gustaf Dalstrom, the moving force behind the calendar venture for many years, the production of the calendar was seriously imperiled. By 1973, the Board of Directors regretfully considered the complete abandonment of this worthwhile annual project.

In the meantime, the news of a possible threat to the publication of the calendar somehow reached Clara MacGowan, former president of the Chicago Society of Artists (1935–1937) who still retains her membership in the Society, although she resides in Oceanside, California. Her letter to the Board Members, written on January 22, 1973, was not only encouraging, but it shed new light upon the history of the publication. With her permission the letter is reproduced verbatim.

> Greetings to the Officers and Members of the Board of the Chicago Society of Artists:
>
> Dear Friends:
>
> Only recently I have learned that the Chicago Society of Artists Calendar, as an activity to be continued, is in a precarious position. Perhaps a few words regarding its history may help to clarify its meaning to the Society over the years and now.
>
> The Chicago Society of Artists had exhibitions of painting and sculpture only, when I was president. When we faced the fact that we could not exhibit unless we found a way to pay for catalogs and exhibition expenses, we were forced to examine our resources. I had the idea that a book of prints put out each year might work. The Society endorsed the idea 100%. I asked Beatrice Levy to be the chairman of this Print Committee. We usually had no car, but together we tramped through the Loop and out to other locations to learn about our chances of selling a volume of prints done by

Left, STREET CAR CROWD, linocut by IRENE BIANUCCI and right, BEANERY, linocut by CHARLOTTE ROTHSTEIN ROSS (Courtesy of the Chicago Society of Artists)

the members. Mr. Kroch, the folks at Donnelley's and Cuneo's and many other interested loyal friends all said 'no.' But they all agreed to help us if we put out an annual calendar with prints. This they felt would sell.

Beatrice Levy and Todros Geller both knew Mr. Charles Kay of the Labor-World Press. When Beatrice and I met with Mr. Kay, he

AMERICAN INDIAN DANCE, linocut by EMIL ARMIN, 1943 (Courtesy of the Chicago Society of Artists)

Left, BEGONIA, linocut by HELEN CORLETT and right, NOCTURNAL REVERIE, linocut by EDWIN BOYD JOHNSON (Courtesy of the Chicago Society of Artists)

said that he had always wanted to print something more than the 'run-of-the-mill' printing jobs, and he would like to work with us. He cut expenses to the bone, and we risked having to pay bills personally, but we agreed to publish the calendar.

There are no words to describe the debt of gratitude we owe to Mr. Kay. Without his personal labor and his willingness to get perfect prints, we could not have started. Our victory in producing an excellent product was indeed a shared achievement.

Our membership was small, and most members held two jobs, as it were. But they were dedicated and had intense pride in what we were accomplishing. Everybody realized that each one must carry his share of tedious practical jobs, if our Society's ideals were to be accomplished. Our group knew the real significance of 'the crash' and W. P. A. days. The Society could easily have 'folded' then!

We telephoned long lists of names to get orders for the calendar. Judge Michael Girten, the Austrian Consul, helped us. We called on prominent business men to convince them that they should have a copy of our calendar on their desks. But we had our reward! We sold out the edition and had a profit for our treasury!

In the years that followed we were grateful to see the demand for our calendar increase. Nobody ever thought of it as more than an aid to the regular program exhibitions of Painting and Sculpture. But, eventually it did earn a place for itself.

It was my privilege to serve also, as president of other art organizations. I soon learned that the organizations that published at least one work annually were more stable and more apt to survive.

A printed work can be handled many times a year. It can go anywhere in the world by mail. It can be kept as a record in libraries. The organization is, as a result, reaching a vast silent public. Our members did send calendars to friends all over the world. In my own case, I have sent to friends in the United States, Canada, Mexico, Japan, China, the Philippines, Hawaii, Spain, France, Germany, Sweden and England—yes, even recently to Tanzania and Ghana. These Christmas gifts have been shown wherever my friends were stationed.

Unfortunately, our Society has had no comparable representation or opportunity for the showing of paintings and sculptures of the members. Not that these do not deserve worldwide notice—simply that we never could afford to reproduce paintings and sculptures in published form.

This Society should have a tremendous future. I cannot see the wisdom of abandoning an activity which is so valuable for keeping the name of the Chicago Society of Artists, at least once a year, paramount in the minds of between 2,000 and 3,000 people in the United States and abroad. Nor can I see why a decent business-like plan cannot be developed for handling the mechanics of addressing, packing and shipping the calendar. To date, the Society has exploited very unfairly, in late years, the energies and time of a few older loyal members.

I suggest that a committee be formed with the purpose of investigating ways and means of marketing the calendar. With all the friends that we have gained through our making a marvelous, genuine contribution to the art of Chicago, it seems to me incredible that some patron could not be found to help with the mechanical work involved in addressing, packing and shipping the calendars. Of course, the Society would not dare delegate the art end of the activity without losing control of the high quality that has been sustained.

Here is one idea, and, I'm sure if we really settle down to think, our members will have others. Offer some firm that has the right equipment to do this sort of thing, an acknowledgment of their help and print this appreciative statement in the calendar that all may know of our partron. There are still people in Chicago who care about our Society. It is astonishing how things unfold when we all work together! We always have had to grow on our merits. Nobody ever has offered to finance a group like ours. But, everybody respects the magnificent record of the Chicago Society of Artists. Keep it up!

Sincerely,
Clara MacGowan
Past President of the
Chicago Society of Artists

IMPRESSIONS OF SAN FRANCISCO, linocut by CLARA MacGOWAN in the Society's 1953 calendar (Photograph by Barbara Lazarus Metz)

ILFORD
2A
HP5
4
4A
SAFETY
5
FILM
5A
7A
HP5
8
8A
9
9A
10
ILFORD
10A
HP5
11A
HP5
12
12A
SAFETY
13
FILM
13A
14
ILFORD
14A
ILFORD
17
HP5
SAFETY

Calendar meeting of the Chicago Society of Artists, 1978 (Photographs by Barbara Lazarus Metz)

The CSA: 1940 to Present

Along with the social, political, scientific and industrial changes which have come about in the last three decades, much has also transpired in the world of art. This is especially true of the United States, where experimentation and innovation became the dominant forces in view and where change and novelty became the basic criteria for recognition—perhaps more than ever before in the country's artistic past. True, the artist's vision has been expanded. Newly discovered phenomena surrounding celestial as well as terrestial matters have emerged. New media, new processes have been discovered. New philosophies of art proliferate the art scene.

CONTEMPORARY TRENDS IN ART

Movements in art have emerged, appeared and disappeared. Some have originated in the city of Chicago as well as in New York. Abstract-Expressionism, hard-edge, pop and minimal art, conceptualism, sharp focus realism, and in effect a melange of other experimental approaches have briefly skirted the scene.

Eroticism and an overindulgent exploration of the libidinous elements, unrestrained and explicit in representation, 'shocking' in essence, and deliberate in its attempt to dislodge the long-established value-judgments and criteria concerning aesthetic matters, have for a period of time become the order of the day, acceptable to some reputable galleries and leading museums in the land.

In a recent review of the Abstract Art in Chicago Exhibition at the Museum of Contemporary Art, Franz Schulze, art critic of the Daily News, expressed a rather indeterminate view of what is the state of art today. He stated:

> ...the 1970's have witnessed an almost total collapse of the once-assured avant-garde esthetic, in the wake of which many observers are not sure any more which way art ought to go, or what art is good, and what art is not, or simply what art is in the first place. Little wonder that contemporary art politics is more fun to talk about than contemporary art; little wonder too that the art itself is more readily catalogued than certainly judged.

In his review of the 72nd American Exhibition at the Art Institute held in 1976, Mr. Schultze did, however, offer a reasonable conclusion which would give the viewer some guiding rationale for accepting what is being done in American art today.

> ...the viewer gets not only a revealing picture of advanced American art, but an impression that art in its most accomplished is about as challenging today as it ever was.
>
> Intellectual challenge, after all, is central to the modern esthetic. This history of art in the 20th century, especially the second half, is mostly a record of men who have sought less to make art than to re-define it or to ask questions about it, to push it past limits reached by previous generations. This may not be your idea of how art should be, but that is how it is, and if you accept this as a starting point, you will find some very remarkable things to see at the Institute.

Represented in the 72nd American Exhibition were many familiar names, some who have been popular since the Post War II years. For example, there were Willem DeKooning and Richard Diebenkorn and others in the early 60's like Jasper Johns, Elsworth Kelly, Kenneth Noland, Claes Oldenburg, Robert Rauchenburg, Frank Stella and Andy Warhol.

There is no denying that the presence of shifting trends has injected a new sense of vitality and freshness into the visual arts. To a degree, these may have affected the artistic performance of old and established painters, printmakers and sculptors. But more important perhaps is the fact that these philosophical currents have stirred into action those who are yet in search for artistic identity or individuality in self expression.

To be sure, a few of the innovative and avant-garde approaches to art have filtered into the aesthetic fiber of the Chicago Society of Artists. Fashion has a way of luring and challenging the receptive mind. Often it stimulates the imagination enough to rock the proverbial boat, even of one who tends to cling tenaciously to the tried-and-proven aesthetic values and thus lead him into previously unchartered paths.

The younger members have no doubt infused a bit of daring and adventure into this group of artists. They may have even ignited a few sparks along the way and churned the Society's intrinsic, substantive and established tendencies.

READING, oil by HARRY MINTZ, 1936. Mintz was invited to exhibit in the Art Institute's Chicago Room.

THE AYIN, casein by A. RAYMOND KATZ. Katz was invited to exhibit in the Art Institute's Chicago Room.

Through its consistency and its qualitative performance, attributes which generally characterized its older and more experienced members, the Society has managed to retain its remarkable steadfast position as a vital organization. Conditioned by time and experience and by a tenacious adherence to artistic values in the last three decades, the Chicago Society of Artists has easily continued to forge ahead to control its essential caliber in a world that is totally pre-occupied with experimental "hodge-podge."

HONORS BESTOWED UPON MEMBERS OF THE SOCIETY

As a group, the Chicago Society of Artists has received more than its share of attention. In fact, it is the only artists' organization which has been accorded official recognition by the Art Institute of Chicago.

In 1963, the trustees of the Art Institute held a tea in honor of the Society's 75th anniversary. This was an unprecedented gesture on the part of the Institute, having never before accorded similar recognition to other long-established artists' groups in the city. However, the Chicago Society of Artists is the oldest group of professional artists in the United States, and it has certainly earned due recognition for its longevity as well as for its noted contribution to the artistic life of the city and the nation.

Honors were also conferred upon individual artists in the group. Aside from the usually coveted awards received for meritorious works of art, some members were invited to hold one-man exhibitions in the Chicago

SPIES AND COUNTERSPIES, oil by JULIO DeDIEGO, 1942. DeDiego was invited to exhibit in the Art Institute's Chicago Room.

Room, a room which the Art Institute had set aside in the 1930's and 1940's for invitational one-man exhibitions by Chicago artists only. Among those C. S. A. members who were so honored were Rowena Fry, Emil Armin, A. Raymond Katz, Samuel Greenburg, Alice Mason, Ivan LeLorraine Albright, Macena Barton, Tressa Emerson Benson, Aaron Bohrod, Frances Strain, Julio DeDiego, Leon Garland, Andrene Kauffman, Julia Thecla, Paula Gerard, Harry Mintz, Gus Dalstrom, Jean Crawford Adams, Beatrice Levy, Frances Foy, Flora Schofield, Laura VanPappelandam, Fred Biesel and Sylvia Shaw Judson.

In the last decade many members of the Chicago Society of Artists have been represented in the Art Rental and Sales Gallery of the Art Institute of Chicago. A jury of painters, sculptors, printmakers, and collectors select the works of local artists who submit their entries to be juried several times a year. Artists are thus provided one more outlet for the sale of their products.

In the last three decades, there have been many group exhibitions sponsored by either civic organizations or by the Chicago Society of Artists. Certainly not all of them need to be chronicled for posterity. The more current activities in which the Society has been duly involved, however, can be examined here briefly.

In 1945 the Chicago Society of Artists held an exhibition of prints at the Riverside Museum in New York. The following quote from the New York Times dated January 14, 1945, represents a brief review of the exhibition:

> An unusually good exhibition of graphic work by members of the Chicago Society of Artists and the Northwest Printmakers is current at the Riverside Museum. Among more than a hundred items one might single out etchings by Frances Foy and Gustaf Dalstrom; lithographs by Paula Gerard and Fred Anderson (especially his 'Dirge for a Dead City'); a fine wood engraving ('Orcas Isle') by R. C. Lee; woodcuts by Elizabeth Warhanik, Fay Chong ('Homage to Ancestors'), and William Klamm ('Evening') and ('Organ Builder') and silk screen prints by Clara MacGowan.

In 1945 also, the Chicago Society of Artists held its 56th Annual Exhibition of Paintings and Sculpture at the Findlay Galleries, Chicago. "The Artist Looks at the Home Front" was the theme of this exhibition in which 57 painters and sculptors participated.

Other exhibitions held by the Chicago Society of Artists were at the New Trier High School Gallery, 1946; Riverside Museum, New York, 1947; Evanston Art Center, 1947; Marshall Field Galleries, Chicago, 1947; Mandel Brothers Gallery, Chicago, 1948 and 1950.

More recently, the Chicago Society of Artists has held exhibitions of paintings, prints and sculpture in galleries whose facilities could accommodate the whole group. Exhibits were staged at The McCormick Place Gallery; M'Kerr Observatory Gallery; the University Club of Chicago; the Triangle Art Center Gallery; the Circle Gallery; the Renaissance Society Gallery of the University of Chicago; the Chicago Public Library; the Monroe Gallery; the Covenant Club; the 4 Arts Gallery, Evanston; Rosary College, River Forest; Triton College, River Grove, Northeastern Illinois University, and other available exhibition areas. These constitute the usual listing of places where the Chicago Society of Artists still holds its annual exhibitions.

SOCIAL EVENTS

Besides those meetings that are held at exhibition openings, the Society also gathers at other special events. These are generally attended by the entire membership and friends.

Once a year a calendar meeting is scheduled. Members who have designed and executed lino-cuts for the anticipated publication of the calendar submit one or two blocks and artists' proofs. The blocks and proofs are then recorded and readied for the printer. Matted prints are displayed on the walls of the meeting area so that the members present may vote to award several prizes for those block-prints which merit special recognition. However, all of the prints submitted, even those designed by artist-members living in cities other than Chicago, are included in the Chicago Society of Artists Calendar published the following year.

Two dinner meetings are also scheduled annually at which time the Society honors noted art critics or art collectors who have made a noteworthy contribution to the art scene of Chicago and have exerted

NATALIE HENRY contemplating her vote for one of the calendar print awards at the annual calendar meeting, 1978 (Photograph by Barbara Lazarus Metz)

LOUISE DUNN YOCHIM, current president of the Chicago Society of Artists, with her husband MAURICE YOCHIM at the Society's Annual Christmas Dinner Meeting at the Drake Hotel, 1976

a great deal of effort in behalf of Chicago artists.

All in all, the yearly schedule of events provides the membership of the Society with a reasonable schedule of activities of professional consequence.

CIRCUMSTANTIAL CHANGES

As may be assumed about any group of artists within a given period of time, changes do occur. And they have occurred in the Society's constituency but not at all in the nature of its activities. Through unavoidable circumstances, the vicissitudes of life, the demise of a number of members, through change in destination and for other personal reasons, some artists have left the organization. Others have achieved national and international attention and found organizational affairs time-consuming or infringing upon their immediate priority, painting or sculpting.

Nevertheless, a number of artists who reside in New York, Kansas, California, Texas, Arizona, Hawaii, New Mexico, Florida and Colorado still retain their membership in the Society and participate in some of the group's activities whether it is in the annual calendar publication or in written communications. For example, Clara MacGowan Cioban, former president of the Chicago Society of Artists, current member living in Oceanside, California, in her annual Christmas Greetings to the Society expressed her feelings in a thought-provoking, beautiful statement worthy of note. It reads as follows:

> A Merry Christmas to Each One! 1976
>
> Christmas with all its expectation, excitement and joy is here again! No matter where we are, there are favorite scenes that endear us to our home areas. In Oceanside, the poinsettias, red pyracanthus berries and the palms supply the rich accents of holiday red and green. Recently, in the afternoons, I have been seeing unusual color effects over the majestic Pacific. Sometimes the water is a sparkling clear blue with a golden ball in the sky of gray; again, the ocean is a dark blue with an irridescent pearl emerging from moving light gray clouds; and occasionally, the waves of heavy dull gray support an orange-red ball dramatically perched on the horizon. And, invariably, as we watch the sun disappear, it leaves us in awe of the wonder of it all. We are deeply stirred by this God-given beauty in nature and thankful for the experience.
>
> This very special year, our Bi-Centennial, has been magnificent! We have learned more about our nation's past and the brave people who envisioned a great government in a new country. The presidential candidates, in their excellent debates, acquainted us with many significant aspects of our national problems and prepared us for carefully planning the actions of future years. We did win the respect throughout the world for our procedures in effectively and efficiently changing to the new term of government.
>
> Making history is inevitable, but building a good history requires the best thinking of every citizen. Each person has a responsible part to play in our government—if we are to survive. It is wise to remind ourselves that we came to this country of our own volition. We either continue to build the quality of life our forefathers established or we destroy it by inertia, indifference and unimaginative actions.
>
> Many ideas in constant use here came from other cultures. James Henry Breasted, America's most famous Egyptologist, stated that Egypt's Delta Civilization in 4241 B. C. introduced the calendar year of 365 days, the earliest fixed date in the history of the world as known to us. Caesar took it to Rome and we got it from Rome. Breasted also said that the Egyptian religious philosophy of a belief in life after death had a direct result in their magnificent architecture: mastabas, pyramids and temples. We profit by knowledge shared by all the people of all the ages.
>
> Communication also plays a tremendous part in our lives. This unknown author has a real gem for us:
>
> THE POWER OF WORDS
>
> A careless word may kindle strife,
> A cruel word may wreck a life;
> A bitter word may hate instill,
> A brutal word may smite and kill;
> A gracious word may smooth the way,
> A joyous word may light the day;

> A timely word may lessen stress,
> A loving word may heal and bless.
>
> As we embark on the New Year, let us all try to make 1977 a better year. With God's help, nothing is impossible and we can go as far as we can envision. More power to you and a truly wonderful 1977.
>
> Always my love,
>
> (Signed) Clara

Despite circumstantial changes in the last thirty years, the Society's membership has remained comparatively stable. Presently, it boasts of a roster of one hundred fourteen painters, sculptors and printmakers. The only obvious change which has occurred is the number of sculptors belonging to the group. It has declined substantially. The number of painters has remained approximately the same. But there has been a decided increase in the number of printmakers in the organization. Limitations put upon the size of exhibiting pieces may have had some affect upon the decision to exhibit smaller works, to which printmaking lends itself admirably. An increase in delivery or shipping expenses may also have had some influence on the nature, size and media used by the artist.

Nevertheless, it is clearly apparent that the Chicago Society of Artists has developed a built-in sense of permanency in its structure, and a workable frame of reference has its roots in the foundation that has been laid by those who have departed, and it is at this point that the writer feels compelled to make pertinent reference to them.

Those who have departed from this earth have left a rich and precious legacy for us, the living for they have laid the corner stone upon which the Chicago Society of Artists stands today. Some have served as this organization's leaders. Others have exerted their creative energies in many capacities, often at great personal sacrifice and far beyond the call of duty. Always in behalf of the Society's welfare, with dedicated fervor and unstinted devotion.

Among them were many well-established painters and sculptors who have been members of the Society for more than thirty years. Their works have contributed greatly to the stature of major art events in the nation.

Indeed, they are sorely missed. Missed, by those whose artistic careers they have invariably inspired as teachers and as friends. Gertrude Abercrombie, Jean Crawford Adams, Emil Armin, David Bekker, Fritzi Brod, Edithe Jane Cassady, Gustaf Dalstrom, Theodore Frano, Maurice Friedlander, Frances Foy, John Emerson, Leon Garland, Todros Geller, Bacia Gordon, V. M. S. Hannell, William Jacobs, Joshua Kaganove, A. Raymond Katz, Beatrice Levy, Alice Mason, Mike Mason, Verne V. Mullen, Tunis Ponsen, Yvonne Pryor, Frederick Remahl, Ceil Rosenberg, Sam Ostrovsky, Morris Topchevsky, Flora Schofield, Ethel Spears, Ivy Steele, Laura VanPappelendam, and Louis Weiner—all have passed away within a period of twenty or twenty-five years; others are gone much longer.

The resonant qualities of the legacy which these painters and sculptors have bequeathed to those whose lives they have touched will resound in the hearts and minds of many of us. With them has

A CALL TO LIFE, linocut by MORRIS TOPCHEVSKY (Courtesy of the Chicago Society of Artists)

gone a substantial portion of the history of Chicago art in which the departed artists played a significant role.

Chicago's history of art has been richly fortified with inordinate pride because of the honors and prestige that the above mentioned illustrious names have brought to the aesthetic climate of the city and the nation and in no lesser measure to the Chicago Society of Artists.

43

CATHERINE CAJANDIG inking a stone, preparing to print (Photograph by Barbara Lazarus Metz)

10

SECTION II

The CSA: Statements and Reproductions

To gain further insight into the innermost feelings and thoughts of individual members of the Chicago Society of Artists, personal statements, credos and philosophical thoughts are delineated in subsequent pages. Included are matters of anecdotal nature, of intuitive perception, of cherished and unshakable beliefs, and of influences which helped to forge each artist's distinct identity.

Through his or her particular medium and personal or unique approach is unfolded an arena of content spawning the broad spectrum of innovation through the creative process, and emerging as the congenial aggregate—the sum and substance of the Society.

Examples of work further illustrate each artist's approach to self-expression, and add visual credence to philosophical notions, reflecting the idiom and subtle nuances which pervade his or her personal views and objectives through two- or three-dimensions.

Biographical notes which follow, provide a further analytical and illuminating index to each artist's record of achievement, and his or her distinctive contribution to the world of art.

Although all members of the Society were extended the invitation to submit personal data for inclusion in this volume, not all have responded to this request. The reasons for exclusion, therefore, rest solely with each artist's decision.

TIGER TREE, *oil*

BERTE ANAPOL

The joy of working at nature in all its variety, and the impact of its color pushed me (rather than inspired) into an almost involuntary need to interpret that with which my senses were being bombarded.

DON J. ANDERSON

"Everything that exists is an expression of an idea." This is my favorite quote and adage. But, it doesn't add age: it adds dimension to everything; for then tools as pencils, pens and pigments help create a tangible expression of life and ideas.

ARIES—CHINESE FRAGMENT, *linocut*

COLLAGE

HOWARD B. ANDERSON

Paper collage orchestrated in neutral tones, varied shape relationships, and in delicate nuances, create subtle contrasts in my abstract schemes.

Unlike this approach and conversely, are the strong value contrasts which characterize my graphics in structured arrangements of objects.

BACHELOR KITCHEN, *tempera*

FRANCES BADGER

My life long interest in nature, birds, plant life and animals has served me well as inspiration for my paintings in which I try to depict the beauty and charm of the good earth's living creatures.

Interiors of every type also have a special appeal for me, as these depict human existence, and the characteristics of each personality that this existence envisages.

QUEST: THE STEPS INTO THE FUTURE, oil

ROBERT L. BAILEY

I am intrigued by celestial and terrestial matters, and my paintings reflect my interest. The three-dimensional character of my work is prevalent whether in a bas-relief construction, oil, acrylic painting or graphics.

THE STORM, oil (Collection of Mr. and Mrs. Robert Cleary)

MACENA BARTON

Only a great ego can produce a great work, whether in art, literature or music; therefore, no work of art can be greater than the one who produces it.

I am intensely interested in color, having an orientalist's passion for it. My art is a personal expression. I paint exactly what I feel and am not influenced by the methods of other artists, even of those whom I admire most. I paint to please myself, to satisfy an inner urge that must find expression. One must live life in order to interpret it. To put this interpretation upon canvas should be the chief aim of the painter.

**Jacobson J. Z. Art of Today—Chicago, 1933, L. M. Stein, publisher, 1932.*

MARCANE, linocut

BETTIE BECKER

Though the artist, musician, poet, writer are given the attribute, rather exclusively, of being creative, I do not feel they are any more 'creative' than anyone else. Man is a thinking, and, as a result, a constantly creating entity . . . he shapes, or creates, the events in his life, his home, his ambitions, his family, his job, his life activity. If the artist is unique in his creativity, it is simply because he—through his use of color, rhythm, harmony, paint and canvas—attempts to distill and record the activity of creativity around him. He pins the fleeting event, idea or likeness onto canvas or paper. True, he has developed a degree of awareness of the seen and unseen universe around, and within him, and he has been willing to spend the time developing the skill and the ability to record this awareness, to develop the techniques to isolate and perpetuate these fleeting aspects of life, on canvas. Man and nature are constantly creating, and the artist is the scribe, interpreter and recorder of this creative activity surrounding him.

TRESSA EMERSON BENSON

As an artist I believe in studying the work of artists of many periods and backgrounds. I have found inspiration in the design and color of oriental art as well as occidental particularly in the sculpture, porcelains and paintings of Chinese artists and especially in the color prints of the Japanese. I can see a relationship between the abstract painting of today and the design of the latter. In western art my interest covers many centuries ranging from the primitive to so-called modern art. I try to keep an open mind believing that I am the loser if I do not try to understand what the artist sees in his subject.

DAGUERREOTYPE DANDIES, oil, 1936 (Courtesy of Art Institute of Chicago)

MIMBRES, acrylic on canvas, 1970, 39½" x 39½"

CLAUDE BENTLEY

My paintings have a point of reference in my appreciation for the antique and primitive art worlds and in the immediacy of the images evoked by those forms.

SAILS, watercolor, 26" x 32"

AILEEN BERG

I have worked in the transparent water color medium for nearly fifteen years, after having worked in mixed media. I found that watercolor is the most challenging and exciting of all the other media. I enjoy the use of India Ink and watercolor and find the use of the ink line in the wet pigments along with the transparent wash, results in a means of communicating to my viewers my reaction to the world around me.

I have also combined Oriental rice paper in collage with the watercolor medium, and have arrived at certain textural effects that can not be obtained otherwise.

It pleases me if my work impressed anyone who cares enough to purchase it, but the important thing is that the experiences in my life are great enough to impress me.

STORM, linocut

SYLVESTER BRITTON

I am primarily a figurative painter who enjoys depicting groups of people involved in the daily routine circumstances of life; people seated in waiting rooms, crowds on the street, friendly confrontations between some and just people relaxed in their home environment.

In landscapes I choose to render the jarring and ominous elements of nature.

IRRIGATION, drawing

GERRI H. BUTLER

I agree with Euripides:
I think that Fortune
Watcheth o'er our lives
Surer than we, But well
said:
he who strives
will find his gods strive
for him equally.

STUDY IN MOVEMENT II, oil

CATHERINE CAJANDIG

Movement in the organization of spacial areas on a canvas, or in a graphic composition is of prime interest to me whether utilized in abstract arrangements or employed in subjective formations. In either case, the object is to achieve a synthesis of all elements which enter into the production of a work of art.

LURE OF THE LUTE, *linocut*

HILDA CAMPBELL

I enjoy painting the 'fruits of nature's labors.' Still life arrangements and figurative compositions executed in watercolors, oils or collage are themes which inspire me most, and which I prefer in painting.

SIDI AHMED, acrylic 36" x 38"

JANINE COLLIER

In my paintings I attempt to inject the interpenetration of geometric planes and the inter-relationships of color values and hues, receding and advancing in space in strong contrasting effects and emotionally charged directions.

C. E. COOPER

I work at my art work because I must. Something inside of me impels and compels me to work, and I am in an unhappy and frustrated state when I can't work. I am a story-teller and much of my work is illustrative, although the story may not always be obvious. I believe in a solidly constructed composition. I believe in solid drawing, I cannot jump on band wagons and do what is chic, popular and/or 'in.' I must do that which feels most natural for me and not mimic others. I won't deny the influence other artists have had on me, but only because there was a kinship in approach and emotionality. A person's art work should be a reflection of himself.

BATHERS, ink on paper

CHESS PLAYERS, etching combined with a series of aquatints

CHARLOTTE DOYLE

The artist looks upon this world with a certain sensitivity, his intellect and senses fully attuned to every aspect of life: the exhilarating, the desperate, the beautiful, the ugly, the joyous and the lonely. He organizes his thoughts into a visual expression which creates in the viewer a new way of looking at the universe, allowing him to draw upon the artist's sensitivity and power to communicate.

STILL-LIFE, collage

MARGARET DRISCOLL

I must create or be miserable. In my later years I have wanted to tell of eternal life and to that end I have concentrated on what might be called religious art. Any art is a sort of 'life line' supporting one on the earthly journey.

Representing a small frame of a visually pleasant moment of pleasure, or beauty is my own concept of composition so that the result presents a painting of serenity and tranquility with fluid strokes of color and rhythm. The movement is lyrical as in a poetic ballet, or colorful—yet quiet in a landscape or still-life.

My work is removed from the violent, the harsh, the ugly aspects of the world. The completed work represents evidence of the world's abundance of beauty.

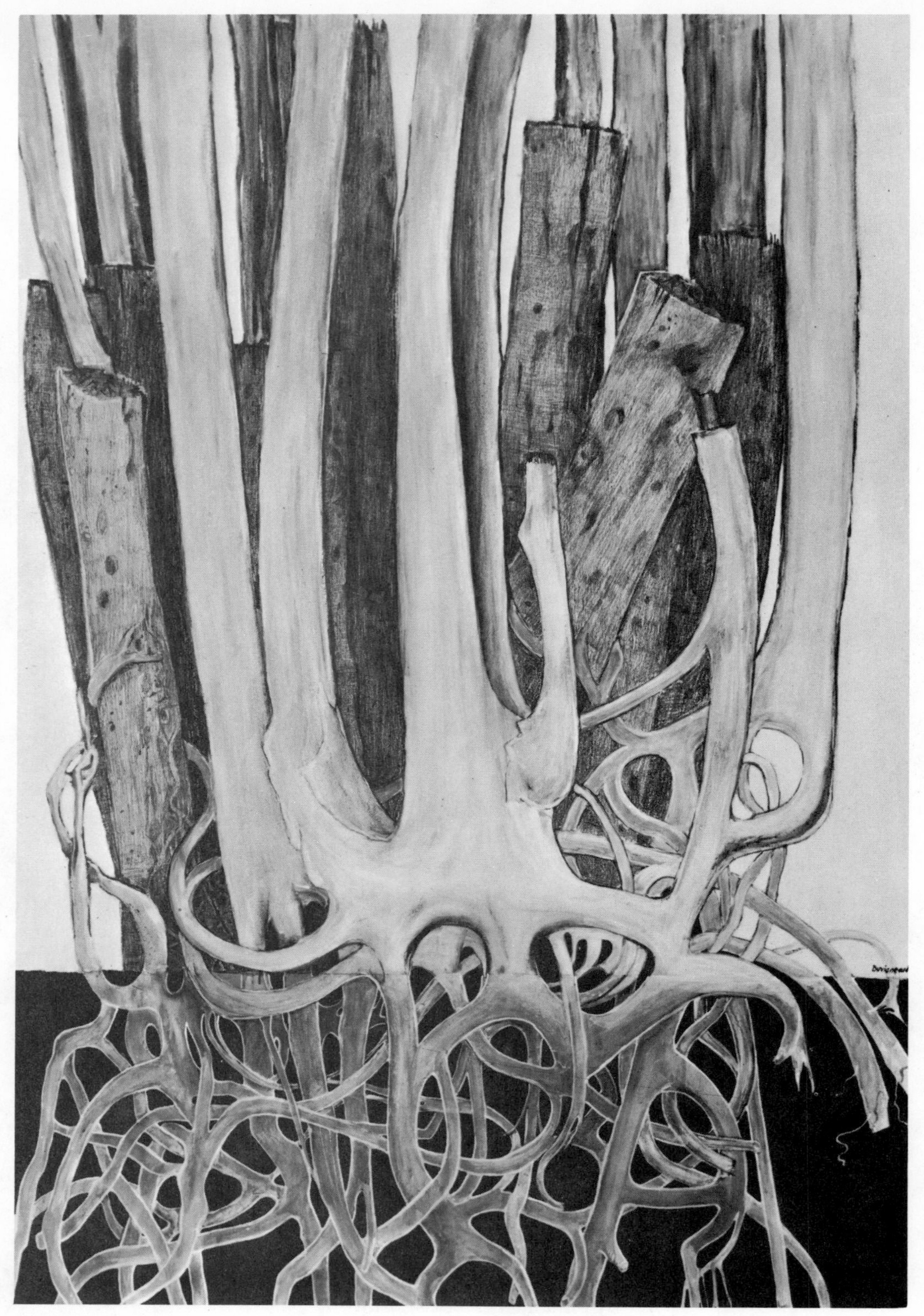

FICUS AND PALM, acrylic

DIANE DUVIGNEAUD

I have been concentrating in my recent work on a special aspect of nature and that is the life-death relationship of all things; to look at a dead tree or an upturned root and to see the life force in that which is called dead, is to increase one's awareness and to enlarge the total life experience—this is what I endeavor to capture in my painting.

GROVE OF THE MAIDENS, *oil*

ELIZABETH EDDY

My process is to sit, perhaps without knowing it, beside the well of my unconscious open and ready for the material to surface. I cannot do this consciously and aggressively, for then the material becomes shy and remains hidden. It is a little like catching butterflies—I must be effortless, so not to scare away my flickering quarry, but at the same time I must be alert.

My desire is to entrap my viewer into a state of wonder—as opposed to know—I think we have too little wonder and too much know, the former is open—the latter closed.

EAGLE, carved wood

JOHN FABION

I have been a painter and sculptor for fifty years, one fourth of our country's Bicentennial. My goal was to add to the culture of America and Chicago in particular as an artist and educator and to incorporate my native heritage into this culture.

BARBARA FAGEN

I believe that each of us must use his or her talent to uplift and inspire those who view the artist's work. It is my aim to achieve an ethereal quality in all my work, whatever the medium—sculpture, painting, mosaics, but particularly in enamel painting on silver and copper.

These works are generally charaterized by gracefully floating human forms, rendered in delicate nuances of color, creating illusions of infinite space and arranged in ambiguous settings of fantasy.

THOUGHTS ASCENDING, fired enamel on copper, 10" x 17"

GAME MASTER, lithograph

SHERRI Z. FELDMAN

I believe that my art work is a non-verbal conversation between myself and the viewer. It is through my art that I make a personal statement. A combination of my statement and the viewer's response make up the conversation.

BIRD FORM, bronze

EMMA FERRY

I find that my ideas are best expressed through the structure of negative and positive areas in a three-dimensional form, and in the realization of grace of movement in animal or human forms.

ENDLESS CORRIDOR, *collograph*

CHARLOTTE FRIEDMAN

Art should be a joyful experience, but often it is painful and frustrating—as life is—and I accept that fact, being inextricably bound together. It is an extension of oneself—stripped of technical devices—a personal vision, nerve endings exposed.

If one can jog one's audience into an awareness of beauty, humor, or pain—then one is fulfilled. And even without an audience the endless challenge of new media, new plateaus to conquer—new problems to resolve—is fulfillment enough.

AFTERNOON, oil, 1973, 54" x 62" (Collection of Hawaii State Foundation on Culture and Art)

RICHARD FROOMAN

I prefer realism in my work and I find natural elements interesting. The ideas for my paintings are the culmination of various thoughts and impulses related to these elements. Organic and sensual qualities are still important but I find myself becoming more involved with social and psychological significance. Ideas and images are now formed in my mind before I start painting. New structural and color possibilities emerge while working, but are often based on previously learned technical relationships as well as physical and psychological experiences. (Lanikai, Hawaii, 1977)

ITALIAN COURT 1919-1968, serigraph

ROWENA FRY

I have had great help and encouragement from all my teachers, but I think I relate more to American Naive painters than any other school or movement.

I have been often asked how I 'became an artist.' This is always difficult for me to answer. As far back as I can remember, drawing has seemed to me almost as natural as breathing.

Very early I became interested in watercolor painting, but found it a difficult medium for profound study. I have since worked in oils, printmaking and other media.

I believe that any work of art worth its salt, must give the viewer some kind of uplift.

I find nature, people and man-made objects a great source of inspiration, and enjoy the inter-relationship of all these elements in my paintings and serigraphs. I am fascinated by the minutest details which enrich the surfaces and textures of things that I paint.

My hope is that something I paint will live long after I have gone.

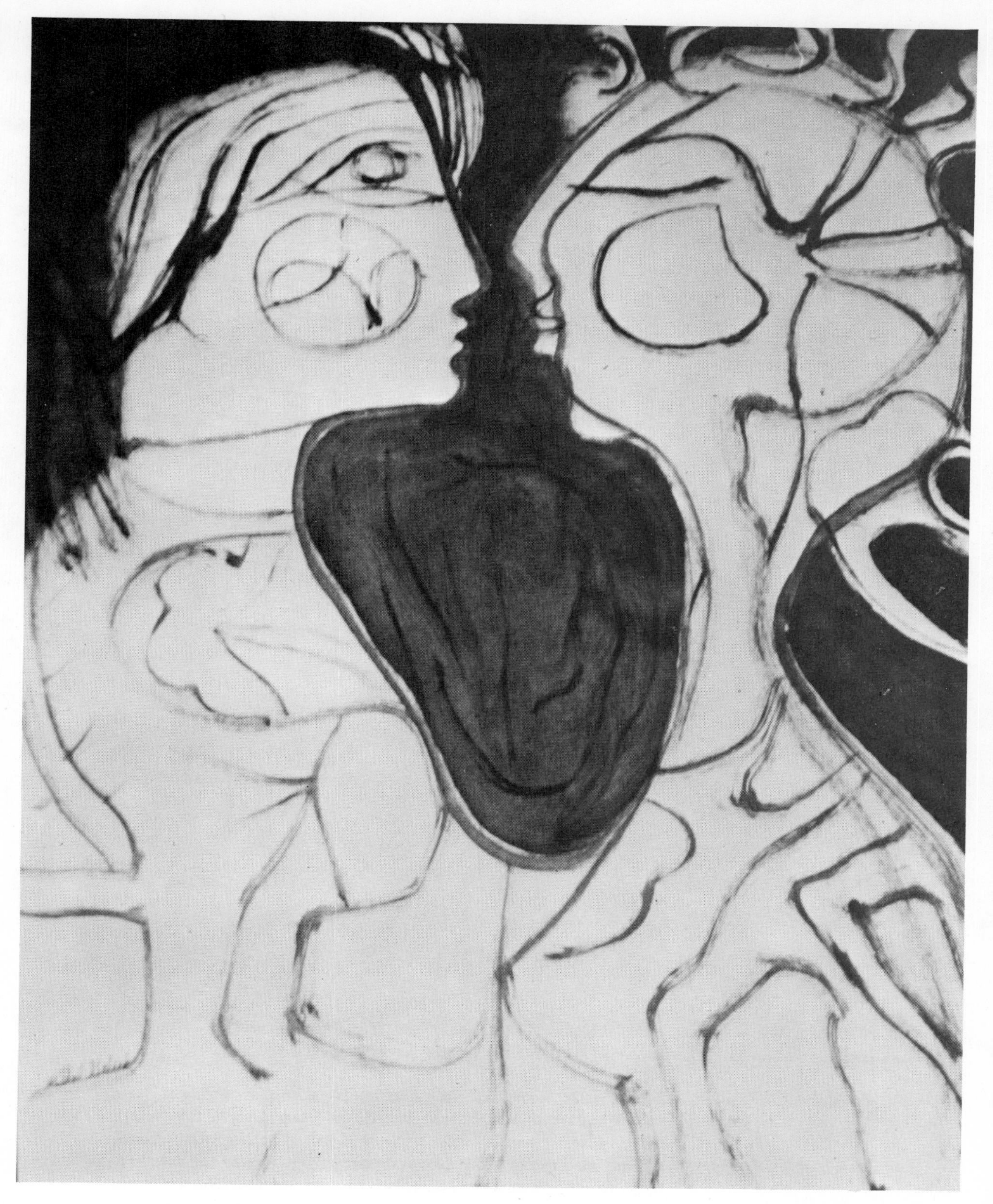

CONVERSATION, oil on paper

ETHEL GELICK

My work enables me to capture and share with others the fleeting moments of everyday life. I am inspired to innovate and portray those elements which provide the necessary resources for my creative outlets. I insist that my work be free and straightforward and that ample room be left for the viewers own fantasy.

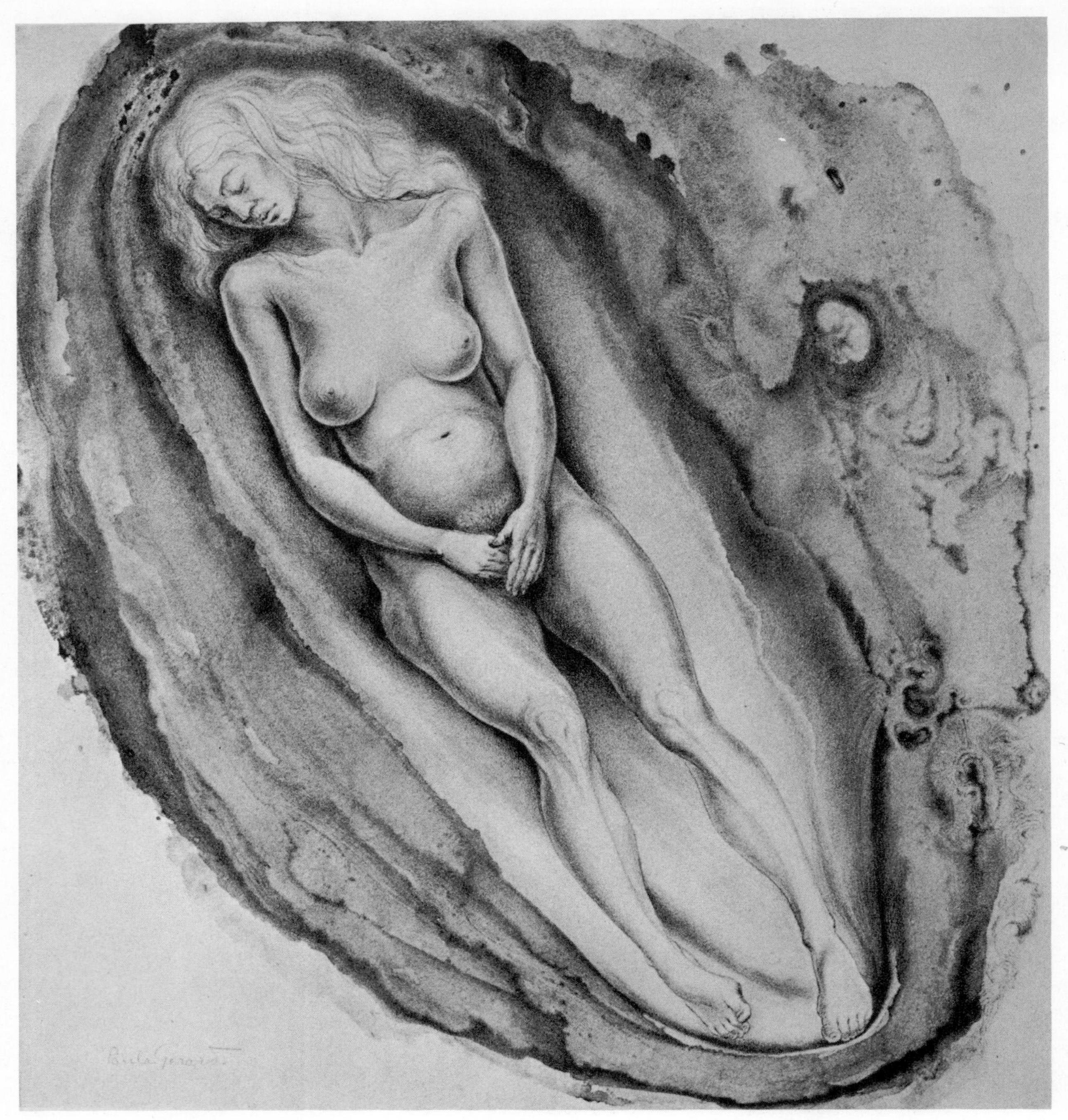

AURA, silver and gold point with watercolor on casein-coated paper

PAULA GERARD

I have never identified with a 'style' or 'school' of thought. I am interested in all new ideas, but do not feel impelled to adopt them, just to prove how 'with it' I am. On the other hand, neither do I make a virtue of conservatism. I prize the integrity of good craftsmanship, but not as an end in itself. Nature is my constant source of material, not to be copied photographically, but to be interpreted and explored in depth. For me, movement of line catches the universal force; the very essence of vitality and this is what I seek to project in visual terms. I like the nude human figure because of its potential for movement, and purity of line. However, these can be found equally in other nature forms, in infinitely fascinating variety of combinations. As far as my work itself is concerned, I prefer to let it stand on its own to trying to 'explain' it.

CHRIST'S FACE ON THE SHROUD, *oil*

THOMAS GIULIANO

My orientation is to all aspects of human feelings, therefore, I paint the basic instincts that are the richest in these feelings—religion, love, fantasy, food, sentiment, sex, fear, survival.

This orientation forces me to accept art and reject illustration. There is a difference between an illustration of man's desire for food and his actual desire. The latter is art; the former doesn't count.

CORRIE-LOU LIVINGSTON GLASS

My philsophy can be espressed in two simple words—'do it.'

THE GROVE, *linocut*

A MOTHER AND HER CHILDREN IN ISRAEL, FROM INDIA, *watercolor*

BACIA GORDON

I believe art is a language that the artist must use to express his reaction to the world around him.

I feel that sometimes through my paintings I can anchor a moment in eternity.

I find that painting for me is a challenge and sometimes there is also fulfillment for which I am eternally grateful.

SPRING, linocut

DIANA GORDON

If the pen was mightier than the sword, the picture can be more powerful than the word.

My imagery is definitely political, critical and involved with our technological milieu.

ZEBRAS, serigraph, 1975

SAM GREENBURG

Artists are peculiar. They say they paint and sculpt not because they're happy when they do, but because they're miserable when they don't. They think art is the most exciting, exhilarating, and engrossing exercise anyone can engage in—from conception to delivery.

Artists respond in different ways to stimuli that move them to produce art, but they all have the same goals. First they seek gratification from within; second, they hope for approval from their peers; and third, they demand adoration from the masses. Some of them expect remuneration, too.

Artists spend years learning their profession; then more years acquiring artlessness to cover up what they learned; and then they end up practicing a very expensive hobby.

Most peculiar of all, artists go on believing the best thing they ever did will be the very next thing they do.

COLOR ZONES, construction, 80" x 69", wood, linen, acrylic over 13,000 sticks

GARNET GULLBORG

My constructions are high-key abstractions which create visual illusions by the use of light, color and form. I think a great deal about color and texture. The wood, laces and other materials stimulate different sensations. At a distance there is a strong thing going that causes one to want to go up to the piece to examine and touch it.

LILLIAN E. HALL

I believe in the importance of knowing one's craft, and in the manifestations of structured special relationships which provide a sound basis for a harmonious relationship of line, form, color, mass and texture.

I am inspired by nature mostly, and intrigued by changes that are brought on by the seasons of the year. Man and his relation to his mechanized environment hold a particular fascination for me. These set in motion a myriad of mental images which readily adapt themselves to creative configurations.

THE HULL SHOP WELDERS, *oil*

CHALLENGE, Collage 24" x 30", japanese paper

MARION HALL

My philosophy in painting is to continually learn and experiment and find new ways of seeing the world around me—nature, people, things, seen and unseen, phenomena, fantasies not yet discovered, and all that make my inner self fulfilled.

HAZEL HANNELL

As an impressionable teenager I read of a woman who required of her children that they should make the world a bit better or more beautiful because they had been in it.

Missionarying did not appeal to me so I settled for the more beautiful.

GALENA, *watercolor*

FLOWERS, *watercolor*

MARJORIE HARTMANN

Watercolor is my favorite medium for it allows for a disciplined permissiveness in the expression of ideas and fantasies.

THE LAW, Byzantine glass mosaic, 8′ x 5½′, one of two equal panels created for the lobby of Temple Beth El, Gary, Indiana, 1959-1960.

HAROLD HAYDON

In the immortal words of Hilla Rebay in a Guggenheim Museum catalogue, "Top of Culture is Where Art Is." It is a privilege and a responsibility to create works of art, especially public works of art.

TRIFOIL, bronze

RICHARD E. HELLER, M.D.

I use sculpture to express my personal response to various emotions, growth in nature, and movement of line, form and texture.

I allow my medium, wax, to influence the form; i.e., its plasticity, adaptability and firmness are used to realize a harmonious and unified arrangement of planes and surfaces.

FOLK DANCE, linocut

NATALIE S. HENRY

The need to illustrate my thoughts was ever present in my very earliest years. Especially, concerning traumatic experiences such as for example, when the town in which I lived passed an ordinance forbidding roller skating on sidewalks. I cannot recall how I drew a protest sketch, but that was the beginning of my early art expressions.

When the war ended I drew boats and planes and soldiers, expecting all of them home the next day. But now I am content to register my reactions to nature—landscape, animals, birds, and people in whatever medium seems best.

MY MOTHER, woodcut

FERN GILBERT HORWITZ

There is personal joy for me in the act of creation. I like to work with color, light and space, interrelating them on the canvas.

I believe that God may be glorified through man's creative abilities, and that He causes me to reflect on the beauty of His creation, and to delight in the gifts He has given me.

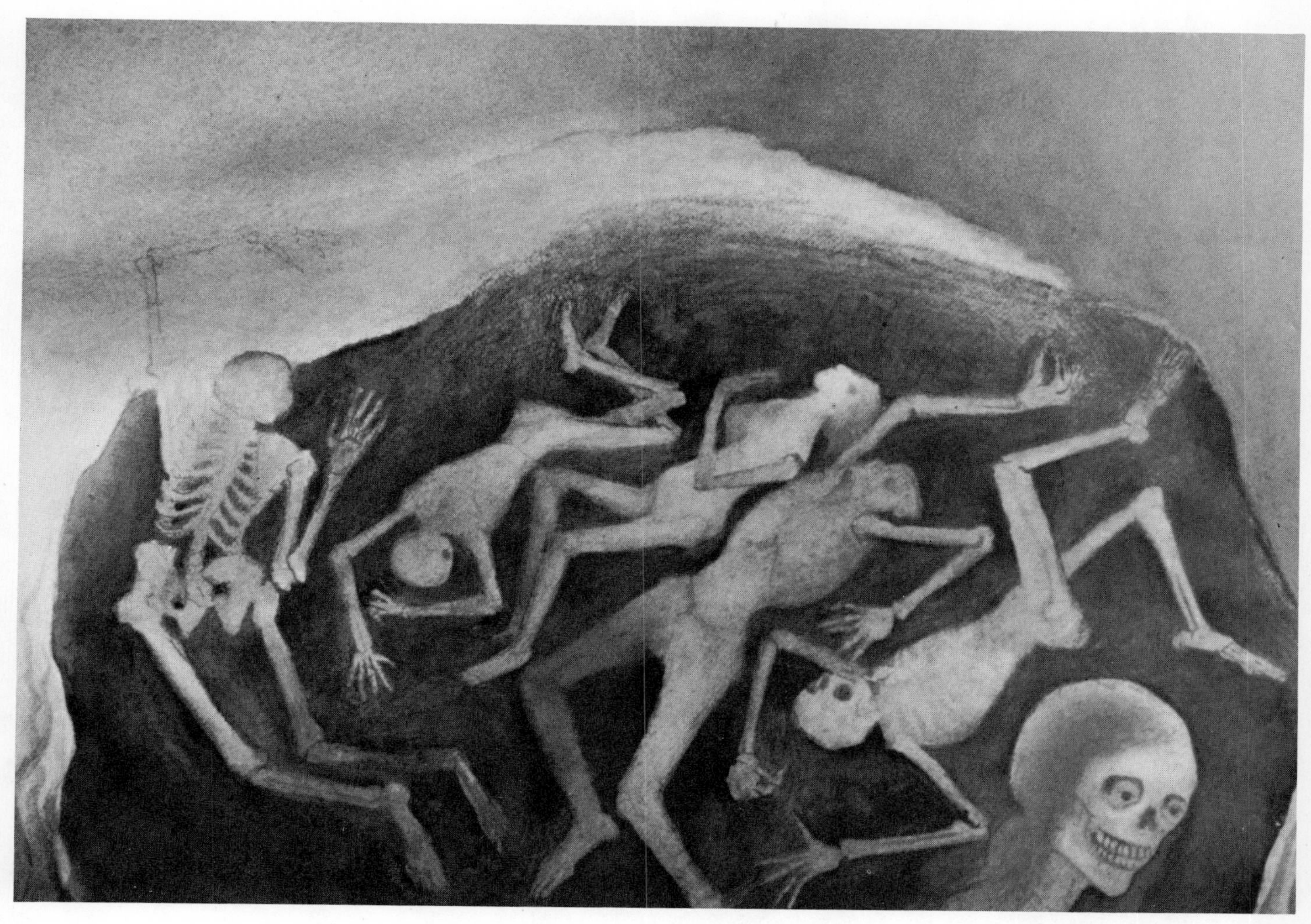

HOLOCAUST #1, watercolor

EMMANUEL JACOBSON

Some of my water color drawings are comments on the discords of our time: the destructive manifestations of the Human Spirit: namely: The Holocaust, Hijackings, Riots: violence employed against the innocent.

Some of my other statements reflect my abiding interest and appreciation of the inspired roles of the Shaman in Primitive Societies.

Tomorrow I shall continue to study some of the myriad natural forms that I discover.

THOMAS HARRY KAPSALIS

I believe that paintings and sculpture are visual statements which project the artist's reactions and his perceptions to everything through his senses.

The artist perceives his world in terms of value, color, form and texture-relationships which he manipulates to achieve an aesthetic totality of an idea conceived in fantasy or reality.

SPICULE STRUCTURE, *welded iron, 7½' height, 1951*

MUSICALE, oil

PORTIA R. KARLSBERG

Besides immediacy and economy, which are the foundation of my work, I must feel the spiritual pull upward, with which the yearning and searching combine to excitingly resolve the painting.

MASADA, oil

MICHAEL KARZEN

As an artist I am less concerned with media experimentation than with developing and deepening my own personal vision of the world. In my view, art can help clarify and re-affirm man and his environment. Art can give man meaning and insight into self. Art is a kind of visual psycho-analysis. The artist through learning about himself rediscovers our collective humanity and restates it in compelling visual terms. Art is the very essence of our spirit, the bedrock of our existence. It is our life's blood. Without it we cease to be human—with it we reach forward toward eternal truth.

ANDRENE KAUFMANN

To place myself philosophically in the present, I would say that I have believed in the approach of Albert Camus. He discusses the human being as the only creature who is able to withstand the tensions or constant flux of living, with growing understanding of it, and with the ability to maintain a functioning balance in it—i.e. a constant made by everchanging balance.

In painting (as in all the arts) these producing, evolving processes work in the same way. A painting evolves and comes to a solution, as problems of life evolve and come to solutions. We are able to understand to a certain point and maintain the tensions of balance. Neither painting nor life has any pre-destined or pre-conceived answers, but each has many possible solutions or absolutes. The structure of life, the expression in painting—the solution is always an evolving tentative one made absolute by work, but which might well be altered or destroyed by the next awareness or lack of it.

Thus an awareness becomes a work of art but also becomes a reality. It expresses an absolute in time, and becomes the union between us and our existence. The greater the insight into this growing awareness or consciousness, the more real or actual the work of art is.

GANDHI, ceramic, 52" x 28", one of 19 murals and large stained glass windows in the Third Unitarian Church of Chicago, 1955-1969

THE POET, oil

FELIX KLUCZEWSKI

The universe is a wonder to me, and its wonderful to be alive. All the wonderous things in the universe, with their rhythmic pattern and order leave me in awe!

My art is a striving expression of the above statements, in the hope that I may create something that may give the viewer 'pleasure and well being.'

SHIRLEY PAPERNO KRAVITT

Art is experimentation, non-conformity, searching and probing; the unharnessed pursuit of these elements being a pre-condition for creativity. Concerning expression and influence, one reaches the stature of an artist when one expresses his personal philosophy through the philosophy of the time in which he is living and working—through the influence of universal man.

To paint the 'essence' one pulls from the guts to create; art flows from the deepest sources of life; the artist must believe in himself and the power of his ideas. I bring to my paintings my emotional and intellectual background uniting with the subconscious element reflecting and projecting my total life experience.

MIRADOR DE DARAXA, ALHAMBRA, GRANADA, *acrylic on canvas 4' x 3'*

CROSS AND RECROSS, acrylic 30" x 40"

ALICE LAUFFER

Severe limitations on the forms with which one is working would seem to be creatively limiting to the artist. Paradoxically, the modular forms that I chose as a self-imposed restriction eventually led to new areas of work I would not have otherwise conceived. Ellipses of two related sizes and straight lines, that I used rather rigidly in my earlier work, I am now adapting in a very uninhibited manner and with great freedom.

The resulting imagery ranges from forms floating in deep, dark mysteriously evocative space to light, airy, softly subtle constructions that cross and recross the thin line between living and non-living organisms. The response of the viewer depends very much on what the viewer brings to the painting. A scientist will see the paintings as symbolic of biological chemical processes. People associated with astronomy, technology or interested in science fiction believe the images are definitely related to outer space. Still others see a metaphysical relationship to their inner life and use mystical language to describe their feelings toward the painting.

The evolution of the imagery I have described could not have been achieved without a concurrent development of technical skill in the use of spray or airbrush technique. The elegantly smooth gradation of tone would be nearly impossible without competent airbrush work.

Thus, after a time of fretting at the restrictions, I finally began to realize how unshackling those restrictions were in reality. Within the unity of a self-imposed discipline, I can now push my imagination and the resulting imagery to the limit.

HUNTER, acrylic

LUCILLE LEIGHTON

Art to me is a way of life—a quest and a fulfillment. It is a bridge, a means of communication with the peoples of this world, for art has its own language, transcending distance, race, creed—it is a bridge, too, to all of the art of the past and to that of the future.

ON A KENTUCKY ROAD, oil

BEATRICE S. LEVY

My life as an artist is a constant struggle to put down adequately on canvas or paper what I think and feel about what I see and learn. As I am constantly seeing and learning, this life, like that of an explorer, is filled with thrilling adventure, for every painting, drawing or etching is a fresh and exciting experience.

Subject matter in my work is usually a starting point and it may or may not continue important as the work progresses... Although most of the time my design begins as an abstraction and could again be resolved into one, I do not do any pure abstractions.

...I paint because of the thrill of fresh vision and independent thought I derive from it. Because I am an American and a Chicagoan, my work must have something in it of the quality of both.

...Quite sincerely I can say that I have not been influenced by the demands of galleries, the art market, or by the opinion of current criticism.

Art of Today, Chicago—1933, L. M. Stein Pub., Chicago, 1932

GREENWICH VILLAGE, emulsion on canvas 46" x 34", 1976

BARBARA K. LEWIS

Artistic endeavor is the expression of one's relationship to the world in visual terms. The response continues, regardless of its reception by others, but is tempered by their reactions just as all expressions are affected by social response.

BOUQUET, *sculpmetal intaglio*

EVELYN LEWY

Although I enjoy working in oils, acrylics, watercolor and other media, I find printmaking most suitable to my temperament since it affords infinite possibilities for experimentation and exploration of media, techniques and processes in the development of innovative ideas.

CLARA MacGOWAN   *Keep learning; keep working; be true to yourself.*

MT. EDITH, BANFF SPRINGS PARK, CANADA, oil

DEMPSTER STREET EL, EVANSTON, mixed media (Courtesy Illinois Bell Collection)

LUCRETIA A. MALCHER

A search for truth—the cause of things; Then, I would like to share my treasures with others.

FULTON FISH MARKET, *oil*

SHIRLEY MANSFIELD

I consider myself extremely fortunate in that I have a talent with which I am able to express my ideas. Art to me is color and subject matter. Through these elements I project my infinite moods and reactions to life, to people and to nature. I particularly enjoy painting landscapes and children. My happiest days are those I spend at the easel composing and synthesizing, color, form and texture in subject matter.

IN THE GARDEN OF EDEN, wool tapestry, 40" x 60"

JANINA MARKS

My art is an extension of myself, of my heritage, my feelings about life, about my surroundings, and about myself.

The joy of watching a sunset, letting dry sand run through my fingers, or touching the colors in my tapestries, sharing, discovering, communicating—that is what my work is all about.

BIRD HAVEN, oil

ALICE MASON

I derive a great deal of inspiration for my paintings from reading poetry, particular Oriental sources. My ideas develop as I go along with them. I study nature because I believe that all art stems from nature and living forms. I never work in front of objects but depict my impressions of nature only after I have looked and found in it the essence of the scene or subject.

CAROL AND SHEILA, oil, 30" x 36", 1943

FRANCES McVEY

I revere Nature in the beauty of her various forms, and consider it the mission of the artist to convey this love and understanding to those less privileged in seeing. There are truths to be disclosed, also, no less by way of the painting or artifact than by the written or spoken word.

My later work has been devoted to compositions representing the better-known saints in aspects of importance to mankind's virtues; for instance, courage, love, sharing, worship, etc. This series is housed in the Art Gallery at Camp Chesterfield, Chesterfield, Indiana.

As music and books are an inspiration to me, it is my hope that my offerings may inspire artists in other fields to some furthering of their knowledge of truth and beauty.

BEATRICE ROITMAN METRICK

Painting is for me a highly charged emotional experience. I paint intuitively, intensely, almost passionately. I never know when I start where a painting will lead me, but I must follow. I suppose what I am trying to do is make each painting a microcosm of the world, a perfect world where all elements merge harmoniously. I somehow feel an aversion to excessive verbosity about painting. After all, as Renoir said, "If you could explain it, it wouldn't be art."

ABSTRACT 2B, *oil collage*

SHIFTING PLANES, lithograph

BARBARA LAZARUS METZ

I believe that art and life are inseparable. The need to express, to communicate, to evoke responses are inherent in man's nature. Each individual is a unique personality and has a valid view of reality to express. An artist can examine nature, society, humanity, and herself critically and then convey her impressions unashamedly and honestly to others, helping in their growth. An artist should be constantly growing in her personality, in her experience, and especially in her art, which is the sum total of her person.

EDGAR MILLER

Art has always been a public affair—man communicating with mankind in visual form language—"Modern Art"—has degenerated to expression of the personal egos of many of the modern artists, has no longer any cultural relation to people—most of whom 'do not understand it.' Most abstract art is an exhibition of skill in the organization of token forms—a similar activity to the literary diagramming of sentences that we went through in the 7th grade—and, of the same empty importance. Great art has been the product of the balance of the two brain hemispheres—a balance of the Intuition and the Rational. Art is the organization of amounts of space, as music is the organization of amounts of sound vibration.

STUDY: CITY DETAIL, oil, 1944 (Courtesy Art Institute of Chicago)

HARRY MINTZ

In a statement about figurative subject matter in art, Harry Mintz said, "I feel that this is healthy, because it expresses a freedom based on knowledge, rather than freedom for freedom's sake."

This explains many of the characteristics of Mintz' paintings, which have always been firmly founded not only on the sensitive initial responses of a person who is sharply aware of the distinctive qualities of specific time and places, but also on a profound awareness of the historic function of all fine art, so far as serious self-realization and demonstrable communication are concerned.

He has demonstrated brilliantly that it is possible to retain and develop many of the resources of contemporary style without ignoring the definition and certainty of intention. His work expresses a sense of dignity and respect for all the elements concerned. This includes not only the artist himself, but his environment, his materials, his audience . . . it is satisfying to observe this work of one who has, indeed, achieved freedom based on knowledge.

Mintz is singularly responsive to his surroundings . . . he has always expressed precisely those two things for which we search in all valid artistic expressions: his own understanding, the accumulated wisdom of a lifetime; and the inherent quality of the original motif.

His work is essentially and profoundly humanistic based as it is on a fusion of understanding and intuition. In recent years his work has broadened in a deeply expressive way . . . and its strength adds a significant sense of authority and content.

Dean Allen S. Weller, Fine and Applied Arts, University of Illinois

ALTAR #8, MEXICO, oil

SEEING EYE, lithograph, 13" x 17"

ANNETTE OKNER

Art is a way of life, not an isolated experience which takes place at the time a piece of work is being created. Everything one perceives, inter-acts with, and experiences, is stored for reference at a later time. The need for re-clarification, maturity, evaluation, perspective and one's place in the scheme of things reflects directly upon the creative process. A basic honesty and dependence upon inner peace and quiet are almost indispensable.

SIAMESE TWINS, *linocut*

ELIZABETH OPPENHEIM

I refuse to write about art, mine or in general. I do it because it is the only thing that gives me satisfaction, regardless of fashions, success or failure.

CHASIDIC MUSICIANS, casein, 1952

VICTOR M. PERLMUTTER

The Impressionists opened my eyes to light and color. Cezanne deepended my knowledge about form and space. Cubism released me from a 'surface reality' vision. The Expressionists took me into their private universe and the abstract artists extended my senses.

Of the many modern artists whom I admire, Marc Chagall is one of my favorites. A forerunner of Surrealism, he was one of the first to demolish the barriers set up by the laws of physics and nature. He released his objects and figures from the law of gravity and retained their fullest liberty, beauty and charm.

Chagall's vision of the world within him is a peculiar blend of the real and the unreal, or realism and fantasy, of life and dreams built upon memories rooted in timelessness. He encompasses the important discoveries of the most significant modern art periods since Impressionism. His ability to reconcile contradictions and to cause the unyielding to yield never fails to excite me.

Chagall builds his art on memories of childhood, Jewish life in Russian villages and above all, Jewish folklore steeped in mysticism. He achieves universal values and a broad human interest because his art penetrates psychic reality.

SCULPTURED WALL

JUDY M. PETACQUE

Life is filled with beauty and humor. Art is an 'attempt' to personally translate this. It is a kind of manifestation of what I feel, see, hear and taste . . . and, also that which I cannot . . . it is a striving for greater and more profound understanding and an expression of same—there is a great joy that comes from the accomplishment of art work.

LOUISE F. PIERCE

I have always found it difficult to express my philosophy of art in words. To me, what a painting has to say is not the same as what the written word has to say. The language of art is in the composition of the plastic means as shapes, forms, dimensions and color, not in the literary expression.

MASKS FROM NEPAL, *linocut (Courtesy of Chicago Society of Artists)*

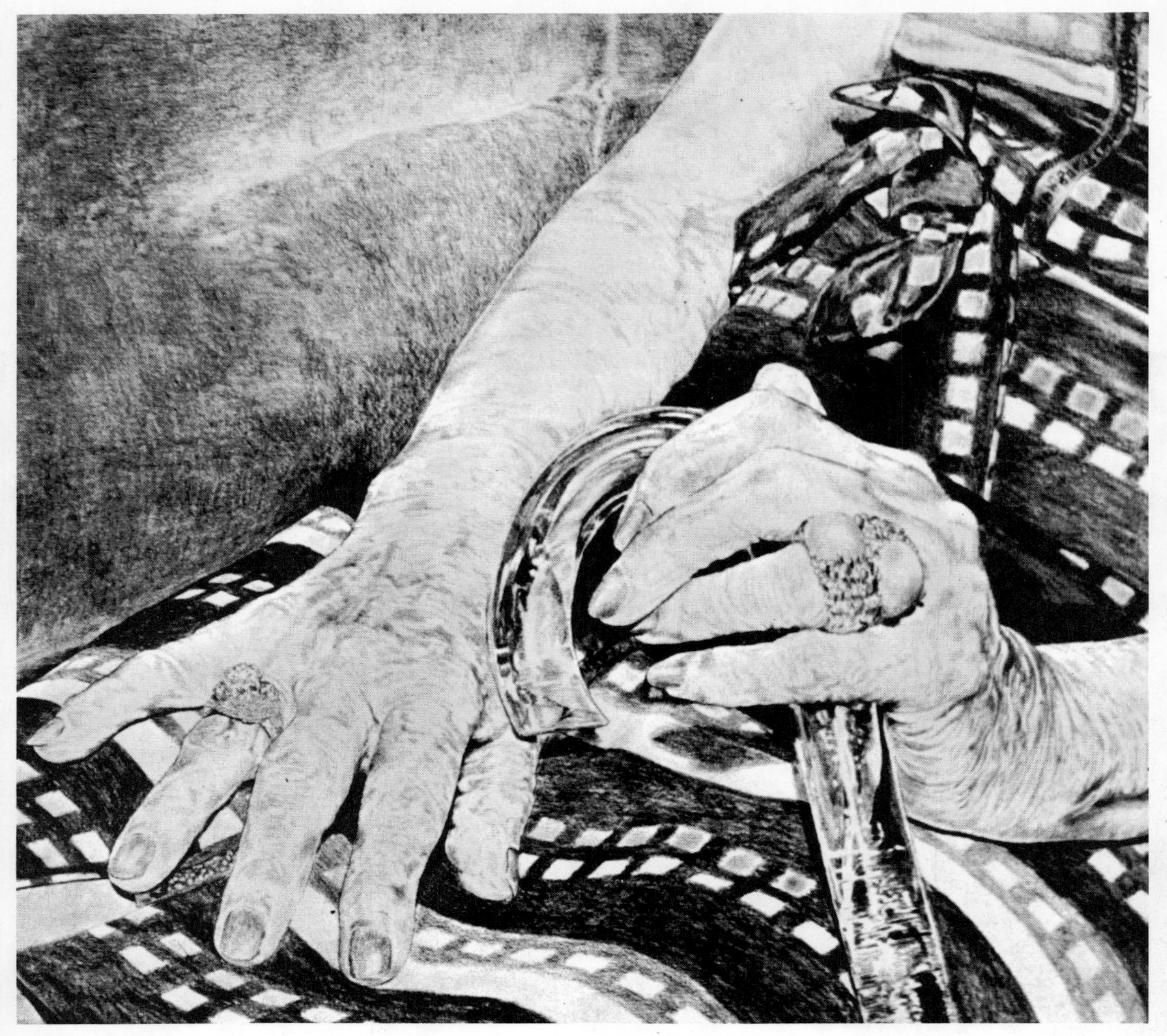

OLD HANDS, graphite

CLAIRE F. PRUSSIAN

The means by which I examine my point of view is derived from aspects of my own life. Since I feel that our dimensionality as human beings stems from the fact that we know that we are eventually going to die. One of the most important themes in my work is time. Much of my work is devoted to games since I feel that these are marvelous devices with which to explore not only the use of time, but also other interesting concepts such as the game as a method of communication and the idea of satire. Most games are highly ritualistic with very ancient origins. Somehow an air of timelessness clings to them and maybe this is partly why they are appealing. One can reach outside a limited span of years to participate in a rite which has both preceded, and will extend beyond a single lifetime. There is a kind of immortality in this.

SEVEN UP, woodcut

FRED RAPPAPORT

Any artistic creation presumes an inherent need to express an emotional reaction to a single or a series of communicated experiences. It is based upon the interaction of the artist and his environment representing a high form of communication.

SARLINDA, oil

LESTER REBBECK

I am devoted to my subject and am constantly searching for and learning new techniques and methods to diversify my teaching and make it more relevant to the students. I have respect for the opinions of others and a willingness to share ideas. I feel that I work well with people, and am willing to accept conscientiously all the responsibilities that would be mine as a member of any teaching faculty.

FOCUS, linocut

MARIE SALWONCHIK

I believe that art has a dual nature of spirit and matter and, as such, it has personal and social relevance. Art is a real and vital force which may be used constructively or destructively. Its origin is in the soul; this psyche is eternal. The conscious and unconscious components of the soul are materialized in the various art forms. Accordingly, art works reflect society and reveal psychic conditions individually and collectively. Art can bring order out of chaos and make ideas clear through representation.

UNTITLED, procion dye on canvas

FERN SAMUELS

My approach to art as well as to life is to be exceedingly open to everything around me. I try to view life through a child's eye. Everything is fresh and exciting. I hope that each piece I create will contain that freshness for the viewer. I don't want to do things in stereotyped ways and I want my thinking to be continually shaken-up so that I will not be trapped into repetitive art.

MARVIN SARUK

I enjoy using the human form in my paintings as it provides me with a continual source of inspiration.

In painting the human form from memory, I find even greater creative possibilities as I re-construct the figure in my mind.

Abstract or Imagery, the underlying tendency is figurative, and for me there is always, a compulsive desire to discover new ideas and concepts that I can express in various mediums.

DANTE'S INFERNO, *mixed media*

DETAIL I-CROWDED PROPS. oil. 32" x 28"

MOLLY J. SCHIFF

I must do my work within a framework that is dictated by knowledge, experience and mood.

Occasionally, these three fragments of my being stir me independently; but, more often, they are a harmonious blend.

FULL BLOOM, graphite

BEATRICE B. SCHILLER

Art is a universal language which is able to cross national boundaries in order to communicate one's feelings to anyone who is willing to receive the message.

I was given a gold palette pin with small stones by my husband, and invariably when I wear it—no matter where I happen to be—fellow artists notice it, and interesting conversations develop—which lead into art, artists, and life, which generate creative thinking, feeling and reacting.

NEAR NORTH SIDE, CHICAGO, oil, 1935, 36" × 40" (Courtesy of the Encyclopedia Britannica)

WILLIAM S. SCHWARTZ

All my life I have been a musician as well as a painter. In both music and art, I believe that the great thing is the creation of harmony in an individual way. In art, among the old masters as well as among the contemporary artists, harmony may be of three sorts of color, of form and of line. When looking at nature, therefore, I search for materials which may be interpreted and manipulated until they become unified wholes and reveal the sorts of harmony which are representative of my own personality—my thoughts and my feelings. I feel that the mastery of only one of these elements—color, form or line—is unsatisfactory. Difficult though it may be, I strive for the simultaneous mastery of all three.

LEOPOLD B. SEGEDIN

I want my work to reflect on 'the human condition' insofar as painted images can evoke a sense of present existence.

BOCHAR, oil, 1951 (Courtesy of Art Institute of Chicago)

BEACH HAVEN MARINA, oil

JANE COALE SHAAR

At this time of my life I am unable to express in words or writing how I feel about my philosophy of art. I have yet too much to experience. I feel I am just breaking the surface. Now that my two little girls are in school all day, perhaps good things are on the way and my art will start to happen.

AT NIGHT, graphite 24" x 16"

LORRE ANN SLAW

Art is a major part of my life. It makes me feel that I can express myself, my thoughts, my fears, my happiness. My most joyous moments are spent working at my craft. Nothing can substitute the "doing" of art for me. I am truly lucky to be involved in this creative process. I plan to work for many years to come, to grow, to learn, to experience all that I can grasp.

FUGUE, collage 24" x 30" japanese papers and old sheet music

RITA SPAULDING

The artist needs basic mastery of his medium, technique, balance, composition and color. In this learning period or, for many artists, at a much later point, creativity can grow, change, and move in any direction that his external and internal experience takes him. New trends and forms of art expression are stimulating and challenging, but they must be integrated into his work in a very personal way if they are to enhance his creative growth. Although the artist, as most people is influenced, often unconsciously, by what goes on around him, both artistically and experimentally, he should strive for motivation that is an honest expression of himself as an individual.

BARBARA S. SPITZ

I believe that art should reflect the age in which it is conceived—civilizations are best represented by man's creativity. Many of my prints have involved the art and architecture of ancient peoples symbolizing the continuity of man. Some of my prints are involved with the loneliness of man who, in today's world, deals with a dehumanized society.

Printmaking offers limitless possibilities for experimentation. I combine methods of etching, engraving and aquatint with innovations drawn from modern technology. I work directly on my plates with power tools and build up surface areas with epoxies and liquid aluminum. Of particular importance is my adaptation of photo-engraving. Images in my photographs are combined, altered and sometimes abstracted in all stages leading to the development of the final print. The image is changed again through color: using inks of varying viscosities, the rolling of surfaces, the inking of depressions, in additional printings and with chine colle. Many proofs are pulled before the edition is printed in its final form.

ANCIENT ENIGMA, *color intaglio*

ARIZONA CANYONSCAPE, watercolor

ROBERT D. SPITZ

To open the viewer's eyes to new realities through the artists cumulative input that is then reorganized and arranged in the private world of paintings, is the purpose and challenge that results in the joy I get from painting.

GRACE SPONGBERG

My paintings and lino-cuts are inspired mostly by the people, landscape and architectural structures which I encountered in my travels in most of Europe, Scandinavian countries, Japan, Cambodia, Thailand and Martinique.

FRESH FISH, MARTINIQUE, *linocut*

ABSTRACTION, linocut, 1950 (Courtesy of the Chicago Society of Artists)

DOROTHY STAFFORD *Art is an individual expression. If it is not creative, it is not art.*

THE FAMILY, bronze

IVY STEELE

I feel deeply the life, movement and interrelationships of my surroundings and feel compelled in the best way for me, to involve myself in the tensions and vitality of my experience. If I can capture and develop a fragment of this experience into something viable, or, in teaching, help establish a climate where others can do this, there will come my greatest satisfaction.

RUBIN STEINBERG

Art is the only constant taking infinite form. It is consistent in its ability to reflect, create and forecast changes in society through the skills of those artists who are involved in its manipulation. I believe in the individual as a supreme being endowed to design and manipulate environment for better existence. My whole life is spent teaching Art in one form or another—in or out of the classroom.

FOREST FANTASY, sculptural weaving, leather, rope, canvas, acrylic

MERCADO, linocut

JANE W. STEINER

My work reflects my experiences and travels in Asia, Africa, the Orient and Mexico. Figurative subject matter in settings indigenous to various cultures, characterizing the daily activities of the natives, is of particular interest to me.

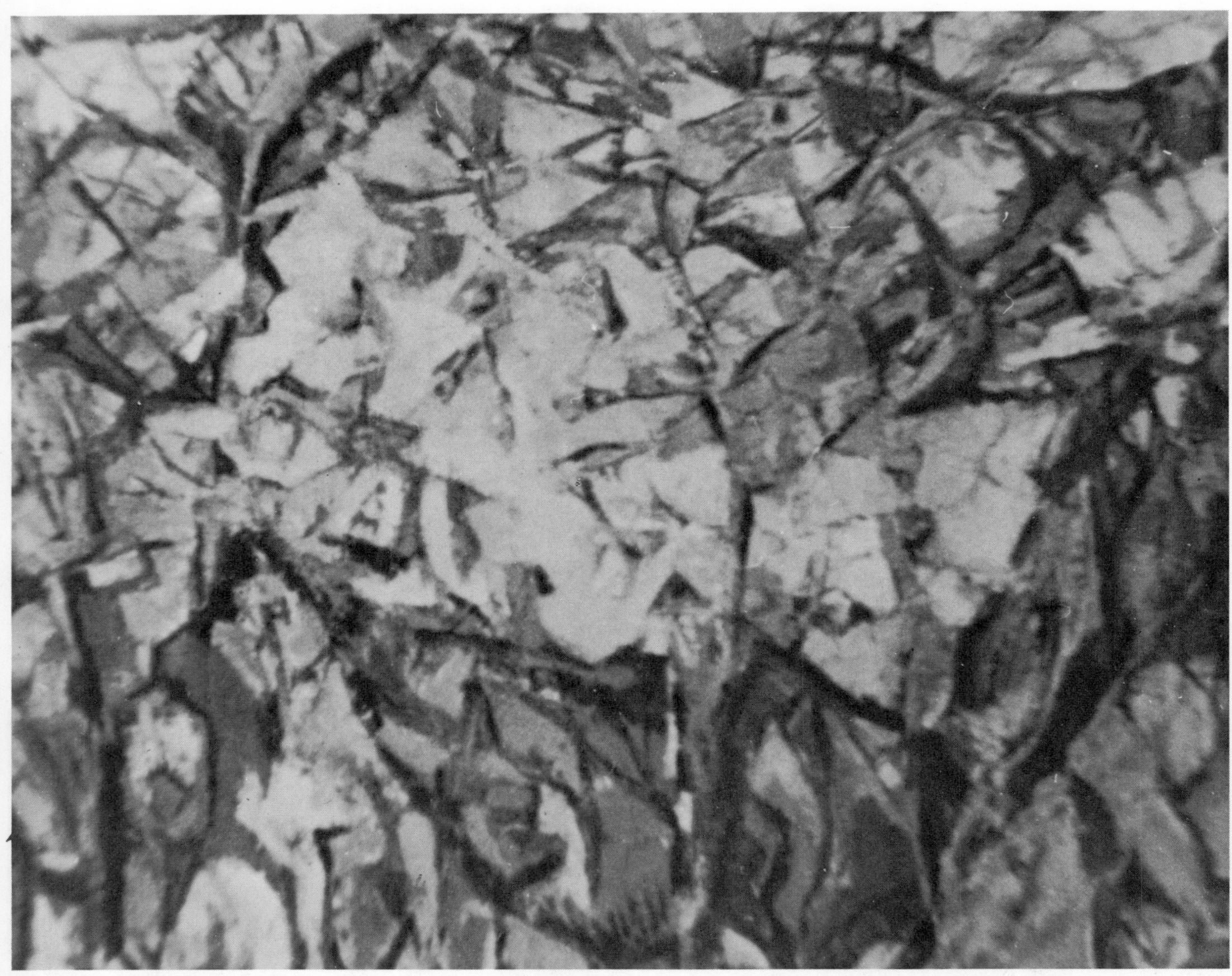

FLORAL PATTERNS, oil

BELLE C. SWEENEY

I paint what I feel, and what I see and what I feel is generally an intuitive response to what crosses my vision. Often, it is the sight of a floral garden that influences my use of color and shapes, or a suggestion of floral shapes in abundant areas of greens and blues, that merely suggest the essence of a garden and more importantly my reaction to the sight. Color is my fort—I use it in brilliant hues and in many variations of each.

PREZIOSI, collage, posters, newsprint, tie dye, stock and bond certificates, stamps from Lincoln's assassination (Collection of Robert A. Kurtenacker)

ELVIE TenHOOR

Thinking of the future, I would like my work to be less labored, in terms of time, allowing more freedom to occur independently. Poetry in motion, ease in expressing an emotion, rhythm of colors and design.

THE HAVE AND THE HAVE-NOTS, oil

ALEX TOPP

I feel that art should contribute to man's enlightenment. Without art there is abject darkness in a drab existence, devoid of the noble aspirations of mankind, and of the enduring passions which give meaning to man's physicial, emotional and spiritual being.

BACK OF THE CHURCH, oil, 1932

LAURA VAN PAPPELENDAM

I never know what kind of subject will thrill me. Very opposite types of subjects are often breath-taking; it is the possibilities I see in existing relations that get me wild to work.

Form plays a very important part in my work and that includes the structural use of volume, line, mass, and color.

I do pure abstractions only as try-outs for larger paintings. My work is personal in the sense that I paint only what I am interested in. I do not think of any contribution to society when I paint. In each painting I try to relate my subject matter to the rectangle within which it is placed.

**Art of Today—Chicago 1933. J. Z. Jacobson, L.M. Stein, Publisher, Chicago, 1932.*

PORTRAIT, mixed media on gessoed muslin

JAMES F. WALKER

My paintings project my intense concern for, and interest in the nature of textured surfaces within the context of meticulously rendered forms, revealing the essence of Magic Realism, a microscopic view of every infinitesmal area upon the canvas.

BEACH HOUSE, *watercolor*

LIONEL WATHALL

The person who finds himself stimulated by the natural world, its phenomena and the works of Man, may if he does something to record his experience, be called an artist. Why an artist wishes to do what he does seems most likely to be a seeking for pleasure. The mystery of pleasure to the visual senses seems to spark a desire for recording, describing or preserving a fleeting moment. Whatever it may be, that tantalizing effort filled with both anguish and joy can result in a work that reveals both the artist and his subject to the beholder. Where the understanding is mutual so is the pleasure.

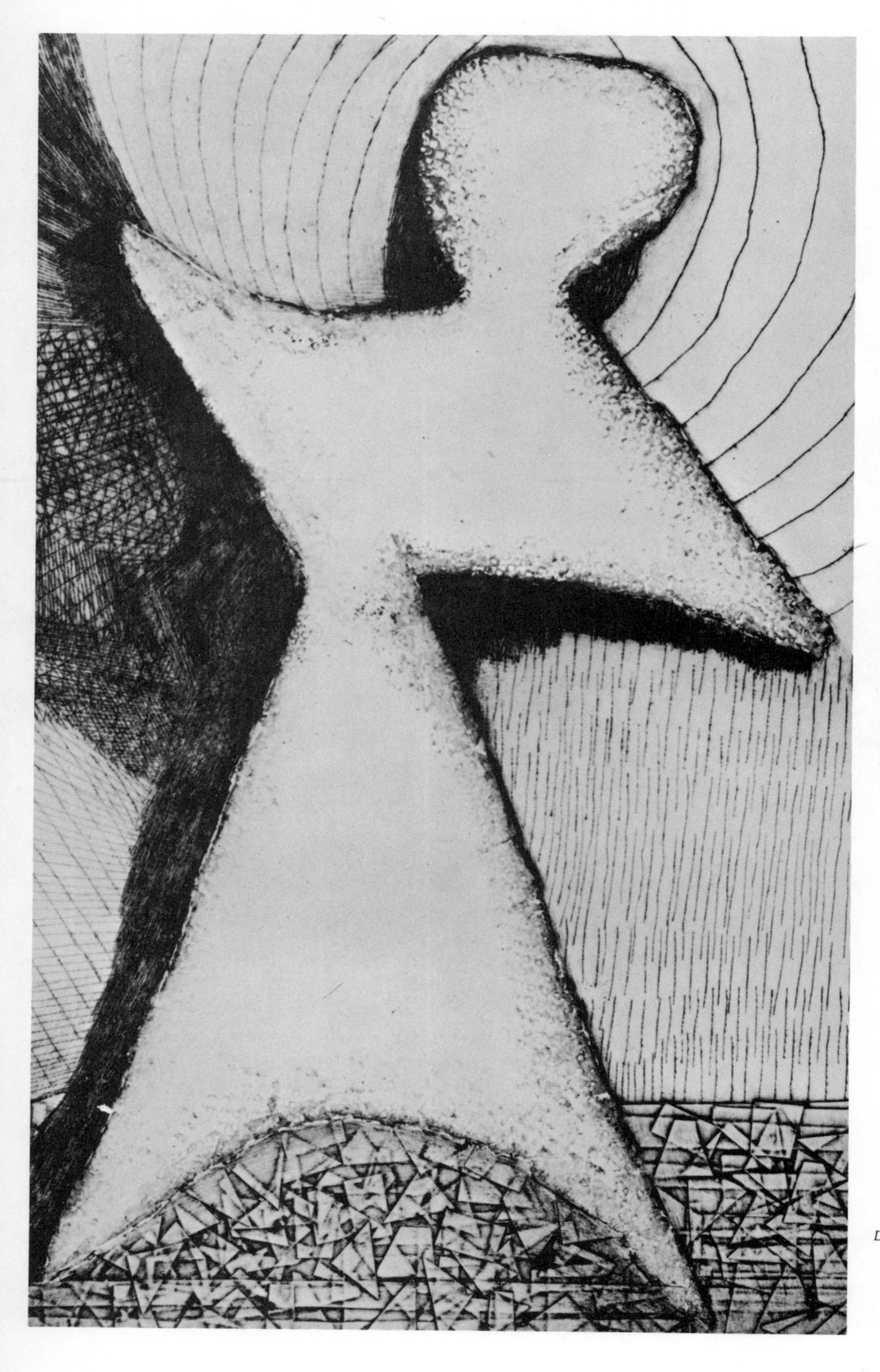

HELEN JOY WEINBERG

In one of Shakespeare's plays a character says: "Shepherd, hath no philosophy?" I sometimes believe that I really have no philosophy or credo. Sometimes I have made the somewhat exaggerated statement that I believe that a true artist's first and last waking thought must be about his or her work. I also came upon the following quotation which I have pasted on the blotter of my desk, (don't know who is author): "the artist has the responsibility, whatever the hazards, of carrying through the demands of his art till death overtakes him; in doing so he re-affirms his allegiance to life." And, I also believe with Columbus that "persistence is the master of destiny."

My work has no message, but I hope it has its own kind of reality — an existence of its own.

DANCER, *collograph and drypoint*

MARCHING MEN, oil

LOUIS WEINER

Subject matter plays an important part in my work. This is born out by such pieces of mine as "Marching Men," "Eagle Dance," and "Corn Dance." . . . Abstraction, entirely as an end in itself, has not concerned me greatly, but I have made use of the "abstract" in molding my designs.

I have a strong feeling for color. Form is of utmost importance to me and I strive continuously to achieve solidity.

I try to paint independently and I am not influenced by the demands of the market. I hope that my thinking in general is independent, whether it be in relation to politics, economics or aesthetics. I have not consciously been affected by the comments of art critics.

I avoid the introduction to my work of national, racial, or religious elements for their own sake. I believe that art is universal and makes use of elements, emotion, and phenomena which are in their essence the same the world over and in all times. *

**Art of Today—Chicago 1933, J. Z. Jacobson, L. M. Stein, Publisher, Chicago, 1932*

SUMA, collage

BETTY J. WEISS (HURD)

I get pleasure in developing a visual creation. That pleasure is enhanced by those who are stimulated by it.

FEBRUARY IS SLATE GREY, collage

MARY LOUISE WEISS-KELLY

The artist's work is always a commentary on his emotional mental and spiritual need and the urge to express creatively. His work should parallel his growth and development in these areas, and if one carefully observes the work it usually does.

IN MEMORIAM, oil (Courtesy Eilat Museum, Israel)

LOUISE DUNN YOCHIM

I find nothing in the cosmos of my existence outside the realm of interest for me. Therefore, I paint that which expresses my feelings, my intuitions, my reflections, my fantasies and my beliefs—all within the context of artistic integrity. I hope that I may never reach the point of abject sterility.

I am ever stirred by a sense of social responsibility and stimulated by humanistic goals and values.

Within the scope of varied media I attempt to achieve a living rationale which demands of me a uniqueness of expression conceived in a harmonious interrelationship of line, form, color and texture—within the limits of a given space.

MAURICE YOCHIM

I believe that a work of art should express an artist's point of view. It may reflect his personal experiences of the visual world, or his reactions to intangible realities which cannot be seen but, nevertheless, are part of his consciousness. The artist, therefore, may depart from optical realities and take liberties with form and color by simplifying, altering, reorganizing and inventing new relationships.

Above all, I believe that design, which is the structure of all art forms, is the organization through which an artist expresses his reactions to life. Design must, therefore, be an integral part of his work in order for it to be complete.

AFFECTION, mahogany 24" x 12" x 4", 1960

LA ROUE DE FORTUNE, linocut

JAN YOURIST *I am particularly interested in figurative yet abstracted subject matter evolved from conjectural fantasy and specific symbolism.*

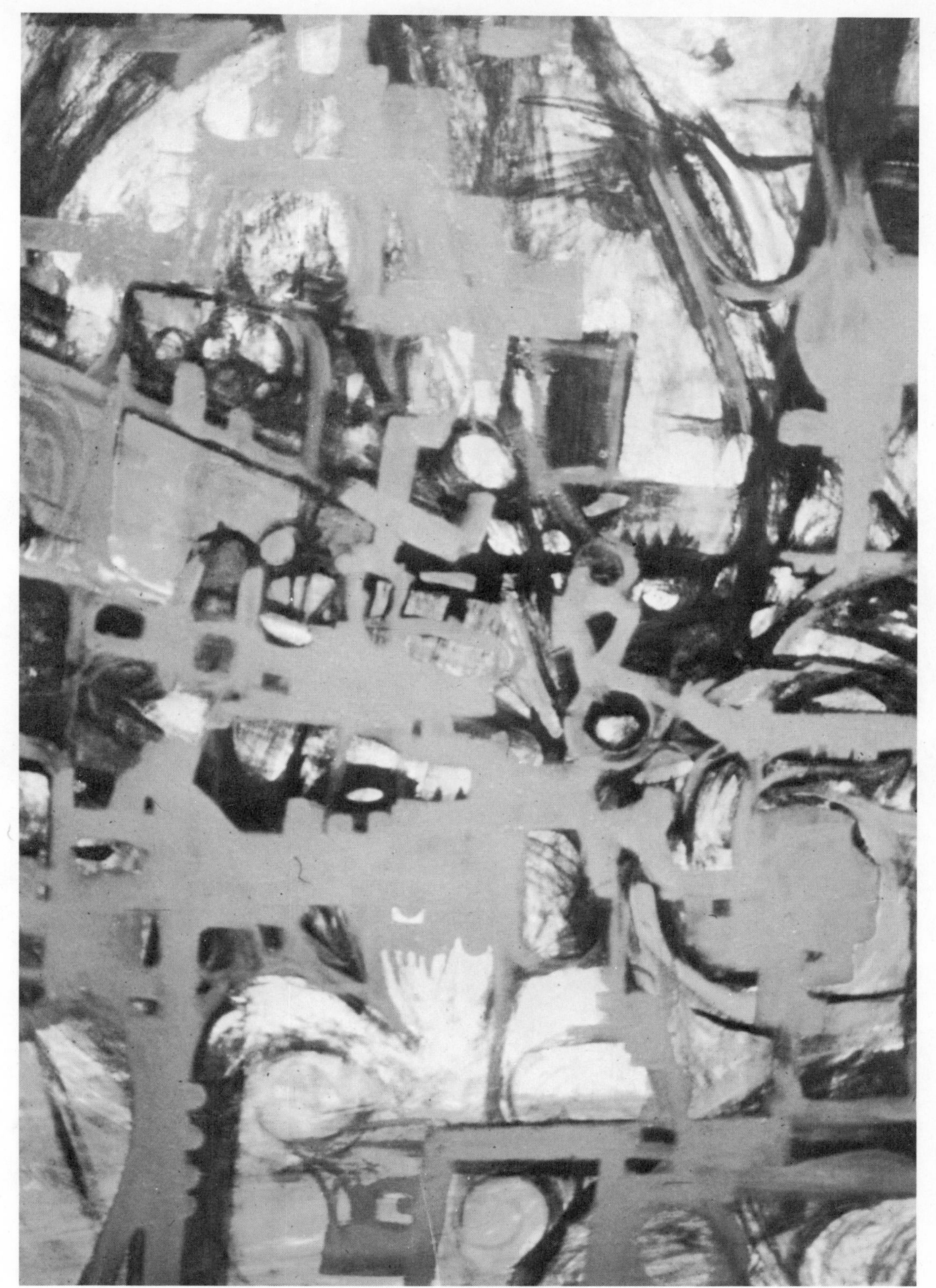

VENICE II, acrylic 5" x 6"

ALOISE AIGNER ZEHNER

Art, is the visually expressed extension of one's self. To deny the artist his right to be seen thru his work, is to deny him his right to be heard.

A sincere work of art is the result of one artist's training and life experiences. It should not be compared with another's.

SHADE TREE, etching, 1976, 10" x 16"

M. GIEDRE ZUMBAKIS

My paintings or prints are a composite of images derived from nature, often combined with free-form or geometric shapes, a rather personal glimpse of nature sometimes revealed in a close-up view, or through a particular feeling and manifested not in a pictorial representation, but in an intimate and unique combination of subject, medium and process.

THE FAMILY, stoneware (Courtesy of Dr. & Mrs. Jerome Yochim)

ROSEMARY ZWICK

I enjoy life and have a temptation to journalize through any art. I view my work as a desire to share my personal experience with others in what I hope is a meaningful way.

SECTION III

Biographical Notes

GERTRUDE ABERCROMBIE
(Painter) was born in 1909. Her family settled in Chicago when she was five years old. She attended the University of Illinois, the Art Institute of Chicago and the American Academy of Art in Chicago.

Her works were exhibited in the International Watercolor Exhibition at the Art Institute of Chicago in 1935; Delphic Studios, New York, in 1935; New Jersey State Museum, Trenton, New Jersey, in 1936; Riverside Museum, New York, in 1939; Contemporary American Painting Exhibition, University of Illinois in 1950 and 1951; Artists of Chicago and Vicinity Exhibition at the Art Institute of Chicago including the shows of 1936, 1937, 1942, 1944, 1945, 1946, 1949 and 1951. In 1977 a retrospective exhibition of ninety-six of her works was held at the Hyde Park Art Center in Chicago.

In 1936 Abercrombie was awarded the Joseph N. Eisendrath prize for her oil painting "There on the Table." In 1946 she received the William and Bertha Clusmann prize for her oil painting "The Past and the Present." Both prizes were awarded in the Artists of Chicago and Vicinity Exhibitions at the Art Institute of Chicago.

She died in 1977.

JEAN CRAWFORD ADAMS*
(Painter) was born in Chicago and studied at the Art Institute of Chicago. She has traveled and painted in Scotland, England, Germany, France, Spain and Italy, New Mexico, California, Florida, Wisconsin, Indiana, Michigan, New York, Pennsylvania, North Carolina and Tennessee.

In Chicago she has had one-woman exhibitions at the Art Institute and the Chester Johnson Galleries. She has also had one-woman shows in Milwaukee, Madison, Kansas City, Dallas, Los Angeles and San Francisco.

She exhibited at the Art Institute of Chicago, the Chester Johnson Galleries in Chicago; the Carnegie Institute; the Pennsylvania Academy of Fine Arts; the Detroit Museum; and the Sesquicentennial Exposition in Philadelphia.

She is represented in permanent collections in Baltimore and Springfield, Illinois. Her work has been written about in Chicago newspapers and periodicals, the New York Times, the New York Herald Tribune, and the **Arts**; and by art critics Forbes Watson, C. J. Bulliet, Inez Cunningham, Marguerite B. Williams, J. Z. Jacobson, Phil Nesbit and Eleanor Jewett.

Adams was awarded prizes by the Art Institute of Chicago, the Englewood Women's Club and the Chicago Society of Artists.

She was a member of 10 artists (Chicago), the Chicago Society of Artists and the Arts Club of Chicago.

Adams died in 1971.

*J. Z. Jacobson, "Art of Today," Publisher: L. M. Stein, Chicago, Pg. 137.

IVAN LeLORRAINE ALBRIGHT
(Painter) was born in Chicago, Illinois on February 20, 1897. He studied at Northwestern University; Illinois School of Architecture; Art Institute of Chicago; the National Academy of Design in New York; the Pennsylvania Academy of Fine Arts and the Ecole des Beaux Arts of Nantes, France.

One-man shows of his works were held at the Walden-Dudensing Galleries in Chicago and the Art Institute of Chicago. The "Portrait of Dorian Gray" and "The Temptation of St. Anthony" were paintings done for films in 1943.

His work was exhibited in the Brooklyn

Museum, New York; Carnegie Institute, Pittsburgh; Dallas Museum of Fine Arts; Library of Congress, Washington, D. C.; Metropolitan Museum of Art, New York; Pennsylvania Academy of Fine Arts; the National Academy of Design, New York; the Art Institute of Chicago; the Detroit Institute; the Whitney Museum of Modern Art, New York and many others.

Albright has been written about by George A. Flanagan in **Understanding and Enjoying Modern Art** published by Crowell, 1962; **The Artist's Voice, Talks with Seventeen Artists** by Katharine Kuh, Harper & Row, 1962; **Break-Up: The Core of Modern Art** published New York Graphic Society, 1965.

Albright was awarded the John C. Shafer prize of $500.00 from the Art Institute of Chicago in 1928; the Silver Medal Award in 1930, the Gold Medal Award in 1931, from the Chicago Society of Artists; the National Institute of Arts and Letters, 1957; Benjamin Altman Prize from the National Academy of Design in 1961; Dunn International Award, Tate Gallery, London, 1963; and many others.

Albright was President of the Chicago Society of Artists in 1934 and Vice-President in 1935.

MALVIN MARR ALBRIGHT (ZSISSLEY) (Painter, Sculptor) was born in Chicago, Illinois, on February 20, 1897, and studied at the University of Illinois, Art Institute of Chicago, Pennsylvania Academy of Fine Arts, the Beaux Arts Institute of Design, New York and Nantes, France.

His works were exhibited at the National Academy of Design; Whitney Museum of American Art; Museum of Modern Art; Pennsylvania Academy of Fine Arts; Carnegie Institute; Art Institute of Chicago; the San Diego Fine Arts Gallery, San Diego, California; and many others.

His works are included in the permanent collections of the Corcoran Gallery of Art; Toledo Museum of Art; Butler Institute of American Art; University of Georgia; Pennsylvania Academy of Fine Arts; and others.

Albright was the recipient of the Chicago Fountain Prize, 1922; Robert Rice Jenkins Prize, 1929; Art Institute of Chicago; Chicago Galleries Prize, 1930; Honorable Mention in the Chicago Society of Artists Exhibition, 1931; the Altman Prize, National Academy of Design, 1942 and 1962; Palmer Memorial Prize, Art Institute of Chicago; Corcoran Silver Medal, Washington, D. C.; Dana Medal, Pennsylvania Academy of Fine Arts, 1965; and others. He is listed in **Who's Who in American Art, 1976.**

He is a member of the National Academy of Design, Fellow of the Royal Society of Arts, International Institute of Arts and Letters, National Sculpture Society, and is a Fellow of Pennsylvania Academy of Fine Arts. He was a member of the Chicago Society of Artists as far back as 1935. He was included in its Annual Exhibition held at the Michigan Square Gallery in Chicago with his sculpture, "Composition."

BERTE ANAPOL (Painter, Graphic Artist) was born in Chicago. She studied at the Art Institute of Chicago, the University of Chicago and the Illinois Institute of Technology. She has traveled extensively.

She has exhibited at Winnetka Women's Club, Winnetka, Illinois, 1949; Little Gallery, Esquire Theater, Chicago, 1950; Robert North Gallery, 1952 through 1955; Mandel Brothers Gallery, 1961; Cromer and Quint Galleries, 1963, 1971, 1972, 1974; Chicago Public Library, 1966-68; Covenant Club Galleries, 1965; Old Town Gallery, 1969; and in the Lyons Township Junior College Gallery, 1961.

She participated in group shows at the Springfield Art Museum, Springfield, Illinois; University of Illinois in Urbana; the Art Institute of Chicago; the Art Institute Art Rental and Sales Galleries; 1020 Art Center; Sherman Hotel Gallery; Kroch's and Brentano's; Stuart Brent Gallery; Magnificient Mile Exhibitions; Fisher Hall Galleries; Covenant Club Galleries; Hillel Gallery of Northwestern University; the University club.

She also exhibited at the Kalamazoo Art Center, Kalamazoo, Michigan; Evanston Art Center, Evanston, Illinois; Rockford Art Center, Rockford, Illinois; Downtown Gallery and Halpern Galleries in New York City; San Diego Art Institute; and the Art Rental Fine Arts Gallery, San Diego, California.

Her awards include First Prize for oil painting from the Spectrum Society of Art, Chicago, 1953; Second Prize from Temple Sholom Professional Artists Exhibition, 1959; Honorable Mention in the Festival of the Americas Exhibition, Covenant Club, Chicago, 1960; First Prize for block print from the Chicago Society of Artists, 1965.

Anapol is a member of the Chicago Society of Artists, American Jewish Art Club, Artists Equity Association and the San Diego Art Institute. She resides in San Diego, California.

ROBERT W. ANDERSEN (Painter) was born in Chicago, Illinois, in 1933. He studied at the School of the Art Institute of Chicago, 1954–1958 where he received the B.F.A. degree. He also attended the Summer School of Painting in Saugatuk, Michigan, DePaul University and the University of Chicago.

Since 1953 he has held several one-man exhibitions and participated in group shows which included the Artists of Chicago and Vicinity, Art Institute of Chicago; Chicago Painters, 1963; Tacoma Art Museum, Tacoma, Washington; Western Museum Association, traveling exhibition, 1964; Chicago Graphics Exhibition Contemporary Art Association, Houston, Texas; Old Town Art Center, Chicago; Bernard Horwich Center; McKerr Observatory Gallery; Lexington Hall, University of Chicago; Rockford College and Sneed Gallery in Rockford, Illinois; and many others. His work was represented by the Ontario East Gallery.

Andersen taught at the Art Institute of Chicago (History of Art); Old Town Art Center, (Painting); Adult Evening School, Oak Park; River Forest High School, Oak Park; and at the Junior School of the Art Institute of Chicago.

Andersen received the Broadus James Clarke Award in 1958 and the William H. Bartels prize in 1960, both from the Art Institute of Chicago.

DON J. ANDERSON (Painter, Writer) was born in South Haven, Michigan. He studied watercolor painting with Ruth Van Sickle Ford at the Chicago Academy of Fine Arts and at the Institute of Design under the personal direction of Laszlo Moholy-Nagy.

Anderson traveled extensively in Africa, the Orient, the Middle East, Europe and Scandinavia in the last five years. One of his memorable experiences was a trip to Egypt with thirty designers where all were detained in Cairo during the October 1973 war. Following each trip he created collages using momentos and sketches inspired by the places he visited, which he has titled "Post Card Art."

For twenty years he has taught private classes to beginners and advanced students. Each summer, he conducts sketching tours with his students to various points of interest in and around Chicago from Lincoln Park to Meigs Field.

Anderson has served as art critic for the **Chicago Today** for ten years. He has written articles about interior design for the **Chicago Tribune**, and he has written and illustrated on travel and design for the **Christian Science Monitor**. His report of his trip to Ireland to observe the arts and crafts program of that country was featured in the March and April 1975 issues of **Townsfolk**. Currently he is writing about the Chicagoland art and cultural scene for **Chicago's Elite** magazine.

HOWARD BENJAMIN ANDERSON (Printmaker) was born in Racine, Wisconsin. He studied at the University of Wisconsin, (B. S.); Art Institute of Chicago and Corcoran Art School, Washington, D. C. His early training was received in Racine, Wisconsin. Teachers who had the greatest influence upon his work were Max Kahn, Art Institute of Chicago, and Eugene Weicz, Corcoran Art School. He has traveled extensively through Europe and the United States. He works in a number of media and processes including collage, photography, lithography and drawing.

He has held one-man exhibitions at the Western Museum, Racine, Wisconsin, 1955; State Teachers College, Kutztown, Pennsylvania, 1957; Illinois Arts Council, 1976. His works have been exhibited in the Art Institute of Chicago, 1948, 1949, 1952, 1961, 1966; the Water Color, Print and Drawing Annuals at the Pennsylvania Academy of Fine Arts, Philadelphia, 1952, 1953, 1957, 1961; National Academy of Design, New York, 1956; Society of American Graphic Artists, New York, 1950, 1959, 1967, 1968; Brooklyn Museum, Brooklyn, N. Y., 1950–1953; Library of Congress, Washington, D. C., 1948, 1953, 1956; 150th Anniversary of Lithography and Print Club of Rochester, Rochester Memorial Gallery, Rochester, N. Y., 1958; Boston Print Makers Annual, Boston, Mass., 1954; 57th and 58th Anniversary of Western Art, Denver Art Museum, Denver, Colorado, 1951–1952; 21st, 22nd, 23rd and 24th, and 26th Anniversary of North West Printmakers, Seattle Art Museum, Seattle, Washington, 1949, 1950, 1951, 1952, 1954; Portland Society of Art, Portland, Maine, 1953, 1955, 1957; 59th and 60th National Exhibition of Watercolor Club of

Washington, National Museum, Washington, D. C., 1956–1957; Wisconsin Art Salons, Wisconsin Members Union, Madison, Wisconsin, 1950, 1951, 1954, 1957; 15th, 16th, 17th, 18th and 20th Anniversary Exhibition of Watercolors, Drawings, and Prints, Oakland Art Gallery, Oakland, California, 1947, 1950, 1952; 18th, 19th, 21st, 22nd, and 23rd Annual Graphic Art and Drawing Exhibitions, Wichita Art Association, Wichita, Kansas, 1949–1954; Drawing and Print Exhibition, San Francisco Museum of Art, San Francisco, California, 1954; America-Japan Contemporary Print Exhibition, Tokyo, Japan, 1967; 75th Annual Chicago Society of Artists, McCormick Place, 1963; Union League Club of Chicago, 1972; Print Club, Philadelphia, Pennsylvania, 1947, 1950, 1952, 1958; 54th Annual Exhibition, Society of American Graphic Arts, Pratt Institute, New York, New York, 1976.

He is represented by the Art Rental and Sales Gallery of the Art Institute of Chicago.

Anderson received the Mrs. Walter, Ela, Anon, Purchase Award for the Wisconsin Union Loan Collection, Wisconsion Artists Salon, 1951. He is listed in **Who's Who in American Art.**

He is a member of the Society of American Graphic Artists.

THOMAS R. ANDERSON (Painter) was born in Michigan City, Indiana, on December 3, 1949. He studied at Cornell University, B.F.A., 1972, California Institute of The Arts, M.F.A., 1974; Whitney Museum of American Art, and in an independent study program 1970–1971, New York City. His early training was received from Stanley Mitruk, Carl Schwartz and Gertrude Harbart. His travels include Scandinavia, Eastern Europe and Mexico.

He has held one-man shows at Cornell University, Ithaca, New York, 1970–1971; Chicago Public Library, 1971; Deerfield High School, 1972; Monroe Gallery, 1968; Dunes Arts Foundation, 1968. His work has been exhibited in the New Horizons in Art, 1971–1973; Eight State Print Exhibition, Speed Art Museum, Louisville, 1973; Critic's Choice, Art Rental, Art Institute of Chicago, 1972; Countryside Gallery, 1971–1972, Benjamin Gallery, 1970.

Anderson is included in the private collection of Kingman Douglass, Jr., and in public collections of Standard Oil, Chicago Bank of Commerce, the Latin School of Chicago and Cornell University. He is represented by the Art Institute Art Rental and Sales Gallery.

He has received numerous awards at Deer Park Art League and North Shore Art League.

EMIL ARMIN (Painter) was born in Radautz, Roumania, in 1883 and migrated to Chicago in 1905. He studied at the Art Institute of Chicago with J. Wellington Reynolds, George Bellows and Randall Davey. He spent much time in the Indiana Dunes, Maine, New Mexico and Mexico painting and carving.

His works were exhibited at the Art Institute of Chicago where he was represented by a one-man show, as well as in the Chicago and Vicinity; the International Watercolor Exhibition; the American Watercolor Exhibition; the Whitney Museum of American Art, New York; the Newark Museum; the Pennsylvania Academy of Fine Arts, Philadelphia; the Brooklyn Museum; the Kansas City Art Institute; Carnegie Institute; the Berkeley Art Museum, Berkeley, California.

Posthumous one-man exhibitions of his works were held at the K.A.M. Temple Community House, Chicago; the Rosenstone Art Gallery, Chicago.

A full-length biographical and critical study entitled **Thirty-Five Saints and Emil Armin** was written by J. Z. Jacobson and published by L. M. Stein, Chicago 1929. He was also written about by poets and fellow artists.

Armin received many awards for his oils, watercolors, prints and wood sculptures.

He was a member of the Chicago Society of Artists, Chicago No-Jury Society of Artists, 10 Artists Group and the American Jewish Art Club.

His works are represented in numerous private and public collections.

As a memorial to her husband, Hilda Armin has established The Emil Armin Revolving Loan Fund for Fine Arts Students in the Department of Art at the University of Chicago, helping young artists through their difficult student days.

Armin died in 1972.

RALPH MOFFETT ARNOLD (Painter) was born in Chicago, Illinois, on December 5, 1928. He studied at Roosevelt University; the School of the Art Institute of Chicago with Vera Burdich; University of Illinois; and collage and painting with W. H. Roland DuVerne.

He has held a one-man show at Concordia College, Seward, Nebraska in 1962 and a two-man exhibition at Flair Studio, Chicago, 1959.

He participated in group shows and was included in the Chicago and Vicinity Show in 1958; the Trend Studio, 1958; the Red Door Gallery, 1959; 7 Arts Studio, 1959; South Side Community Art Center, 1960; "Ad Lib" Studio, 1959 and 1960; Brotherhood Show at Marshall Field Gallery, 1959; Ghana Museum of Art, New Horizons in Sculpture, 1961; McCormick Place Gallery, Chicago, 1961.

Arnold has executed murals for James House, Arthur Rubloff, 1971; and participated in the Violence in American Art Exhibition at the Museum of Contemporary Art, Chicago, 1969; American Prints Today, Museum of Art, Utica, New York, 1970; Afro-American Arts, 1800–1969, Museum of Philadelphia Civic Center, 1970; Contemporary Black Artists in America, Whitney Museum of American Art, 1971; Cornell University, 1975; All Collage Exhibition, Ball State University, Muncie, Indiana, 1972.

His work is included in the permanent collections of the Whitney Museum of American Art, New York; Fisk University, Nashville, Tennessee; Rockford College, Illinois; Commonwealth Pennsylvania; Illinois Bell Telephone Company, Chicago.

Arnold taught painting at Rockford College, 1969–1970; was Assistant Professor of Art, Barat College in Lake Forest, 1970; and taught at Loyola University in Chicago, 1970, where he is currently Chairman of the Art Department. He also serves on the advisory boards of the Arts, and Sales Rental Gallery, Art Institute of Chicago; and the Illinois Arts Council.

His work has been reproduced in the book **Collage and Assemblage** by Elvie TenHoor and Dona Meilach, Crown publisher.

In 1969 Arnold was awarded involvement in Artists in Residence program sponsored by the Illinois Arts Council to help underprivileged children.

He is a professional member of the Arts Club of Chicago and has been a member of the Chicago Society of Artists since 1961.

FRANCES BADGER (Painter) was born in Kenilworth, Illinois. She studied at the Junior School of the Art Institute of Chicago (then called the Winnetka Extension and located in the basement of the Winnetka Woman's Club) and graduated from the Roycemore School, Evanston, Illinois (then the day school of the Art Institute of Chicago). In 1925 she was awarded a diploma from the Fine Arts Department of the Art Institute of Chicago and in 1949 a B.F.A. degree. Frances Badger also attended the University of Chicago and Northwestern University. She studied mural painting with John W. Norton.

One-woman exhibitions of her works were held in the Art Room of the Chicago Public Library; Chicago Woman's Club; Cordon Club; the University Club of Chicago; Monroe Gallery; Chicago Woman's Aid; Roycemore School and the Evanston Public Library.

She has exhibited at the International Watercolor Exhibition, Art Institute of Chicago, 1934 and 1936; Delphic Studios Exhibition, New York, 1935; New Jersey State Museum Exhibition, Trenton, New Jersey, 1936; Riverside Museum Exhibition, New York, 1939; Chicago Artists and Vicinity Exhibitions, Art Institute of Chicago; International Etching Exhibition, Art Institute of Chicago; Print Club of Philadelphia; Union League Club of Chicago; University Club of Chicago; Monroe Gallery, Chicago; and other galleries in New York and San Francisco.

Badger has designed murals for the Trustees Lounge entitled "Gay Nineties"; A Century of Progress; the Joliet Township High School; the Robert Louis Stevenson Playground, Oak Park, Illinois; the Treasure Island murals, and several for the Federal Art Project.

Her paintings are included in private collections of Mr. & Mrs. John Ross, Chicago; Mr. & Mrs. David A. Bridewell, Winnetka, Illinois; Mr. & Mrs. Jonathan Laing, Evanston, Illinois; Mr. John Meyer, Chicago; and many others. One of her paintings is in the collection of the Bohemia Club Grove in San Francisco. Two paintings were purchased by the Society for the Encouragement of Local Art for the City of Chicago.

Her works are represented by the Art Rental and Sales Gallery, Art Institute of Chicago, and the Vanderpoel Gallery in Beverly, Chicago.

Her teaching experiences include the

Saturday Junior School of the Art Institute of Chicago and Roycemore School, Evanston, Illinois. Currently, she is serving as Gallery Director of the Old Town Triangle Art Center.

Badger is a member and past president (1942) of the Chicago Society of Artists, professional member of the Arts Club of Chicago, and the Art Rental and Sales Gallery of the Art Institute of Chicago. Currently, she is serving on the Board of Directors and acting as chairman of the Society's membership and exhibition committees.

ROBERT L. BAILEY (Sculptor) was born in Hutchinson, Kansas, on July 20, 1923. He entered the U. S. Air Force in 1943 and was discharged in 1946. He spent over 2½ years in India, during which time he designed and executed the stage backdrops and props for a Hindu religious celebration honoring the God Vishnu and completed the designs for a chapel for the service in Assam, India. He studied at the Art Institute of Chicago, 1946–1951; the University of Chicago, 1947–1951; and the Summer School of Painting, Saugatuck, Michigan, 1956–1957.

One-man exhibitions of his works include Forester's St. Almo on North State, 1949; Cromer and Quint Galleries, 1955; TV show of works on Channel 9, WGN-TV, 1956; Evanston Township High School, photography, 1959; Riccardo's Restaurant Gallery, photography, 1959; Chicago Public Library Branch, 939 West Fullerton, 1966; Mid-North Gallery, print show, 1966; Chicago Society of Artists Gallery, 1968; Blackhawk Restaurant, 1970; J. Walter Thompson Company, John Hancock Building, Chicago, 1970; Wood Dale Administration Building, Wood Dale, Illinois, 1970. Bailey has participated in group shows with the Chicago Society of Artists since 1955. He has had exhibitions at the Mandel Brothers Art Galleries; Cromer and Quint Galleries; Evanston Art Center; Latin School; Cordon Club; Todros Geller Gallery; Momentum Show, 1956; shows in Nippersink, Wisconsin, 1956; Wayne, Indiana, 1956 and 1957; Renaissance Society at the University of Chicago; McCormick Place Gallery; National Design Center at Marina City; The Monroe Gallery; National Arts Club, N. Y., 1965; the University Club of Chicago; Chicago Midwest Cultural Show, photography, 1963–1965; Covenant Club Gallery of Chicago; Hunterdon County Art Center, New Jersey, 1970 and 1971; American Embassy in Singapore, 1967–1969; 12th National Print Exhibition, Hunterdon County Art Center, 1968, Clinton, New Jersey; State Museum of New Jersey in Trenton, 1968; Morgan Park Academy, 1968; Public Library of Newark, N. J., 1969, 1971; Cultural Center of Ocean City, N. J., 1969; Bernard Horwich Jewish Community Center, Chicago, 1969, 1970; Old Town Art Center, 1969, 1970, 1971; Bergen Community Museum, Paramus, N. J., 1970; Morris Museum of Arts and Sciences, Morristown, N. J., 1970; St. Alexius Hospital, Elk Grove Village, Illinois, 1970 and 1971; The Village Art Gallery, Pentwater, Michigan, 1970 and 1972; Juliann Studios, River Forest, Illinois, 1971 and 1972; Continental Can Company, Inc., 1972; Federal Court Building, Chicago, 1972; Rackham Gallery University of Michigan, Ann Arbor, Michigan, 1974; Ann Arbor Library, Ann Arbor, 1974; V. A. Hospital, Ann Arbor, 1974 and 1975; City Hall Show, Ann Arbor, Michigan, 1975.

His works are included in several major public collections such as Playboy, 1958; Illinois Bell Telephone, 1966 and 1970, and Blue Cross, 1970.

Bailey received the International Design Award in 1963 for sculpture. He was included in the 9th edition of the **International Arts Directory**.

In 1957, Bailey helped organize Exhibit "A." He also served as vice-president of the Chicago Society of Artists, 1957 and 1958, and member of the Board of Directors for many years.

MACENA (ALBERTA) **BARTON** (Painter) was born in Union City, Michigan on August 7, 1901. She is the daughter of Henry James and Jessie (Rogers) Barton. She graduated the Art Institute of Chicago in 1924. She married Francis Robert McNeilan on January 17, 1953.

She has held one-woman shows at the Art Institute of Chicago, 1928; Knoedler Galleries in Chicago, 1931; Findley Galleries in Chicago, 1933–1936; Chicago Galleries Association, 1932, 1935, 1943, 1948, 1951.

She participated in group shows at the Art Institute of Chicago, 1933, 1937, 1939, 1944, 1943; Virginia Museum of Fine Arts, Richmond, Virginia, 1946; Museum of Fine Arts, Kansas City Art Institute; Riverside Museum, New York; Carnegie Institute, Pittsburgh, Pennsylvania; Minneapolis Institute of Art, Minneapolis, Minnesota; Los Angeles Museum, Los Angeles, California.

Her work was exhibited at the Century of Progress Exhibition of Paintings and Sculpture, Art Institute of Chicago, 1933, and at the Half Century of American Art, Art Institute of Chicago, 1939.

In the 1960's she exhibited at Galerie International New York; The Arts Club of Chicago; the Union League Club, Chicago; the Illinois State Museum, Springfield, Illinois.

Her work has appeared in **World Biography 1948**; **Who's Who of American Art, 1933–1965**; **Art Masterpieces of 1933 and 1934** by C. J. Bulliet, Art Critic, **Chicago Daily News**. She has been written about in numerous publications and newspapers in Chicago and New York and in the **Dictionary of International Biography**, London, England.

Her awards include the August Peabody prize, Art Institute of Chicago, 1927; Chicago Woman's Aid prize, Art Institute of Chicago, 1931; Chicago Woman's Club prize, Art Institute of Chicago, 1932; Chicago Galleries Association, first prize, 1945–1956.

She is a Fellow of the International Institute of Arts and Letters, F.I.A.L., and is listed in **Who's Who of American Women**; **The World Who's Who of Women**; **The Blue Book Leaders of the English Speaking World**. Barton is a member of the Chicago Society of Artists, Arts Club of Chicago, the Alumni Association of the School of the Art Institute of Chicago.

BETTIE BECKER (Painter, Graphic Artist) was born on September 22, 1918, in Peoria, Illinois. She studied at: the University of Illinois, Champaign-Urbana, B.F.A.; Art Institute of Chicago; Art Student's League, N.Y.; Institute of Design, Chicago.

She held one-woman shows at Esquire Gallery, Chicago, 1950; Chicago Fine Arts Center, 1964; Featured Artist, Countryside Gallery, Arlington Heights, 1967; Michelini's Gallery, Evanston, 1970–1972; Lake Forest Academy, Lake Forest, Illinois, 1973; Crossroads Gallery, Art Institute of Chicago, 1973.

She participated in two-woman exhibitions in Stouffer's Gallery, Old Orchard, 1968; Monroe Gallery, Chicago, 1971; Deer Path Gallery, Lake Forest, 1960; exhibition sponsored by Continental Can Company, Chicago, 1971.

She also participated in the following juried shows: Art Sales and Rental, Art Institute of Chicago; Evanston-North Shore Artists Exhibitions, 1964, 1965, 1967, 1968, 1972; Union League Art Competitions, 1967, 1972, 1974; Second Annual Exhibit of Art Miniatures, Artist's Guild Gallery, 1971 and 1972; "Critic's Choice," Art Institute of Chicago, ARSG, 1972; Mead Paper Corporation's Ninth Annual Painting of the Year Competition, 1963; Professional Exhibition, State Fair, Springfield, Illinois, 1962, 1963, 1967; Fifth Annual Tippecanoe Regional Exhibition, LaFayette Art Center, LaFayette, Indiana; 16th Annual Area Show, Lakeview Center of Arts and Science, Peoria, Illinois; Drawings, U.S.A. touring museums and galleries throughout U.S., 1966–1968; Christmas Art Competition, Marymount College, Union Carbide Gallery, N.Y.C.; Louisiana Watercolor Society Fourth International Exhibiton, Louisiana Art Commission Gallery, Baton Rouge, La.; Festival DeArte DeLas DosBanderas, Douglas, Arizona, 1972.

She was included in group shows in Chicago at National Design Center, Marina City, McCormick Place Gallery, University Club, Covenant Club, McKerr Gallery, Harper Gallery, Renaissance Gallery, University of Chicago, New Center for Continuing Education, University of Chicago and others. She was in a four-person show in the Chicago Society of Artists Gallery in 1968.

Becker's works are represented in many private and public collections including the Witte Memorial Museum, San Antonio, Texas; Union League Club, Chicago; Standard Oil Building, Chicago.

Becker has been awarded the Newcomb Prize, Art History, University of Illinois, Urbana, Illinois; Regional Painting, Painting of Merit Award, Mead Paper Corporation's Ninth Annual Painting of the Year Competition, 1963; Honorable Mention, Monoprint, Summer Show Alumni Association Art Institute of Chicago; First Prize, Modern Oil, Evanston, North Shore Artist's Exhibition, 1964; First Prize, Evanston North Shore Artist's Exhibition, 1965; Special Distinction Award, Marymount College Christmas Art Competition, Union Carbide Gallery, New York, 1965; Mr. & Mrs. Donald Erickson Purchase Prize, Union League Show, 1967; Third Prize Evanston North Shore Artists's Exhibition, 1967; First Prize, Calendar Print, Chicago Society of Artists, 1967, 1971, 1974; Third Prize, Calendar Print, Chicago Society of Artists, 1976; Second prize, Festival of Religious Art, Evanston Council of Churches, 1968; Honorable Mention, Second Annual Exhibit of Art Miniatures, Artists Guild of Chicago, 1972; George R. Bailey Purchase Prize, Union League Show, Chicago, 1972; H. Barry McCormick Purchase Prize, Union League of Chicago Show, 1974.

DAVID BEKKER (Painter) was born in Vilna, Poland, on May 1, 1897. He studied at the Antokolsky School of Art in Russia, the Pann Free Academy and the Bezalel Art Academy in Palestine. Later he continued his studies in Paris and the Denver Academy of Art in Colorado. He has painted and carved in Russia, Turkey, Palestine, Egypt, Bulgaria, Roumania, Germany and France.

His works are included in the Library of Congress, Washington, D. C., in several Chicago public schools; State Capitol Building, Boston, Mass.; Oak Forest, Illinois Hospital; Tel Aviv Museum, Israel. He is represented in private collections in Chicago, Boston, Bucharest and Jerusalem. He designed stained glass windows for several synagogues in Chicago and elsewhere.

Bekker was awarded prizes in Jerusalem, 1911 and 1912; Colorado State Fair, 1923; Honorable Mention in the International Watercolor Show at the Art Institute, Chicago, 1942; Martin Kahn Award in the 53rd Annual Exhibition of American Painting at the Art Institute, Chicago; Maurice Spertus Award at the 28th Annual Exhibition of the American Jewish Arts Club, 1955.

Bekker has authored two portfolios: **Myths and Moods**, wood cuts, 1932; **Two Worlds**, etchings.

He was a member of the Connecticut Academy of Fine Arts; Chicago Society of Etchers; Chicago Society of Artists; American Artists Congress; American Jewish Art Club.

Bekker died in 1956.

EUGENE BENNETT (Painter) was born in Central Point, Oregon, on December 20, 1921. He studied at the Art Institute of Chicago, 1946–1954, (BAE and MAE); University of Chicago; DePaul University; University of Oregon, 1940–1943; Park College, Missouri.

One-man shows of his works were held at the Portland Art Museum; Mandel's, Chicago, 1955; Bordelon's, Chicago; Brooklyn Museum Print Show; Museum of Modern Art Print Show (also in permanent collection). He participated in Chicago exhibitions at Momentum, Feingarten, Pritchard and Roberts, Merchandise Mart (permanent collection).

He taught life drawing and children's art classes at the School of the Art Institute of Chicago. He taught at New Trier High School, Winnetka; Katherine Lord's, Evanston; Eugene Bennett Summer classes, 1947–1953; Medford, Oregon; 414 Art Workshop; Abbott Laboratories, North Chicago.

Bennett won the Pauline Palmer Prize, Art Institute Chicago and Vicinity Exhibition, 1956.

He is a member of the Art Institute Alumni Association, Portland Art Museum, Museum of Modern Art, National Art Education and Western Arts Association. He joined the Chicago Society of Artists in 1956.

TRESSA EMERSON BENSON (Painter) was born in Bucksport, Maine, on June 28, 1896. She studied at Syracuse University, B. F.A., 1923; and with Charles Hawthorne and C. Ambrose Webster in Provincetown, Massachusetts. In 1923 she received a Fellowship from Syracuse University, which enabled her to study abroad. She studied in Paris and in other cities in Europe and traveled in Italy, Switzerland, Belgium and England. She is married to Ben Albert Benson, a retired commercial artist (advertising art and design) who for many years had studios at Superior and Michigan.

One-woman exhibitions of her work were held at the Art Institute of Chicago, 1932; Jocelyn Memorial, Omaha, Nebraska, 1943; University of Syracuse, Syracuse, N. Y., Mandel Brothers Art Gallery in Chicago, 1941.

Her work was included in group shows in The American Artists Exhibition, Art Institute of Chicago, 1937, 1938; The International Water Color Exhibition Art Institute of Chicago, 1935; The Century of Progress Exhibition, Art Institute of Chicago, 1933, 1934; Chicago and Vicinity shows, 1931–1941.

Several of her painting were chosen from the Art Institute shows for traveling exhibitions to other museums in the United States.

Private collections in which her works are included are many. A portrait of Preacher Smith is owned by Dakota Wesleyan University.

Benson was Professor of Painting at the University of Nebraska, 1925–1930; Instructor of Art Education Program, Downers Grove, Illinois, 1952–1953; and taught in her private studio from 1941–1968 at Downers Grove, Illinois.

Benson was awarded the Hiram Gee Fellowship, Syracuse University, 1923; Kansas City Art Institute medal, 1929; Mr. & Mrs. Frank Armstrong Prize, Art Institute of Chicago, 1937. She is listed in the second edition of **Who's Who of American Women** and **Who's Who in American Art**.

She is a member of The Lincoln Artists Guild, Lincoln, Nebraska; Chicago Society of Artists; New York Association of Women Artists, New York; Renaissance Society of Chicago.

CLAUDE BENTLEY (Painter) was born in New York City on June 9, 1915. He studied at Northwestern University and the Art Institute of Chicago. From 1941–1945 he served with the armed forces in North Africa and France. He has made many trips to Mexico where he became interested in the Indians and the pre-Columbian cultures. This along with his interest in the "primitive" arts of Africa, Oceania and the American Indian has had a profound influence on his painting. His current style, which began to take form in the mid-1960's, relates to perceptual abstraction. The forms often refer to geometric shapes and frequently relate to those of "primitive" art which deals generally with bold simplifications. He is a collector of African, Oceanic and pre-Columbian art.

One-man shows of his works were held in the Gallery Studio, Chicago, 1949; Well of the Sea Gallery, Chicago, 1950; Boyd Britton Gallery, Chicago, 1950; Chicago Public Library, 1951, 1961; Laurel Gallery, New York, 1951; Baldwin-Kingrey Galleries, Chicago, 1952; Frank Ryan Gallery, Chicago, 1953; Boutique Fantasque Gallery, Chicago, 1955; Layton School of Art, Milwaukee, Wisconsin, 1956; Northern Illinois State College, 1956; Duveen-Graham Gallery, New York, 1957; Art Institute of Chicago, 1959; Feingarten Galleries, Chicago, 1960; Feingarten Galleries, New York, 1960; Parsons College, Fairfield, Iowa, 1962; Adele Rosenberg Gallery, Winnetka, Illinois, 1962; Rosenstone Art Gallery at Bernard Horwich Center, Chicago, 1963, 1973; Milwaukee Jewish Community Center, 1964; Chicago Teachers College, North, 1965; Kasha Heman Gallery, Chicago, 1966; Jacques Baruch Gallery, Chicago, 1973; Hokin Gallery, Chicago, 1975. He has been represented in various group shows in Europe and America since 1941 numbering well over 100. Included are: Art Institute of Chicago, 1941, 1948, 1950 through 1966, 1968; Denver Art Museum, 1941, 1948, 1951, 1954, 1960, 1963, 1964; Seattle Art Museum, 1947; Brooklyn Museum, 1948; Library of Congress, 1948; Pennsylvania Academy of Art, 1948; University of Illinois, 1949, 1951, 1952, 1957; Joslyn Memorial Art Museum, Omaha, 1949; Carnegie Institute, 1949; Milwaukee Art Institute, 1951, 1955, 1956; Metropolitan Museum of Art, 1953; Corcoran Gallery, 1953, 1958, 1961; Whitney Museum of American Art, 1955; University of Wisconsin, 1954; Butler Art Institute, 1953; San Francisco Museum of Art, 1960; Walker Art Center, Minneapolis, 1959.

His paintings are included in public collections of University of Illinois (Krannert Museum); Metropolitan Museum of Art; Art Institute of Chicago; Santa Barbara Museum; Sarasota Art Association; Illinois State Museum; Denver Art Museum (two paintings); Government of France; International Mineral and Chemical Corporation, White-Weld Company; Bendix Corporation; Borg-Warner, Inc., North Advertising, Inc., Mel Boldt and Associates, Inc.; Commerz-bank AG, Chicago, and Continental Illinois National Bank, Chicago.

He was commissioned to do murals for 3600 Lake Shore Drive Building, 1960; was Design Consultant for Plaza del Lago Shopping Center, Wilmette, Illinois, 1966–1968, and has worked on other architectural design projects.

Bentley taught at Layton School of Art, Milwaukee, Wisconsin; Art Institute of Chicago; Old Town Art Center, Chicago; at North Shore Art League, Winnetka, Illinois, 1976–1977. He has given lectures and demonstrations to Evanston Art Center; Oak Park River Forest Associates of the Women's Board of the Art Institute of Chicago; Art Institute of Chicago; Milwaukee Art Center; Lawrence College, Appleton, Wis.; Ft. Wayne Art School, Fort Wayne, Indiana; Parsons College, Fairfield, Iowa; Suburban Fine Arts Center; Lisle Artists Guild, Lisle, Illinois; South Shore Commission Art League, Chicago; Wingspread Conference, Kenosha, Wisconsin.

Bentley was awarded Honorable Mention for a lithograph, Print Club, Philadelphia, 1948; Mural Competition Second Award, Taxco, Mexico, 1949; Purchase Award for Painting, University of Illinois, 1949; Honorable Mention for lithograph, Art Institute of Chicago, 1949; Honorable Mention for painting, Art Institute of Chicago, 1950; Honorable Mention for painting, Terry Art Institute, Miami, Florida, 1952; Watercolor Award, Metropolitan Museum of Art, 1952; Purchase Award for painting, Denver Art Museum, 1954 and 1960; Pauline Palmer Award for painting, Art Institute of Chicago, 1955; Magnificent Mile Award for painting, Chicago, 1955; Milwaukee Journal Award for painting, 1957; First Prize for painting, Brotherhood Week, Chicago, 1959; First Purchase Award, Sarasota Art Association National Exhibition, 1959; First Purchase Award for painting, Village of Oak Park, Illinois, 1959; First Prize for painting, Evanston Art Show, 1960; Second Prize for painting, Old Orchard Art Exhibition, 1961; First Prize for painting, Old Orchard Art Exhibition, 1963; John G. Curtis Award for painting, Art Institute of Chicago, 1963; Purchase Award for painting, Illinois State Museum, 1964; Purchase Award for collage painting, Government of France, Paris, 1971. He is listed in **Who's Who in American Art**.

Bentley became a member of the Chicago Society of Artists in 1949.

AILEEN BERG (Painter) was born in Danville, Illinois, on April 24, 1916. She studied at the School of the Art Institute, receiving the B.F.A. in Art Education.

She has held a one-woman exhibition at the City Administration Building, Waukegan, Illinois. Her work was exhibited in The Pennsylvania National Art Show, Pittsburgh, Pennsylvania; Wisconsin Art Festival, Madison, Wisconsin; Old Capital Art Fair, Springfield, Illinois; Ann Arbor, Michigan Art Festival; Deerpath Art League of Lake Forest; Glenview Art Associaton; and many other exhibits in the North Shore area.

Berg is represented in private collections of: A. C. Nielsen Company; First National Bank of Libertyville, Illinois; First National Bank of Lake Bluff, Illinois; First Federal Savings and Loan Association of Wilmette, Illinois; and the Tower Park Gallery of Peoria, Illinois.

Her work is represented by the Deerpath Gallery, Lake Forest, Illinois; Toronto Art Gallery, Ontario, Canada; Art Institute Sales and Rental Gallery, Chicago, Illinois; Carnegie Memorial Art Gallery, Pittsburg, Pennsylvania; Tower Park Gallery, Peoria, Illinois; and all Merrill Chase Galleries in the Chicago area.

She has taught at the Deerpath Art League; Lake Forest children's classes; Adult Evening School, Winnetka Public School Sytem; Adult Evening School, Lake Forest School System; and Kindergarten through grade 12 in the Waukegan School System.

Her awards include First in Watercolor, Penn-National, Ligonier, Pa.; Purchase Award, North Shore Art League; Purchase Award, Libertyville Art League; First Award in Watercolor, Deerpath Art League, Lake Forest, Illinois; Best of Show award, Libertyville Art League, Libertyville, Illinois; First Award in Watercolor, Lake County Art League; First Award in Watercolor, Skokie Art Exhibit.

KATHLEEN BLACKSHEAR (Painter, Graphic Artist) was born in Navasota, Texas, June 6, 1897. She studied at Baylor University (B. A.); Art Institute of Chicago (M.F.A.) and Art Students League of New York, N. Y.

Blackshear is a painter, graphic artist, craftsman, educator and lecturer. Her works have been exhibited in various museums in the country. She has illustrated and diagramed Helen Gardner's **Art Through the Ages**. She held the position of Professor of Art History at the School of the Art Institute of Chicago, 1926–1961. She lectured at Witte Museum and School of McNey Art Institute, San Antonio; School of the Museum of Fine Arts of Houston, Texas; presented a lecture series at the Centennial Museum, Corpus Christi, 1965; also, an annual series for members of the Museum of Fine Arts, Houston, since 1961.

Blackshear has been a member of the Chicago Society of Artists for nearly a half century. Since 1937 until the present Ms. Blackshear has been contributing lino-cuts to the Chicago Society of Artists Annual calendar. She now resides in Navosota, Texas, but continues to participate in some of the activities of the Chicago Society of Artists.

AARON BOHROD (Painter) was born in Chicago on November 21, 1907. He studied at Crane College, 1925–1926, the Art Institute of Chicago, 1927–1929 and the Art Student's League, New York with John Sloan, 1930–1932.

By 1949 he had become known as one of the finest water-colorists and gouache painters in the country. In 1942 he was commissioned by the U. S. Engineers and later by Life Magazine to record the ravages of World War II in Normandy, Cherbourg, England, Luxembourg, Germany and in the South Pacific. His completed works now hang in the Pentagon and remain as dramatic and powerful statements of the tragedy of war.

In 1942–1943 Bohrod served as Artist-in-Residence at Southern Illinois, Carbondale University and in 1948 he was appointed Artist-in-Residence at the University of Wisconsin in Madison until 1973. Following his appointment, he painted the rural regions of Wisconsin and Michigan. Out of these experiences emerged his Magic Realism approach to painting. He is one of the most important Trompe l'Oeil painters today.

Bohrod is represented in numerous private and public collections of: the Army Historical Collection, Washington, D.C.; Art Institute of Chicago; Brooklyn Museum, New York, Metropolitan Museum of Art, New York; Library of Congress; Butler Art Institute, Youngstown, Ohio; Corcoran Gallery of Art, Washington, D. C.; Cranbrook Museum, Michigan; Detroit Art Institute, Michigan; Encyclopedia Britannica Collection; Evansville Museum of Arts and Science, Indiana; Madison Art Center, Wisconsin; Museum of Fine Arts, Springfield, Massachusetts; Museum of Fine Arts, Boston, Massachusetts; New Britain Museum of American Art, Connecticut; Oshkosh Public Museum, Wisconsin; Pennsylvania Academy of the Fine Arts, Philadelphia; Philippines Museum of Art, Manila; Truman Library and Museum, Independence, Missouri; Walker Art Center, Minneapolis, Minnesota; Whitney Museum of American Art, New York; Witte Memorial Museum, San Antonio, Texas; University of Arizona; Syracuse University, New York; Phoenix Art Museum, Arizona; Milwaukee Art Center, Wisconsin; Davenport Municipal Gallery, Iowa; Sheldon Swope Art Gallery, Terre Haute, Indiana; Ripon College, Wisconsin; John Nelson Bergstrom Art Center, Neenah, Wisconsin; and others.

Bohrod was written about by Harry Salpeter "Bohrod: Chicago's Gift to Art," **Esquire Magazine**, 1940; **Life Magazine**, 1941 and in other publications.

He has written **A Pottery Sketch Book**, 1959, and **A Decade of Still Life**, 1966, published by the University of Wisconsin Press.

He received the following awards for meritorious achievement in art: the Carr Landscape prize, 1935; Clark Prize of $1,500.00 and Silver Medal, Corcoran Gallery of Art; $1,000.00 prize in the "Artists for Victory" Exhibition, Metropolitan Museum of Art; Guggenheim Fellowships 1936–1937 and 1937–1938; San Francisco Golden Gate Exhibition, 1939; Art Institute of Chicago, 1933, 1934, 1935, 1936, 1937, 1945, 1947; First Watercolor Prize, Pennsylvania Academy of the Fine Arts, 1942; California Watercolor Society, 1940; Carnegie International Exhibition, Pittsburgh, 1939; Saltus Gold Medal, National Academy of Design, 1961; Childe Hassam Purchase Prize, American Academy of Arts and Letters, 1962; Kirk Memorial Prize, National Academy of Design, 1965; Wisconsin Governor's Award for Achievement in the Fine Arts, 1969; and others.

MARY S. BORNARTH (Painter) was born in Chicago, Illinois, on October 26, 1900. She studied at the Wisconsin State Teachers College, Milwaukee School of Fine and Applied Arts, 1917; Minnesota University, 1918–1919; and the Art Institute of Chicago, 1919–1924 and 1941–1942. She studied with Leon Kroll, Anisfeld, Seiffert, J. Wellington Reynolds; she studied three summers at Saugatuck, one at Provincetown. Bornarth was a pupil of Charles Hawthorne and F. Fursman and a private pupil of Mr. Frederic Victor Poole. She graduated from the Illinois Institute of Technology "Special" in mechanical engineering, 1944, and did research in optionics at M.I.T., Cambridge, Mass., 1944 and 1955.

One-woman exhibitions of her works were held at the Evanston Art Center, Rogers Park Women's Club, Skokie Library, Wheaton Library, Wilmette Women's Club, University Club of Chicago, the Cordon Club and many others.

She participated in group shows at Mandel Brothers, Chicago; Art Institute of Chicago; Grand Central Gallerie, New York; Indiana Print Makers, Indianapolis; Kansas City Print Makers, Kansas City; traveling exhibits through all of Illinois and through the East.

She taught Color Theory, Dynamic Symmetry, Painting and Anatomy as assistant to Frederic Poole in his private classes and as assistant to Ethel Louise

Coe in her private art school in Evanston.

Bornarth conducted her own school of Painting (Mary Bornarth Studio) from 1936–1941. She was a guest lecturer in Dynamic Symmetry at the Art Institute of Chicago, 1953–1954.

Bornarth designed war memorials, West Portico of Flagstaff Terrace in city Hall of Evanston. She was one of seven engineers who designed the Museum of Science and Industry; Bell and Howell; Mark IV Supersonic Trainers.

Bornarth received the following awards: First Prize for pastel portraits from the North Shore Art League, Winnetka; First Prize for pastel, oil, watercolor portraits and scultpure, Evanston; First Prize from watercolor group at Mandel Brothers Gallery; three prizes from the Skokie Art Guild.

She was a member of the Cordon Club (president), Women Emergency Engineers and Designers; Secretary of Art Institute Alumni; Municipal Art League; All-Illinois Society; Alumni Illinois Institute of Technology and the Chicago Society of Artists for many years.

EDGAR BRITTON (Sculptor, Muralist) was born in Kearney, Nebraska, on April 15, 1901. He studied at the University of Iowa, 1918–1920, and with Grant Wood, 1920–1924. He is a sculptor and works in bronze primarily but also is known for his many frescoes. A one-man show of his works was held in the Denver Art Museum, 1972, and one-man and group shows at the Fine Arts Center, Colorado Springs.

His work in public collections includes Doors and Tower, United Bank of Denver, Colorado; Column for Federal Court Building, Denver; Orpheus, Colorado Springs Library, Colorado; Genesis, Antlers Plaza, Colorado Springs; The Family, Denver General Hospital.

His works were included in the International Watercolor Exhibitions at the Art Institute of Chicago, 1934 and 1935, and in the American Painting and Sculpture Exhibition at the Art Institute of Chicago, 1941, as well as in the Artists of Chicago and Vicinity Show in 1936.

He has done frescoes for Chicago Heights High School and Deerfield Sheilds High School during the Works Project Administration, 1935; frescoes for Lane Technical High School, Chicago, Illinois, 1937; and frescoes for Waterloo Post Office, Iowa, 1940; and for the United States Interior Fine Arts Commission.

He taught art at the Fountain Valley School for Boys, Colorado, and at the Colorado Springs Fine Arts Center.

Britton received the Anne Evans Memorial prize for painting, Denver Art Museum, 1948; First Prize for painting, Pasadena Art Institute, 1949; award from Denver Chapter of American Institute of Architects, 1971.

Edgar Britton is president of the Artists Equity in Colorado Springs and was a member of the Fine Arts Commission of Denver from 1967–1971 and Arts and Humanities 1967–1968.

GERRI H. BUTLER (Painter, Printmaker, Textile Designer) was born in Detroit, Michigan. She has received her training at the School of the Art Institute of Chicago, B.A., M.A.E., De Paul University, Roosevelt University, University of Chicago, Post-graduate work at Harvard University where she studied with Dr. Benjamin Rowland. Currently she is an art and design consultant. She has traveled extensively in the Carribean, Mexico and the United States.

She has participated in juried group shows held by the Chicago Artists League, Art Institute of Chicago, Illinois State Fair Exhibitions, Hyde Park Art League, Chicago Public Library, Covenant Club Gallery, Monroe Gallery, University Club of Chicago, Triangle Art Center and Door County, Wisconsin art shows. Also, at the Boston, Massachusetts Fine Arts Festival; Roosevelt University, Chicago; Renaissance Society Gallery at the University of Chicago; Rubino Gallery, Chicago and at the St. Luke's Presbyterian Art Gallery in Chicago.

Her works are represented by the Sales and Rental Gallery of the Art Institute of Chicago and are included in private and public collections of A. K. and G. G. Butler, William F. Heiskell, F. Lackey, J. H. Butler, Dr. S. A. Hinchliff of New York, D. & M. Corbin, Dr. S. M. Woods, Donald, Howard and Morris Goldstein, Charlotte V. Olson, Saxon Construction Corporation and others. She is listed in **Artists U.S.A.**

She taught art in the Chicago Public Schools on an elementary and secondary level, on the teacher-training and professional level, and was Art Consultant for the Chicago Public Schools for the past fifteen years in Districts #4, #7 and #11, and Areas B and C (approximately 150 schools.)

She has served as judge at many art events such as the White Sox Art Competition, National Scholastic Competition, Navy Pier Show and the Mayor Daley's Buckingham Art Contest.

She has served on two state committees, the State of Illinois Aerospace Committee, and the Illinois Art Curriculum Committee, participated on panels at art education conferences and arranged organizational exhibits.

Butler has received the Delta Sigma Theta Scholarship, Huntington Hartford Fellowship, the North Michigan Boulevard Water Tower Association prize. She has been elected to membership of Delta Kappa Gamma Society.

Butler is a member of the Society of Typographical Art, Chicago Artists Guild, Chicago Society of Artists, North Shore Art League, Evanston Art League, American Craftsmen, Midwest Artists and Craftsmen, International Art Education Association, National Art Education Association, Western Arts Association and the Illinois Art Education Association. Butler is a member of the Civil Air Patrol, has a pilot's license and participated in various air force maneuvers and visits to SAC bases.

CATHERINE CAJANDIG (Painter, Graphic Artist) was born in Chicago, and studied at the Art Institute of Chicago (B.A.E. & M.A.E.) and at the Instituto Allende, Mexico (M.F.A.). She has traveled and painted throughout the United States, the Caribbean, Asia, Europe, Mexico, Central and South America.

She has held one-woman exhibitions at the Lake Forest Academy; Monroe Gallery, Chicago; North Park College; Old Town Art Center, Chicago, and in Mexico.

She participated in group exhibitions at Art Institute of Chicago; Chicago Public Library; Covenant Club; Harper Court Gallery; Rosenstone Gallery of Bernard Horwich Center, Chicago; LaFayette College, Easton, Pa.; National Design Center; Old Town Art Center, Chicago; University of Chicago, University of Illinois; University Club of Chicago.

Currently she is teaching art in the Chicago Public School System and lithography to evening adult classes at Jane Addams Hull House.

Cajandig won several awards for linocuts submitted to the Chicago Society of Artists' Annual Calendar publication. Her work is represented by the Art Rental and Sales Gallery of the Art Institute of Chicago, Standard Oil and other private collections.

Cajandig has served as President of the Chicago Society of Artists for two years and as Vice-President and Corresponding Secretary for several years. She has served on its Board of Directors and has been in charge of publication and distribution of the Society's Annual Calendar as co-chairman of the calendar committee.

HILDA E. CAMPBELL (Painter) was born in New Jersey on April 5, 1915. She studied at Greenbrier College, Lewisburg, West Virginia; New York School of Interior Design; Samuelson and Pinto Institute deAllende, Mexico; and with Kip Nielsen, New Jersey; Elvie TenHoor, Chicago, Illinois; Art Institute of Chicago, Academie N. D. Des Champs, Paris, France, and with Stanley Mittrick at the Commonwealth Art Center. She has traveled to Europe, Mexico and the Orient.

Hilda E. Campbell has exhibited in the Garland Building; Rehabilitation Institute of Chicago; Art Originals Lutheran General Hospital; The Covenant Club Gallery; Continental Can Company, Technical Center; Little Gallery, Palos Park, Illinois; Dunes Art Foundation, Michigan City, Indiana; Montessori Benefit, Lake Tower Inn, Chicago; B'nai Torak Temple, Highland Park, Illinois; Artists Guild of Chicago.

Her work is included and written about in the book **Collage and Assemblage** by Meilach and TenHoor, Crown Publisher.

She is a member of the Chicago Society of Artists, Art Institute Alumni Association; Municipal Art League; Artists Guild of Chicago; The Renaissance Society at the University of Chicago; and the Mid-American Art Association.

EDITHE JANE CASSADY (Painter) was born in Chicago. She graduated from the Art Institute of Chicago (B.A.E., M.F.A.).

Her works have been exhibited in the Century of Progress Exhibition, Art Institute of Chicago; Artists of Chicago and Vicinity shows, 1936, 1949 and other years; in the annual professional member's exhibitions of the Arts Club of Chicago; the Smithsonian Institute; the National Academy of Design; and numerous other museums.

Cassady's work has been written about by Chicago art critics Eleanor Jewett, C. J. Bulliet, and in J. Z. Jacobson's book **Art of Today–Chicago**, L. M. Stein, Publisher, 1932.

For a brief period of time she taught in the Chicago Public Schools. Later, she taught Anatomy at the Academy of Fine Arts in Chicago and at the school of the Art Institute of Chicago, where she was a member of its faculty for 16 years. In 1961 she was appointed Professor of Art, Art Institute of Chicago. In the more recent past she served as Chairman of the Junior School of the Art Institute of Chicago.

Cassady was a member of the Chicago Society of Artists since 1958; the Association of Painters and Sculptors; Art Institute of Chicago Alumni; the Arts Club of Chicago; The South Side Art Association of Chicago; the National Art Education Association; and the Illinois Art Education Association.

She was awarded the Union League Club Prize, 1929; the All Illinois Society of Fine Arts Bronze Medal, 1937; the South Side Art Association of Chicago, First Prize, 1944, 1945; the Flora M. Witkowsky Prize, 1947; Mr. and Mrs. Maurice Joseoff Prize, 1947; the Chicago Critics Exhibition Prize, 1948, 1949, 1950; and the Magnificant Mile Art Festival Prize, 1952.

Cassady died on September 2, 1977.

JANINE COLLIER (Painter) was born in France. She was educated in Paris and studied privately with French painters until going to work in Washington, D. C., for the French government. Later, when living in New York, she again studied with private teachers. In 1960 she moved to Chicago and took additional courses at the Old Town Art Center, Contemporary Art Workshop, Art Institute of Chicago and in the studios of local artist-teachers.

She has held one-woman shows at the M & M Art Gallery, Chicago, 1968; Chicago Public Library, 1968; Compass Gallery, Nantucket, Massachusetts, 1968; the Covenant Club of Illinois, 1973.

Juried exhibitions in which her works were included are Countryside Gallery, 1963–1967; McKerr Gallery, Chicago, 1963; Illinois State Museum (Invitational), Springfield, Illinois, 1964; Illinois State Fair, Springfield, Illinois, 1964; Suburban Fine Arts Festival, 1964; Art Institute of Chicago, Sales and Rental Gallery, 1964 to 1976; Old Town Art Center, 1966; Niles West Small Paintings Exhibition, 1967; Raymond Duncan Prix de Paris, France, 1967, 1968; 54th Annual Exhibition, Allied Artists of America, New York City, 1967; Old Orchard Art Festival, 1968; Mainstreams U.S.A., 1971; Fourth Annual Marietta College International Competition; North Shore Art League, 1973.

Collier has exhibited extensively in the Chicago area, the East Coast and Europe, with her work featured on the cover of Paris **Revue Moderne** in 1964 and 1968.

Galleries which represent her work are the Newman Galleries in Philadelphia, the Woodland Gallery in Palm Springs, and the Rental and Sales Gallery of the Art Institute of Chicago. Numerous paintings are in private collections.

Collier has received the following awards: Winners Circle, Plum Grove, Illinois, 1963; Honorable Mention, Skokie, 1963; Second Prize, Niles, 1964; Second Prize and Honorable Mention, Countryside Gallery, Spring of 1965, 1967; Second Prize, Illini Union University, Chicago, 1965; First Prize, Randhurst, 1965; First Prize, Niles, 1966; Second Prize, Randhurst, 1966, 1967; Best in Show Award, Duncan Gallery, New York City, 1967; Honorable Mention and First Prize, North Shore Art League, 1967; Purchase Prize, Niles, 1967; Third Prize, Print Show, Chicago Society of Artists, 1973.

CHARLES E. COOPER (Painter) was born in Chicago, November 5, 1922. He received his training at the Art Institute of Chicago, (B.A.E.); studied at Institute of Design with Moholy-Nagy, Archipenko, Hugo Weber, Harry Callahan, and did graduate work at Loyola University; Illinois Institute of Technology; Corcoran Gallery of Art, Washington, D. C.; Honolulu Art Academy, Honolulu, Hawaii.

He held one-man exhibitions at Club St. Elmo; Morris B. Sachs-North; Northwestern University Hillel Foundation; Robert North Gallery; Kerrigan-Hendrix Galleries, and at Alpha Gallery in Chicago.

His works were included in group shows at Exhibition Momentum, Chicago Art Institute, in Chicago and Vicinity exhibitions; Rental and Sales Gallery of Art Institute; American Jewish Arts Club Annual Exhibitions; Navy Pier No-Jury Shows, 1957; Old Town Triangle Art Fair, 1948–1965; 57th Street Art Fair, 1948–1965; Highland Park Art Fair,

1951, 1952; Webster Street Winter Walk Open Studio Show, 1975; Chicago Society of Artists Exhibitions; Art Student League, 1941–1951; Albany Park Library, 1946, 1948, 1950; American Veterans Committee Exhibition at Institute of Design, 1947.

His work has been represented by the Art Institute of Chicago Rental and Sales Gallery for the last 17 years, Gallery 750, House of Arts, Kerrigan-Hendrix Galleries, and Alpha Gallery in Chicago. Also, in private collections of: J. Belka, Winnetka; S. Rifkin, Los Angeles; E. Friedman, New York; R. Schiller, Chicago; M. Golden, Chicago; and in public collections of Congregation Beth El, Grand Rapids, Michigan; St. Elizabeth in Chicago; Oir Israel, Miami, Florida.

He has taught art in the Chicago Public High Schools for the last twenty-four years and in the Agudas Achim North Shore Congregation, Camp Greenwoods, J.P.I. Day Camp, and Camp Waupaca. He has served as art consultant for the Board of Jewish Education.

Cooper received the Maurice Spertus Award; the Nathan Schwartz Award; the Raymond Schiff Award, and the Morris DeWoskin Award for paintings. He is listed in **Who's Who in the Midwest**; Silver Anniversary Issue of Art Digest's **Who's Where in American Art**; **Dictionary of International Biography.**

HELEN CORLETT (Painter) was born in Oak Park, Illinois, in July 1893. She studied at the Church School of Art, Chicago, Illinois, graduating in 1916. Emma Church, Anita Burnham, Rudolph Pen and others were influential in her artistic development.

She has held one-woman exhibitions at the Saugatuck Art Gallery, Cordon Club, and participated in many Village Art Fairs sponsored by the North Shore Women's Club.

GUSTAF DALSTROM (Painter) was born in Gotland, Sweden, in January 18, 1893. He studied at the Art Institute of Chicago where his outstanding teachers were George Bellows and Randall Davey. He has painted in Sweden, France, Italy and Germany. He worked in oil, watercolor and graphics.

For many years he served on the staff of the Field Museum of Natural History in Chicago where he directed, planned and executed authentically documented settings for various world-wide wild life displays.

One-man shows of his paintings were held at the Art Institute of Chicago, the Woman's Aid, the Renaissance Society of the University of Chicago and many others.

He was represented in numerous juried group shows in New York, Ohio, Iowa, Illinois, Washington, D. C., Michigan, Indiana and other states.

His works have been included in the following international, national and regional exhibitions: A Century of Progress Exhibition of Painting and Sculpture, Art Institute of Chicago, 1933; International Watercolor Exhibition, Art Institute of Chicago, 1934, 1935; New Jersey State Museum Exhibition, Trenton, New Jersey, 1936; Riverside Museum Exhibition, New York, 1939; American Art Today Exhibition, New York World's Fair, New York, 1939; and in many Artists of Chicago and Vicinity Exhibitions at the Art Insitute of Chicago.

His work has been written about in various Chicago publications, in **The Arts** magazine and in the book **Art of Today, Chicago, 1933** by J. Z. Jacobson, L. M. Stein, publisher, 1932.

Dalstrom received the Logan Award and Gold Medal from the Art Institute of Chicago, and the Gold Medal Award from the Chicago Society of Artists.

He was a loyal and dedicated member of the Chicago Society of Artists since 1927 and served as its president for a number of years. Until the end of his life he gave unselfishly of his time and energy in order to expedite the production and distribution of the Chicago Society of Artists Annual Calendar. Gustaf Dalstrom contributed lino-cuts to the annual publication since its inception in 1937.

Dalstrom died in 1971.

JULIO DeDIEGO (Painter) was born in Madrid, Spain, May 9, 1900, and studied in Madrid, Paris and Rome. He has painted in France, Germany, Italy, Portugal, North Africa, the Balearic Islands, the Canary Islands, and the Midwest and South of the United States. He works in watercolors, tempera, metals and jewelry.

DeDiego held one-man exhibitions at the Art Institute of Chicago, 1935; Surrealist Exhibitions in Paris, France and London, England, 1947; International Cultural Affairs Exhibit, Department of State, Paris, London and Rome, 1948;

Pennsylvania Academy of Fine Arts, Philadelphia and Carnegie Institute, Pittsburgh, several years.

He was commissioned to execute murals and chapel doors for the St. Gregory Church in Chicago, 1929; Bullfight (mural) Hotel Sherman, Chicago, 1933; Fort Sheridan (mural) Fort Sheridan, Chicago, 1936; Story of Wine (mural) Hotels Ambassador and Sherman, Chicago, 1937; metal sculpture and murals, Ling Nang Restaurant, New York, 1959, and others.

His works are included in a number of public collections at: Metropolitan Museum of Art, New York; Washington University, St. Louis, Missouri; Montclair Art Museum, New Jersey; Encyclopedia Britannica, New York; Santa Barbara Museum of Art, California, plus others.

He was professor of painting at the Art Institute of Chicago, 1939–1940, University of Denver, 1948–1952, Artists Equity Workshop, 1955–1957.

He has written and illustrated several books.

DeDiego received the following awards for his etchings, painting and sculpture: a medal for etching at Lespocion Nacional deBellas Artists; First Prize, Men and Steel Show, 1954; First Prize, Cotton Exhibit, 1956, Birmingham Museum, Alabama; First Prize for the Figure, Arvida Corporation, Sarasota, Florida, 1971 and many others.

Until 1941 he was a member of the Chicago Society of Artists, the Chicago No-Jury Society of Artists, and LosAmericus in Spain. Later, he became associated with Artists Equity Association in New York (became its president), and the Sarasota Artists Association.

AVINASH N. DESAI (Graphic Artist) studied at Guyarat College of Arts and Science. He has traveled through most parts of India and in the United States. His primary interests are block printing, watercolor and line drawing.

He has held one-man exhibitions at the Gallery of Folk Arts in India and the Taj Mahal Restaurant in Chicago.

He taught History of Indian Arts and Fundamentals in Pen Drawing and Watercolor.

Currently he is working as a medical technologist.

CHARLOTTE DOYLE (Painter) was born in Chicago, Illinois, and studied at the University of Wisconsin, Madison, where she received her M.A. degree in Art. Doyle participated in a six week traveling seminar on Christian Iconography in Italy and Switzerland and six weeks at the Kordas Painting Workshop on the Island of Samos, Greece, in the summer of 1974. The summer of 1976 was spent in a six week painting workshop at the Aegean School of Fine Arts on the Island of Paros, Greece. Her favorite media are painting and graphics.

She has held one-woman exhibitions at Rosary College, River Forest, and at the Aegean School of Fine Arts, Paros, Greece. She also participated in an exhibition of graphics at Kitchener, Waterloo Gallery, Canada, and in a two month traveling exhibition in Ontario, Canada.

She participated in juried group shows in Mount Mary College, Milwaukee, Wisconsin; Northland College; University of Wisconsin; Playboy Club, Lake Geneva; Wisconsin State Fair; Park Forest Art Fair; Moraine Valley Community College Art Fair; Evanston Art Center. She has participated in shows in the March Gallery, Western Springs; Fine Arts Gallery, Hinsdale; Evanston Art Center, Monroe Gallery; University Club; Astor Hotel, Milwaukee; Jewish Community Center, Milwaukee; Marina Towers Gallery, Chicago; Circle Gallery; Old Town Art Center; Covenant Club, Chicago; Kordos Painting and Workshop Exhibit at Samos, Greece.

Doyle's works are also included in numerous private collections. Private showings have been held in Whitefish Bay, LaGrange and Hickory Hills, Illinois.

Her work is represented by the March Gallery, Western Springs, Illinois, the Evanston Art Center and Collector's Showroom, Chicago. Her work is included in public collections of the Queen of Peace High School, Oak Lawn, Illinois, and Dominican High School, Whitefish Bay, Wisconsin.

Prizes include an Honorable Mention at the 1972 Illinois State Fair where she won a prize for an etching. In 1971 she won Best in the Show in Madison, Wisconsin, at the West Town Art Fair and Best of Graphics in Brookfield, Wisconsin. She has been awarded a prize for painting at DePaul University; prizes for etchings at Northland College, Mount Mary College and the University of Wisconsin Shows.

She is presently teaching art at Lyons Township High School in LaGrange, Illinois, and has taught in adult education programs as well. For nine years she served on the National High School Scholastic Awards Committee.

MARGARET DRISCOLL (Painter) was born in Chicago, Illinois, in 1916, and studied at Northwestern University in the Department of Education and with artist-teachers Kwok Wai Lau and Stanley Mitruk. Her favorite media are oil and collage.

Her works are represented by the Art Rental and Sales Gallery of the Art Institute of Chicago and the Two-Thirty Seven Gallery and were exhibited in group shows at the Thor Gallery, Louisville, Kentucky; Harper Gallery, Chicago; Old Town Art Center, Chicago; University Club of Chicago; Merchants and Merchandise Mart Club, Chicago; Allentown Museum, Pennsylvania, Commonwealth Art Center; and Architects League in Chicago.

Her paintings and collages are included in the collections of the President and Mrs. Allen Wallis of Rochester University; Mr. & Mrs. Thomas Duffron, Editor of New York Times, Paris, France; Civic Center Bank, Chicago; Mr. & Mrs. Burton Foley, Alabama; Dr. & Mrs. Graham of Grosse Pointe, Michigan; Dr. & Mrs. Stanley Lawton of Pomona, California; and in the public collection of the Civic Center Bank, Chicago.

She is a professional member of the Arts Club, Commonwealth Art Center and the Chicago Society of Artists.

DIANE DUVIGNEAUD (Painter) was born in Manitoulin Island, Ontario, Canada, and studied at the Massachusetts School of Art (B. S. of Ed., 1939), Northwestern University (M.F.A., 1950), the Art Institute of Chicago, 1946–1948, the American Academy, 1945 and the Hans Hoffman School of Fine Arts, Provincetown, Massachusetts, 1945.

She has held one-woman exhibitions at the Werbe Gallery, Detroit, Michigan; Newman Brown Gallery, Chicago; La-Boutique Fantasque, Chicago; Sidney Rafilson Gallery; and at North Central College, Naperville, Illinois.

Her works were exhibited in group shows at the Corcoran Gallery, Washington, D. C., 22nd and 23rd Biennials, 1951–1953; Pennsylvania Academy, Philadelphia, 51st Annual Watercolor Exhibition, 1953; Ohio Valley Oil and Watercolor Exhibition, 11th Annual, 1953; Chicago and Vicinity Exhibition, Art Institute of Chicago, 1946; 59th Annual American Exhibition, Art Institute of Chicago, 1949; Brooks Memorial Art Gallery, Memphis, Tennessee, 1940; Museum of Fine Arts, Boston, Massachusetts, 1952; Illinois State Fair, 10th Professional Art Exhibit; Werbe Gallery, Detroit, Michigan. In Chicago at the Newman Brown Gallery; LaBoutique Fantasque; Sidney Rafilson Gallery; 1020 Art Center; Well of the Sea; Renaissance Society at the University of Chicago; North Shore Art League, Fine Arts Faculty Gallery; Benjamin Gallery, Circle Gallery, and University Club.

Gallery representation includes the Art Rental and Sales Gallery, Art Institute of Chicago.

Her works are included in the Dow Collection, New York City, New York; and in the permanent collection of Phillips Memorial Gallery, Washington, D. C. Honors and awards conferred upon her works are: Chicago Critics Award, Spectrum, 1st prize, 1953; 2nd prize, 1954; American Federation of Arts Traveling Exhibition, 1955–1956; Chicago Critics Award, Perspective, 3rd prize, 1957; Chicago Artists Award, Perspective, 1st prize, 1957; Alumni Association of Art Institute, Playboy Award, 1964 and in 1966; Honorable Mention, Watercolor, 1st prize, 1966; 7th Annual Union League–Martin D. John Purchase Prize, 1967; and Municipal Art League, Honorable Mention, 1971.

She is author of **Guide to the Visual Arts** (workbook on terminology and processes); **What is a Painting?** (essay); "An Approach to Creativity" (address).

She taught at the James Lee Academy of Art, Memphis, Tennessee, and is currently chairman of the Art Department, North Central College, Naperville, Illinois.

She is listed in **Who's Who in the Midwest**, **Directory of American Scholars**, and recipient of the Outstanding Educators of America Award, 1972.

Duvigneaud is a member of the Artist's Equity, Renaissance Society, Perspective, Alumni Association, Art Institute of Chicago, College Art Association, Municipal Art League, and Chicago Society of Artists.

ELIZABETH EDDY (Painter) was born in Cleveland, Ohio, on November 27, 1907. She studied at Cranbrook

Academy of Art, Bloomfield Hills, Michigan; Art Institute of Chicago; Cleveland Museum of Art and Cleveland Art School with Zoltan Sepesky and Arshile Gorki. She works in many media including oil, watercolor, acrylics, gouache, lithography, woodcut and drawing.

Her one-woman shows include The Door Gallery, 1964–1968; McCormick Theological Seminary, 1962–1967; Lincoln Park Branch Library, January 1966; Park Forest Art Center, September 1965; Art Department of Chicago Public Library, July 1965; 59 Gallery, 59 East Monroe, Chicago, 1964; Eldred Hall, Western Reserve University, Cleveland, Ohio, 1964; No Exit Cafe, Evanston, Illinois, 1961; Lexington Hall, University of Chicago, 1961; Lake Meadows Art Gallery, Chicago, 1961; Ft. Wayne Art Museum, 1952; Lyman Brothers Gallery, Indianapolis, 1951; Harper College, Palatine, Illinois, January 1971; Isaac Delgado Museum, New Orleans, La., 1933.

She participated in group shows with Momentum, 1952–1957; Society of Washington, D. C. Printmakers, National, 1958–1960; Art Association of Newport Rhode Island, National, 1958–1960; Honolulu Printmakers, 1959; Bradley University, National Print Show, Peoria, 1952; Brooklyn Museum Print Show, National, 1951; Albright Art Gallery Print Show, Buffalo, New York, 1951; Northwest International Printmakers, Seattle, Washington, 1948; American Drawing VII, Albany, New York, Institute of History and Art, 1947; Philadelphia Annual Watercolor Exhibition, Pennsylvania Academy of the Fine Arts, 1933; Ohio Printmakers Annual, Dayton Ohio Art Institute, 1947, 1950–1952, 1958–1961; Cleveland Ohio Annual May Show, 1945 through 1950, 1953, 1959; Michigan Artists Annual, Detroit Institute of Arts, 1930–1932, 1950; Butler Art Institute Annual National, Youngstown, Ohio, 1948; Ecclesiastical Crafts Exhibition of Church Architectural Guild of America, Pittsburgh, 1961.

Invitational shows in which she took part were Baptist Graduate Student Center at University of Chicago, 1963, 1964, 1967, 1970–1973; Moholy Nagy Memorial Show and Auction, Institute of Design, 1954–1957, 1962; Cranbrook Academy of Art Alumni Exhibition, 1952; Ball State Teachers College, Muncie, Indiana, Exhibition, Indiana Painters, 1952; J. B. Speed Art Museum, Louisville, Ky., Print Show, 1951; Old Northwest Territory Art Exhibit, 1950, 1951.

Her work is included in public collections including The Museum of Cranbrook Academy of Art, "Drawings of Contemporary Artists," McCormick Theological Seminary, oil gift of 1965 graduating class; Northwestern University Methodist Graduate Student Chapel, two woodcuts; Cleveland Print Club, drawings and print; Fort Wayne Art Museum, oil; North Side High School, Fort Wayne, watercolor; South Bend Art Association, lithograph; Midwest Fine Art Colorslide Collection, Art Department, Chicago Public Library; Colorslide collection, Cleveland Museum of Art.

She taught at Cranbrook Academy of Art; was chairman of Upper School Art Department, Laurel School in Shaker Heights, Ohio; Fort Wayne Art School, on college level; Arts, Crafts, and Shop at Evanston Receiving Home for emotionally disturbed children; and private classes. She lectured on art in Fort Wayne, and wrote articles for Fort Wayne newspapers, catalogues and radio releases.

Her work has been published periodically in **Motive** magazine, and she was the featured artist in the magazine **Liberation.**

Her awards include Fellowship, Cranbrook Academy of Art, graduate, 1944; prizes from South Bend Art Association, Michiana Regional, 1950, 1951, 1955, 1958; Ohio Artists Drawing Exhibition, Canton Art Museum, 1950, Honorable Mention; Cleveland May Show, third prize, 1945; drawing, Honorable Mention, 1949; Indiana State Fair Art Exhibit, first and third prizes for drawings, Honorable Mention for print, 1947; Fort Wayne Annual, 1954, for drawing; 1952 for watercolor; 1951, for casein.

Eddy also writes poetry. She has appeared on a number of TV interviews reading her poetry while showing her paintings.

JOHN W. EMERSON (Painter) was born in New York City on April 4, 1921, and studied at the Art Institute of Chicago (B.A.E., 1950 and M.A.E., 1952) and at the Institute of Design, Illinois Institute of Technology. Emerson worked in oils, gouache, jewelry, watercolors, woodcuts and monoprints.

His works have been shown in many local galleries and art fairs.

He joined the faculty of Chicago Teachers College in 1951 and served as chairman of the Art Department from 1953 to 1958. He also taught drawing and painting at the Hyde Park Art Center, 1951, 1953, and at St. Joseph's College, Calumet Center, 1956. In 1959 he was appointed Assistant Director of the Institute of Design. In 1965 he became Associate Professor at the Institute of Design while continuing his administrative responsibilities.

He was a member of the following organizations: Chicago Watercolor Club; Chicago Society of Artists; International Society for Education through Art, National Art Education Association; Illinois Art Education Association; Chicago Art Educators Association; American Association of University Professors; Western Art Association and National Committee of University Professors; Western Art Association and National Committee on Art Education. He served as president of the Chicago Society of Artists in 1960.

Emerson died at Odgen Dunes, Indiana, on September 4, 1966.

JUDITH ESAROVE (Painter, Sculptor) was born in Chicago, Illinois, and studied at Benet Academy in Illinois, Connecticut School of Art, Westport, Connecticut, and the Art Institute of Chicago. She is primarily interested in creating mixed media constructions.

She has held one-woman exhibitions at the Artists Showcase, Lincolnwood, Illinois; Continental Bank, Chicago; Indian Hills Country Club, Indian Hills, Illinois; Gallery II, Fox Valley; Oakbrook Theatre, Oakbrook, Illinois; Northern Illinois Gas Company, Aurora, Illinois; Concordia College, River Forest, Illinois,

Group shows in which she participated include Anita Gordon College, Montreal, Quebec; Fort Wayne Museum of Art, Fort Wayne, Indiana; Fields Contemporary Gallery, Santa Fe, New Mexico. Her work is represented by the Art Institute, Art Rental and Sales Gallery; Bodinet Gallery, Evanston, Illinois; House of Fine Art, Chicago; Art and Inc., Cincinnati, Ohio; Park Forest Art Center, Park Forest, Illinois; Inmergluck Gallery, Lincolnwood, Illinois.

She participated in art festivals at the Glenview Invitational; Golf Mill Art Fair; Cincinnati Art Festival; South Bend Art Fair; Yorktown Festival of Art; Lisle Art Show, Town and Country Art Fair; Lawrencewood Art Fair; Lisle Fall Show; Randhurst, Autumn Festival; Eastgate Art Festival; Villa Park Art Fair; duPage Art League; Deerbrook Art Festival, Deerfield, Illinois; Oakbrook Promanade, Oakbrook, Illinois; Gallery in the Forest, Four Lakes Village; and Carol Stream Arts Festival, Carol Stream, Illinois.

JOHN FABION (Painter, Sculptor) was born on October 31, 1905, in Vienna, Austria, of Polish parentage. He studied at Art Institute of Chicago; Master Studio, Krakow, Poland; Royal Academy, Florence, Italy, 1930; Kuntsgewerbecshule, Vienna, Austria, 1931; and in Paris, 1932. Teachers who have influenced John Fabion mostly were Boris Anisfeld, Albin Polasek, Anton Hanak of Vienna and Xavery Dumkowski of Krakow, Poland. He has traveled to twenty countries in Europe, the near-East and the Orient.

His work is represented in public collections in Poland and in the U. S. Marine Corps Museum; U. S. Navy Museum, Racine, Wisconsin; Polish Museum of America, Annapolis, Maryland.

He also exhibited at juried exhibitions in Philadelphia, in other American shows, and in Warsaw and Krakow in Poland.

He taught at the School of the Art Institute of Chicago for twenty-four years.

In 1934 he received the Ryerson Fellowship of $2,500. He received four prizes at the Art Institute of Chicago, and other awards at various exhibitions.

BARBARA FAGEN (Painter, Ceramist) was born in Cleveland, Ohio, on October 26, 1913, and studied at the Cleveland School of Art and the Art Institute of Chicago. Her major media include enameling, ceramic sculpture, painting and mosaics. In her early years she had been a ballet dancer performing with the Russian Ballet in all major cities in the United States.

She has held one-woman exhibitions at the Chicago Public Library, 1951–1961, Downers Grove Public Library, 1960–1963, Bensenville Library, 1973, Oakbrook Theatre, and a number of other places.

Her works have been exhibited at the Sixth Annual Ceramic Exhibit, Syracuse Museum; National Academy of Design, New York City; Connecticut Academy of Art; Butler Museum of Art, Youngstown, Ohio; International Invitational Ceramic Exhibit, Syracuse Museum, New York; juried into American House, 1966–67, New York City. Figurines have been featured in George Jensen's, New York City, Peacock's, Chicago and New York, Marshall Field, Chicago. She has received recognition for her paintings and ceramic sculpture in group shows.

She directed her own ceramic school in Westmont from 1947–1953, taught mosaics at Downers Grove High School, and was art director of the Illini Ceramic Service for ten years. Her works, i.e. ceramic figurines and enamel paintings, are in many private collections. A mosaic mural 12′ x 6′ is installed at the Rex Restaurant in the Teakwood Room, Austin, Illinois.

Her works are represented by the Art Rental and Sales Gallery of the Art Institute of Chicago.

SHERRI Z. FELDMAN (Graphic Artist) was born in Chicago, Illinois, on December 30, 1931. She studied at: the University of Illinois, B. A., 1953; University of Wisconsin, Madison, Wisconsin, 1949–1950; and Art Institute of Chicago, 1972–1976. She also studied with Fred Berger of Evanston Art League, 1973; Dennis McWilliams, Ox-Bow School of Painting, Saugatuck, Michigan, 1966–1975, in private studios of Lillian Desow-Fishbein, Heidi Bak, Studio #22, Shelley Canton, 1968–1970, Kwok Lai Lau, Commonwealth School of Art, 1964–1966.

Her work is represented in Chicago by the Art Institute Sales and Rental Gallery; Tower Gallery, Marina City; Chicago Society of Artists Gallery; L'Affaire D'arte, New Town; in the Left Bank Gallery in Saugatuck, Michigan; Deerpath Art League Gallery, Lake Forest, Illinois; Harmon's Galleries, Clayton, Missouri; Cain Gallery, Oak Park, Illinois; Douglas, Michigan; Station Gallery, Crown Point, Indiana; and many others.

She participated in Art Fairs at Old Orchard, 1970, 1974; Randhurst; 57th Street; Howard and Western; Golf Mill; Gold Coast New Horizon Shows; Deerpath Art League; Anshe Emet, Temple Beth El; Evanston Woman's Club; Hubbard Woods; Lincolnwood Fair; Edgebrook; The Great Midwest; Illinois State Fair and Bernard Horwich J.C.C. Annual.

She exhibited in group shows with The North Shore Art League, Skokie Art Guild, Chicago Society of Artists, Evanston Art League, American Jewish Arts Club, Covenant Club, Triangle Art Center, Woman's Club of Evanston, Deerpath Art Gallery.

She has taught in the Chicago Public Schools for seven years, and gave lecture demonstrations in graphic arts for the National Council of Jewish Women, Ort, B'Nai Brith, and various organizations, sisterhoods and church groups.

Her awards and honors include Third Prize, Skokie Art League, 1965–1969; best in show 1966; First and Third Prize, North Shore Art League Print and Drawing Show, 1967–68; Second Prize, Woman's Club of Evanston; Second Prize Lincolnwood Art Fair, 1969, 1972; Honorable Mention, Woman's Club of Evanston, 1970; First Prize, Woman's Club, 1971; Honorable Mention, Deerpath Art Show, 1972; Third and Second Prize, Annual American Jewish Art Club, 1973, 1974; North Shore Art League Print and Drawing Show, 1974; Honorable Mention Annual American Jewish Art Club, 1975.

She is member of the Chicago Society of Artists, North Shore Art League, Evanston Art League, Deerpath Art League, Skokie Art Guild, Art Institute of Chicago, and American Jewish Art Club.

EMMA FERRY (Painter, Sculptor) was born in St. Louis, Missouri, in September, 1923. She studied at the Art Institute of Chicago and with Constantine Pougialis, Lucile Leighton, David Packard and Robert Hurdlebrink. Her favorite media are oil and sculpture.

Her work has been represented by Distelheim Galleries, Chicago; Art Wagon, Scottsdale, Arizona, and the Art Institute Sales and Rental Gallery of Chicago.

She has exhibited her paintings and sculptures in juried exhibitions at Ball State Teachers College Gallery, Muncie, Indiana; Illinois State Fair, Springfield, Illinois; and the Chicago and Vicinity Show at the Art Institute of Chicago; also at the University Club of Chicago, Monroe Art Gallery, Federal Court Building, Continental Can Company, Chicago; Old Town Art Center, Old Town Art Fair and many others.

Her works are included in private collections of William Martin, Nashville, Tennessee; Mrs. Maurice Perlstein, La Jolla, California; Mrs. M. Colby, La Jolla, California; Mrs. Harry T. Lewis, Littleton, Colorado; Mr. & Mrs. Edward Parmacek, Atherton, California; Roberta Gerry, New York City, New York, and a number of others.

LILLIAN DESOW-FISHBEIN (Painter, Graphic Artist) was born in Detroit, Michigan, on February 1, 1921. She studied at Cranbrook Academy of Art, Bloomfield Hills, Michigan, and Wayne University, 1941. Her favorite media are oil, ink, intaglio, lithography and drawing.

Her works have been included in juried exhibitions in the Detroit Institute of Arts; European Traveling Exhibition (sponsored by U.S.I.S. and the Art Institute of Chicago, 1957, 1958, 1959); Art Institute of Chicago Vicinity Shows 1950, 1957; Rental and Sales Gallery of the Art Institute of Chicago since 1955; Rental Gallery May Festival, 1956; San Francisco Museum of Art, 1957 Print Show; Butler Institute of American Art, Youngstown, Ohio, 1957; Library of Congress, Washington, D. C., 1958; Charles Feingarten Galleries, 1956, 1957; Garelick's Gallery, Detroit, Michigan, one-woman show in 1957, continuous showings 1956, 1957, 1958, 1959; A.C.A. Gallery, New York, 1957, 1958; Mandel Bros. Gallery, one-woman show 1956; group shows 1956, 1957; Renaissance Society, 1955, 1956, 1957, 1958; Illinois State Fair, 1956, 1958; Hyde Park Art Center, 1956; Schwartz Gallery Exhibition, 1957; American Jewish Arts Club, 1956, 1957, 1958; Union League Exhibition, 1959.

Her work is represented by the Garelick Gallery, Detroit, Michigan, and the Art Rental and Sales Gallery of the Art Institute of Chicago.

She has taught art in her studio for more than twenty-five years.

Desow-Fishbein won awards from the Detroit Institute of Arts — Booth Purchase Award, 1939, Art Institute of Chicago, Armstrong Award for painting, 1957; and the Palmer Award for drawing in 1959; two awards at Old Orchard Art Festival; the American Jewish Arts Club, Spertus Award, 1957 and the Fried Award in 1958; S. R. Schwartz Gallery Art Competition, Roth Award, 1957; A.C.A. Gallery, New York, National Competition Show, 1957; Library of Congress, Pennell Purchase Award (Permanent Collection, 1958); North Shore Art League, Hahn Memorial Prize, 1958.

Fishbein joined the Chicago Society of Artists in 1959.

RICHARD A. FLORSHEIM (Painter, Graphic Artist) was born in Chicago, Illinois, on October 25, 1916, and studied at the University of Chicago. His preferred media are oil and lithography.

His works have been exhibited in many museums in the world, the most recent being the Rejksakademie, Amsterdam, 1968; Art Institute of Chicago, 1970; American Academy of Arts and Letters, New York, 1971; Illinois State Museum, Springfield, Illinois, 1971; National Academy of Design, New York, 1972; plus many other group and one-man exhibitions.

His works are included in public collections of the Museum of Modern Art, New York, N. Y.; Metropolitan Museum of Art, New York; Art Institute of Chicago; Library of Congress, Washington, D. C.; Musee Nationale d'Art Moderne, Paris, France, as well as others.

He was a member of the staff of the Layton School of Art, Milwaukee, 1949–1950; the Contemporary Art Workshop in Chicago, 1952–1963; artist-in-residence at the High Museum, Atlanta, Georgia, 1964. He also held positions as Assistant Director of the Arts Center Association, Chicago, 1951–1952; board member of the Illinois Arts Council, 1965–1973.

He has been written about by A. Eliot in an article "Richard Florsheim" in **Time** magazine in 1959; by N. Kent, "Color Lithographs of Richard Florsheim" in the **American Artist** magazine, 1966; by E. Barry, "The Artist is Busy" in the **Chicago Tribune Magazine**, 1970; **Richard Florsheim** by August L. Freundlich, A. S. Barnes & Co., South Brunswick and New York; Thomas Yoseloff, Ltd., London, 1976.

Florsheim has published articles in the **College Art Journal**, **Art League News**, **Motive**, **Chicago Sun-Times**, **Cape Cod Standard Times**.

Florsheim received the Chicago Newspaper Guild Award, Art Institute of Chicago, 1954; the Pennell Fund Award, Library of Congress, 1956; Silvermine Guild Artists, 1959. He is a member of the National Academy of Design; the Society of American Graphic Artists; the Audubon Society of Artists; the Provincetown Art Association (trustee and vice-president), 1962–1971; Artists Equity Association (president 1953–1954—now honorary president). Florsheim joined the Chicago Society of Artists in 1947.

FRANCES M. FOY (Painter) was born in Chicago on April 11, 1890, and studied at the Art Institute of Chicago with George Bellows. She painted in Sweden, France, Italy and Germany and exhibited her oil paintings and watercolors throughout the United States.

One-artist exhibitions of her works were held at the Art Institute of Chicago, the Romany Club, the Walden Gallery, the Chicago Woman's Aid, and the Increase Robinson Studio Gallery in Chicago.

Paintings of Frances M. Foy have been included in the following International, National and Regional Shows: A Century of Progress Exhibition of Paintings and Sculpture, Art Institute of Chicago, 1933; International Watercolor Exhibition, Art Institute of Chicago, 1934; International Exhibition of Contemporary Prints, Art Institute of Chicago, 1934; International Watercolor Exhibition, Art Institute of Chicago, 1935; Delphic Studios Exhibition, New York, 1935; New Jersey State Museum Exhibition, Trenton, New Jersey, 1936; Artists of Chicago and Vicinity Exhibitions, 1936, 1949, and others.

Her work has been written about in Chicago and New York newspapers and magazines and in the book **Art of Today**, Chicago — 1933, by J. Z. Jacobson, L. M. Stein, publisher, 1932.

Foy won the Marshall Fuller Holmes prize, the Jules F. Brower prize and the Frank G. Logan prize at the Art Institute of Chicago and the Chicago Society of Artists Gold Medal Award.

Frances M. Foy died in 1963.

MAURICE FRIEDLANDER (Painter, Graphic Artist) was born in Chicago, and studied at the Art Institute of Chicago; The Chicago Academy of Fine Arts; Summer School of Painting at Saugatuck, Michigan; and with teachers Frederick Fursman, John Norton, Todros Geller, Robert VonNeuman, Emil Armin and Alexander Archipenko. He worked in oils, watercolors, engraving and silk screen.

He started his art career as an apprentice in the art department of his uncle's engraving company. Subsequently he worked in art departments of engraving houses and studios.

He exhibited at the Art Institute of Chicago, the Pennsylvania Academy of Fine Arts, the Riverside Gallery in New York, and the State Museum in Springfield, Illinois. He received awards from the College of Jewish Studies in 1948, and the Mussart Club of Chicago.

Friedlander served on the faculty of the Institute of Design of the Illinois Institute of Technology for a number of years.

He was a member of the Chicago Society of Artists, and the American Jewish Art Club, and elected president of both organizations. He died in 1971 while serving as president of the Chicago Society of Artists.

CHARLOTTE FRIEDMAN (Painter, Graphic Artist) was born in Chicago, Illinois, on October 2, 1918, and studied at the University of Chicago, Art Institute of Chicago and Barat College. She also worked with Lillian Fishbein, Kwok Lau, Dennis McWilliams, Hedi Bok, Thurman Nicholson and Tony Giliberto. Her present interests are printmaking-etching, embossment, collograph, dry point, lithography, monoprinting, serigraphy, and oil and acrylics in painting.

She has held one-woman exhibitions at The South Shore View Hotel, 1967; Mart Inn, 1969; Devonshire Library Learning Center, 1970; Argonne National Laboratory, 1970; Ferry Hall, Lake Forest, 1970; Bank of Highland Park, 1971; and Briarwood Country Club, Highland Park, 1971.

Other exhibitions in which her paintings and prints were included are The Northshore Art League Gallery, 1969–1971; Suburban Fine Arts Center, 1970, 1971; Art Institute Rental and Sales Gallery, 1969, 1970, 1971 through 1975; Anshe-Emet, 1973; Old Orchard Festival and Old Orchard Bank, 1971; Northwestern University Library, 1972; Beth-El, 1972; University Club, 1972, 1973; District #68 School, Skokie, 1972; Covenant Club, 1969, 1972; Barat College, 1972, 1973; University Club of Chicago, 1973; Oakbrook Festival, Sheraton Hotel, 1972, 1973; Art for Israel Exhibition, 1974; B'Nai Emunah Exhibition, Skokie, 1973 and many others. Her work is also included in the public collection of Caesarea Gallery in Israel.

She has taught printmaking and painting at the Suburban Fine Arts Center, Lincolnwood Art Workshop and currently at her studio.

Galleries representing her works include: Larew, Evanston, Countryside Gallery; Arlington Heights, International Gallery, Orlando; Surf & Surrey, Chicago; Art Institute Rental. and Sales Gallery.

Friedman is the recipient of the following awards: The Illinois State P.T.A.

Convention, First prize for painting, 1967; Lincolnwood Spring Festival, First prize for mixed media, 1970; Lincolnwood purchase prize award for graphics, 1971; Skokie Art Fair, Second prize for graphics, 1969; Great Midwest Fair, Third prize for graphics, North Shore Art League, Second prize for graphics, 1970; and several Honorable Mentions in local shows.

RICHARD FROOMAN (Painter) was born in Chicago, Illinois, on September 1, 1930, and graduated from the Art Institute of Chicago in 1952 (B.F.A.). He was awarded the Anna Louise Raymond Traveling Fellowship in 1953. He traveled, studied and painted in Europe, Mexico, New Zealand and Japan. From 1953 to 1955 he served in the Army Corps of Engineers as Corporal in Special Service.

One-man shows of his works were held at the Oehlschlager Galleries, Chicago, 1961, and at the Gilman Galleries in 1964, 1968, 1969; Illinois Teachers College, 1966; Washington Gallery of Art, Washington, D. C., 1970; the Chicago Public Library, 1972; Honolulu Academy of Art, Artists of Hawaii, 1972, 1973, 1974.

Juried exhibitions in which his works were included are the Art Institute of Chicago, 1952 (Seven Young Artists); Art Institute of Chicago, 1960, 1962, 1965; Arts Festival — Silvermine Guild, New Canaan, Connecticut; Boston Arts Festival, American Drawing, 1959; Chicago Society of Artists, 1960; Detroit Insitute of Art, American Oil Painting, 1959; Illinois State Fair Exhibitions, 1956, 1958, 1960; Illinois State Museum, North Mississippi Valley Exhibition, 1959, 1961, 1964; National Academy of Design, New York, 1962; Pennsylvania Academy of Art, American Oil Painting, 1959, 1961; Union League Club of Chicago, 1959; Butler Institute of American Art, American Oil Painting, 1959; Brotherhood Week Drawing Exhibition, 1960; DesMoines Art Center, 1967; Honolulu Academy of Art, National Print Exhibition, 1973; Hawaii Painters and Sculptors League, 1973, 1974, 1975; Honolulu Printmakers, 1973, 1974; Fine Arts Gallery of San Diego, California Hawaii Biennial, 1976.

He has done portrait commissions of George Sax, Board Chairman, Exchange National Bank; Edgar Heyman, President, Exchange National Bank; Mark Brown, former President, Harris Trust and Savings Bank; Webster Corlett, Board Chairman, Standard Screw Company; Edward Sparling, Founder and President, Roosevelt University; Philip Thorek, Surgeon; DeBeers Diamonds; Playboy Jazz Poll Winners; Margaret McDowell, Miss Chicago; and Reverend Miyama, Harris United Methodist Church. He was also commissioned to do the cover for the Hawaiian Telephone Directory, 1975.

Frooman's works are included in public collections of the Harris Trust and Savings Bank; Playboy; the Upjohn Company; Roosevelt University; DeBeers Diamond Collection; Union League Club of Chicago; Hawaii State Foundation on Culture and the Arts; Honolulu Advertiser and in numerous private collections.

He has also contributed editorial art to the following publications: **Playboy**, **Show Business Illustrated**, **Lions International Magazine**, **Elks Magazine**, **University of Chicago Magazine** and **Kiwanis Magazine**.

In addition to the above, he has done advertising illustrations for N. W. Ayer, Young & Rubican, Leo Burnett, Ruthrauff and Ryan, and advertising illustrations for Admiral TV; Armour Meats; DeBeers Diamonds; Western Auto Supply; Northwest Orient Airlines; Santa Fe Railroad; Hamilton Watches; Zenith; Motorola; Abbott Laboratories and others.

His work is to be included in a traveling exhibition of Hawaii Artists sponsored by the U. S. State Department. The exhibition will be shown in Bucharest, Romania.

He taught art at the Y.M.C.A.; the Bernard Horwich Center in Chicago; Lake Michigan College, Benton Harbor, Michigan, 1965–1968; University of Hawaii and University of Hawaii College of Continuing Education, 1972, 1973, 1975; and Honolulu Academy of Art, 1972, 1973. He has lectured in the Evanston Art Center, Evanston, Illinois; the Chicago Public Library; and for Windward Artists Guild in Hawaii, 1976.

Frooman received the following awards: the National Academy of Design, Julius Hallgarten Prize, 1962; Art Institute of Chicago, Chicago and Vicinity Show Awards, 1960, 1961, 1962; Chicago Society of Artists Award, 1960; Brotherhood Week Drawing Exhibition Award, 1960; Chicago Sun-Times Blossom Time Award; Union League Club of Chicago Award, 1959.

Frooman received illustration awards from Artists Guild of Chicago; Art Directors Club of Chicago; Art Directors Club of Philadelphia; C/A, Commercial Art Annual, New York; and work reproduced in various other annual award publications.

He appeared on **Jim Conway Show**, WGN-TV, Chicago and on Harry Bouras **Critic's Choice**, WFMT, Chicago.

Since 1972 Richard Frooman has been residing in Hawaii.

ROWENA FRY (Painter, Graphic Artist) was born in Athens, Alabama, and studied at the Watkins Institute in Nashville, Tennessee, the Art Institute of Chicago, and the Hubert Ropp School of Art in Chicago. Her favorite media are oil, watercolor, serigraphy, linoblock printing and caligraphy.

She has held two one-woman exhibitions at the Art Institute of Chicago in 1944 and 1972; Chicago Woman's Aid, and at the University Club of Chicago, twice.

She participated in group and juried exhibitions at the American National and International watercolor shows, both at the Art Institute of Chicago; in the Art Institute Chicago and Vicinity Shows, Art Institute of Chicago and many other exhibitions.

She has executed paintings and murals in the city of Lake Forest; Abbott Laboratories; Oscar Meyer Company (bought for them by Bert Meyer); and murals for the American Mareitta Paint Company.

One of her prints was loaned to the State Department for our embassy in Oslo, Norway. She also participated in the art section of Channel 11 auction for the past few years. Recently three of Rowena Fry's serigraphs were purchased for the Standard Oil collection.

Her work is currently represented by the Art Rental and Sales Gallery. Her paintings and serigraphs are included in private collections of Joseph Ryerson, Graham Aldis, Roy Porters, Gordon Bent, Mrs. Frank C. McAuliffe family, Miss Adele Morel, Louise and Maurice Yochim, and many others in the United States and Europe.

For many years she taught painting and serigraphy in her studio. From 1938 to 1939 she served in the Painting Division of the W.P.A., and from 1941–1946 during World War II she worked in the Arts and Skills Program in the Great Lakes Naval Hospital.

Fry is a professional member of the Arts Club of Chicago, Chicago Society of Artists, and the Renaissance Society of the University of Chicago.

She has been awarded three First, four Second and two Special awards in block calendars published by the Chicago Society of Artists; Purchase Awards in Union League Exhibitions, 1971; Second Prize for watercolor, Chicago Society of Artists Exhibition, 1970.

LEON GARLAND (Painter) was born in Borbruisk, Russia, and arrived in the U. S. in 1913. He studied at the Art Institute of Chicago and attended classes at Hull House. There he met Sadie Ellis whom he married in 1927. Together they traveled and painted in Germany, Switzerland, Lithuania, Italy and studied at the Andre Lothe School in Paris.

He was extremely interested in textile designing, in batik, and in metal crafts, all of which he taught at the Hull House. Lithography and stained glass were processes in which he also excelled.

Early struggles and experiences of oppression in Russia left him with a passion to see a better world, and he became ardently devoted to the cause of dignity of man. His paintings, rendered in subdued and subtle color, sensitive and serene, reflected memories of his experiences and subject-matter reminiscent of his youth, his family and his people in villages in Russia, themes expressed in a poetic manner.

His paintings were included in the Art Institute of Chicago and Vicinity exhibitions and in three of its circuit shows: at the M. H. De Young Memorial Museum, San Francisco, California; the Museum of Modern Art, New York; New York World's Fair; Carnegie Institute, Pittsburgh, and in two one-man shows at the Increase Robinson Gallery in Chicago and the Chicago Woman's Aid. Forty of his paintings are in public buildings throughout the nation, placed through the Federal Art Project.

Garland is represented in the permanent collections of the Jewish Museum of New York, the Museum of Tel Aviv, Bezalel in Jerusalem, Haifa and Ain Harod in Israel.

In 1942 the Art Institute of Chicago paid him the posthumous honor of opening and dedicating its "Chicago Room" with a one-man show of his paintings. In 1942 the San Francisco Museum of Art held a memorial exhibit; in 1948 the American Jewish Art Club held a retrospective show of his works; in 1951 the Witte Memorial Museum of San Antonio as well as the William Rockhill Nelson Gallery of Art in Kansas City, Missouri, honored him with memorial exhibits.

Garland died in 1941.

MARY GEHR (Painter, Printmaker) was born in Chicago, Illinois, and studied at Smith College, Art Institute of Chicago with Paul Wieghart, Institute of Design of Illinois Institute of Technology with Misch Kohn. She prefers working in intaglio, oils and acrylics.

Her paintings and prints are included in public collections at the Art Institute of Chicago; Philadelphia Museum, Pa.; Library of Congress, Washington, D. C.; Nelson Rockefeller Collection and the Free Library of Philadelphia.

In 1967 she was commissioned by the International Graphic Arts Society to produce "Golden Santorini," intaglio-edition of 210 etchings printed by Leterio Calapai.

Her paintings and prints were included in the Chicago and Vicinity Exhibition and the Society of Contemporary American Art at the Art Institute of Chicago; Brooklyn Museum National Print Exhibition; Boston Printmakers, Mass., and in Print Club, Philadelphia, Pa., Exhibition.

Her works are represented by the Jacques Baruch Gallery in Chicago.

Her work was written about in an article by John Fink entitled "The Greece of Mary Gehr," **Chicago Tribune Magazine**, 1967; by T. J. Carbol, Editor, "The Printmaker in Illinois," Illinois Art Education Association, 1971–1972; plus many articles in local papers.

She has illustrated, designed and edited **Exploring the World of Archaeology**, 1966 and **Exploring the World of Pottery**, 1967.

Gehr received the Print Fair Award, Philadelphia; First Purchase Award, Artist Guild of Chicago; Award for Graphics at Old Orchard Festival in Chicago.

She is a member of the Arts Club of Chicago; Print Club of Philadelphia; Alumnae of Art Institute of Chicago; Society of Typographic Arts; Archaeological Institute of America (Chicago Branch), and was a member of the Chicago Society of Artists from 1954–1962, contributing block-prints to its annual calendar publications.

ETHEL GELICK (Graphic Artist) was born in Chicago, Illinois, on December 4, 1916. She studied at the Art Institute of Chicago, Evanston Art Center, North Shore Art League, and Ox–Bow School of Painting in Michigan. She works in graphics, oils and sculpture.

One-woman exhibitions of her works were held in the Chicago Public Library (Loop), 1971; First Federal Gallery, 1971; Evanston Public Library; Evanston Community Center; Michelini's Gallery; Palmer House Gallery; Northtown Public Library and other libraries.

Group shows include The Tennessee National, 1961; Illinois State Museum, North Mississippi Valley Show, 1964, 1969; Small Painting National, Purdue, 1964; Oklahoma Print and Drawing Show, 1964; East Room of Art Institute Drawing Show; Chicago Society of Artists show at Harper Gallery, 1966; Pan American Art Festival at Roosevelt College, Chicago, 1961; Peoria Collects Exhibition, 1965; Peoria Area Sculpture at Lakeview Museum, 1966; Union League, 1972; American Jewish Arts Club, 1967, 1973; Chicago Printmakers at Chicago Public Library (Loop), New Horizon Show, 1959, 1960, 1970, 1974; Wustum Museum, Racine, Wisconsin Religious Show, 1970; North Shore Print and Drawing Show, 1970, 1971, 1973; Oklahoma Print and Drawing Show, 1964; Marina City Tower Gallery, 1973; Old Town Triangle Center Gallery, 1974; Religious Show at Judson College, Elgin, Illinois, 1974; Sun-Times Area Show Magnificent Mile Competition, 1961; Evanston Art Center Three Woman Show; and New Trier Exhibits.

Invitational shows include Ravinia Art Festival, Highland Park, 1967; Religious show, J.C.C.; and Milwaukee and Baptist Graduate Student Center, Chicago, 1967; Marymount Christmas Show, 1975; J.C.C., Milwaukee Exodus Show, 1975.

Her work is represented in collections and galleries of Library of Congress, Washington, D. C.; Marymont College, Tarrytown, New York; Borg Warner Collection; Municipal Building Collection, Springfield, Illinois, painting and sculpture; Northern Illinois University Collection; Art Rental and Sales Gallery of Art Institute of Chicago; Deerpath Gallery, Lake Forest; Park Forest Gallery, Park Forest; Knoxville Gallery, Peoria; Burpie Art Museum, Rockford, Illinois; Wustum Museum Art Rental and Sales, Racine, Wisconsin; and Neville Sargent Gallery in Evanston.

Gelick's works were also included in the North Shore Art League's Print and

Drawing Show, Woman's Show and Photo Image Show in 1976, and in the Illinois Institute of Technology Exhibition in 1977.

Awards for painting, graphics and sculpture include Old Orchard, First Prize, 1961; Milwaukee Art Festival, First Prize for sculpture, 1965; Golf Mill Festival, First Prize for graphics, 1965; Evanston Art Center, First Prize for painting, 1965; Susan Fried Award, Hillel, 1968; Park Forest Library, Purchase Award, 1963, 1964; A. G. Beth Israel, First Prize, 1967; Northbrook Festival Purchase Award, 1971; Riverwoods Festival, Purchase Award, 1971; Women's Winnetka Club Art Festival, First Prize, 1968; North Shore Art League, First Prize, 1972; Lincoln Village Art Festival, First Prize, 1964; Second Prize, 1975; Countryside Gallery Art Festival, 1967; All Media Illinois Festival of Arts, McCormick Place, award; Deerpath Print and Drawing Show, Second Prize, 1968, 1969, 1974; Waukegan Art Festival, First Prize for graphics, 1967; Second Prize, 1968; New Horizons Show award for graphics, 1974; Kankakee Art Festival, First Prize for graphics, 1974; North Shore Art League, Third Prize in graphics, 1974; Artists Guild Miniature, Purchase Award, 1974; Deerpath Show of Graphics, First Prize, 1974.

TODROS GELLER (Painter, Graphic Artist) was born in Vinnitza, Ukraine, and migrated to Montreal, Canada, in 1906 where he attended art school. He married in 1913 and moved to Chicago. For five years he studied at the Art Institute of Chicago.

Since 1925 Geller participated in major national and local exhibitions. He held five one-man shows in the U. S. and Canada.

Group exhibitions in which his paintings, wood cuts and lithographs were included were the Metropolitan Museum, New York; Art Institute of Chicago; Pennsylvania Academy of Fine Arts; San Francisco Museum of Art; Los Angeles Museum; Carnegie Institute, Pittsburgh; National Academy, New York; Whitney Museum, New York, and many others.

His works are represented in permanent collections at the Art Institute of Chicago; Library of Congress, Washington, D. C.; Princeton University, New Jersey; Osage Museum, Oklahoma; New York Public Library; Wichita Art Museum; Board of Jewish Education, Chicago.

Several books of his wood engravings and wood cuts have been published, and he has illustrated about forty other publications. Many synagogues and temples throughout the nation are enhanced by stained glass windows that he designed. He was a leading authority on Jewish Art.

For many years he served as a member of the Supervisory Staff of the Board of Jewish Education in Chicago.

Geller taught art at the Jewish People's Institute in Chicago for a number of years. Later he began to conduct classes in his studio. Many well known Chicago artists studied drawing and painting with Todros Geller.

For three consecutive years Todros Geller received awards for his woodcuts and wood engravings at the Annual Library of Congress National Print Exhibitions.

Geller was a member of the Artists Equity, the Around the Palette, the Chicago Society of Artists, and the American Jewish Art Club, serving as president for the latter two organizations for a number of years.

Geller died in 1949.

PAULA GERARD (Graphic Artist) was born in Brighton, England. She received her basic training in private studios in Europe. She attended the University of Florence and the Institut Francais, a branch of the University de Grenoble in Florence; completed art studies as a special student at the School of the Art Institute of Chicago, where she studied fresco with Melvin Pollock and advanced figure painting with Boris Anisfeld.

One-woman exhibitions of her work were held in the Department of Prints and Drawings, the Art Institute of Chicago; Earlham College, Richmond, Indiana; Layton Art Gallery, Milwaukee, Wisconsin; Museum of Fine Arts, Montgomery, Alabama, 1971; Gallery 2111, Milwaukee, Wisconsin, 1972; Ripon College, Ripon, Wisconsin, 1972; Covenant Club of Chicago, 1973; Auburn University, Alabama, 1975, and others.

Her work was included in juried shows at the Art Institute, 6th International of Lithography and Wood Engraving; Chicago and Vicinity, 1946, 1949, 1955 and 1977; 59th Annual American Exhibition of Watercolors and Drawings, 1948; 1st Biennial of Prints, Drawings and Watercolor, 1961; also in the Audubon Society, N. Y.; National Academy of Design, N. Y.; Philadelphia Art Alliance; American Color Print Society, Philadelphia; San Francisco Art Association; Denver Art Museum, 56th Annual; Wichita Art Association, Wichita, Kansas; Sarasota Art Association, 10th Annual; Annual Exhibition of Watercolors, Prints and Drawings, Washington Watercolor Association, Smithsonian Institute, Washington, D. C., 1963; Images on Paper "70," Jackson, Mississippi; National Print and Drawing Exhibition, Oklahoma Art Center, Oklahoma City, Oklahoma, 1972.

Her invitational shows include North Mississippi Valley Art at the State Museum in Springfield, Illinois, 1948, 1951, 1961; 2nd Annual Chicago Arts Festival at McCormick Place, 1963; Mount Mary College in Milwaukee, 1974; "Art on Paper" exhibition at the Jacques Baruch Gallery, 1974; Faculty Exhibits of Layton School of Art and School of the Art Institute of Chicago. She participated in membership shows of the Renaissance Society at the University of Chicago, Chicago Society of Artists, Artists Equity, the Arts Club of Chicago, represented in the Art Rental and Sales Gallery of the Art Institute of Chicago.

She did botanical illustrations for the Field Museum, Chicago; also, illustrations for **Is Contemporary Painting More Temporary Than You Think?** by Louis Pomerantz; jacket and illustrations for **The Great Speckled Bird** by P. H. Lowrie; she served on juries for Annual Local Artists Exhibition, Fort Wayne, 1963, 1966; judged Dixie Annual of Prints, Drawings, Watercolors, Montgomery, Alabama, 1970.

Her work is included in the public collections of The Library of Congress; Smart Gallery; University of Chicago; Museum of Evansville, Indiana; Earlham College, Richmond, Indiana; George F. Harding Museum, Chicago; Ringling Museum, Sarasota, Florida; Standard Oil of Chicago, as well as many private collections.

She was head of Art Department, North Central College, Naperville, Illinois, 1944–1945; Instructor at Layton School of Art, Milwaukee, Wisconsin, 1945–1962; Visiting Instructor, Midway Studios, University of Chicago, 1958–1965; Art Institute of Chicago (figure drawing, figure-structure-anatomy), 1962–1975, Professor Emeritus.

She is listed in **Who's Who in American Art**, **Who's Who in the Midwest**; **Who's Who in American Women**; and **Dictionary of International Biography, 1974**.

Gerard is a life member of the Alumni Association of the Art Institute of Chicago; Board Member, Renaissance Society, University of Chicago, 1964–1975; now Honorary Member; Director, Chicago Chapter Artists Equity, 1972–1977; Director, Artists League of the Midwest, 1944–1977; member of Chicago Artists Coalition.

Currently she maintains her studio in her home in Chicago where she lives with her husband, pianist and teacher Herbert Renison.

THOMAS GIULIANO (Painter) studied at the Art Institute of Chicago for five years and received his degree in 1959. The same year he was awarded the Edward L. Ryerson Foreign Traveling Fellowship in the amount of $2,500.00. He works almost exclusively in oils. His graphics have included both lithography and etching.

He has exhibited paintings and graphics in many shows throughout the country including Chicago and Vicinity, Library of Congress, Princeton University and Allentown (Pennsylvania) Museum.

CORRIE-LOU LIVINGSTON GLASS (Painter) was born in Chicago on April 19, 1939. She graduated with honors from the Institute of Design, Illinois Institute of Technology (B. S.) and also attended the School of the Art Institute of Chicago. She has traveled to Mexico, Central America, Europe, North Africa and in the Caribbean.

A one-woman exhibition of her works was held at the Cordon Club. She participated in juried shows at South Shore Commission, Little Gallery; University of Chicago; FOTA Exhibit; Macomb College; Midwest Drawing Exhibition, Artists Guild of Chicago; Drawing, Watercolor and Fine Art Exhibit, Libertyville Arts Club; Chicago Society of Artists Gallery; Old Town Triangle Center; Monroe Gallery; Covenant Club; University Club and Rosary College.

She is represented by the Rental and Sales Gallery of the Art Institute of Chicago.

For ten years she has worked in Advertising Art for Visual Art Studios in Chicago.

She was recipient of awards for watercolors, drawings, and acrylics at Artist Guild Exhibitions, and for lino-cuts from the Chicago Society of Artists.

BACIA GORDON (Painter) was born in Vilna, Russia, March 16, 1904, and studied at the Art Institute of Chicago, the Institute of Design, and for a number of years with Todros Geller. She has traveled extensively and painted throughout the United States, Mexico, and in Europe, Spain Italy and Greece. Since 1955 she has made yearly trips to Israel where she painted the ancient and the ultra-modern, the aged and the young, and the in-gathered. Her favorite media are oils, watercolor, acrylics and lithography.

She held numerous one-woman exhibitions. A partial list includes the Chicago Public Library (Loop); YWCA; University of Michigan, Ann Arbor; Northwestern University; University of Chicago; Circle Campus, University of Illinois; IIT; Maurice Sternberg Gallery; Spertus Museum Gallery; Spertus College of Judaica; Sheldon Swope Art Gallery, Terre Haute, Indiana; Youngstown, Ohio; and three one-woman exhibitions in Tel-Aviv, Ashkelon, and Kiryat Gat, Israel.

She participated in juried shows of The Union League Club; the Art Institute of Chicago; Spertus Museum; Herzl Institute in New York City; Sternberg Gallery; St. Paul, Minnesota; Des Moines, Iowa and San Francisco, California.

Her work is represented by the Harper Gallery, Maurice Sternberg Gallery, Siegel Gallery, and the Art Rental and Sales Gallery of the Art Institute of Chicago. She is included in private collections of Ida and Richard Conti of Chicago, Rabbi Raskes of St. Paul, Rabbi and Mrs. Bonder and Sara Feder Keyfitz of Jerusalem and others.

She held seminars and taught art classes at the Circle Pines Center for thirty years; the YMCA, senior classes for seventeen years; and the Triangle Art Center for several years.

Gordon was the recipient of the All Illinois Award and the Triangle Art Center Award for painting.

Gordon died in 1977.

DIANA GORDON (Painter) was born in New York City on April 29, 1922. From 1940–1942 she attended the Kings Hospital School of Nursing, Brooklyn, New York, and completed psychiatric affiliations at Bellevue Psychiatric Hospital, New York. In 1968 she was awarded the B.F.A. degree in Design and Crafts at the Art Institute of Chicago, and in 1970 an M. S. degree in Visual Design, Printmaking, at the Illinois Institute of Technology, the Institute of Design. She studied further at the University of Texas in El Paso and Rosary College in River Forest, Illinois.

She held five one-woman exhibitions at Concordia College, 1964; Hillel Chapel, Northwestern Campus, 1964; St. Xavier College, Chicago, 1965; Aquinas Institute of Philosophy, River Forest, Illinois, 1967; Rosary College, River Forest, Illinois, 1963–1965; Washington Cathedral, Mount Saint Alban, Washington, D. C., 1968; Designer Craftsmen of Illinois, Bienniel, Illinois, 1968.

She participated in group shows at Exhibition Momentum, 1957; McCormick Place "Art in Government," Chicago, 1962; Perspective, 1963; University of Chicago Festival of the Arts, Baptist Graduate Center, 1963, 1966, 1973; Artists Equity, "Art in Government," Springfield, Illinois, 1963; North Central College, Naperville, Illinois, 1963; Alumni, Art Institute of Chicago, National Design Center, Marina City, Chicago, 1964; Perspective; Temple Beth Emet, Evanston, Illinois, 1964; "Artist and the Atom," in conjunction with Hiroshima Show from Seattle World's Fair, 1964; New Horizons Show; North Shore Art League, 1965–1973; Maryknoll Seminary, New York, 1965; Third Annual, Northern Illinois University, 1965; Fine Art Faculty Gallery, Chicago, 1965, 1966; Art Institute Rental and Sales Gallery, 1966, 1973, 1974, 1975; Fine Arts Faculty Gallery, Chicago, 1965, 1966; Garrett Theological Seminary, Evanston, 1968; American Baptist Assembly, Green Lake, Wisconsin; Washington Cathedral, Mt. Saint Alban, Washington, D.C.; Designer-Craftsman of Illinois, Biennial, Illinois State Museum; Rosary College, River Forest, Illinois, 1964; University of Texas at El Paso, 1970; the Art Institute of Chicago Textile Galleries, "Forms in Fibers," 1970; Laguna Beach Art Association Invitational Crafts, 1971; Northern Baptist Theological Seminary, Oak Brook, Illinois, 1973; Mayer Kaplan Jewish Community Center, Skokie, Illinois, 1973; Chicago Society of Artists, University Club of Chicago, 1973; Kriegs Gallery, Lombard, Illinois, 1973.

Her work is included in public collections of A. E. Stevenson Elementary School, 1963; Aquinas Institute of Philosophy, River Forest, 1964; Rosary College; Concordia Teachers College, River

Forest, 1967.

From 1973–1975 she taught Painting and Design at the College of DuPage, Glen Ellyn, Illinois; Lecturer, creativity-studio and Supervisor of Art Student-Teachers, University of Illinois, Chicago Circle Campus, Chicago; 1971–1973, Supervisor of Adjunctive Therapy, Riveredge Hospital, Forest Park, Illinois; 1969–1970, Instructor, Drawing and Design, University of Texas, El Paso, Texas; 1963–1965, Instructor, Drawing and Painting, Rosary College, River Forest, Illinois. She has also taught mentally disturbed high school patients and the under-priviledged.

She received an Award of Merit in 1968 from the Christian Art Association for a woven wall-hanging; a Citation of Appreciation for Liturgical Banners from the Chapel of Aquinas, 1968; a print-making award, A.J.A.C., 1973.

SAMUEL GREENBURG (Painter, Graphic Artist) was born in the Ukraine, Russia, on June 23, 1905. He studied at the Academie Andre Lhote in Paris, the Bezalel Art School in Jerusalem, at the University of Chicago (B. A. & M. A.), and at the Art Institute of Chicago.

Greenburg has traveled extensively in Europe, the Mediterranean, Mexico, Guatemala, Africa, the Orient, and the United States. He lived in Israel and Egypt for 2½ years, working in Cairo as a poster artist, cartoonist, and caricaturist for a theatrical magazine.

One-man exhibitions of his work were held in the Creative Gallery in New York in 1950 and 1951; in the Room of Chicago Art, Art Institute of Chicago; the Todros Geller Art Gallery at the College of Jewish Studies; Northeastern Illinois University in 1963; Hillel Foundation at Northwestern University in 1961 and 1966; and a retrospective exhibit at the Covenant Club Gallery in 1975.

His works were included in juried group exhibitions at Library of Congress Print Shows; Pennsylvania Academy; Philadelphia Print Club; International Watercolor Show and many Chicago and Vicinity shows at the Art Institute of Chicago; also in the New York 1939 Worlds Fair; Illinois State Museum in Springfield; Art Museums of Brooklyn, Cleveland, Birmingham, San Francisco and Seattle; National Gallery and Corcoran Gallery, Washington, D. C., Carnegie Institute, Pittsburgh; and Traveling Exhibits of American Federation of Arts.

Public collections in which his paintings, prints and drawings are represented include the Library of Congress, Washington, D. C.; Bezalel Museum, Jerusalem; Tel-Aviv Art Museum; Ein Harod Museum and Fighters of the Ghetto Memorial Museum in the Galilee, Israel; College of Jewish Studies, Chicago; California College of Arts and Crafts in Oakland, and the Art Institute of Chicago.

During 1932 and 1933 (with A. R. Katz), Samuel Greenburg owned and operated the Little Gallery in the Auditorium Tower where many Chicago artists, now well established, held their first one-man exhibitions.

He has written the book **Making Linoleum Cuts** and co-authored **Arts and Crafts in the Jewish Schools.** His articles have appeared in **Life** Magazine and **New York Times.**

From 1932–1962 he taught art in the Chicago Public High Schools. From 1962–1970 he served as a Supervisor of Art for the Chicago Board of Education. For many years he taught private adult classes in his studio, and more recently, at the Commonwealth Art Center.

His paintings, posters and prints have won many awards including those at the Illinois State Fair, Second Prize for Oil Painting, 1956; First and Second Prize Prints at the Chicago Society of Artists in 1960 and 1961, and another First Prize print in 1973; Union League Club Purchase Prize in 1972; and awards in 1954, 1956, 1961, 1968, 1970 at the American Jewish Art Club Annuals.

Greenburg was included in **Who's Who in American Art, 1936–1962,** in **Who's Who in America 1950 to 1967** and is currently in **Who's Who in World Jewry** and **Who's Who in the Midwest.**

From 1937 to date, he has contributed blockprints to the Chicago Society of Artists annual calendars.

EMILE JACQUES GRUMIEAUX (Painter) was born in Gosslies, Hainaut, Belgium, on May 17, 1897. He studied art in various European and American cities. He has painted in Belgium, France, England and in the United States.

One-man shows of his works were held at the Chicago Woman's Aid.

He has exhibited at the Art Institute of Chicago, the Toronto Art Museum, the Illinois Academy of Fine Art, the University of Michigan, the Kansas City

Museum and the Detroit Museum.

His work is represented in the Springfield, Illinois, Museum.

He has been written about in Chicago publications by R. A. Lennon, Irwin St. John Tucker, Tom Vickerman and J. Z. Jacobson.

He received the Chicago Society of Artists Gold Medal and the Eamer MacVeagh Purchase Prize (in the Illinois Academy).

He was a member of the Chicago Society of Artists, the Chicago No-Jury Society of Artists, the Illinois Academy of Fine Art and 10 Artists, (Chicago). Grumieaux was president of the Chicago Society of Artists in 1928.

GARNET GULLBORG (Painter) was born in Iowa and studied in Public Adult Classes, Los Angeles, California; Chappell House Fine Arts, Denver, Colorado; Art Institute of Chicago with Andrene Kauffman, LeRoy Nieman and Isabel McKinnon, among others. She works primarily in laminated wood and acrylics creating two and three-dimensional constructions.

Her work is represented in collections at I.O.O.F. Orphan Home, Mason City, Iowa; Lake Shore National Bank, Chicago; Peat, Marwick, Mitchell & Company, C.P.A., Chicago; Newman, Williams, Anderson & Olson, Chicago; Standard Oil of Indiana; Mr. & Mrs. Irving Sten Jr., Chicago.

Exhibitions include Invitational, opening of First National Bank of Chicago Plaza, 1973; North Shore Art League "New Horizons," 1971, 1973, 1975; Union League Civic and Art Foundation, Chicago "3-D 1975," Chicago and Vicinity Exhibit, Art Institute of Chicago, 1973; 'Ten Year' Invitational Art Rental and Sales Gallery of Art Institute of Chicago, 1975; plus many other group and one-woman exhibitions.

Gallery representation includes Art Rental and Sales Gallery, Art Institute of Chicago; N.S.L.A. Corporate Art Rental Service, Winnetka, Illinois.

Awards received are First Prize, West Suburban Art League, 1960; Alumni Association of the Art Institute of Chicago, 1961 and 1965; Second Prize, Technical Center of Continental Can Company, 1972; Purchase Award, Standard Oil of Indiana, 1975.

Gullborg is a member of Alumni Association of the School of the Art Institute of Chicago; North Shore Art League; Chicago Society of Artists, Inc.; Chicago New Art Association; DuPage Textile Arts Guild; Life Member of Art Institute of Chicago; Chicago's Museum of Contemporary Art and National Standards Council of American Embroiderers.

LILLIAN HALL (Painter) was born in Waukegan, Illinois, on May 15, 1905 and studied at the Illinois Institute of Technology, Institute of Design (B. S.), DePaul University (graduate work), the Metropolitan Art School, New York, and Glouchester, Massachusetts.

During the W.P.A. days she painted murals for various public and government institutions. For two years, Lillian Hall served as assistant to Beatrice Levy who directed a W.P.A. Gallery in which works executed under the auspices of the Project were exhibited periodically.

She taught art at the Institute of Design; life drawing at the Chicago Academy of Art; arts and crafts for the Chicago Park District, and served as director of the Weaving Center there. She also held private classes at her studio.

For many years she has skillfully served as treasurer of the Chicago Society of Artists, keeping the financial records of the organization in meticulous order and dispensing and collecting funds with personal and legal accountability. She has been one of the most loyal members of the Society dedicated to the smoothly functioning business of the organization. Since 1940 she has been a contributor to the Society's Annual Calendar, a publication consisting of original lino-cuts, designed and executed by members of the Society. Since the death of Gustaf Dalstrom, Lillian Hall, Janine Collier and Catherine Cajandig have handled the distribution of the calendar. The apparent success of this venture is no doubt due to the untiring efforts of all three members in the promotion and sales end of this annual publication.

MARION HALL (Painter) was born in Gary, Indiana, on January 13, 1914. She studied at the Academie Notre Dame de Champs, Paris; Instituto Allende, San Miguel, Mexico; Contemporary Workshop, Chicago; and with Elvie TenHoor, Chicago. Her travels include the entire United States and Canada, Mexico, Jamaica, Austria, Poland, Switzerland, Italy, France and Portugal.

One-woman shows of her work were

held at Hartford Plaza, and the Garland Building in Chicago, 3 exhibits at Town Gallery, Munster, Indiana, 10 at Gary Country Club, Gary, Indiana; Indiana University; Little Art Gallery, Raleigh, North Carolina; Arts Center, Wilson, North Carolina.

Juried exhibitions in which she participated include the Northern Indiana Art Salon, Hammond, Indiana; Dunes Art Foundation; Michiana Shores, Indiana; Southern Shores, Gary, Indiana; Michiana Regional Art Exhibit, South Bend, Indiana.

Group exhibitions in which her work has been included were held at Harper Court; Charles Quint Gallery, both in Chicago; Gary Post Tribune; Bank of Indiana; Main Library of Gary, Indiana. She has served on many juries of art exhibits and fairs.

She is represented in the Rental and Sales Gallery of the Art Institute; in numerous private collections throughout North and South America, Puerto Rico and Jamaica; and in public collections in the Griffith Library, Griffith, Indiana; Gary Country Club, Gary, Indiana; and Indiana University. Marion Hall received awards for her oil paintings, acrylics, watercolors and collages.

Her work was reproduced in **Contemporary Collage and Constructions** and **How to Create Your Own Designs,** Crown Publishers. The American Cancer Society selected one of her collages to be reproduced on a Christmas card in 1975.

HAZEL HANNELL (Painter) was born in La Grange, Illinois, and studied at Church School of Art and Art Institute of Chicago. She has traveled extensively in France, Finland, Ireland, Canada and the United States.

She is represented in private collections in Finland, England, France, Brazil, in the United States, and in the public collection of the Standard Oil Building.

Her work is represented by the Art Rental and Sales Gallery of the Art Institute of Chicago.

She received awards at exhibitions of Northern Indiana Art Salon, the Dunes Arts Foundation, Southern Shores Exhibition, and the Chesterton Women's Club exhibit. Mrs. Hannell works in watercolors primarily, but enjoys working in lino-cuts and ceramics.

She has been a member of the Chicago Society of Artists since 1940 and has been contributing lino-cuts to the Annual Chicago Society of Artists Calendar since then.

V.M.S. HANNELL (Painter, Sculptor) was born in Negaunee, Michigan, on January 22, 1896, and studied art in Abo, Finland, and in Chicago. He has painted in Finland and in France, and in this country in Florida and the East.

In the thirties he turned from painting to sculpture, working mostly in wood, and was represented in that medium by the Feingarten Galleries in Chicago and San Francisco. A number of his works are included on the Purdue University Westville Campus and in many private collections. He was a member of the Chicago No-Jury Society of Artists and 10 Artists (Chicago), and has exhibited at the Art Institute of Chicago and the No-Jury shows. A one-man show of his work was held at the Little Gallery in Chicago.

His paintings have been commented upon in Chicago newspapers and magazines and in the **Arts** of New York.

Hannell died in 1964.

MARJORIE HARTMANN (Painter) was born in Chicago on December 3, 1913, and studied at the School of the Art Institute of Chicago and at the Illinois Institute of Technology.

Her interest in drafting led her to study with Kathleen Blackshear at the Art Institute of Chicago when Blackshear taught mechanical drawing as an approach to Cubism. This stimulated Hartmann's interest in drafting, so she pursued it further at the Illinois Institute of Technology.

Teachers who were most influential in the development of her career as an artist were: Andrene Kauffman, Kathleen Blackshear, and Margaret Artingstall, all of whom were on the faculty of the Art Institute of Chicago. She works in several media—oils, watercolors, serigraphs, and lino-cuts.

Her works have been shown at the Art Institute of Chicago in the Artists and Vicinity shows; the Wichita Art Museum, Wichita, Kansas; the North Mississippi Valley Artists at the Illinois State Museum in Springfield; the University Club in Chicago; the Triangle Art Center and other exhibition galleries.

As a member of the Chicago Society of Artists, she has been contributing lino-cuts to the Chicago Society of Artists Annual Calendar since 1943 when she joined the group.

HAROLD HAYDON (Painter, Muralist) was born in Fort William, Ontario, Canada, on April 22, 1909, and studied at the University of Chicago (PhB, 1930, M. A. 1931), and at the School of the Art Institute of Chicago, 1932–1933. He has traveled in Canada, Mexico, England, France and Italy.

Haydon has held twenty-two one-man exhibitions including the following: Pickering College; Chicago Public Library; George Williams College, Chicago; Wheaton College, Wheaton, Illinois; St. John's College, Annapolis, Maryland; Richard Feigen Gallery, Chicago; One Illinois Center Gallery, Chicago; Chicago Teachers College, North; and North Shore Art League.

His works were included in juried exhibitions at the Art Institute of Chicago, 1937, 1938, 1944, 1949, 1950, 1967 and in invitational shows — the 58th Annual Exhibition of American Painting, Art Institute of Chicago, 1947; Society for Contemporary Art, Art Institute of Chicago, 1947–1949–1950; the Museum of Contemporary Art, Chicago, 1968.

His work is included in private collections of Gladys Campbell, Leonard Horwich, Robert and Jean Allard, P. T. Elsworth, Lotte Drew-Bear, Albert Dahlberg.

Haydon works in oils, mosaic, hooked wool, graphics, and stained glass. His major commissions have been a mural for Pickering College, Newmarket, Ontario, 16′ X 40′ oil, 1932–1933; Tapestry Ark Cover, Temple Beth Am, Chicago 8′ X 22′, wool, 1958; Temple Beth El, Gary, Indiana, two glass mosaic murals 8′ X 5½′, 1959–1960; ceramic tile murals, Sonia Shankman Orthogenic School, University of Chicago, 3 floors of stairhall, 1971. Also, brick mosaic mural, 3 floors of stairhall, 1966; stained glass wall 90′ long, 1966; glass enamel on steel mural, 6′ X 36′, 1977; glass mosaic mural 45′ long, St. Cletus Church, La Grange, Illinois, 1963; glass mosaic mural 10′ X 12′, Temple Beth Am, Chicago, 1968; ten stained glass aisle windows, Rockefeller Memorial Chapel, University of Chicago, 1972; Parochet (Ark Veil), Niles Township Jewish Congregation, Skokie, Illinois, 1976.

Haydon has been the art critic for the **Chicago Sun-Times** since 1963. He wrote **Great Art Treasures in America's Smaller Museums**, which was published by Pitnam in 1967.

He taught at George Williams College, Chicago, 1934–1944; University of Chicago, 1944–1975; Director of Midway Studios, 1963–1975; currently Professor Emeritus of Art, University of Chicago; Adjunct Professor of Fine Arts, Indiana University Northwest; Visiting Lecturer, School of the Art Institute of Chicago. He served as Artist in Residence, Pickering College, Newmarket, Ontario, 1933–1944.

He was appointed to the Cultural Advisory Committee of the Mayor's Committee on Economic and Cultural Development of Chicago. He is also a member of the National Society of Mural Painters; Phi Beta Kappa; Honorary life member of the Artist's Guild of Chicago and the Alumni Association of the Art Institute of Chicago.

Haydon is past president of the Artists League of Chicago; Artists League of the Midwest; Artists Equity Association, Chicago Chapter; Chicago Society of Artists; and the Renaissance Society at the University of Chicago.

DR. RICHARD E. HELLER (Sculptor) was born in Chicago on August 20, 1907. He studied at the University of Chicago (B. S. and M. D.). In 1960, he became a student of Si Gordon, a Chicago sculptor. Since 1961 he worked many summers in Rome and studied with Robert Cook and John House. His favorite medium is wax which he utilizes in preparation for his abstract sculptural forms — later executed in bronze and finished with various patinas. He has traveled extensively in the United States and Europe.

His works are included in a number of private collections in Chicago, the East Coast and California.

He is represented by the Art Rental and Sales Gallery of the Art Institute of Chicago.

As a surgeon he has had a long-standing interest in human anatomy, and now that he has retired he is teaching anatomy at Northwestern Medical School.

Heller has been a member of the Chicago Society of Artists since 1966.

NATALIE HENRY (Painter) was born in Malvern, Arkansas, and studied at the Art Institute of Chicago and at the Hubert Ropp School of Art. Her favorite media are watercolor, oil, drawing and lino-cutting.

Her works were exhibited in the Chicago and Vicinity, American and in the International Watercolor exhibitions at the Art Institute of Chicago.

She has also exhibited in group shows with the Chicago Society of Artists, the Women's Salon and the Renaissance Society of the University of Chicago. She has executed a number of murals for private clients, and one for the post office in Springdale, Arkansas.

For twenty-three years she has been manager of the Art Institute School store guiding students in the purchase of art supplies, tools and materials for their creative endeavors.

She contributed lino-cuts to the Chicago Society of Artists annual calendar for more than twenty-five years, receiving special recognition for some.

Henry has served on many committees, and held the office of treasurer of the Chicago Society of Artists for many years. She has been generous in her efforts to facilitate the planing and arranging of group exhibitions for the entire membership.

FERN GILBERT HORWITZ (Painter, Graphic Artist) was born in Chicago, Illinois, on January 28, 1943, and studied at Washington University, St. Louis, Missouri (B.F.A.), 1964, and Art Institute of Chicago. She has traveled in the United States, British Isles, Caribbean Islands, Cayman Islands, South America, and the Orient.

She works in acrylics, pen and ink, oil pastels, mixed media and woodcuts.

She has held one-woman exhibitions at the William Kastan Gallery, Denver, Colorado, 1974; West Nebraska League of Arts, Scottsbluff, Nebraska, 1974; 2-man exhibits at the Wazee Restaurant, Denver, Colorado, 1975 and Northeastern Junior College, Sterling, Colorado, 1976.

Juried shows in which her works were included are 27th Annual Gilpin County Art Exhibit, Central City, Colorado, 1974; Larimer Square Sunday Art Market, Denver, Colorado, 1974; Jewish Community Center, 14th Annual Collectors' Mart, Denver, Colorado, 1974; Monroe Gallery, Chicago, 1977.

Invitational shows in which she was included are: William Kastan Gallery, Denver, Colorado, "Car Art" group exhibit, 1974, and "Highlights of 2 years" group exhibit, 1974; Colorado Women's College, Drawing Exhibit, 1974; Arapahoe Community College, Littleton, Colorado, League of Women Voters Annual Art Show, 1974; the Library Restaurant, Denver, Colorado, 1975–1976.

She has taught art in the Chicago Public Schools at Wicker Park and Yates Upper Grade Centers. She is currently involved in graphic arts, advertising layout, illustration, and design and other related areas of the commercial arts.

Horwitz received the following awards for her paintings and drawings: Second Prize for drawing and Third Prize for painting at Littleton, Colorado Annual Art Fair, 1974; with Award Exhibits at Bemis Library, and Southglenn Mall in Littleton, Colorado.

Her work is represented by the William Kasten Gallery, Denver, Colorado, and included in private collections throughout the United States.

LOUIS H. HUEBNER (Painter) was born in Chicago on May 23, 1922, and studied at the University of Illinois (B.S. and F.A. degrees). He has traveled around the world including Africa, Mexico, China, Japan, Phillipines, Italy, France, England, Spain, Austria, Switzerland, Denmark, Canada and Greece.

Five of his paintings are in the permanent collection at the Continental Bank of Chicago. He has held two one-man shows, one at Maine South High School, and another at Edison Park Library. He was included in forty juried art fairs during the last three years and sold 121 paintings in the last four.

He has taught two years at the University of Illinois, Architectural Design; three years at the Art Institute of Chicago; one year at Illinois Institute of Technology and two years at Maine Township Evening School. He has also had some Gallery and Curatorial experience.

He received eight First Prizes in various art exhibitions, nine Second Prizes and three Third Prizes.

EMMANUEL JACOBSON (Painter) born in Chicago, received his training at the School of the Art Institute of Chicago, (B.A.E. & M.A.E.), University of Chicago, Northwestern University and University of Colorado. He has traveled and painted in the Eastern United States, Mountain States, Hawaii, Mexico, Guatemala, England, France, Italy, Switzerland, Spain and Morocco. His favorite media are watercolor, drawing and mixed media.

A one-man show of his works was held at the Paul Theobald Gallery in Chicago.

For a time he was employed on the W.P.A. art project where he designed and executed murals. Among these were murals for a school in Oak Park, Illinois, and one mural panel which was installed in the Henry Street Settlement in New York City. He also completed a drawing which was included in the **Index of American Design.**

Jacobson's works were exhibited in the Chicago and Vicinity Exhibitions in the International Watercolor Exhibition at the Art Institute of Chicago, in the Art Rental and Sales Gallery of the Art Institute of Chicago in 1975; also, with No-Jury Exhibition, the North Shore Art League, and the Chicago Society of Artists in 1976.

Jacobson has taught art in the Chicago Public Schools, 1946–1972, Saturday classes at the Junior School and currently at the Young Artists Studios of the Art Institute of Chicago, 1946 to the present; at New Trier East Extension program, 1947–1977; North Shore Art League, 1975; Mundelein College. In 1945 while in the armed services he conducted a course in the United States Armed Forces Institute under the auspices of the University of Hawaii.

For a brief period of time Mr. Jacobson was Supervisor of Art for the Chicago Public Schools. He has served on the North Central Association Committee which accredits schools in Chicago and elsewhere, and as juror for the Scholastic Art Competition, a nationally sponsored event.

His works are included in the private collections of Arthur Heun (a Chicago collector); Harriet Monroe (editor of **Poetry Magazine**); C.J. Bulliet (a Chicago Art Critic); Inez Cunningham (a Chicago Art Critic); Eliabeth Stein, and others.

SYLVIA SHAW JUDSON (Sculptor) was born in Chicago, Illinois, on June 30, 1897 and studied at the Art Institute of Chicago with Albin Polasek and at the Academy Grande Chaumiere, Paris, France, with Antoine Bourdelle. She is a sculptor and craftsman and prefers to work in bronze and stone primarily.

Judson has held one-woman exhibitions at the Art Institute of Chicago, 1938; Arden Gallery, New York, 1940; Sculpture Center, New York, 1957; International Sculpture Exhibition, Philadelphia Museum; American Shows, Art Institute of Chicago, Museum of Modern Art, New York; and Whitney Museum of American Art, New York.

Her works are included in public collections such as the Art Institute of Chicago; National Academy of Design, New York; First Lady's Garden, White House, Washington, D.C.; Brookgreen Gardens, Georgia; Kosciasco Park, Milwaukee, Wisconsin.

She was commissioned to execute the Memorial Fountain to Theodore Roosevelt, Brookfield Zoo, 1954; Violinist, Norman Ross Memorial, Ravinia Park, Chicago, 1955; monument to May Dyer, State House, Boston, Massachusetts Art Commission, 1959; group of granite animals, Fairmount Park Association, Philadelphia, Pennsylvania, 1965; gate posts and drinking fountain, Morton Arboretum, Lisle, Illinois, 1970.

Judson is author of **The Quiet Eye**, 1954 and **For Gardens and Other Places**, 1968, Regnery, Publisher.

In 1963 Judson served on the faculty of the American University in Cairo as an Instructor of Sculpture.

She won the Logan Prize, Art Institute of Chicago, 1929; Purchase Prize, International Sculpture Show, Philadelphia Museum, 1949; Milbrook Garden Club Medal, 1957.

From 1948 to 1950 she was president of the Chicago Public School Art Society, and vice-president of Women's Board of the Art Institute of Chicago, 1953–1954; clerk of Lake Forest Friends Meeting, 1956–1957; member of Humanities Visiting Committee of the University of Chicago, 1962 to 1974. She is a member and Fellow of the National Sculpture Society, New York, N.Y.; Academician of National Academy of Design, New York, N.Y.; Arts Club of Chicago; honorary member of the National Academy of Interior Decorators, Cosmopolitan Club, New York.

Judson died at the age of 81 in 1979.

THOMAS HARRY KAPSALIS (Painter, Sculptor) was born in Chicago, Illinois, on May 31, 1925, and studied at the School of the Art Institute of Chicago B.A.E., 1949; M.A.E., 1957. He received a Fulbright Grant to Germany, 1953–1954.

Kapsalis has exhibited at the Pennsylvania Academy of Fine Arts Annual Watercolor and Print Exhibition, Philadelphia, 1946; Contemporary Drawings from twelve countries, Art Institute of Chicago, 1952; Barone Gallery Group Show, New York, 1956; Twenty Seventh Biennial Exhibition of Contemporary Painting, Corcoran Gallery of Art, Washington, D. C., 1961; Illinois Arts Council Traveling Exhibition, 1971.

His works were reproduced in **Direct Metal Sculpture** by Meilach and Seiden, Crown Pub., 1966, and **How to Create Your Own Designs,** Meilach and Hinz, Doubleday Pub., 1975. His name is in **Who's Who in American Art,** 1973; **International Who's Who in Art and Antiques,** 1976; and **Who's Who in American Art,** 1976.

He has taught as Associate Professor of Drawing and Painting, School of the Art Institute of Chicago, 1954 to present, and has lectured on painting, Northwestern University, Chicago and Evanston, 1958–1971.

He received the Huntington Hartford Foundation grant in 1956 and 1959; the Pauline Palmer Prize, 1960; and Jule F. Brower Prize in 1969 from the Art Institute of Chicago.

PORTIA R. KARLSBERG (Painter) was born in Chicago on October 7, 1916, and studied at the Memphis Academy of Art; the Art Institute of Chicago; Studio School of Art Chicago; Chicago Academy of Art; and Watkins Institute, Nashville, Tennessee. She works in several media — oil, watercolor, acrylic, and collage.

Karlsberg has held eight one-woman shows at Memphis and vicinity, 1961–1963; Hillel Foundation, Northwestern University, Evanston, Illinois, 1964; Winnetka Public Library, 1974; One of "Ten Chicago Artists," Gary, Indiana, 1965.

She participated in juried shows at the Delta Regional (six states) Art Exhibit, Arkansas Art Center, Little Rock, Arkansas, 1961, 1962; Nashville, Tennessee Art Festival (six states), 1962; Dogwood Arts Festival, Chattanooga, Tennessee, 1962; included in Ten Best Paintings, American Art Week, Memphis, Tennessee, 1960–1962; Renaissance Society, University of Chicago, 1966; Mid-South Art Festival (six states), Brooks Memorial Museum, Memphis, Tennessee, 1963; Corcoran Art Gallery of Washington, D.C., slide Library of prominent American Painters, 1962; Art Rental and Sales Gallery, Art Institute of Chicago, 1965–1975 and in the San Diego Watercolor Society National Show, 1977.

Other exhibitions in which Portia R. Karlsberg's works were included were: several invitationals at the Rosenstone Gallery of Horwich Center, Chicago; and annual exhibitions of the Chicago Society of Artists; Renaissance Society, University of Chicago; Artists Equity; American Jewish Arts Club and Perspective, (a Society of Artists).

One of her paintings is included in the Telegraph Savings and Loan Association, Chicago, and one-hundred-seven paintings are in private collections in the U. S. and abroad.

Awards received for her oil paintings are one of ten top paintings, American Art Week, Memphis, 1960, 1961, 1962; Second Prize Motorola Regional, Memphis, Tennessee, 1960 and 1962; First and Second Prizes, Memphis Art Academy Fellowship Shows, 1962, 1963; Second Prize for oil painting, Barrington Art Festival, 1966.

Karlsberg is a member of Artists' Equity, Chicago Society of Artists, Perspective, Musarts and other artists groups, such as the San Diego Fine Art Guild; San Diego Art Institute; La Jolla Museum of Contemporary Art Rental and Sales Gallery; Knowles Art Center, La Jolla, California; and Tipton Richards Art Gallery, San Diego.

MICHAEL KARZEN (Painter) was born in Chicago on February 18, 1932, and studied at Roosevelt University, B. A., University of Chicago, M.F.A. He did post-graduate work at the Art Institute of Chicago and U.C.L.A. He has painted and traveled in Europe and Israel, 1959; Mexico, 1962; Canada, 1960 and 1975. His favorite media are oil, acrylic and ink.

Karzen has participated in a two-man exhibition at the Hillel Foundation of Northwestern University in 1965 and in group shows at Harper Court Gallery, Chicago Society of Artists, I.I.T. Phalanx Show, the No-Jury Exhibition at Navy Pier, University of Chicago, Art Institute of Chicago, Northwestern University, Fisher Hall Gallery, Spertus Museum, University Club, Covenant Club, Rosary College and others.

His works are included in a dozen private collections and in the Co-Op Gallery of the Evanston Art Center.

He taught art at Kelly High School, 1958–1959; Tuley High School, 1959–1973; Northeastern Illinois University,

1966; and is currently teaching at Clemente High School in Chicago.

From 1964 to 1972 he received eight awards for paintings in the American Jewish Art Club annual exhibitions: two Maurice De Woskin Awards, two Maurice Spertus Awards, two L. M. Stein-David Bekker Awards, the Alexander Spaulding Award, and the Emily J. Bernstein Award.

Karzen is a member of the Chicago Society of Artists, the American Jewish Arts Club and the Artists Coalition.

A. RAYMOND KATZ (SANDOR) (Muralist) was born in Kassa, Hungary, in 1895 and came to the United States at an early age. He studied at the Art Institute of Chicago and the Academy of Fine Arts. His outstanding teachers were St. John, Forsberg, and Gunther. Katz has traveled and painted abroad in England, France, Switzerland, Austria, Hungary, Italy, Germany, Czechoslavakia and in the United States.

He has painted in oil, watercolor, and casein which he is credited with pioneering in this country. More recently he has developed work in new materials, using additives, polymers and epoxies.

Major one-man shows of his works were held in many leading institutions, including the Art Institute of Chicago, 1946; Milwaukee Art Institute; the Jewish Museum of New York, 1956; Museum voor Sierkunst, Ghent, Belgium, 1963; Butler Institute of American Art, 1962; and four galleries in New York City. Mr. Katz also has had one-man shows in hundreds of colleges, snynagogues and community centers.

As a muralist, he worked in mosaic, fresco graffito and designed in stained glass. 170 houses of worship in the United States have incorporated in their architectural structures his stained glass windows, bas-reliefs or three-dimensional pieces of scultpure he created for interiors or facades of exteriors in collaboration with sculptors.

He was commissioned to paint a mural for the Century of Progress in Chicago, 1933, 1934; History of the Immigrant, Madison Post Office, 1936; Ten Commandments Frescoes, 1936; exterior murals, Temple Beth-El, Baltimore, Ohio; stained glass windows (with Alfonso Ianelli and Don Benardon), Vaughn Army Hospital, Illinois.

He has exhibited in major museums, art galleries and traveling exhibits. Among them are the Carnegie Institute International; Corcoran Gallery of Art; Pennsylvania Academy of Art; Los Angeles Museum; Newark Musuem; San Francisco Museum; Golden Gate Exposition; Museum of Contemporary Crafts; Architectural League of New York; Painters in Casein; National Academy of Design; American Jewish Tercentenary Travel Exhibit; "Art U.S.A., 1958."

He held positions as Director of Poster Department, Paramount, Chicago, 1926 to 1931; member of staff for **Chicago Magazine**, 1928 to 1931; Director of Posters, Chicago Civic Opera, 1930–1933.

Katz has published three books and four portfolios of his works. One of them, **A New Art For an Old Religion** has appeared in three editions.

He received the following awards: First Prize for poster, Century of Progress, 1934; First Prize from the Mississippi Art Association.

Katz left for New York in the 1950s, but while in Chicago he was a member of the Chicago Society of Artists, the Art Institute Alumni Association, No-Jury Society of Artists, the All-Illinois Society of Artists, the Artists Guild of Chicago, and "Around the Palette."

Katz died in 1974.

CAMILLE ANDRENE KAUFFMAN (Painter, Muralist) was born in Chicago on April 19, 1905, and studied at the Art Institute of Chicago, (B.F.A. & M.F.A.); University of Chicago, M.F.A.; Illinois Institute of Technology, University of Illinois, Chicago; and with Andre L'Hote in Paris, France.

One-woman exhibitions of her paintings were held at the San Diego Museum and in La Jolla Fine Arts Gallery, 1950; Bernard Gallery, Chicago, early 1960s; Mount Mary College, 1964; 350 works at Third Unitarian Church, Chicago, 1967; Vanderpoel Museum, Beverly Art Center, Chicago, 1970; 57 paintings and drawings, University Club of Chicago, April 1974; Triangle Art Center in Chicago and New Trier, Wilmette, Illinois, 1976; Elmhurst College, 1977.

She has executed the following mural and sculpture commissions: 20 murals in oil on canvas, Works Progress Administration and United States Treasury Department, Burbank and Hirsch High Schools, Cook County Hospital, Chicago; Ida Gove, Iowa, Post Office Building; 7 bas-reliefs in wood or stone,

Administration Buildings, schools and field houses, Oak Park and Highland Park, Illinois (1934–1942). Two murals were done in ceramic tile for the Department of Public Health Building of Winnebago County, Rockford, Illinois, 1951–1952. Nineteen murals in ceramic tile and a large stained glass window were done for Third Unitarian Church, Chicago, 1955–1969. An acrylic mural was done for the Forest Park Library, Forest Park, Illinois, 1972.

Her works are included in public collections of the Art Institute of Chicago, Vanderpoel Gallery, Beverly Art Center, Chicago; Rockford College, Rockford, Illinois; Mount Mary College, Milwaukee, Wisconsin; also many easel paintings and bas-reliefs in schools and public buildings throughout Midwest; Jane Addams' Hull House; Circle Campus, University of Illinois.

She is represented by the Art Rental and Sales Gallery, Art Institute of Chicago.

Her works were reproduced and written about by Robert B. Johnson, **Sermon Results in Murals**, Unitarian Register, January, 1959; Professor John Hayward, narrator: **Church Trilogy** (TV program), Channel 11, Chicago, August 1959; Donald Key (author); **Kauffman Show Rich in Color**, Milwaukee Journal, September 17, 1961.

She taught art at the Art Institute of Chicago, Professor of Drawing and Painting, 1927–1967; Chairman of the Division of Fine Arts, 1963–1966; Professor Emeritus, 1967. She also held Professorships at Rockford College and at Valparaiso, Indiana.

Kauffman's awards include the John Quincy Adams Fellowship, Art Institute of Chicago, 1927; Honorable Mention, Chicago and Vicinity Exhibition, Art Institute of Chicago, 1946; Second Prize, Block Print Calendar, Chicago Society of Artists, 1973.

She is a professional member of the Arts Club of Chicago; National Society of Mural Painters; Chicago Society of Artists; Art Institute of Chicago Alumni, University of Chicago.

MARY LOUISE WEISS KELLY (Painter) was born in Chicago, Illinois, on March 24, 1929, and studied at the School of the Art Institute of Chicago for four years, at Loyola University, and at the American Academy of Art. She has traveled and painted in the Southwest, West Coast, East Coast and Midwest areas of the United States and Canada. She enjoys working in mixed media and likes the challenges and variables these offer.

She has held two one-woman shows at Exhibit "A" Gallery in Chicago and at the Gallery in Springfield, Virginia. Her work was included in juried group shows at the Illinois State Fair, Chicago and Vicinity Show, Butler University and at Rosary College, University of Illinois, Center for Continuing Education, University of Chicago, New Trier High School, Evanston High School, Highland Park High School, Oak Park High School, Navy Pier-University of Illinois, Jewish Education Center, National Design Center, Well of the Sea Gallery, Swartz Art Gallery, McCormick Place Gallery, Monroe Art Gallery, Main Street Gallery, Visitation High School, Exhibit A Gallery and others.

Her work is included in private collections of Dr. Jerome Rubin of California, Sammy Davis, Jr., of California, Mr. William M. Ward, Jr., of Winnetka, Illinois; Mr. William J. Carrigg, Springfield, Virginia and in the public collection of Vanderpool Art Gallery.

Her work is represented by "the Gallery" in Springfield, Virginia.

She has taught for the Bureau of Parks and Recreation in Chicago, at the Vanderpool School of Art, Beverly Hills; Reavis High School, Oak Lawn, Illinois; Argo High School, Argo, Illinois; Maryville Academy, Des Plaines, Illinois, and in the Chicago Parochial Schools.

Kelly was the recipient of the Elizabeth Stein Award while attending the School of the Art Institute of Chicago.

FELIX KLUCZEWSKI (Painter, Sculptor) was born in Wagrowiecz, Poland, on October 22, 1906, and studied at the School of the Art Institute of Chicago, the University of New Mexico and at the Institute of Design with Laslo Moholy Nagy. He has traveled and painted in Mexico, Canada and in most of the United States.

His works have been exhibited at the Art Institute of Chicago and in five Artists of Chicago and Vicinity Exhibitions. He has also exhibited at the Allied Artists of America exhibition in New York; the Chicago No-Jury Society of Artists; Mandel Brothers Gallery; Navy Pier Art Show; Covenant Club; University Club of Chicago; Triangle Art Center of Chicago.

Kluczewski has served as treasurer of

the Chicago No-Jury Society of Artists for a number of years. He has retained his membership in the Chicago Society of Artists since 1943 and has participated in most of its major annual exhibitions.

SHIRLEY PAPERNO KRAVITT (Painter, Lecturer) received her formal education at the Art Institute of Chicago and the Ecole Nationale Superieure des Beaux-Arts in Paris.

She has had twenty-two one-woman shows and has exhibited in museums in the United States and Europe. She has participated in group shows held in leading galleries in the United States and Europe.

She is a member of the International Platform Association and is listed as a Specialist on Art in Eastern Europe. She has presented her lecture with slides entitled "The Art and People of Russia" on a national tour and throughout the entire Chicago area to universities, art groups, and women's clubs. She was commended for her work in foreign relations through art in Washington, D. C. Her lectures are in the Library of Congress.

She has participated in the Art in Embassies sponsored by the State Department and has shown her paintings in embassies around the world.

She has created art education programs for TV and radio and has been interviewed frequently on talk shows.

She is an expert on gold art objects and was the leading art witness for the defense in the case "United States versus One Solid Gold Object in the Form of a Rooster."

She has authored two books and many articles on art.

Kravitt was awarded the People's Choice Prize, the Prix de Paris, the Silver Medal of Paris, the Gold Medal of Athens, and First Prize in the print show of the Chicago Society of Artists. She is listed in **Who's Who of American Women**.

Kravitt is a member of many art organizations, French clubs and charitable groups.

ALICE LAUFFER (Painter, Graphic Artist) was born in Frankfort Township, Illinois, on October 25, 1919, and studied at the Chicago Academy of Fine Arts, Original Hull House Workshop; the School of the Art Institute of Chicago; and with Paul Weighart at the Evanston Art Center.

For the past nine years she has been doing experimental work with airbrush. It has been used by the artist in doing lithography at Landfall Press. Using modular forms and watercolors she has airbrushed large drawings which have been shown nationwide. Currently the artist is airbrushing acrylic paintings on canvases four feet by five feet, still developing the modular forms. In 1973 she served as artist in residence at the Blackhawk Mountain School of Art.

One-woman and small group shows in which she participated are Four Arts Gallery, 1971; Continental Can Company, 1972; Deson-Zaks Gallery, group show, Chicago, June 1972; Five-artist Summer Show at Mayer Kaplan, J.C.C. Skokie, Illinois, 1972; Chicago Public Library at Randolph & Michigan, Art Room, October 1972; Women of Distinction, Skokie Public Library, Summer, 1973; Lobby Gallery, Illinois Bell Building, Chicago, April 1974; Women in the Arts, Donnelley Library, Lake Forest College, May 1974; Illinois Arts Council, Chicago, 1975; Hyde Park Art Center, Retrospective, Chicago, 1976; Critics Choice, 1134 Gallery, Chicago, 1976.

She has exhibited in the following national or international exhibitions: Drawings, U.S.A., Drawing Biennal, Minnesota Museum of Art, St. Paul, 1968, 1973; Traveling Exhibition Drawings, U.S.A., 1973–1975; Watercolor U.S.A., Springfield Art Museum, Missouri, and Traveling Exhibitions, 1968, 1970; Chicago and Vicinity 72nd Annual Exhibition, Art Institute of Chicago, 1969; National Drawing Exhibition, San Francisco Museum of Art, 1970; American Drawing Biennial XXIV, Chrysler Museum, Norfolk, Virginia, 1971; Smithsonian Institute, Washington and Smithsonian Traveling Exhibition, selected from the American Drawing Biennial to travel the U. S., 1972–1974; National Print and Drawing Competition, Dulin Gallery, Knoxville, 1970, 1973; National Gallery of Fine Arts, Washington, D. C., and Smithsonian Traveling Exhibition, selected from National Print and Drawing Competition to travel the U. S., 1973–1975; First New Hampshire International Graphics Annual, Rivier College, 1973; 17th Annual National Exhibition of Prints and Drawings, Oklahoma Art Center, 1975; National Print and Drawing Exhibition, 2nd St. Gallery, Charlottesville, Virginia, 1975.

Her paintings and prints were exhibited in group exhibitions at Northern Illinois

University; Wake Forest University; University of Redlands; St. Edward's University of Texas; University of S. C., Adams State College of Colorado; East Tennessee State University; Quincy College; Montgomery Museum of Fine Art; Ball State University; New Horizons, Chicago; Circle Gallery, Chicago; Critics Choice of the Art Institute of Chicago; Minnesota Museum of Art; Smithsonian Institute; Bowling Green State University; Montgomery College of Maryland; Coe College; Memphis State University; University of Nebraska; University of Colorado; Milliken University; Riviera College of New Hampshire; Joslyn Art Museum; Carleton College, University of Kentucky; Sweet Briar College; Memphis Academy of Arts; Columbia Museum of Art, S. C., Pa. State University; Central Michigan University; Anchorage History and Fine Arts Museum; Rochester State College; Fine Arts Center of Colorado Springs; Indiana University Art Museum; Tweed Museum of Art; Oklahoma Art Center; and Second Street Gallery of Virginia.

Her work is included in permanent collections of: Art Institute of Chicago Print and Drawing Collection; Minnesota Museum of Art Permanent Collection, St. Paul; Gould Fine Arts Collection, Chicago and abroad; Winnetka City Hall, Village of Winnetka; Northwest Industries, Chicago; Tatham, Laird and Kidner, Chicago; Block-Steel Corporation, Forest Park, Illinois; Mid-America Media, Illinois, Mr. C. Wolcott Henry III, Lake Forest, Illinois; Dr. Saul Machoff, Chicago; Mr. & Mrs. Evan Frances, New York; Gloria Steinem, New York and others.

Lauffer is represented by the Zaks Gallery and by the Art Institute Art Rental and Sales Gallery.

Lauffer has a number of social and political interests. For example, she has been instrumental in the organization of "The Rights of Spring," an ecologically oriented exhibit for the students at Northwestern University at the "New Library" in 1970. She was also one of the organizers of The First Annual Mid-West Conference of Women Artists in 1973.

She served as political liaison between the W.E.B. and the E.R.A. Central to help implement the passage of the Equal Rights Amendment in Illinois for the past three years.

Lauffer received the James Broadus Clarke Award, Art Institute of Chicago, 1969; Continental Can Company Award, 1972; Drawings U.S.A., Purchase Award, Minnesota Museum of Art, St. Paul, 1973.

She is listed in **Who's Who in American Art**, 1976.

LUCILE LEIGHTON (Painter, Graphic Artist) was born in Chicago and stud ied at the Art Institute of Chicago, Evanston Academy of Fine Arts, Chicago Academy of Fine Arts, and the Illinois Institute of Technology with Misch Kohn. She has traveled throughout Europe, Japan, India, Taiwan, Indonesia, Malaysia, Hong Kong, Bangkok, Singapore, Greece, Turkey, Ceylon, Egypt, Mexico, Ecuador, Peru, Israel, Iran, Afghanistan and Borneo. She is the wife of Robert Leighton, well known for his documentary films. Lucile Leighton works in oils, acrylics, drawing, watercolor and printmaking.

She has done private teaching for thirty-five years, and has been a founder-member of Exhibit A Gallery, a first cooperative gallery in Chicago. She lectures on art and travel and served on the Speaker's Bureau of the Adult Education Council, and the Council of Foreign Relations.

She has held one-woman shows at the Chicago Public Library (main); the North Shore Art League; Chicago Woman's Aid; Sherman Hotel Galleries; Deaville Galleries, Atlantic City; M & M Club, Merchandise Mart, Chicago; Covenant Club, Chicago, and the University Club of Chicago.

She participated in juried shows at the Art Institute of Chicago in the Chicago and Vicinity, and Print and Drawing Shows; Butler Museum, Ohio; Pennsylvania Academy of Fine Arts, Philadelphia; Springfield Museum, Massachusetts; Corinthean Gallery, Philadelphia; Galerie Nouvelle, Detroit; Tower Gallery, Hyde Park Art Center, Chicago; Chicago Area Artist, Winnetka, Illinois; Illinois State Fair; Museum of Fine Arts; Rochester, New York; Cayuga Museum of Fine Arts, New York; Old Orchard Festival, Skokie, Illinois; Magnificent Mile, Chicago; Renaissance Society, University of Chicago; Wilmette Library; Union League Club; Oehlschlaeger Gallery; Sun-Times Chicago Artists Exhibit; Suburban Art Center; Evanston Art Center; Rosary College, Lake Forest, Illinois.

She was invited to exhibit in the Wayne, Illinois Annual; North Shore Art League; Chicago Arts Festival; Contemporary Artists, Lake Forest; Old Town Art Fair; Anshe Emet Temple; West Suburban Temple, Winter Show; Deerpath Art League; Rosenstone Art Gallery, Bernard Horwich Center; Kaplan Center; Sears-Vincent Price Galleries.

Her work has been represented by Oehlschlaeger Galleries, Merrill Chase, Collectors Showroom, Art Institute, and the Art Rental and Sales Gallery, Art Institute of Chicago. Also, included in private collections throughout the United States and in the Vincent Price and Arenberg collections.

Leighton has received First Prize for a painting and Second Prize for a print, from the Chicago Society of Artists.

She was nominated "New Talent in the United States" by **Art in America** magazine. Listed: in the **Dictionary of International Biography**; **Who's Who of World's Women**; **Who's Who of American Women**; **2,000 Women of Achievement**; **Who's Who in the Midwest**; in the **Bicentennial Edition of Community Leaders and Noteworthy Americans**; and in the 1975 edition of **Who's Who in the United States**.

BEATRICE S. LEVY (Painter, Graphic Artist) was born in Chicago in 1892. She studied at the Art Institute of Chicago. Her outstanding teachers were Vojtech Preissig, Charles Hawthorne and Ralph Clarkson. She has painted in France, Corsica, Italy, England, Germany, Switzerland, North Africa, Spain and Canada, and in this country in New Mexico, Massachusetts, California, Louisiana and Kentucky.

One-artist exhibitions of her work have been held in New York, Boston, the Philadelphia Print Club, the Washington, D. C. Art Club, the Smithsonian Institute of Washington, D. C., the Art Institute of Chicago, the Layton Gallery of Milwaukee, and in San Francisco and Grand Rapids.

She exhibited at Art Institute of Chicago, 1917, 1919, 1922, 1923, 1928, 1929–1940, 1946; Carnegie Institute, 1929; Pennsylvania Academy of Fine Arts, 1923, 1924, 1931; National Academy of Design, 1945, 1946; Society of American Etchers, 1938, 1940, 1944, 1945; Chicago Society of Etchers, 1914–1919, 1922–1931, 1935–1945; Library of Congress, 1945, 1946, Fifty Prints of the Year, 1932, 1933; Chicago, 1953; Davenport Municipal Art Gallery, 1953; Des Moines, Iowa, 1953; Grinnell, Iowa, 1953; San Diego Fine Arts Guild, 1953–1963; University of New Mexico, 1957; (one artist) Long Beach Museum, Arizona Traveling Print Exhibition, 1959–1960; traveling drawing exhibition, 1960–1961; traveling ceramic exhibition, Yokohama, Japan, 1963–1964.

She has exhibited in Paris, London and Florence, Italy.

Her works are included in public collections of: Chicago Municipal College; Bibliotheque Nationale, Paris; Art Institute of Chicago; Library of Congress; Fine Arts Gallery of San Diego; La Jolla Museum of Art; Davenport Municipal Art Gallery; Smithsonian Institute; University of New Mexico; Long Beach Museum of Art; Vanderpoel College.

Levy was awarded a gold medal by the Chicago Society of Artists in 1928, the prize of the Chicago Society of Etchers in International Etching Exhibition in 1930; Honorable Mention in Exhibition of American Art at the Art Institute of Chicago in 1930, the Robert Rice Jenkins, Springfield, Illinois Academy, 1928; Coronado Artists Association, 1952, 1956, 1957; Del Mar, California, 1953; San Diego Fine Arts Guild, 1955, 1957.

She was a member of the Chicago Society of Artists since 1928, the Chicago Society of Etchers, the Arts Club of Chicago, the Art Institute of Chicago Alumni Association, the Renaissance Society of the University of Chicago, San Diego Fine Arts Guild, the La Jolla Museum of Art.

Levy died in 1974.

BARBARA K. LEWIS (Painter, Graphic Artist) was born in Oak Park, Illinois, on November 21, 1925, and studied at the University of Illinois (B.F.A.), and at the Institute of Technology, Institute of Design (M. S.). Lewis has traveled to Mexico, Canada, throughout the U. S., Alaska, Hawaii, England, France, Switzerland and Portugal. She works in oil, acrylic, watercolor, all print media and photography.

She taught adult watercolor classes, children's painting classes and held printmaking seminars at the College of Du Page. She was Curator of Prints, Morton Arboretum Library and is currently Gallery Assistant, Richard Gray Gallery. She has conducted lectures on contemporary art, served as a docent at the Museum of Contemporary Art for three years, and was a juror for the Evanston Art Center Festival of Art in 1973.

One-woman shows of her works were held at the Studio Gallery, Geneva, Illinois, 1961; Rose Paintings, Morton Aboretum, Lisle, Illinois, 1966; Nashville, Tennessee, 1967; Whitnall Park, Milwaukee, Wisconsin, 1967.

Lewis has participated in juried shows in Newport, R.I., Painting and Sculpture, 1958; Pennsylvania Academy of Fine Arts, Painting, 1958; Bodley Gallery, N.Y., Drawing Show, 1958; Oak Brook Festival of Arts, 1963; Ball State Art Gallery, Drawing, 1958, 1959; Old Orchard Festival of Arts, 1971; "Women 71," Northern Illinois University, 1971; Wayne Art Show, 1971, 1972, 1973; Illinois Invitational, Illinois State Museum, 1973; Eight State Prints Exhibition, J. B. Speed Museum, Louisville, Ky., traveling; Tulsa, Oklahoma, Mid-Western Graphics, 1973; Bradley Print Show, Peoria, Illinois, 1975; seven watercolor panels, Blackhawk Restaurant, Chicago, September 1975.

Other exhibitions in which her work was included were with the Chicago Society of Artists at Cromer and Quint Gallery; McCormick Place Galleries; Monroe Gallery; the University Club Gallery; and in an exhibition of graduate students of Misch Kohn held at the Social Services Building, University of Chicago.

Her works are included in private collections of Mrs. Charles Salmon, Chicago; Dr. Jack Kleinman, Chicago; Arnold Bisbee, Wayne; Mrs. Ruth Gwinn, Wilmette; Mr. & Mrs. Terry Lord, Hoffman Estates; Dr. & Mrs. William Barclay, Elmhurst; Ms. Elizabeth Chapman, Chicago; Mr. William McKenna, New York; Mr. & Mrs. S. Moser, Florida.

Her works are in public collections at the Pennsylvania Academy of Arts; Elmhurst Public Library; Walter Frank Organization; Morton Aboretum Reading Garden (tiles).

In 1972 she received a grant from the Illinois Arts Council to write and illustrate a **Handbook for the Development of Art in Public Places**, which she completed in 1973.

Her works have been represented by the Art Rental and Sales Gallery of the Art Institute of Chicago continuously since 1971. She is also represented by Joy Horwich Gallery in Chicago and Prairie House Gallery in Springfield, Illinois.

EVELYN LEWY (Painter, Graphic Artist) was born in Pittsburgh, Pennsylvania, on July 6, 1919. She is a graduate of Carnegie-Mellon University, B.F.A. (1940), and studied with Constantine Pougialis (1955) and Hans Hofmann (1956). In 1965, she attended the Chicago Teachers College, South. She did graduate work at the Institute of Design, IIT, working with Misch Kohn (1960–1961) and others in 1972. She also studied at Instituto Allende, San Miguel, Allende, Mexico, (1965). She has traveled extensively in the United States, Mexico, Caribbean, Israel, Europe and the Orient.

She participated in juried shows at the Art Institute of Chicago in the Chicago and Vicinity Show, 1952; Hyde Park Art Center, 1956; S. R. Schwartz Chicago Artists First Annual Competition, 1957; Second Annual Chicago Artists Competition Chicago Sun-Times, 1961; Boston Printmakers 14th Annual, Boston Museum of Art, 1961; Northwest Printmakers 34th International Seattle and Portland Art Museum, 1963; 7th Annual Exhibition of Prints, Drawings and Sculpture, Dept. of Art, University of North Dakota, 1963; Invitational Division, 2nd Annual Arts Festival, McCormick Place, 1963; Invitational Fine Arts Festival, Highland Park, Illinois 1964; Chicago Printmakers Invitational, Chicago Public Library, 1965; Artists Members, Renaissance Society, University of Chicago, 1966; Old Town Art Center, 1966; "The Body," Hyde Park Art Center, 1968; "New Horizons," North Shore Art League, 1970.

Invitational shows include the Artists Equity-McCormick Place and City Hall, 1962; Art in Government, Springfield, Illinois, 1963; University of Chicago Shorey House, 1964; McKerr Observatory; Monroe Gallery; Covenant Club; Mandel Bros.; Studio 22; Urban Gateways; Anshe Emet Synagogue; Bernard Horwich Center; K.A.M. Collectors Show; Hillel at Northwestern University; Art Expo, Isaiah Israel Temple, 1968–1970; Continental Can Company; Rosenstone Art Gallery; Bernard Horwich Center; A.J.A.C., Prize-winners, 1963.

Lewy's work is represented by the Art in Embassy Program, American Embassy Prague, 1966–1968; American Embassy, Haiti, 1969–present; Mr. & Mrs. John Kenneth Galbraith — shown in American Embassy, India; Peoples Gas Light & Coke Company, Chicago; Lanzit Corrugated Box Company; Frederick Chusid & Company; Donald R. Booz Association, Inc.

Galleries representing her work include

The Art Rental and Sales Gallery, Art Insitute of Chicago, 1960; Renaissance Society at the University of Chicago "Art for Young Collectors" annual sale since 1955; Fairweather-Hardin Gallery, Chicago, 1962–1965; Bresler Gallery, Milwaukee, 1962–1965; Ontario East Gallery, Chicago 1965–1967; Arts Club of Chicago, Professional Members Annual, since 1965; Town Gallery, Munster, Indiana, 1965–1968; Alter Gallery, Indianapolis, 1968–1970.

She has given demonstrations on collage and printmaking for many worthy causes, appeared on television, served on numerous Boards of Directors, served as volunteer for political candidates, and for various community services. During World War II, she was Gray Lady, Red Cross Nurses Aide.

For a brief period of time she taught art in the Chicago Public Schools and for a number of years printmaking at Roosevelt University. She also taught printmaking and painting at the Hyde Park Art Center and at the South Shore Commission Art Workshop.

Currently she is serving as Director of the Circle Art Gallery in Chicago.

Her work has been reproduced in the Chicago Society of Artists Block Print Calendar since 1968 and written about in **Printmaking** by Dona Z. Meilach, Pitman Publishing Company (New York, 1965); **Creating Art From Anything** by Dona Z. Meilach, Reilly & Lee, (Chicago, 1968); **Collage and Assemblage** by Dona Z. Meilach and Elvie TenHoor, Crown Publishers, Inc., (New York 1973).

Awards received for her paintings and prints include the John L. Porter Prize for Progress in Art Studies, Carnegie-Mellon University, 1939; Leon Garland Prize, American Jewish Art Club, 1960; South Shore Commission Art League, numerous awards, 1961–1965; including Second Prize for all three entries, 1963; Todros Geller Award, Third Prize, A.J.A.C., 1963; L. M. Stein Award, A.J.A.C., 1968; Honorable Mention, A.J.A.C. 1969.

She is a member of the Arts Club of Chicago; the Chicago Society of Artists; and the Artists Equity Association, Inc.

SIDNEY LOEB (Sculptor, Painter) was born in Chicago in 1904 and studied at the Art Institute of Chicago; University of Illinois at Champaign with Lorado Taft, noted American sculptor in Chicago and at the Cooper Institute and the Art Students League in New York City.

His works have been exhibited at the Sculptor's Guild in New York, The Carnegie Art Museum, Pittsburgh, The Art Museum of Philadelphia, The Brooklyn Art Museum, The Whitney Museum in New York, the Art Institute of Chicago, Boston Art Museum, paintings and sculpture at the Westport Art Gallery, painting and sculpture at the "Gallery," Williamstown, Massachusetts. Since 1950 the artist has devoted some time to painting landscapes, flowers and abstracts, but did mainly portraits in sculpture. Among these were portraits of David Smart, publisher of **Esquire** magazine, Shepard Vogelgesang, Chicago architect, Mrs. Mathews of San Clemente, California, and a sculpture portrait of Hillel for the Hillel Foundation of New York. In 1937 he did two bas-reliefs of American Farm and Pioneer Families for the Treasury Department which have been installed in the post office at Royal Oaks, Michigan.

His paintings and sculptures are included in the collections of Norman G. Shidle of Roxbury, Connecticut, Mrs. Harriet Amanda Chapman of Pompano Beach, Florida, Pierre Gildesgane, K.B.E. (Knight of British Empire) of London, England, Mr. & Mrs. Warner Smith of Williamstown, Massachusetts; Dr. & Mrs. Elliot M. Greenfeld of Pittsfield, Massachusetts and Mrs. V. A. Sweeney of North Adams, Mass.

In 1926 he submitted his first piece of sculpture to the Artists of Chicago and Vicinity Exhibition at the Art Institute of Chicago where he won the coveted Robert Rice-Jenkins Prize.

In 1929 while teaching at the Art Student's League in New York, he was awarded a Guggenheim Fellowship for study in Paris, with a renewal the following year. Upon his return to the United States in 1931, he opened a studio in New York City, but later returned to Chicago.

During World War II, in 1942, Sidney Loeb volunteered for the Air Force. While stationed in Baton Rouge, La., he served in a hospital teaching art to disabled veterans and helping in their rehabilitation.

Before joining the Air Force, however, he had completed his over life-size statue of Abraham Lincoln which he submitted to the 47th Annual Exhibition by Artists of Chicago and Vicinity at the

Art Institute of Chicago. Here it was awarded the Mr. & Mrs. Frank Logan Prize and Medal and an Honorarium of five hundred dollars. He also received an Honorable Mention and Medal for a reclining nude he exhibited at the New York World's Fair. Sidney Loeb was also invited to exhibit his Lincoln statue at the International Sculpture Show in the Philadelphia Art Museum — the only midwestern artist included among 100 sculptors from all over the world.

A bronze cast of his Lincoln statue was recently unveiled in Ramat Gan, Israel. It was a gift from the American people to the people of Israel, so designated by an Act of Congress in a joint resolution and President Ford. The bill was signed on December 16, 1976.

Upon his release from the Air Force, Sidney Loeb returned to his studio in Chicago where he resumed his life work and teaching.

In 1953 Loeb moved his studio to Westport, Connecticut where he continued to paint and exhibit. Eighteen years later he moved to Williamstown, Massachusetts. He was about to establish a studio when he died in June, 1972.

CLARA MacGOWAN (CIOBAN) (Painter, Graphic Artist) was born in Montreal, Canada, on September 15, 1894. She studied at the University of Washington, Seattle, Washington (M.F.A.), and at the Academie Moderne, Paris, France with Fernand Leger; L'Hote Academie, Paris, France with Andre L'Hote; Kunstgewerbe Schule, Vienna, Austria with Franz Cizek (special work); Chicago Bauhaus School of Art with L. Moholy-Nagy and G. Kepes; University of Hawaii-Hawaiian Culture with Dr. Kenneth Emory; San Carlos School of Fine Arts (graduate school) Valencia, Spain with Professor D'Alos; Upholstery-private class with Professor Rudolph Siegrist, Washington, D.C.; and acquired all California credentials for teaching and supervision of art. She traveled extensively around the world in Europe, Mexico, Cuba, Hawaii and Canada. MacGowan works in oil, watercolor, graphic arts and designs in many materials and media.

One-woman exhibitions of her works were held in Frauenkunst, Vienna, Austria, abstract oils, 1931; American Library, Paris, France, abstract oils, 1931; Delphic Studios, New York City, abstract paintings and landscapes, 1931, 1935, 1936, 1937, 1938; Gima Gallery, Waikiki, Honolulu, Hawaii, oils and landscapes, 1948.

Juried shows in which her paintings were included are the Art Institute of Chicago; Denver Museum, Colorado; Henry Museum, Seattle, Washington; Findlay Galleries, Chicago; Evanston and North Shore Artists; Chicago Society of Typographic Artists; Woman's Salon of Chicago; Evanston Art Center; Wilmette Woman's Club; Cornell University Gallery, Ithaca, New York.

Invitational shows of her work were held in the Albert Roullier Galleries, Chicago, portrait exhibition, 1944; Chicago Woman's Aid Gallery (one of ten invited), 1944; Marshall Field & Company Gallery, Chicago, (one of seven invited, 1945; Riverside Museum, New York, 1945; invited to do block print for cover of folder, "The Cross at Kole Kole Pass, Oahu," in the first Easter Service at the Pass after World War II, 1948.

Her works are included in private collections of Mrs. Daniel B. Hayden, Chicago; the Mountaineer Society, Seattle, Washington; Mrs. James B. Eyerly, Chicago; Mrs. Patricia Newman, Chicago; Mr. Mark Gruber, El Chorro Lodge, Scottsdale, Arizona; Mrs. Jane Wilson MacGowan, Seattle, Washington; Mrs. John N. MacGowan, Royal Oak, Maryland, Mr. & Mrs. Douglas MacGowan, Beaverton, Oregon, The collection "Design in the Minor Arts" given to the Carlsbad City Library, Carlsbad, California was installed in 1977.

She co-authored the book **Chicago — A History in Block Print** with Dean James Alten James of the History Department at Northwestern University. The prints were executed under her direction. These were exhibited in Vienna, Paris, Mexico City, and Washington, D. C. in 1936–1937. In 1933 and 1934, the College Art Association circulated the prints in exhibitions in the United States. A second book, **The Social History of Chicago in Blockprint,** with text by Professor Arthur J. Todd, head of the Sociology Department at Northwestern University, was published in 1935. Advanced Students in Design created the blockprints under the direction of Clara MacGowan, then head of the Department of Theory and Practice of Art at Northwestern University. MacGowan has also written the following articles: "Polynesian Treasures in the Bishop Museum in Honolulu" for **Design** magazine, January 1949, and "Pursuit of Tastelessness in Design," for **Design** magazine, 1967.

She was President of the Department of Art Education, Washington, D.C., 1938–1940; editor of the annual Bulletin of the Department of Art Education, National Education Association, 1937–1944 inclusive; advisory editor of **Design Magazine** for many years until 1972; art editor and art director of "The Trumpeteer" in San Francisco, 1950; owner and director of school, "Studio of Art Interpretation" in San Francisco, California, 1950–1954.

She was Associate Professor of Art at Northwestern University and was head of the Department of Theory and Practice of Art, 1928–1949. While on leave of absence from 1947–1949, she taught at the Branch of University of Hawaii, Schofield Barracks. From 1956–1963 she served as Consultant in Art for the public schools of Washington, D.C., and in 1964 she taught at the College of the Desert, Palm Desert, California.

MacGowan received the following awards: First prize, Charles H. Dennis Award (for watercolor) Evanston and North Shore Artists Exhibition, 1934; Honorable Mention, Chicago Society of Artists (for oil painting), 1934; Carnegie grant to cover cost of publication of her study, **A Statement of Problems for Determining Teacher Qualifications in Art** published by the National Education Association, Washington, D.C. 1951; listed in **Who's Who in Chicago and the Midwest,** 1972–1973.

President of the Chicago Society of Artists, 1935–1937, and member of the Board for a number of years. She inaugurated the Calendar of the Chicago Society of Artists in 1937, to which she has contributed a print since then. She was responsible for presenting to the Trustees of the Art Institute of Chicago a plan for continuous shows of Chicago artists, which resulted in the establishment of the Chicago Room in 1941. She was President of the American Friends of the Austrian Werkbund, Chicago.

MacGowan is currently a member of the Arts Club of Chicago, the American Association of University Women, the American Association of University Professors, and the Soroptimist Club of San Francisco. Her works have been written about by art critics Frank Holland of the **Chicago Daily News**, Eleanor Jewett of the **Chicago Tribune**, Howard Devree of the **New York Times**, Jean Ten Broeck of the **Wilmette Life**, and Yukon Mau of the **Honolulu Advertiser**.

LUCRETIA A. MALCHER (Painter) was born in Chicago. She was graduated from the Drawing, Painting and Illustration Department at the Art Institute of Chicago and studied in Munich, Germany with Professor Y. Heymann and at the Atelier Delecluse and Colorassi, Paris, France. She has traveled throughout the United States and to many countries throughout the world, visiting every major museum in each main city.

She has held one-woman exhibitions of her paintings at the Evanston public Library; Evanston Community Center; Tally-Ho Gallery in Evanston; Monroe Gallery; Newman Brown Gallery; and Esquire Little Gallery in Chicago.

Juried group exhibitions in which her paintings were shown are the Art Institute of Chicago, the Renaissance Gallery of the University of Chicago; Magnificent Mile of Chicago; Cromer and Quint Gallery, Freed Gallery, Marshall Field Gallery; Riccardo Gallery, Mandel Brothers Gallery, Well of the Sea Gallery, Oak Street Gallery, Monroe Gallery,—all of Chicago, and in Evanston at the House of Commerce, Orrington Hotel, Old Orchard Gallery and Pan-American Gallery.

Gallery representation of Malcher's work includes the Art Rental and Sales Gallery of the Art Institute of Chicago, the Evanston Art Center, and Evanston Public Library. Her work is also represented in private collections in Chicago, Evanston, Springfield, Illinois, and Los Angeles, California.

Malcher has illustrated 15 books and many family magazine stories. She has done commercial art work and has lectured for the Federation of Women's Clubs throughout Chicago and suburbs.

Her teaching experience includes twenty years in Tree Studio Building, (Malcher Studio); two years at Harvard School for Boys; also, Gardner-Doing Progressive School; and fifteen years at Loyola Field House for the City of Chicago.

She received a $500.00 award for cover design of Illinois Bell Telephone Company, Evanston, Illinois, and a prize for "Sights of Evanston" painting, also, for a HAT design for Marshall Field and Company, in Chicago.

SHIRLEY MANSFIELD (Painter) was born in Chicago, Illinois, on June 2, 1922, and studied at the Art Institute of

Chicago, American Academy of Fine Arts, Chicago Academy of Art, and the University of Wisconsin (B. S.) in Art Education.

She has traveled extensively in the United States and in Italy, France, British Isles, and Mexico. Although her favorite medium is oil, she also enjoys welding sculpture.

One-woman exhibitions of her work were held at the Sherman Art Gallery; Winnetka Women's Club; Glencoe Library; Illinois Corperative Gallery; Hitching Post Gallery in Kalamazoo, Michigan.

Mansfield exhibited in juried group shows New Horizons Exhibits, 1959, 1960; New Trier Exhibit, 1958, 1959, 1961; Illinois State Fair in Springfield, Illinois, 1960; Chicago Watertower Exhibit, 1961; Roosevelt University, 1961; 57th Street Art Fair 1960–1972; Old Town Art Fair 1958–1972, and many others.

For the past fifteen years she has taught three classes of adults and teenagers in her private studio. She has held a one-woman exhibition of her works at the Sherman Art Gallery and at the Illinois Cooperative Gallery in Chicago. She participated in group shows at the Evanston Woman's Club Annuals, the S. R. Schwartz Gallery, North Shore New Horizons shows, and the Oak Park Art Fair. Her work was included in the Oak Park traveling collection and at the University of Wisconsin, 1957.

Mansfield won an Honorable Mention and later First Place in the Evanston Woman's Club Annual 1958, 1961; an Honorable Mention in the S. R. Schwartz Gallery exhibit 1957, a Purchase Award at the Oak Park Art Fair, 1961; the University of Wisconsin, 1957; Libertyville Arts Club, 1958; North Shore Art League Summer Fair, 1959.

JANINA MARKS (Painter, Graphic Artist) was born in Radvilishis, Lithuania, on September 21, 1923, and studied at Lithuanian National Theatre Drama College, Lithuania, and the Ecole des Arts et Metier in Freiburg, Germany. She studied tapestry weaving with Ovis Tamojaitis, Kingston, Canada. Her favorite media are oil, graphics, and weaving. She prefers to use bright colors in primitive organic designs.

She has traveled and painted in many lands, including the Caribbean Islands, Mexico, Central America, Hawaii, European countries, U.S.S.R., Lithuania, Latvia, Helsinki, Czechoslovakia, Germany, Austria, Belgium, Netherlands, France, Japan, Taiwan, Hong Kong, Bangkok, Bali, and Israel.

One-woman exhibitions of her works were held in Harper Galleries, Blackhawk Restaurant, Lithuanian Youth Center, Marillack High School Gallery, Balzehas Museum of Lithuanian Culture, Sun-Times Gallery and Bonwit-Teller Gallery.

Juried exhibitions in which her works were included are Chicago and Vicinity at the Art Institute of Chicago; Dunes Art Center; Renaissance Society of the University of Chicago; DePaul University; Hyde Park Art Center; Old Orchard Art Fair; New Horizon's Show; Beverly Art Center; Barrat College; Gary Art Center, and many invitational group shows. Her works are currently represented by the Art Rental and Sales Gallery of the Art Institute of Chicago.

Her works are included in private collections of Mr. & Mrs. Robert Buckfinder, Dr. & Mrs. Ovis Albert Potts, Dr. & Mrs. Paul Williams, Dr. & Mrs. Albert Dorfman, Mr. & Mrs. Leon Depres and others, and in public collection of Balzehas Museum and Rehabilitation Institute in Chicago.

Marks has been the recipient of awards from the Dunes Art Foundation; North Shore Art League; State of Illinois; YMCA; Hyde Park Art Center; New Horizons Show; Motorola Company; Lithuanian Youth Center.

Marks has served on the Board of Directors at Hyde Park Art Center. She is a member of Women's Guild at Balzehas Museum of Lithuanian Culture. She was Exhibitions chairwoman of Lithuanian-American Women Artists and Ethnic Visual Arts Advisor for the Illinois Arts Council.

ALICE MASON (Painter, Graphic Artist) was born in Chicago on January 16, 1895. She studied at Northwestern University (B. S.), 1917; Art Institute of Chicago (B.F.A.) 1935, (M.F.A.) 1944; Chicago University for several years; Summer School of Painting Saugatuck, Michigan, 1925; Vienna, 1925; and with Frederick Poole, Frances Chapin, Edgar Rupprecht, and Maroger. She traveled in Europe for fourteen months in 1920; Vienna, Austria, 1925; Spain and England, 1954; and Scandinavia and England, 1958. Her favorite media are oils, watercolor, and lithography.

She has held one-woman shows at the Art Institute of Chicago, Room of Chicago art, 1943; Chicago Public Library Print Show, 1961; New York Argent Gallery, 1940; Chicago Society of Artists, Cromer and Quint Gallery, Chicago; Quincy Illinois Art Association, 1950–1966; Stone-Brandel Center of Chicago, 1967.

Mason participated in juried exhibitions at the Art Institute of Chicago, 1937, 1938, 1939, 1940, 1946, 1949, 1951, 1952, 1954, 1955, 1956. In 1951 by invitation to Chicago Show; International Lithography Show, Chicago Art Institute, 1937; Metropolitan Museum, N.Y.; Artists for Victory 1942 and 1952 print exhibitions; Pennsylvania Academy Oil Show, 1938, 1939, and print shows 1953, 1956; Corcoran Gallery, Washington, D. C., oil show, 1941, Library of Congress Print Shows, 1952, 1953, 1954, 1955, 1957; Cincinnati Art Museum Biennial International Lithography shows, 1950, 1952, 1954, 1956; New Britain, Connecticut Art Museum, 1952; 1953; Society of American Graphic Artists, N.Y., 1952, 1953, 1954, 1955, 1957; Print Club of Philadelphia, 1951, 1952, 1953, 1954, 1955, 1957; Illinois State Fair, 1956, 1957, 1958; Illinois State Museum, by invitation, 1958; Union League Club of Chicago, 1957, 1961, 1963, 1965; Chicago Public Library, by invitation to Print show, 1965; University of Illinois, Graphic Arts U.S.A. by invitation, 1954; in Lithography shows of Buffalo Print Club Silvermine Guild of Artists, Dallas Texas Museum, Wichita Art Museum, Society of Washington Printmakers, Connecticut Academy, Hunterdon County Art Center and Rackhem Gallery of University of Michigan, 1973.

Traveling shows of the American Federation of Arts included her lithographs in the Metropolitan Museum, N.Y., 1952; Library of Congress, 1952; Cincinnati Art Museum, 1954; Print Club of Rochester, 1954.

Her lithographs were purchased by The Metropolitan Museum, N. Y., 1952; Library of Congress, 1952, 1953; University of Chicago for print collection; Cincinnati Art Museum International Print Show, 1950, 1952, 1956; Society of American Graphic Artists, N.Y., 1953; New Britain Art Museum Conn., 1952, 1953.

Her lithographs were on view in the American Embassy in Singapore, 1966, and Rabat, Morocco, 1970.

In 1949 the Chicago Society of Artists commissioned Mason to do a color lithograph, the "Print of The Year."

She taught lithography at Ox Bow Summer School of Painting, Saugatuck, Michigan, 1954–1955, and lectured on color lithography to Clubs and Renaissance Society of the University of Chicago.

Mason received the following awards: the Art Institute of Chicago, Alumni Show, Honorable Mention, 1949; Society of American Graphic Artists, New York, Honorable Mention, 1953; Municipal Art League of Chicago Prize, 1957; Print Club of Philadelphia, Honorable Mention, 1952; New Britain Art Museum, Connecticut, First Prize, 1953; Honorable Mention, 1952; Illinois State Fair, Honorable Mention, 1956.

Since 1940 she has been a member of the Chicago Society of Artists and was its president from 1954 through 1959. She is also a member of the Arts Club of Chicago; Cordon Club, (president for three years); Renaissance Society of the University of Chicago (Board of Directors), honorary director since 1969; Connecticut Academy of Fine Arts since 1956; Hartford Connecticut Hunterdon County Art Center, New Jersey; Ann Arbor Art Association; Ann Arbor City Hall, 1974.

She is represented by the Art Rental and Sales Gallery of the Art Institute since 1955, and has been listed in **Who's Who in America** since 1956. She is also listed in **Who's Who in Art in the Midwest; International Directory of Art,** 9th edition; **Who's Who of American Women,** first edition; **Dictionary of International Biography,** London, England, 1968, and in the Smithsonian Institute in Washington, D.C., 1977.

Mason died in 1977.

FRANCES McVEY (Painter) was born in Muncie, Indiana, on October 1, 1903. She studied at the Art Institute of Chicago and was graduated in 1925. Later she studied with Boris Anisfeld (1935–1936) and at the Goodman Theatre on a Fellowship (1945). In 1936 she was married to Richard C. McVey, Assistant Superintendent of the Chicago Public Schools, who died in 1966. She is known mainly for portrait and figure painting in oil and in pastels.

Her works have been exhibited in the Art Institute Chicago and Vicinity Exhibitions; Riverside Museum, New York; Library of Congress, Washington, D.C.; and is included in many private collections. A number of her religious paintings are in the Gallery of Chesterfield Spiritualist Camp, Chesterfield, Indiana.

She is currently teaching in her studio and exhibiting with various Indiana groups.

Since 1939 McVey has been a member of the Chicago Society of Artists and of the United Scenic Artists Association. She has been a regular contributor of lino cuts to the Chicago Society of Artist's annual calendar.

BEATRICE ROITMAN METRICK (Painter) was born in Chicago, Illinois, and studied at the Art Institute of Chicago; Institute of Design, Old Town School of Art; Contemporary Art Workshop; and Ox-Bow Summer School of Painting. Among her instructors have been Louis Ritman, Constantine Pougialis, Paul Wieghardt, Emerson Woelffer, and Copeland Burg. She has traveled extensively throughout Europe, Canada, Mexico and the United States. Beatrice Metrick is employed as Technical Illustrator and Electronic Draftswoman for Zenith Radio Corporation.

She has held one-woman exhibitions at Lake Meadows and at the Rubino Gallery. She exhibited in group shows at the Art Institute of Chicago; Union League Club of Chicago; the University Club, Palette and Chisel Academy; Artists Guild; Campanile Gallery; Municipal Art League Show; Old Orchard Bank; Gold Coast Art Fair; University of Chicago; Harper Gallery; Northwestern University; Illinois Grand Salon Show; Sun-Times Gallery; Artists Equity Group Show in Springfield; Spiesberger Gallery; Germania Club; McCormick Place Gallery; M.A.A.A. Biennale; Old Town Triangle Gallery; North Shore Art League; Rosary College; 4 Arts Gallery, Circle Gallery.

She is represented in the Permanent Archives of American Artists-Smithsonian Institute, Washington, D. C. and in private collections throughout the country.

She received the following awards for painting: the Municipal Art League, Honorable Mention, 1971; Municipal Art League, I.F.W.C. Cash Award, 1973; Mid-America Art Association, Biennale, 1973, Honorable Mention and Cash Award.

Metrick is a member of Artists Equity, American Jewish Art Club, North Shore Art League, Chicago Society of Artists and the Chicago Artists' Coalition.

BARBARA LAZARUS METZ (Printmaker, Photographer) was born in Chicago, Illinois and received a certificate in Interior Design from the Chicago Academy of Fine Arts (1950). She returned to school at Fullerton Junior College (A. A. 1970) in California and in Chicago at Mundelein College (B.F.A. 1973) and the School of the Art Institute (M.F.A. 1977). She has traveled throughout the United States, the Caribbean, Mexico, Brazil, Europe, and recently in the Orient.

One woman exhibitions of her work were held at Mundelein College in Chicago and Pacific Telephone in California. She participated in a two-person show at A.R.C. gallery in Chicago in 1978.

Metz has been in the following national juried shows: Dulin National Print and Drawing Show, Knoxville, Tennessee, 1977; Bradley National Print and Drawing Show, Bradley University, Peoria, Illinois, 1977; Mitchell Museum, Mt. Vernon, Illinois, 1977; Color Print USA, Texas Tech University, Lubbock, Texas, 1976.

Other juried shows in which her works were included are the Illinois Photographers '78, Illinois State Museum, Springfield, Illinois; Artists Books, School of the Art Institute Library, Chicago; Book Week, Chicago Cultural Center; Chicago Photo Works, Valpariso University, Valpariso, Indiana, 1977; Evanston Art Center, 1977, 1976, 1975; North Shore Art League, Winnetka, Illinois, 1975; Circle Gallery, 1975; Lakehurst Art Show, Waukegan, Illinois 1975, Rubino Gallery, Chicago, 1974; Mundelein Alumnae, Chicago 1974; Rosary College, River Forest, Illinois, 1973, New Horizons in Art, Chicago, 1972, 1973; and numerous shows in Southern California from 1965 to 1970.

Metz is a member of A.R.C. (Artists, Residents of Chicago), a women's cooperative gallery. Her work has been represented by the Art Rental and Sales Gallery of the Art Institute of Chicago since 1971 and is in the Standard Oil collection in Chicago as well as various private collections in Chicago, New York, Texas, California and Florida.

She taught lithography at the Jane Addams Center of Hull House and is presently teaching etching and bookbinding there. She gave a photo serigraphy workshop at Valpariso University in Valpariso, Indiana in 1977. Metz was a teaching assistant in lithography and photo mechanical processes while getting her masters degree at the School of the Art Institute of Chicago and did substitute teaching for the Chicago Public Schools. While in Cincinnati she helped organize and direct the Brentwood Art Center as a school and gallery for the local area. Before returning to school Metz worked as an Interior Designer for the Architectural firms of A. Epstein and Sons and Holabird and Root in Chicago.

Metz has received awards for her ceramics, prints and paintings in California and Chicago.

EDGAR MILLER (Painter, Muralist) was born at Eagle Rock, Idaho, on December 17, 1899. He briefly attended the School of Mines, Ballarat Art School in Australia, and later studied with George Bellows and Alfonso Ianelli. He was graduated from the Art Institute of Chicago in 1918. He has traveled and painted in Australia, the South Seas, Central America, Mexico and western United States. His favorite media are painting, sculpture, and wood carving. He has painted murals, portraits and easel paintings.

He has held one-man shows at the Art Institute of Chicago and Art Center Bellaire, Florida.

His work is represented in many public collections including the Art Institute of Chicago. His commissioned works are sculpture on the North Dakota State Capitol; Northwestern Technological Institute, Evanston, Illinois; 13 bronze figures in Evergreen Park, Chicago; bronze figure and jardinieres, in Henrotin Hospital, Chicago; sculpture and murals, Pierce Hotel, New York; murals, Marco Polo Club, Waldorf, New York and mural for Tavern Club, Chicago.

Miller also designed the building at 155 Burton Place in Chicago. It was the first structure which led to the movement that became "Old Town." The building has been made a landmark in that area.

For three years Miller taught at the Art Institute of Chicago.

Miller was awarded five bronze Logan medals from the Art Institute of Chicago, and at the time of World's Fair in Chicago in 1933, he was chosen one of 52 portrait painters. He was also awarded the Society of Graphic Arts Award, FAIA mural painting in 1955.

HARRY MINTZ (Painter) was born in Warsaw, Poland, in 1909 and studied at the Warsaw Academy of Fine Arts (M.F.A.). He was awarded a Fellowship from that institution. He has traveled and painted extensively in Europe, Mexico, South America and Israel.

Mintz has held 33 one-man shows, including those at Feingarten Galleries, Los Angeles, 1961; Feingarten Gallery in Chicago in 1961; Studio Gallery, Madison, Wisconsin; Werbe Gallery, Detroit in 1955; Cliff Dwellers, Chicago, 1954; Palmer House Galleries, Chicago 1952–1953; Galeria Escondida, Taos, New Mexico, 1953; College of Jewish Studies, Chicago, 1953; John Heller Gallery, New York, 1952; Steven Gross Galleries, Chicago, Illinois, 1951; Cowie Gallery Los Angeles, 1948; the Art Institute of Chicago, 1945; Evanston Art Center, 1942; Woman's Aid Society of Chicago, 1938; Abbot Gallery, Chicago.

His paintings were included in over 300 invitational and juried national and international group exhibitions. From 1934–1963 consecutively he has exhibited in local, national and international exhibitions at the Art Institute of Chicago. He has also exhibited in other noteworthy events held in museums and other institutions such as the Carnegie International, Pittsburgh, Pennsylvania; Whitney Museum of American Art, New York; Venice Biennale; Pennsylvania Academy of Fine Arts, Philadelphia, Pa.; Corcoran Gallery of Art, Washington, D.C.; Palace of the Legion of Honor, San Francisco; Museum of Cincinnati, Cincinnati, Ohio; Milwaukee Art Institute, Milwaukee, Wisconsin; Half Century of American Art, Art Institute of Chicago, 1940; New York's World Fair, 1939; University of Illinois, American Exhibition, 1948, 1949, 1950, 1953, 1961, 1963; Pepsi-Cola Competitions; Denver Art Museum, Denver Colorado, 1963; Sarasota Art Association, Sarasota, Florida; St. Louis Art Museum, St. Louis, Missouri, Los Angeles County Museum, Los Angeles, California.

From 1955 to present he has served on the staff of the School of the Art Institute of Chicago. As Associate Professor of Advanced Painting he taught senior and graduate students.

From 1954–1955 he was Visiting Professor of Painting at Washington University, St. Louis, Missouri, from 1944–1964 he taught at the Evanston Art Center, Evanston, Illinois, and from 1949–1959 at the North Shore Art League, Winnetka.

Mintz was awarded the following prizes at the Art Institute of Chicago: Silver's Prize, 1962; Jules F. Brower Prize, 1952, 1954; Honorable Mention, 1953; Flora M. Witkowski Prize, 1949; Town and Country Arts Prize, 1946; William H. Bartels Prize, 1939; Honorable Mention, 1938; Joseph N. Eisendrath Prize, 1937. Other prizes he received are First Prize, Old Orchard Art Exhibit of Chicago Artists, 1959, 1962, 1963, Second Prize, Sun-Times Exhibit of Chicago and Vicinity Artists in 1963; Honorable Mention, Old Orchard Exhibit of Chicago and Vicinity, 1958, 1960, 1961; Purchase Prize, Union League Art Exhibit, 1959; Cash Award, Magnificent Mile, Chicago, 1955; First Prize, Evanston Woman's Club, Evanston, Illinois, 1953, 1949, 1948; Honorable Mention, Terry National Exhibit, Miami, Florida, 1952, First Prize, American Jewish Arts Club, Chicago, Illinois, 1948; Cash Award, Old Northwest Territory Exhibit, Springfield, Illinois, 1948; Silver Medal, Palace of Legion of Honor, San Francisco, California, 1946, and others.

Mintz's works are included in public collections of the Art Institute of Chicago, 1962; New Evansville Museum, Indiana, 1959, 1961; University of Notre Dame, Notre Dame, Indiana, 1961; Whitney Museum, New York, 1957; Art Institute of Chicago, 1954, 1946; Downtown Gallery, New York, 1954; Tel-Aviv Modern Museum of Art, Israel, 1944; Hackley Art Gallery, Muskegan, Michigan, 1942; Rio de Janerio Museum of Art, Brazil, 1929; Warsaw Academy of Fine Arts, Poland, 1928.

Publications in which he was included are **Who's Who in America,** 1962–1963; **Who's Who in American Art,** 1947–1977; **Who's Who in World Jewry,** 1964–1965; **International Dictionary of Who's Who,** 1964–1965; **Dictionary of International Biography,** 1977 and the **Israel Honorarium.**

LeROY NEIMAN (Painter) was born in St. Paul, Minnesota, on June 8, 1927, and studied at the School of the Art Institute of Chicago, 1945–1949, painting with Boris Anisfeld; at the St. Paul Art Center, 1944–1945, painting with Clement Haupers at the University of Chicago and the University of Illinois. His favorite media are enamels, oils, serigraphs, and etching.

One-man exhibitions of his works were held at Oehlschlager Gallery, Chicago, 1961; O'Hana Gallery, London, 1962; Galerie Bosc, Paris, 1962; Hammer Gallery, N. Y., 1963, 1965, 1967, 1968; Heath Gallery, Atlanta, 1969; Gallery of Modern Art, N. Y.; The Choate School, Wallingford, Connecticut, 1969; French Center, Chicago, 1965.

His works were exhibited at the Carnegie Institute, 1956; Corcoran Gallery of Art, 1957; Art Institute of Chicago, 1957, 1960; Herron Art Museum, 1956; Chicago and Vicinity Exhibitions, Art Institute of Chicago, 1954–1960; St. Paul, 1952, 1954; Walker Art Center, Minneapolis, 1957; Toledo Museum of Art, 1957; Ringling Museum, 1959; Butler Institute of American Art, 1960; Des Moines Art Center, 1960; Tobu Gallery, Tokyo, 1974; Minnesota Museum of Art, St. Paul, 1975 (Retrospective 1949–1975); Knoedler Galleries, London, 1976; Fahlnass Konstsalon Gallery, Goteborg, Sweden, 1976.

His works are included in the permanent collection of the Illinois State Museum, Joslyn Art Museum, Woodham College, Oxford, England; National Museum of Sport in Art, New York; Hermitage Museum, Leningrad U.S.S.R., and Harding Museum, Chicago.

He has executed murals for the Continental Hotel, Chicago, 1963; Mercantile National Bank, Hammond Indiana, 1965; Swedish Loyd Ship—"SS Patricia," Stockholm, Sweden, 1966; Madison Square Garden N.Y., 1969; Sportsman's Park Clubhouse, Cicero, Illinois, 1976; Olympiads, Montreal, Canada, 1976.

He served as Instructor of Drawing, Art Institute of Chicago, 1950–1960; Painting, at Wintson-Salem Art Center, 1964; Drawing and Painting at Atlanta Art Council, 1968–1969; Atlanta Poverty Art Program, 1967–1968.

He held the position as Resident Artist, New York Jets Professional Football Team, 1968–1970; as artist reporter, ABC-TV Wide World of Sports, 1969; Official Artist, Major League Baseball Promotions, 1971; ABC-TV Official Artist, Olympiad, Munich, Germany, 1972.

Neiman's works have been reproduced on **Time Magazine** covers March 1, 1968, and January 17, 1972, and on the **Newsweek** cover of December 4, 1972. His work has been published in **Countdown to Superbowl** (with Dave Anderson), Random, 1969; **This Great Game** Prentice-Hall, 1971; **LeRoy Neiman Art and Life Style** Felicie Press, 1974; **Moby Dick** (artists limited edition), 1975.

Neiman has received the following

awards: Gold Medal from Salon d'Art Moderne, Paris, 1961; First Prize at Twin-City Exhibition, Minneapolis, 1953; Minnesota State Exhibition, 1954; Clark Memorial Prize, Art Institute of Chicago, 1957; Municipal Prize, Chicago Show at Art Institute, 1958; Ball State University, 1958; Mississippi Valley Exhibition Purchase Prize, 1959; AAU (Amateur Athletic Union), Award of Merit as the nation's most outstanding sport's artist, 1976; Honorary Doctor of Letters Degree, Franklin Pierce College, N. H., 1976.

Neiman was a member of the Renaissance Society of the University of Chicago, the Artists Equity, Faculty Association of the Art Institute, Chicago, and the American Association of University Professors. He became a member of the Chicago Society of Artists in 1958.

ANNETTE OKNER (Printmaker) was born and educated in Chicago, Illinois. She received a B.F.A. degree from the Art Institute of Chicago and a Master's degree from the Illinois Institute of Technology, School of Design. She attended the Instituto, San Miguel, Mexico, and has done post graduate work in several schools. She has traveled in Europe, Israel, Greece, Yugoslavia, Mexico, Canada and the United States. Although she concentrates primarily on etching, she also works in woodblock, lithography, serigraphy, and collography. Her background includes watercolor and other media.

One-woman exhibitions of her works were held at The Octagon Art Center, Ames, Iowa; Triton College, River Grove, Illinois; Northeastern Illinois State College, Chicago; Chicago Public Library, art room, main branch; Paul Theobald Gallery, Chicago; Green Earth Gallery, Evanston, Illinois; and Palmer House, Chicago.

National shows in which she participated are the J. B. Speed Art Museum, 8 State Print Show, Louisville, Kentucky; Library of Congress 23rd National Print Exhibition; 17th 18th and 19th National Print Exhibits Hunterdon Art Center, New Jersey; 4th International Art Exhibit, New Orleans, Louisiana; Contemporary Graphics, Chauncy Center, Princeton, New Jersey; Ohio Arts Council, Columbus, Ohio; Indiana Arts Commission, Indianapolis, Indiana; Carroll Reece Museum, Johnson City, Tennessee; Morris County College, Dover, New Jersey; and New York State College Museum, Binghamton, New York.

Other juried shows include New Horizons; Old Orchard; Art Institute Sales and Rental Gallery; Winnetka Schools Gallery; Harper College, Palatine, Illinois; Collector's Choice, Kaplan, J.C.C. Center; North Riverwoods Gallery, Chicago; Hyde Park Art Center, Chicago; and West Suburban Invitational, River Forest, Illinois.

Okner also participated in exhibits at Village Art Fair, Oak Park, Illinois; Park Forest Fair, Illinois; Chroma Art Festival; Highland Park Art Festival; Spring Art Festival, Beth Israel Temple, Skokie; and Chroma Art Festival, Downers Grove, Illinois; group shows with the Chicago Society of Artists and the American Jewish Art Club.

Her works are in public collections of New Jersey State Museum, Iowa State University, Standard Oil Company, Chicago Rehabilitation Center, Continental Illinois National Bank, Oak Park; River Forest High School, and St. Lukes Hospital, Chicago. She also had work included in a limited edition folio of original works of 13 artists, published by IIT, School of Design. Many private collectors have purchased her work.

Galleries representing her works are the Art Institute Sales and Rental Gallery; Venable Gallery, Washington, D. C.; Springfield, Illinois Musuem Gallery; Art Today, Elmhurst, Illinois; Cain Gallery Oak Park, Illinois, and Eye Corporation, Chicago, Illinois.

She was chairman of the Art Department at Austin High School before she resigned to devote more time to her art. Currently she is an art instructor at Triton College, River Grove, Illinois.

Awards received for her prints and drawings include the Purchase Prize 16th National Print Exhibit, Hunterdon, New Jersey; Dreikurs Memorial Award, American Jewish Art Club; Honorable Mentions Deerbrook Art Festival, North Shore Art League Print and Drawing Show, and First Prize 1977 C.S.A. Calendar prints.

ELIZABETH OPPENHEIM (Painter) was born in Vienna, Austria, in 1913. She received her early art training in Vienna and in the United States studying with A. Kikuchi, John Fabion, A. Uchima and others. She has traveled extensively in Europe, the Near East, Japan, Mexico and the U.S.A.

One-woman exhibitions of her works were held at the Little Gallery, Chicago;

Glencoe Women's Club, Glencoe, Illinois; Center for Continuing Education, University of Chicago; Chicago Public Library; and Park Forest Academy, Park Forest, Illinois.

She participated in juried shows of the North Shore Art League; Biennial Watercolor and Print Show of the Art Institute of Chicago; Allied Artists, New York; Albany Print Club; Renaissance Society of the University of Chicago; Chicago Artists Guild; Old Orchard Festival, Skokie, Illinois; and in group shows at the Crawford Gallery; Arts and Riverwoods, Milwaukee; Art Festival, Beth El Temple, Skokie, Illinois; Young Collectors Shows; and in the Chicago Society of Artists Annual Exhibitons.

Her works are included in public collections of the Chase-Manhattan Bank, New York; Standard Oil Building, Chicago; several in Canada, Israel and many more in the United States.

She has won several prizes from the North Shore Art League, the South Shore Commisssion Art League, and the Chicago Society of Artists.

In 1973 she moved to Berkeley, California. Prior to her move to California she was represented by the Rental and Sales Gallery of the Art Institute of Chicago; now, by the Arts and Crafts Co-Op in Berkeley, California.

VICTOR PERLMUTTER (Painter) was born in New York City on July 1, 1910, and studied at the New York School of Fine and Applied Arts (1931 diploma); College of the City of New York (1939, B. S.), also graduate work, Design Laboratory, New York, 1934–1935. His favorite media are oil, casein, and graphics.

One-man shows of his oils and watercolors were held at the Contemporary Art Center, New York City, 1939; Exhibit A Gallery, Chicago, 1957; Todros Geller Art Gallery, Chicago, 1952, 1954, 1955, 1956; Mandel Brothers Gallery, Chicago, 1953, 1955, 1956; New Trier, Wilmette, Illinois, 1957; Cliff Dwellers Art Gallery 1959; Anne L. Werbe Galleries, Detroit, Michigan, 1959; Northwestern University, Evanston, Illinois, 1961; Adele Rosenberg Gallery, Winnetka, 1962; Bernard Horwich Center, Chicago, 1963; Gilman Galleries, Chicago, 1968; Rosenstone Gallery, Chicago, 1970.

Group exhibitions in which his works were included are the Brooklyn Museum, 1942; Chicago and Vicinity Exhibition at Art Institute of Chicago, 1959, 1961; Art Institute of Milwaukee, 1950; Des Moines Art Center, 1955; Butler Institute of American Art, 1958; Society Contemporary Art, Art Institute of Chicago, 1959, 1960; American Watercolor Society, Rockefeller Center, New York, 1953; Well of the Sea Gallery, Chicago, 1950; Rockefeller Memorial Chapel, University of Chicago, 1953; Old Orchard Art Festival, 1960; Los Angeles Museum of Art, California, 1975.

His works were represented by the Art Rental and Sales Gallery of the Art Institute of Chicago from 1956 to 1974 and included in numerous private and public collections such as the Chicago Park District, St. Paul Federal Savings and Loan; National Boulevard Bank; Harry X. Winston collection, Chicago; Herman Spertus collection, Glencoe, Illinois, Allan Goldscmidt, Glencoe, Illinois, David Sac, Palo Alto, California; Herbert Friedlander, Raleigh, N. C., Sigmund Cohen, Skokie, Illinois, Helen Lawton, Flossmoor, Illinois, Donald McPherson, New Canaan, Connecticut, Max E. Meyer, Wilmette, Illinois; Eugene Spertus, Los Angeles, California, Charles Gershenson, Bethesda, Maryland; Robert Zimmerman, Park Forest, Illinois.

From 1933–1940 he taught art at the Educational Alliance Art School, Contemporary Art Center, and Design Laboratory, New York City.

Perlmutter served as Art Director of the college of Jewish Studies, Art Supervisor for the Board of Jewish Education, and Director of the Todros Geller Gallery in Chicago from 1949–1957. He was Director of the Art Program at Bernard Horwich Jewish Community Center in Chicago. He taught painting to adults, lectured on Contemporary Art and Artists and served as Director of Rosenstone Art Gallery at the Center from 1959–1974.

He authored several articles on art, and illustrated a number of books.

He was invited to serve as Art Consultant at the Jewish Material Claims against Germany Commission Ford Foundation, Humanities and Arts Program in 1954, 1955, 1956 and 1957.

In 1954 he was appointed Co-Chairman of the American Tercentenary Exhibition in Chicago; Director of Chicago Artists No-Jury Exhibition in 1957; Secretary of Executive Committee for Chicago Artists Exhibition in 1958. In

1958–1959 Victor Perlmutter was appointed Director of the Festival of the Americas of Chicago, an inter-American cultural exchange program, held in conjunction with the Pan-American games.

He has served as juror on the National Scholastic Arts Competitions for the Chicago Board of Education, Art Institute Sales and Rental Galleries, South Shore Commission Annual Exhibition, the National Polish Art Exhibition and the Bnai Brith Art Competition in 1956.

Perlmutter received art critics awards at Annual Exhibitions of the American Jewish Arts Club at the Todros Geller Gallery in Chicago, 1953, 1954, 1955, 1957, 1958, 1960, 1961, 1962 in the Chicago and Vicinity Exhibition at the Art Institute of Chicago in 1956; Brower Award, Art Institute of Chicago, 1957; Art Institute of Chicago Purchase Award of the John Barton Payme Fund, 1964.

Perlmutter has been written about in **Art News**, **Who's Who in the Midwest**, **Chicago Sun Times**, **Chicago Daily News**, **Chicago Herald American**, **Chicago Tribune**, **The Art League News**, **Chicago American**, **Des Moines Register**, **Detroit Times** and the **Sentinel.**

JUDY M. PETACQUE (Designer) was born in Chicago, Illinois, and studied at the Art Institute of Chicago and the University of Chicago (B.A.E., and M.F.A.). She has traveled extensively in Samoa, Fiji Islands, Cambodia, Indonesia (Bali), Thailand, India, Ceylon, Japan, Hong Kong, Europe and Israel.

She has held one-woman shows at the downtown Public Library, Lake View Public Library, Sheffield Public Library, Marina City, Sun-Times Building and in local small galleries.

Juried shows in which she participated include the Bi-Annual Print Shows, Art Institute of Chicago; New Horizon Shows; Old Town Triangle Center; Hyde Park Art Center; North Shore Art League; Old Orchard Art Festival; Cinema Arts Festival; Temple Shows; Museum of Science and Industry Pan American Exhibit, and many others.

Recent commissions include 15 designs for Edward Fields Custom Rug Company, and two wallpaper books for Louis DeJonge Company, Inc., current ads featuring the designs "Bubble Up" are in **Architectural Digest**, **Interiors**, and **Interior Design.** She is presently working on collages and batik wall hangings.

Approximately 300 of her illustrations are sold each year at Old Town and Hyde Park Art Fairs.

Galleries which have represented her works are Sun-Times Gallery; Art Institute Rental and Sales Gallery; Bendel Gallery, New York; Marina City Gallery; Coronet, Peoples Gas & Coke Company; Old Town Triangle Center.

She taught in the Glenview Public Schools, Art Institute Junior School, Chicago Public Schools and from 1966 at the Old Town Triangle Art Center (Silk Screen and Design). She is presently teaching Design at the Ray-Vogue School of Design. For the last fourteen years she has been a free lance designer and illustrator of children's books and films. Her textile designs have been purchased by Schumacher, Katzenbach and Warren, United Desota, Fieldcrest, Columbus Coated Fabrics, Everfast, Bates Fabrics, Charles Bloom, Inc., Bob Mitchell, Elenhank, Edward Fields, Craftex Mills, United Merchants, Warner Wallpaper, and more designs for rugs, drapery and wallpaper.

Petacque received awards for design and silk screening and fabric designs in New York showrooms and collections and Museum of Science and Industry Pan American Exhibit.

LOUISE PIERCE (Painter) received her art education at Mac Murray College, Jacksonville, Illinois, (A. B.), and at Art Institute of Chicago (B.F.A.). She also studied with Paul Wieghart. She has traveled and painted in Europe, as far east as Hungary and Yugoslavia, Canada, Mexico, most of the United States, Alaska and the Carribean. She works in oil, watercolor and graphics.

One-woman exhibitions of her works were held at Evanston Art Center, Evanston Community Center, Mac Murray College, Jacksonville, Illinois, and Old Town Art Center, Chicago.

Pierce participated in group exhibitions at the Federal Court Building; Continental Can Company; Covenant Club; Monroe Gallery; University Club of Chicago and Women's Club of Evanston.

For many years she was employed in advertising and has taught at the Ray-Vogue Art School.

CLAIRE F. PRUSSIAN (Painter) was born in Chicago, Illinois, on May 22, 1930, and studied at: Wellsley College, Wellsley, Mass., and Art Institute of Chicago. She has traveled in France, Italy, England, Canada, Mexico and in the

United States. Her favorite medium is acrylic, but she also enjoys drawing and photography.

She has held one-woman exhibitions at the Winnetka Bank, 1971; Arlington Heights Public Library, 1972; and two-women shows at Northbrook Public Library, 1973, Winnetka Women's Club, 1972.

Juried shows in which her paintings were included were the Chicago and Vicinity, Art Institute of Chicago, 1965; New Horizon, 1962; Union League of Chicago, 1965–1972; Women, 1971; Northern Illinois University, De Kalb, Illinois; North Shore Landmarks, 1972; Old Orchard Art Fair, 1972, 1973; Bernard Horwich Jewish Community Center, 1973; Evanston Art Fair, 1972; Critics Choice, Art Rental and Sales Gallery, Art Institute of Chicago, 1973; 35th Exhibition — Society for Contemporary Art — "Drawings of the '70's" Art Institute of Chicago; Davidson National Print and Drawing Competition, Davidson College, Davidson, North Carolina; Artists Guild of Chicago; Quincy College, Quincy, Illinois; Women in the Arts, 1974, West Bend Gallery Fine Arts, West Bend, Wisconsin; Madison Art Center, Madison, Wisconsin; East Tennessee State University. By invitation: A Drawing Exhibition, Slocum Gallery, Johnson City, Tennessee; Hunter Museum of Art, Chattanooga, Tennessee. Four group shows, Artemesia Gallery, Chicago; One Two-Person Show, Artemesia Gallery, Chicago, Group Show, Van Straaten Gallery, Chicago.

Other exhibitions in which she participated were the North Shore Art League, since 1968; Chicago Society of Artists annual exhibitions; Hyde Park Art Center, 1973; Country Side Art Center; Artemisia Gallery, 1973.

Prussian's work is included in public collections of the Continental Illinois National Bank and Trust Company of Chicago, Rehabilitation Institute of Chicago; Winnetka Public School System, Winnetka, Illinois.

She is represented by the Artemisia Gallery, Art Rental and Sales Gallery, Art Institute of Chicago, and the Van Straaten Gallery, Chicago.

Currently, she is teaching at Countryside Art Center, Arlington Heights.

Claire F. Prussian won First Prize for paintings at the Deere Path Art Fair, 1972; Women's Club of Evanston, 1969; and several Honorable Mentions at the North Shore Art League.

Prussian is a member of the Arts Club of Chicago and the Chicago Society of Artists.

FRED RAPPAPORT (Painter) was born in Vienna, Austria, on June 8, 1912, and studied at the Vienna Academy of Fine Arts (M. A.) and University of Illinois (O. D.). He has traveled in the United States, Mexico, Europe and Israel. His favorite media are oil, graphics and mosaic. He also enjoys writing and music.

One-man shows of his paintings and graphics were held at the Newman Brown Gallery, Studio 47 Gallery, Oehlschlager Gallery, Harper Gallery, Old Town Art Center, College of Jewish Studies, Northwestern University, K.A.M. Temple, Suburban Fine Arts Center, Evanston Art Center, Hillel Foundation of Northwestern University.

He has exhibited in group shows at the Art Institute of Chicago; Art Institute Rental and Sales Gallery; Union Art League; North Shore Art League; Winnetka Community Center; Evanston Art Center; Suburban Fine Arts Center; Welna Gallery; Sun-Times Gallery; Old Orchard Art Festival; 57th Street Art Fair; Evanston Art Fair; Oak Park Temple; Temple Judea; Illini Club; Renaissance Society of the University of Chicago; University of Illinois; Spertus Museum of Judaica, and in many other exhibitions in the United States, Vienna, Austria, Israel and England.

His works are included in private collections in this country and in Europe and in public collections of the Union Art League and Civic Foundation, K.A.M. Temple, Oak Park Temple, West Suburban Temple, University of Illinois and the Bernard Horwich Center in Chicago.

Galleries which represent his work are the Langsdorff Gallery, Vienna, Austria; Museum of Modern Art, Jerusalem, Israel; Park Gallery, Detroit, Michigan; Scott Richards Gallery, New York; Art Rental and Sales Gallery, Art Institute of Chicago; Welna Gallery and Harper Court Gallery in Chicago.

Rappaport is a registered Art Therapist. He has taught art in the Suburban Fine Arts Center, Jewish Community Centers, and in his private studio. He has served as Psychiatric Art Therapist at the Chicago State Hospital, Veterans Administration West Side Hospital and in private practice.

Rappaport received three Union League Purchase Awards, five Maurice Spertus Awards, three Todros Geller Awards, two Old Orchard Art Festival Awards, the Bernstein Award and others.

LESTER REBBECK (Painter) was born in Chicago, Illinois, on June 25, 1929, and studied at Art Institute of Chicago (B.A.E.) and University of Chicago (M.A.E.) He has traveled in Austria, Bahama Islands, Belgium, England, France, Germany, Greece, Holland, Italy, Liechtenstein, Mexico, Monaco, Switzerland and Yugoslavia. His favorite media are oils, acrylics, graphics and sculpture.

He has held one-man exhibitions in St. Elmo, 1953; Borg Warner, 1964; Baird and Warner, 1964; Evanston High School, 1965; William Rainey Harper College, 1970; Lake Forest Academy, 1973.

He participted in juried group shows at Creative Galleries, New York, 1954; Concordia Teachers College, 1956; Boston Society of Independent Artists, 1956; Sculptor Gallery, St. Louis, 1967; G. I. Show Art Institute of Chicago, 1953, 1954, 1957; Momentun 1956; Alumni Association, School of the Art Institute, Mc Cormick Place 1963; Chicago National Design Center, 1964, 1965; Harper Gallery, 1966; Union League Club, 1969; Art Rental and Sales Gallery Art Institute of Chicago, 1962–1973.

Other shows in which he participated were those held at John M. Smyth Company, 1965–1966; Covenant Club, University Club, Fund for Florence, 1967; Compas, 1968; Old Town Triangle Center, 1969.

His works are included in private collections of Dr. Alan Green, Mr. Harvey E. Meyer, Dr. Mellach, Mr. Seymour K. Wollack, Mr. William Fischer.

Galleries which represent Rebbeck's paintings and sculpture are Countryside Art Gallery, Chicago Society of Artists Gallery, Art Rental and Sales Gallery of the Art Institute of Chicago, and Sculptors Gallery of St. Louis, Missouri.

His works are reproduced in the book **Creating Art From Anything** by Dona Z. Meilach.

He has taught in Chicago public high schools; South Junior High School, District #25, Arlington Heights, Illinois; Adult Education, Arlington Heights High School; William Rainey Harper College; Countryside Art Center.

He has served as director of Countryside Art Gallery, 1963–1968; Chairman of the Directors, 1964–1965; and Chicago Society of Artists Gallery, 1967–1968.

Rebbeck's awards include Class Honorable Mention for still life painting, 1949–1950, Art Institute of Chicago; G. I. Show, Art Institute of Chicago, Medal Award, 1953; Mc Henry Art Fair, First Place oils, 1960; Third Place in 1961; Best in Show, 1962; Countryside Art Festival, Honorable Mention, 1966; and Third Prize in Sculpture in 1967.

SHANE E. REITMAN (Painter) was born in Los Angeles, California, on March 14, 1950, and studied at the University of Illinois (B.F.A. and M. A.). She has traveled to Paris and Israel. Her favorite medium is watercolor, usually done on canvas.

She has held a one-woman exhibition at Aurora College, 1974, and a watercolor exhibit at the University of Illinois.

Her teaching experience includes Painting, Maine Adult Evening School, 1970, 1971; Drawing, Design and Painting — Art for Elementary Teachers, Aurora College, 1973 to present. She also served as designer for Marshall Field and Company, 1962–1972.

FREDRICK REMAHL (Painter) was born in Bohuslan, Sweden, on June 18, 1901, and studied in Europe and America. He has painted in the Scandinavian countries and in Germany and France and in this country in Montana, North Dakota, Minnesota, Wisconsin, Indiana, Ohio, Pennsylvania, New York and Massachusetts.

One-man exhibitions of his works have been held at the Morton Galleries in New York, the Minnesota State Fair and, in Chicago, at the Midland Club, the Chicago Woman's Aid, Weisenborn's Studio and the Gaulios Galleries.

He has exhibited in the Corcoran Gallery of Art, Washington, D. C., the Pennsylvania Academy of Fine Arts, the Brooklyn Museum, the Minneapolis Art Institute and the Art Center in New York, the Chicago Artists and Vicinity Shows at the Art Institute of Chicago in 1942 and 1949 and in the Delphic Studios Exhibition, New York, 1935, New Jersey State Museum Exhibition, Trenton, New Jersey, 1936, the Riverside Museum Exhibition, New York, New York, 1939 and many others.

His work has been written about in New York, Chicago and Swedish newspapers and in **The Arts** by Forbes Watson, C. J. Bulliet and others.

He has been twice awarded prizes by the Swedish exhibitions and is represented with two paintings in the Gothenburg Museum in Sweden.

Remahl has been a member of the Chicago Society of Artists since 1940, the Illinois Academy of Fine Arts, the Swedish-American Art Association and the Minneapolis Society of Fine Arts.

INCREASE ROBINSON (Painter) was born in Chicago in 1890 and studied at Wellesley College, the University of Chicago, the Art Institute of Chicago and in Woodstock, New York. Her outstanding teachers were John Norton, Ernest Thurn and Hans Hofman. She has painted in various parts of the United States.

She has had one-artist shows in the Cordon Club, the Chicago Woman's Aid, and several others in Chicago and elsewhere.

She has exhibited at the Art Institute of Chicago in A Century of Progress Exhibition of Paintings and Sculpture in 1933, the Pennsylvania Academy of Fine Arts, and throughout the United States, in various circuit exhibitions sponsored by the Art Institute of Chicago and the American Federation of Arts.

Robinson was Director of the W.P.A. Art Project and of the prestigious Increase Robinson Studio Gallery in Michigan Square, Diana Court where many prominent Chicago artists held their exhibitions.

Robinson has been a member of the Chicago Society of Artists since 1928, serving as president for several years.

THEODORE ROSZAK (Sculptor, Painter) was born in Poland on May 1, 1907. His family settled in Chicago in 1909. He studied at the Art Institute of Chicago, 1922–1929; University of Chicago; University of Illinois and Columbia University.

One-man shows of his works were held at the Matisse Gallery, 1950, 1952; at the Venice Biennale, 1960; and the Art Institute of Chicago, 1961.

His commissions include The Spire and Bell Tower, Massachusetts Institute of Technology, 1956; U. S. Embassy, London, 1960; Invocation V, Maremont Building, Chicago, 1962; Flight, New York World's Fair, 1964; Sentinel Public Health Laboratories, New York, 1968.

His works were exhibited in the Whitney Museum of American Art Retrospective, 1956; Tate Gallery, London, 1959; U. S. National Exhibition in Moscow, USSR, 1959; Venice Beinnale, 1960; Guggenheim International, New York, 1964, and in many other museums and galleries.

His paintings and sculpture are part of permanent collections of the Guggenheim Museum and the Museum of Modern Art, New York; Whitney Museum of American Art, Yale Gallery of Art, New Haven, Connecticut; Pennsylvania Academy of Fine Arts; Smithsonian Institute; and Hirshhorn Museum, both in Washington, D. C.

He has authored and illustrated **In Pursuit of an Image** published by the Art Institute of Chicago, 1955, and his lecture "The New Sculpture" was published by the Museum of Modern Art.

He has been written about by Peter Selz, **Theodore Roszak**, published by the Museum of Modern Art in 1959; by Michael Conil Lacolste, "Theodore Roszak," **Dictionary of Modern Sculpture**, 1960; by H.H. Arnason, "Theodore Roszak, Sculptor," in **Art of America**, 1961; "Profile of Theodore Roszak" by Belle Krasne in **Art Digest** and in **Current Biography**, June, 1966.

Roszak served as Professor of Sculpture at Sarah Lawrence College, 1940–1956, and Visiting Critic for Graduate Seminar, Columbia University, 1970–1972.

He served on the International Architectural Sculpture Commission, 1957, the National Advisory Commission, National Council on Arts and Government, U.S. Delegate to the International Congress of Arts in Vienna, 1960; President's Fine Arts Commission, Washington, D. C., 1963–1968; New York City Fine Arts Commissioner, 1969–1975.

He was recipient of awards from the Art Institute of Chicago, 1928, 1929, 1934; Campagna Award, 1961, Whitney Museum of American Art, 1934; medals, World's Fair, Poznan, Poland, 1930; Art Institute of Chicago, 1951; Pennsylvania Academy of Fine Arts, 1956; a prize in Sao Paulo, Brazil in 1951; Logan Award, Art Institute of Chicago, 1947 and 1951; Ford Foundation National Grant, 1959.

Roszak has been a member of the Drawing Society, 1972; Louis Comfort Tiffany Foundation, Trustee, 1964; Skowhegan School of Painting and Sculpture, the

Board of Governors, 1960; National Institute of Arts and Letters, vice-president, 1970.

He has been a member of the Chicago Society of Artists since 1928 when he participated in its Autumn Exhibition with a painting "Nude" and a lithography "Nude with Lilly" at the Stevens Hotel in Chicago. He is an Honorary Fellow, Vienna Secession, Austria.

MARIE SALWONCHIK (Designer, Printmaker) was born in Chicago, Illinois, on May 25, 1930, and studied at Loyola University of Chicago, Ph.D., and the School of the Art Institute of Chicago, B.A.E. and M.A.E., winning a number of scholarships as a student. She has traveled in Canada, U.S.A., the Soviet Union, Mexico, South America, Greece, Portugal, Spain, Italy and France. Her favorite medium is batik.

Her work is included in the private collections of Helen Radican and Raymond W. Garbe and is in the Artists Equity Midwest Fine Art Color Slide and the Chicago Public Library slide collections.

She has taught at the elementary, upper-grade center and high school levels and the 414 Art Workshop. She has served as supervisor of art for five years in the Chicago Public Schools.

She was a guest on the TV Contemporary Art Education course from Chicago Teachers College, North on Channel 11, 1963, presenting Batik. She has been curriculum guide illustrator, Bureau of Curriculum Development and Teaching, Chicago Public Schools, and guest speaker at St. Joseph's Calumet College, East Chicago, Indiana.

Salwonchik won second prize for a Chicago Society of Artists Calendar print, 1962.

For a number of years Salwonchik has served as Corresponding Secretary and Chairman of the Membership Committee of the Chicago Society of Artists.

FERN SAMUELS (Painter) was born in Chicago, Illinois, on February 16, 1931, and studied at Mudelein College, (B.F.A., 1973—with a minor in Education) with post graduate work at the Art Institute of Chicago.

She has traveled to Mexico, Caribbean Islands, Hawaii, Israel, England, Greece and Peru. Her favorite media are oil painting, fabric design and weaving. She also enjoys reading and transcendental meditation, the theatre and ballet.

She has participated in juried group shows at Mc Allen International Museum, 1971; New Horizons Show, 1973; Countryside Art Gallery, 1975; Evanston Art Center, 1970, 1971 and 1972; Moraine Valley Community College, 1976; Mundelein College, 1976; Art Rental and Sales Gallery, Art Institute of Chicago since 1968.

Currently she is teaching two courses at Columbia College: "Fabric Arts" and "Art in Chicago, Now," a seminar on the Chicago art scene. She also conducts a bi-annual ten-week course in weaving for adults and another for senior citizens; and a bi-annual ten-week course in copper enameling for ten students.

During the past three years she has conducted workshops at the Art Institute of Chicago, Columbia College, Oakton Community College and the Martin Luther King Lab School. These workshops were in copper enameling, weaving, textile design, psychology and art, and art enrichment.

She is the head of the planning committee for "Teachers of Adult Workshops" since 1975 and the Chicago Regional Representative for "Surface Design Conferences" in 1976 and 1977.

Samuels won Third Prize at Old Town Triangle Art Center for a print in 1969; Second Prize for serigraph from North Shore Council of Churches Show, 1970; Third Prize for wood collage from Evanston Women's Club, 1970. She has won the Judges Selection for exceptional quality at the Fabric Design International Competition 1976.

MARVIN SARUK (Painter) was born in Chicago, Illinois, on September 10, 1925, and studied at the American Academy of Art, the University of Notre Dame and at the School of the Art Institute of Chicago. He has traveled and painted in Canada, Mexico, Scotland, England, Holland, France, Spain, Italy, Switzerland and Israel. He works in oils, watercolor, pen and ink, acrylic and small sculpture.

In 1962–1963 he participated in a work-study program in Mougins, France, and was involved in a radio-interview in 1963, Cannes Film Festival Bldg. on the Nice-Matin, Magazine Blue.

He has held one-man exhibitions at the Parnasse Gallery, Cannes, France, 1963; Parsons College, Fairfield, Iowa, 1969; The South Bend Art Center, South Bend, Indiana, 1965 (three-man show).

Juried shows in which his works were included are the Butler Institute of American Art, Youngstown, Ohio, 1968; the Union League Club of Chicago, 1972; the Art Institute Sales and Rental Gallery, 1968–1976; the Artists Guild of Chicago, 1964–1975; Societe Des Independants, Grand Palais, Paris, France, 1964; the Chicago Society of Artists; the Arts and Riverwoods, Deerfield, Illinois, 1971; the Wayne Art Show, Wayne, Illinois.

His works are represented by the Parnasse Gallery, Cannes, France; Ontario East Gallery, Chicago; Art Institute Sales and Rental Gallery; the Artists Guild of Chicago; and included in private collections in Mexico City; Dublin, Ireland; Nice, France; Jerusalem, Israel and in the U. S.

Saruk was the recipient of the Artists Guild of Chicago, First prize in the Fine Art Exhibition, 1970; Honorable Mention, 1971; Purchase Prize, Drawing Exhibition, 1970.

MOLLY J. SCHIFF (Painter) was born in Chicago, Illinois, on October 19, 1927, and studied at the School of the Art Institute of Chicago (B.F.A., M.F.A., M.A.E.) and Illinois Institute of Technology (post grad graphics). Her travels include United States, England, France, Spain, Portugal, Greece, Yugoslavia, Turkey, Israel, West Indies, Canada, Mexico, Guatemala, Peru, Bolivia, Bulgaria, Argentina, Brazil, Trinidad, Japan, Belgium, Taiwan, Hong Kong, Hawaii, Puerto Rico, Russia, Holland and India. She works in oil, watercolor, lithography, serigraphy, etching and drawing.

One-woman exhibitions of her works were held at Sky Room Gallery, Wisconsin, 1963; Michellini's Gallery, Evanston, 1964; Chicago Public Library, 1967; Illinois Visually Handicapped Institute, 1968; Markal Corporation Teacher's Convention, New York, 1969; Evanston Township High School, 1971; Burlington Iowa Art Center, 1972; Barat College, 1971; Stanislaus State College, California, 1973; Blackhawk Restaurant, 1972; and Middletown Ohio Art Center, 1968; New Trier East High School, 1976; Illinois Arts Council, 1976.

She participated in juried group exhibitions of the Evanston Art Center, North Shore Art League, Old Town Art Fair, Evanston Art Fair, Old Orchard Art Fair, New Horizons; Balzekas Museum; Hull House Arts Festival; New Trier East High School; Chicago Art Institute Travel Exhibition; Alumni Exhibition, S.A.I.C.; Gary Art League; Evanston Library; Hubbard Woods Art Fair; Hinsdale Grace Church; Mayer Kaplan Print Exhibition; Werbe Gallery, Detroit; B'Tzalel Gallery, California; Delta Phi Delta Honor Society; American Jewish Arts Club; and Illinois Institute of Technology.

She is included in private collections in Greece, Israel, England, Canada, California, New York, Arizona, Michigan, Ohio, Florida, Wisconsin, and Standard Oil of Chicago.

Schiff's work is represented by the Art Rental and Sales Gallery of the Art Institute of Chicago, Peoria Art Museum Rental Gallery, Roy Boyd Gallery and Joy Horwich Gallery.

She has taught in elementary and high schools; park district; Jewish Community Centers; adult evening school; Illinois Visually Handicapped Institution; Governors State University, New Trier High Schools.

Schiff has received awards from the Chicago Crippled Children's Society; School of the Art Institute of Chicago; Arts Day at Industry, Meister Brau; South Shore Commission; North Shore Art League Members Show, paintings and graphics; Hubbard Woods Fair, graphics; American Jewish Art Club.

BEATRICE B. SCHILLER (Painter, Printmaker) was born in Chicago, Illinois, and studied at the Institute of Design and Illinois Institute of Technology; the Art Institute of Chicago; and privately with Richard Florsheim, Jack Kearny, Herbert Davidson, Kwak Wai Lau, and Stanley Mitruk. She has traveled extensively throughout the U.S., Europe, Israel, the Caribbean, and the Hawaiian Islands. Much inspiration for her art work came from her travels. Her favorite media are watercolor, drawing, acrylic, woodblock, and oils.

She has held one-woman exhibitions at Stuart Brent Book Shop, 1964; Commonwealth Art Center and Gallery, Chicago, 1965; the Chicago Public Library, 1967; The Covenant Club of Chicago, 1971.

Juried shows in which she participated are The Art Rental and Sales Gallery, Art Institute of Chicago; National Exhibit of Springfield Art League, Museum of Fine Arts, Springfield, Mass.; National Exhibit of Small Paintings, Purdue University, 1964; Sixth Union League, Chicago, 1965; Illinois State Fair Professional Art Exhibit, Springfield, Illinois,

1963, 1964; Suburban Fine Arts Festival, Highland Park, Illinois, 1964; the Golden Mile of Art, Northwest Art League, Chicago, 1964; the North Shore Art League Print and Drawing Show, Winnetka, Illinois, 1966; Suburban Fine Arts Center Festival of Arts, 1966; invitational, First Annual Exhibition, Chicago Society of Artists, Chicago, 1966; Old Town Art Center Exhibition "Flowers," Chicago, 1966; 17th Annual National Exhibition of Realistic Art, Springfield, Mass.; Seventh Union League Art Show, Chicago, 1967; The Butler Institute of American Art, Youngstown, Ohio, 1967; 12th Annual Winnetka Public Schools Art Library, 1967; Wayne 18th Annual Exhibiton, Wayne, Illinois, 1968; North Shore Art League Drawing and Print Show, 1968, 1969; Anshe-Emet Cinema Arts Festival, Chicago, 1968; New Trier High School Painting Exhibition, Winnetka, Illinois, 1969; New Horizons in Sculpture and Painting, Chicago, 1970; Catherine Lorillard Wolfe Art Club; National Academy of Design, New York, 1971; "Gallery M. Inc.," Farmington, Connecticut, 1971; Beth El Art Show, Hartford, Connecticut, 1971; Municipal Art League, 1972; Ninth Union League Art Show, Chicago, 1972; New Trier High School Painting Exhibition, Winnetka, Illinois, 1972; Municipal Art League, Chicago, 1973.

Her works are included in private collections of "Miss Alice," New York City; Mr. & Mrs. Samuel H. Marcus, Wichita, Kansas; Mr. & Mrs. Bertram M. Rubenstein, Milwaukee; Dr. & Mrs. Alex J. Arieff, Chicago; Mr. & Mrs. David Studner, Scarsdale, N. Y.; Dr. & Mrs. Burton J. Winston, Palm Springs, California; Dr. & Mrs. Benjamin Boshes, Chicago; Mr. & Mrs. Arnold Cohn, Toronto, Canada; Mr. & Mrs. Daniel J. Epstein, San Diego, California; Dr. & Mrs. Emanuel J. Wexler, Wilmette, Illinois; Mr. & Mrs. Joseph Minow, Palm Springs, California, and in the collection of MBPXL Corporation, Wichita, Kansas.

Her paintings, prints and drawings are included in public collections of the Standard Oil Company, Chicago; Excel Packing Company, Wichita, Kansas; Michael Reese Hospital, Chicago, Illinois. She is listed in **Who's Who in American Art**, 1973 and 1976.

Schiller's work is represented by the Art Rental and Sales Gallery of the Art Institute of Chicago; "Gallery M. Inc." Farmington, Connecticut; "Collector's Gallery," Chicago.

Schiller received The Reinhardt J. Jahn Purchase Prize, Sixth Union League Art Show; Honorable Mention, North Shore Art League Annual Exhibition, 1966; Second Prize, Suburban Fine Arts Center Members' show; the Herbert C. Brook Purchase Prize, Seventh Union League Art Show; Honorable Mention, the Municipal Art League of Chicago, 1971, 1973; Honorable Mention, the Chicago Society of Artists, 1974, for calendar print.

FLORA SCHOFIELD (Painter) was born in Lanark, Illinois in 1871, and studied at the Art Institute of Chicago. She spent many summers in Provincetown, Massachusetts, and in Woodstock, New York. She also maintained a studio in Paris for about nine years at which time she was a colleague of a number of painters and sculptors who achieved international fame. Her outstanding teachers were Albert Gleizes, Andre Lhote and F. Leger. She painted in various parts of the United States and in France, Germany, Italy and Spain.

One-artist exhibitions of her work have been held at the Art Institute of Chicago and Gallerie Carmine in Paris.

Her paintings were exhibited in the Carnegie International, the Detroit, Cleveland, Brooklyn, and Boston museums, and the Art Institute of Chicago. She has exhibited in the Salon D' Automne, Salon des Independents and Sur Independents in France.

Schofield accumulated a fine collection of paintings by Juan Gris, Survage and sculpture by Chana Orloff when they were still struggling painters and sculptors. Some of their works were purchased from her estate for the Art Institute of Chicago when she died.

She was awarded the Jules Bower prize for landscape in 1929 and the Harry Frank prize for figure composition, both from the Art Institute of Chicago.

Schofield was greatly interested and much stimulated by the exciting Armory Show of 1913 which had a decided influence on painters in America. She was a long time member of the Chicago Society of Artists, the Cordon Club, the Renaissance Society of the University of Chicago, the New York Society of Women Artists, Ten Artists (Chicago) and the Provincetown Art Association.

She was represented by the Norton Gallery of West Palm Beach, Florida, and included in many public and private collections throughout the country. Her studio residence on East Pearson Street was a gathering place for Chicago artists and a focal place of interest in the art world of Chicago for many years.

Schofield died in 1960.

HAROLD A. SCHULTZ (Painter) was born in Grafton, Wisconsin, on January 6, 1907, and studied at the Layton School of Art in Milwaukee, Northwestern University (B.S. & M.A.). He traveled and painted in Mexico during the summer of 1936. During other summers he painted in various parts of the United States and Canada.

One-man exhibitions of his work have been held at the Layton Art Gallery in Milwaukee.

His works were exhibited at the International Exhibition of Watercolors, Art Institute of Chicago; 1928–1932, 1934–1936, 1938, and 1939; Annual Exhibition of American Paintings and Sculpture, Art Institute of Chicago, 1929, 1932, 1935, 1937, 1939, 1940, 1941; Annual Exhibition of Artists of Chicago and Vicinity, Art Institute of Chicago, 1930–1935, 1938, 1940–1942; Brooklyn Museum Exhibition of Watercolors, New York, 1931; Ferargil Galleries, Watercolor Exhibition, 1940; Chicago Society of Artists Exhibition, 1931 to 1942 annually; Central Illinois Art Exhibit, Decatur, Illinois, Winner of a $25.00 watercolor prize, 1946.

Schultz's work has been included in the Art Institute of Chicago traveling exhibitions and exhibited in the Increase Robinson Studio Gallery in Chicago.

He exhibited regularly in the annual Faculty Exhibitions on campus and in traveling exhibitions, University of Illinois at Urbana-Champaign.

His work is represented in numerous private collections including those of Nathan Cummings, Chicago, and Nelson Eddy (estate), Hollywood.

A biographical statement and a painting were reproduced in the book, **Art of Today** — Chicago, 1933, by J. Z. Jacobson.

With J. Harlan Shores he wrote, **Art in the Elementary School,** University of Illinois Press, 1948. He contributed to such journals and publications as **Art Education, College Art Journal** (reviews), **Encyclopedia of Educational Research,** and the **Mental Measurements Yearbook.**

Schultz was head of the art department in the Francis Parker School in Chicago, 1932–1940, and Professor of Art and Design at University of Illinois, 1940–1975; Professor Emeritus, 1975.

He lectured on Art and Education to many groups, including the National Education Association and the Western Arts Association. Some of these presentations have been included in the published proceedings of these groups. On three occasions he organized the Art Sections of the National Conferences of the Progressive Education Association. On various other occasions he organized conference programs for the National Art Education Association.

Schultz was twice a recipient of Honorable Mention awards in exhibits sponsored by the Chicago Society of Artists. In 1976 he was the recipient of an award for "outstanding contributions to the profession of art education" by the National Art Education Association.

Schultz has been a member of the Illinois Art Education Association, National Art Education Association and International Society for Education through Art (UNESCO). He served the Chicago Society of Artists as Treasurer for the years 1935 and 1936 and as President in 1937.

WILLIAM S. SCHWARTZ (Painter, Printmaker) was born in Smorgen, Russia, on February 23, 1896, and studied at the Vilna Art School in Russia, 1908–1912. At the age of sixteen he emigrated to America and three years later entered the Art Institute of Chicago where he was awarded a scholarship. To help support himself he worked 16 hours a day waiting on tables, ushering in theatres, singing in concerts and operas. In 1918, the year after graduation from the School of the Art Institute (with honors in life study, portraiture, and general excellence in painting), he was represented in the annual show of Artists of Chicago and Vicinity. Since that time his work has been seen in national and international exhibitions held in this country and abroad. Schwartz worked in oils, watercolors, lithography, and sculpture.

His works have been exhibited in the Metropolitan Museum of Art; Museum of Modern Art; Whitney Museum; Pennsylvania Academy; Art Institute of Chicago; Joslyn Museum; Oklahoma Museum; Dallas Public Museum and State Museum of Illinois; Associated Artists Gallery and many other museums.

Schwartz's works are included in many

private collections and represented in the following permanent public collections: the Art Institute of Chicago; the San Francisco Museum, the Joslyn Art Museum, Omaha; Pennsylvania Academy of Fine Arts, Philadelphia; Santa Barbara Museum of Art; Denver Art Museum; Art Alliance of Philadelphia; Encyclopedia Britannica, American Peoples Encyclopedia; Dallas Museum of Fine Arts; Library of Congress and Department of Labor, Washington, D. C.; Henry Gallery; Des Moines Art Center; Montclair Art Museum; Elgin Academy; Detroit Institute of Arts; Musee Juif, Paris, France; Ein Herod Museum; Tel Aviv Museum, Israel; Biro-Bidjan Museum, Russia; Collections of Universities of Illinois, Chicago, Nebraska, Montana, Wyoming, Minnesota, Monticello College, Bradley, Chicago Public Schools, Oshkosh Public Museum, Union League Club of Chicago and others. William S. Schwartz's works are owned by fifty-three museums and university galleries.

He has done murals at the Chicago World's Fair of 1933; Cook County Nurses Home, Chicago; and in Post Offices at Fairfield, Eldorado, and Pittsfield, Illinois.

Since 1922, Schwartz's works have been written about and reproduced in more than one-hundred publications by every major art critic in the nation.

He received awards for paintings and lithographs at the Detroit Institute of Arts; Art Institute of Chicago (on five different occasions from 1927–1945); the Scarab Club of Detroit; Honorable Mention; Monticello College, Godfrey, Illinois; First Prize; Albert Kahn Prize, Temple Beth El, Detroit, First Prize; Covenant Club, Chicago, Prizes, 1936–1941; First National Lithography Exhibition, Oklahoma Art Center, Honorable Mention; 4th National Lithography Exhibition, Oklahoma Art Center, First Prize; Corpus Christi Art Foundation, Corpus Christi, Texas, Honorable Mention; Union League Club of Chicago, First Prize.

Schwartz died on February 10, 1977.

LEOPOLD B. SEGEDIN (Painter) was born in Chicago, Illinois, on March 22, 1927 and studied at the University of Illinois (B.F.A., 1948, and M.F.A., 1950) and at Roosevelt University 1950–1952. He has traveled and painted in France, England, Italy, Greece, Mexico and Canada. His favorite media are acrylic, pen and ink, oil and watercolor.

One-man exhibitions of his works were held at Malihini Gallery, Chicago, 1955; Hillel Foundation, University of Chicago, 1955; Fauve Gallery, Chicago, 1956; Anna Werbe Gallery, Detroit, Michigan, 1957; Exhibit "A" Gallery, Chicago, 1958; Suburban Fine Arts Gallery, Highland Park, Illinois, 1971, 1972; Rosenstone Gallery, Chicago, 1970; Spiesberg Gallery, Skokie, Illinois, 1972. Northeastern Illinois University, 1978.

His work has also been exhibited at Little Studio, 1950; Plaza Theatre, Washington, D. C., 1954; "Five" at Todros Geller Gallery, 1957; Chicago and Vicinity, Art Institute, Chicago, 1950, 1951, 1952, 1953, 1954, 1955, 1956, 1957–71; in the 60th National Annual Show at the Art Institute of Chicago, 1952; Decatur Art Institute, Illinois, 1949; Milwaukee Art Institute, 1952; Corcoran Art Gallery, Washington, D.C., 1953; Terry Art Institute, Miami, 1952; Philadelphia Y.M.H.A.; Des Moines Art Center, 1957; Museum of Fine Arts, Springfield, Massachusetts, 1957; Hyde Park Art Center of Chicago.

Other shows in which his works were included are the U.S. Information Traveling Exhibition in France and Germany, 1957–1959; Scott-Richards Gallery, Chicago, 1962; Zolla-Lieberman Gallery, 1965, 1966; Fine Arts Faculty Gallery, Harpers Court, Chicago, 1965, 1966; Chicago Invitational Highland Park, 1972; Wyman Gallery, Chicago, 1972; Critics Exhibition, Chicago Art Institute, 1972.

He has taught Art at the University of Illinois 1948–1950; the Chicago Public High Schools, 1954; Austin Evening School, 1955, 1956; Chicago Teachers College, 1955. Currently he is Profesor of Art at Northeastern Illinois University.

Segedin received Second Prize, Decatur Art Institute, Illinois, 1949; Honorable Mention, Philadelphia Y.M.H.A.; Town and Country Arts Club Award, Chicago Art Institute, 1951; Honorable Mention, Terry Art Institute, Miami, Florida, 1952; Honorable Mention, Corcoran Gallery of Art, Washington, D. C. He ws included among the "New Talents U.S.A." in **Arts in America,** 1956, and was president of "Exhibit A," Chicago artists organization.

Segedin joined the Chicago Society of Artists in 1957.

JANE COALE SHARR (Graphic Artist) was born in Philadelphia, Pennsylvania, on July 29, 1939, and studied at West Chester State College, West Chester, Pa., (B. S.); University of Rhode Island; and Corcoran Gallery, Washington, D. C. She has traveled in France, Holland, Belgium, Germany, Austria, Switzerland, Italy and most of the United States. Her favorite media are woodcuts, lino-cuts, oils, pastels, macrame and photography.

She has held one-woman exhibitions at Northern Michigan University, Marquette, Michigan; Union National Bank, Marquette, Michigan; Faculty Exhibit, Shippensburg State College, Shippensburg, Pennsylvania; and participated in juried group shows at Acquinas Institute, West Chester Art Center, Hyde Park 57th Street Art Fair, Oak Park Art Fair, annual exhibitions of the Chicago Society of Artists, student show at Corcoran Gallery, Washington, D. C., and University of Rhode Island.

Her work is included in public collections of Oak Park River Forest High School, the Union National Bank of Marquette, Michigan, and in private collections in Rhode Island, Pennsylvania, Maryland, North Carolina, Illinois, Indiana, Colorado, Wyoming, Florida, Michigan, Wisconsin and Texas.

Her work is included in private collections of J. Hartzell, High Point, N. C.; D. Hedlund, Oak Park, Illinois; A. Elbert, Chicago; G. Papich, Denton, Texas.

Galleries representing her works are Erie Depot, Oak Park, Illinois, and Gallery, San Jose, California.

She taught primary art in the public schools of Wilmington, Delaware and Marquette, Michigan, and has lectured on printmaking to primary children as well as college students.

Sharr has lectured on Art in European Museums to art clubs in Marquette, Michigan. She illustrated **The Happy Book** used in Children's Memorial Hospital, Chicago, with young patients; **Cook Book** for St. Edmunds Church, Oak Park, booklet commemorating art recognition year; and many programs for Northern Michigan University, Marquette, Michigan. She has also made several large banners for churches.

Shaar received First Prize in Marquette, Michigan, 1965; Honorable Mention, West Chester, Pa., 1962; Purchase Award, Oak Park Art Fair, 1969.

LORRE ANN SLAW (Etcher) was born in Chicago, Illinois, on July 16, 1934, and studied at the school of the Art Institute of Chicago, (B.F.A. and M.F.A.). She has traveled in Canada, England, Scotland, and Italy, Her favorite medium is etching. She also enjoys photography.

She has participated in "Artists Invite Artists" exhibition in the North Suburban Fine Arts Center, Highland Park, 1974; Lakehurst First Juried Show in 1973, and in Student and Faculty Show at the Art Institute of Chicago.

Slaw's work is represented by the Art Rental and Sales Gallery of the Art Institute of Chicago, the Evanston Art Center, and is included in a number of private collections.

She has taught in Glenview, Deerfield and Northbrook Public Schools.

GEORGE MELVILLE SMITH (Painter) was born in Chicago on May 12, 1879, and studied at the Art Institute of Chicago and at the Lhote School of Paris. He traveled and painted in France, Spain, England and Italy and sketched in the New England and Midwestern States in the United States.

His work has been exhibited at the Art Institute of Chicago and in the Chicago Society of Artists annual exhibitions. He was awarded the Fine Arts Building Purchase Prize of 1932 at the Art Institute of Chicago. Smith was a member of the Chicago No-Jury Society of Artists, the Arts Club, and the Chicago Society of Artists, which he joined prior to 1928.

RITA SPAULDING (Painter) was born in Odessa, Russia, in 1907 and studied at the University of Chicago (B.A. & M. A.) and at Art Institute of Chicago, Hyde Park Art Center, and privately with prominent Chicago painters. She has traveled and painted in Western and Eastern Europe, Israel, North and East Africa, the Orient, India, Mexico, Panama, Brazil, and Scandinavia. She works in oils, acrylics, collage and several graphic techniques.

She held one-woman exhibitions at the Covenant Club; the Hillel Foundation, Northwestern University, University of Chicago; Homewood Public Library; Monroe Gallery; Little Gallery, Esquire Theatre, Chicago.

Juried group shows in which she participated were the 65th Annual Chicago and Vicinity Exhibition, Art Institute, Art Rental and Sales Galleries of the Art Institute of Chicago; Renaissance Society of the University of Chicago, North Shore Art League, South Shore Art

League, Dunes Art Foundation, All Illinois Art League and Chicago Society of Artists.

Among other shows in which Rita Spaulding participated are galleries in Paris, New York, Springfield, Illinois, Munster, Indiana; Rosenstone Gallery; McCormick Place with Art Institute Alumni Show; Sun-Times Gallery, Marina City Gallery; Palmer House; Hyde Park Art Center.

Her works are represented by the Art Rental and Sales Gallery of the Art Institute; the Park Forest Art Center; Collectors Showroom, Chapultepec Gallery, Chicago; 4 Arts Gallery, Evanston, Illinois; and included in private collections in Los Angeles; San Francisco; Miami; Ann Arbor, Michigan; St. Louis; Paris, France; Geneva and Lugano, Switzerland; Gary, Indiana; Cleveland; Greensboro, North Carolina; Denver, Colorado; New York City; Chicago.

From 1963 to 1973 she has served on the Faculty of the University of Chicago as Assistant Professor in the Department of Psychiatry.

Spaulding received the Margaret R. Dingle Award for most original work, 1952; First Prize in oils, All-Illinois Fine Arts League; Cash Awards and Honorable Mentions in North Shore Art League, South Shore Art League, School of the Art Institute Alumni, American-Jewish Art Club, Dunes Art Foundation and others. She is represented in permanent Archives of the American Artists at the Smithsonian.

ETHEL SPEARS (Painter) graduated from the Art Institute of Chicago, Design Department, studied in Europe and at the Art Student's Leauge in New York, exhibiting at the Weyhe Gallery there. She returned to Chicago in 1930 and resumed post-graduate work at the Art Institute, graduating from the Fine Arts Department.

Examples of her work are owned by many private collectors in Chicago and elsewhere. Her easel painting and murals were designed and executed for the Nettlehorst Elementary School, Carl VonLinne Elementary School, and many others in the Chicago area.

Since 1937 she contributed blockprints to the Chicago Society of Artists Annual Calendar publication. In honor of her many years of dedicated service on the Board of Directors of the Chicago Society of Artists on the Calendar Committee, and as Treasurer in 1973, Ethel Spears was voted an honorary membership in the Chicago Society of Artists. She continued her membership until her health began to fail. She died on August 2, 1974, in Navasota, Texas, where she has lived since 1961.

BARBARA SPITZ (Printmaker) was born in Chicago on January 8, 1926, and studied at Francis W. Parker School, the Art Institute of Chicago, Brown University, the Rhode Island School of Design and with area painters and printmakers. She has traveled and photographed in Europe, the Far East and in the United States.

Her one-woman shows have been held at the Benjamin Galleries in 1971 and again in 1973. In addition to yearly group exhibitions at the Workshop Gallery of Letterio Calapai from 1969 through 1977, she had a two-woman show in 1971. Other one-woman shows were held in 1973 at Kunsthaus Buhler; R.S.T. Galerie in Scottsdale, Arizona, in 1974; VanStraaten Gallery in 1976 and at the Elca London Studio in 1977.

Other exhibitions of her work were Exhibition Momentum, 1956; Wadsworth Atheneum, Hartford, Connecticut, 1968, Silvermine Guild of Artists, New Canaan, Conn., 1968, 1972; State University College, Potsdam, N.Y., 1969; Hunterdon Art Center, New Jersey, 1969; Dickenson State College, 1969, The Print Club, Philadelphia, 1969, 1972, 1973, 1975 and 1976; Society of American Graphic Artists, N.Y.C. 1971; Bradley University, Peoria, Illinois, 1975; Honolulu Academy of Arts, Hawaii, 1975; Speed Art Museum, Eight State Print Exhibitions, Louisville, Ky., 1974–1975; Library of Congress and National Collection of Fine Arts Print Exhibitions, 1973–1974, Smithsonian Institute Traveling Exhibitions.

Her prints are included in the collections of the Art Institute of Chicago; DeCordova Museum, Lincoln, Mass.; Oklahoma Art Center, Oklahoma City, Albany Institute of History and Art, Albany, N.Y.; Dulin Gallery of Art, Knoxville, Tennessee; Smart Gallery, University of Chicago; Bradley Collection, Milwaukee Art Center, Milwaukee, Wisconsin, and in many private and industrial collections.

Her gallery affiliations are VanStraaten Gallery, Chicago, Art Rental and Sales Gallery, Art Institute of Chicago; Workshop Gallery of Letterio Calapai,

Glencoe, Illinois, A.D.I. Gallery, San Francisco, Lumley Cazalet, Ltd., London, Elca London Studio, Montreal, Canada, and Kunsthaus Buhler, Stuttgart, Germany.

Her teaching included Highland Park High School and studio demonstrations for student groups from area schools and from the inner city for various study groups and organizations. In the 1940's she worked for the Benjamin Galleries and for the A.A.A. Galleries in Chicago.

Spitz has received Purchase Awards in 1972 from the Oklahoma Art Center; in 1973 from the Dulin Gallery of Art; in 1971, 1972, 1974 and 1975 from Boston Printmakers and an Honorable Mention in 1972. From the North Shore Art League, she received the Lindenthal Award in the first New Horizons Exhibit in 1975 and Third Prize in 1958, the Manel Hahn Award in 1959, Second Prize in 1969, Honorable Mentions in 1960, 1966, 1967 and 1968. She received the George May Purchase Award from New Horizons in 1975. Ms. Spitz was awarded the Municipal Art League Prize from the 71st Chicago and Vicinity Show held at the Art Institute in 1968. In 1973, she received a grant from the State of Illinois, under the Illinois Print Commission Program and received the Childe Hassam Purchase Award from the American Academy of Arts and Letters in New York City in 1973.

Spitz is listed in **Who's Who in American Art**, **Who's Who in American Women**, **International Directory of Arts**, **Dictionary of International Biography**, **Printmakers in Illinois**, and **Illinois Printmakers I.**

She is a professional member of the Artists Equity Association, Inc. Arts Club of Chicago, Chicago Society of Artists, Print Club of Philadelphia, and Boston Printmakers.

ROBERT D. SPITZ (Painter) was born in Vienna, Austria, on March 31, 1933, and studied at the Chicago Academy of Fine Arts (certificate), Northwestern University and the Art Institute of Chicago. He has traveled and painted in Mexico, Israel, Canada, French West Indies, England, Scotland, Denmark, Holland, Austria, Italy, France, Spain, Germany, Belgium, Switzerland and the United States. He works in oil, watercolor, acrylic and pen and ink.

He has held one-man shows in the Little Gallery, Ft. Smith, Arkansas, and the Deerpath Gallery, Illinois.

Juried shows in which he participated are the Art Institute of Chicago First Biennial; University of Chicago Festival of the Arts Show; Butler Institute of American Art, Youngstown, Ohio; Fifth National Jury Show of Chautauqua, New York; Watercolor U.S.A.; Art Institute May Festival Exhibit; Norfolk Museum; Norfolk, Virginia; Society of the 4 Arts Exhibition of Contemporary American Paintings; Third National Polymer Exhibition; Illinois State Museum, Springfield, Illinois; Old Orchard Art Festival; Northwestern University; Chicago Society of Artists 4-man show.

He is represented by the Art Institute Sales and Rental Gallery, Ontario East Gallery, Cellar Gallery, Welgart Gallery and is in numerous private collections. Public collections in which his works are included are West Texas Museum, Artists Guild of Chicago and Science Research Association, Inc.

His teaching experience includes the Academy of Applied Arts, Vienna, Austria; Village Art School, Skokie, Illinois; Commonwealth Art Center, Chicago.

Spitz received the Artists Guild of Chicago Monsen Award; A.G.C. Watercolor Exhibition Purchase Award; A.J.A.C. Exhibition, Nathan Schwartz Award; Watercolor U.S.A., West Texas Museum Purchase Award; Science Research Association Purchase Award; A.G.C. 31st Annual Fine Art Show Second Prize Jury Award; 1972 A.G.C. Watercolor and Drawing Show Purchase Award.

GRACE SPONGBERG (Painter, Printmaker) was born in Chicago, Illinois, on April 25, 1904, and studied at the School of the Art Institute of Chicago; Ox Bow Summer School, Saugatuck, Michigan; and with area painters and printmakers. Her travels include most of Europe, the Scandinavian countries, Japan, Cambodia, Thailand and Martinique. Her works were greatly inspired by her travels. She works in oil, watercolor, serigraphy, lithography, ceramics and enamels.

Spongberg exhibited in juried exhibitions at the Art Institute of Chicago, i.e., in the Chicago Artists and Vicinity Exhibitions, International Watercolor Shows; the Pennsylvania Academy of Arts, Cincinnati Museum; print shows in Seattle, Kansas City, and other museums in the country.

Group exhibitions in which she participated were those sponsored by the Chicago Society of Artists, the Swedish Artists of Chicago and in many Art Fairs around Chicago and Suburbs.

For many years Spongberg has been contributing block prints to the Chicago Society of Artists annual calendar publication.

DOROTHY STAFFORD (Painter) was born in Chicago, Illinois, on May 22, 1902, and studied at Rosary College, Art Institute of Chicago, and with Helen Hudson Below and Rudolph Weisenborn. She has traveled and painted in Europe, the Mediterranean, Russia, Mexico, and Canada. She has taught privately in her own studio. Her favorite media are oil, watercolor, acrylic, clay and sculpture. Her style is highly abstract.

A one-woman exhibition of Dorothy Stafford's paintings is currently on view at the Stuart Library in Florida. She has held several shows in the Stuart, Florida area where she has been residing for the last twenty years.

Her work was included in the Chicago Artists and Vicinity Exhibitions at the Art Institute of Chicago, and in group shows with the Chicago Society of Artists for more than 25 years. She has held several two and four-woman exhibitions while in Chicago and has contributed lino-cuts to the Society's annual calendar publication for many years. Her works are included in many private collections.

While in Stuart, Florida, she organized a group of artists "Art Associates" and was its first president.

More recently she has been spending her summers painting in the Carolina Mountains. Here she organized another group of artists, the Art Guild of the Highlands, and was elected its president.

Her studio is affectionately known as the 'Little Louvre' and accommodates ten local painters who work with Dorothy Stafford. Exhibitions of their works are held in the studio gallery periodically.

Stafford has been awarded four First Prizes and three Second Prizes for her paintings shown at local art exhibitions in Stuart, Florida.

JOHN STARR (Painter) was born in O'Neill, Nebraska, on February 14, 1939, and studied privately with Elvie TenHoor and others. He has traveled and painted in Japan, Taiwan, Hong-Kong, Israel, Greece, Italy, Iran, India, England, Spain, Switzerland, Netherlands, Germany, Mexico and Canada. His favorite medium is collage, but he also enjoys jewelry designing.

He participated in juried shows at Naperville and in the Dunes Art Foundation exhibitions; the Museum of Contemporary Crafts, N.Y.C.; Kroch's and Brentano's, Campanile Gallery, Chicago; University Club of Chicago; Wayne Art Exhibit; Michigan City Bank, Indiana; Town Gallery and John Michael Kohler Art Centers Exhibition in Indiana, in Old Town Triangle Center and Rubino Galleries in Chicago and others.

He is included in private collections in Japan, Los Angeles and Beverly Hills, California; New Jersey; and Rochester, New York.

His work is represented by the Campanile Gallery, Chicago; Kohler Gallery, Sheboygan, Wisconsin; Town Gallery, Munster, Indiana; Museum of Contemporary Crafts, New York City.

His works have been reproduced in **Contemporary Leather** by Dona Meilach and **Collage and Assemblage** by Dona Meilach and Elvie TenHoor. He has appeared on the **NBC Morning Show,** a television program.

Starr has received awards from the Dunes Art Foundation, Michiana Shores, 1971, and the Municipal Art League, 1971 and 1972.

IVY STEELE (Sculptor) was born in St. Louis, Missouri, on April 15, 1908. She studied at Wellesley College (B. A.). She has traveled to Europe, Mexico, Central America, Japan, India, Pakistan, Thailand, Turkey and Spain. Her special media were sculpture and drawing. She was also interested in archeological research.

She has held one-woman exhibitions at the Benedict Gallery, Hull House; American Institute of Architects (Chicago Chapter); Chicago Public Library at Lakeview Branch; Paul Theobald Gallery.

Her sculpture was included in the Chicago and Vicinity Shows at Art Institute of Chicago; Old Orchard Art Festivals; New Horizons in Sculpture; Oklahoma Art Center, Oklahoma City; Grand Rapids Art Gallery; I.I.T., Grover Herman Hall; Contemporary Sculpture by Chicago Artists, Renaissance Society, University of Chicago.

Other exhibitions in which her works were included are the Ruth White Gallery, New York; Sculpture by Chicago

Artists, Art Institute of Chicago; Society for Contemporary American Art, Art Institute of Chicago; McCormick Place; Contemporary Art Workshop Gallery; Sun-Times Gallery; National Design Center, Chicago; McKerr Observatory Gallery Chicago; Studio Gallery, Geneva, Illinois; Renaissance Society of University of Chicago; Arts Club of Chicago.

Her works are included in private collections in New York, Los Angeles, Washington, D. C., and St. Louis, and in public collections of Wellesley College Art Museum; Highland Park (Illinois) Hospital, (wall relief); Ravinia (Illinois) Nursery School (exterior relief); Covenant Methodist Church, Evanston (exterior relief).

Chicago galleries which represented her sculpture are Nancy Lurie Art Gallery; Art Rental and Sales Gallery of the Art Institute of Chicago; Charles Feingarten Gallery; Devorah Sherman Gallery; and Bressler Gallery, Milwaukee; Sculptors Gallery, St. Louis, Missouri.

She taught at the Frances W. Parker School, Chicago; Children's Art, Hull House; Lower North Center, Art Department; Sculpture at Psychosomatic and Psychiatric Institute, Chicago.

She has lectured to various groups on travel, archeology, and appeared on NBC Channel 5 programs **Whys and Otherwise** and **Children Work With Clay.**

Ivy Steele died in 1975.

RUBIN STEINBERG (Painter, Sculptor) was born in Chicago, Illinois, on May 31, 1934, and studied at the Art Institute of Chicago (M.F.A., 1968); Roosevelt University, Chicago (M. E., 1961; Chicago Teachers College (B. E., 1957); Institute of Design Illinois Institute of Technology (1959–1960). He has traveled, painted and sculpted in Jamaica, Mexico, Israel, Ecuador, Galapagos Islands, Australia, New Zealand, Tahiti, Figi, France, Spain, Germany, Austria, Switzerland, England and the United States. His favorite media are sculptural weaving, assemblage, collage and stained glass.

Steinberg has held one-man shows at the Oak Park Library, Oak Park, 1975; Park Forest Art Center, Park Forest, 1974; Northbrook Racquet Club, Northbrook, 1974; Deerfield High School, Deerfield, 1974; Mayer Kaplan Jewish Community Center, Skokie, 1973; Kroch's & Brentano's, Chicago, 1973; Suburban Fine Arts Center, Highland Park, 1973; Bonwit Teller, Chicago, 1971; University of Illinois, Circle Campus, Chicago, 1966; Lake Forest Academy, Lake Forest, 1965.

He participated in juried group shows of the American Jewish Arts Club, 1970 to present; Old Orchard Midwest Crafts Festival, 1974; Old Orchard Art Festival, 1971; Gold Coast Association 1967 to present and in various art fairs in the Chicago area from 1961 to present.

His work is represented by the Sourcerists Unlimited Gallery in Chicago and in private collections of Sudler and Company, Hancock Center, Chicago; McDonald's Corporation Oakbrook, Illinois; Continental Bank of Chicago; Samuel Sax, Exchange National Bank, Chicago; James J. Barrett, Director, J. J. Barrett, Inc., Communications, Chicago; L. P. Slotkowski, Jr., Slotkowski Sausage Company, Chicago; Ru-Go Container Corporation, Kansas City, Missouri; Irving Malow, Malow Rope and Cordage Co., Elk Grove Village, Illinois; L. A. Morgan, Madison Steel Company, Skokie; Mr. & Mrs. Edward Labelson, Dance Fashions, Chicago; Herman Batko, Contract Interiors for Business, Inc., Chicago; Joseph Riha, Office Equipment Co., Chicago; Hy Spector, Aval Corporation (Lava Light), Chicago; and in the collection of Mr. & Mrs. Maurice Yochim of Evanston, Illinois.

His works were reproduced in the following books: Sunset Books: **Macrame: Techniques and Projects,** 11/75 Revision; **Art From Anything, Contemporary Leather, Modern Approach to Basketry with Fibers and Grasses, Fibers and Fabrics,** all by Dona Meilach; **Collage and Assemblage,** by Meilach and TenHoor; **Telephone Engineer & Management** by Communications for Comtech Corporation.

Since 1959 he has taught art in the Chicago Public Schools, elementary and high school students. He has instructed teachers in the Art Enrichment Program Workshops sponsored by the Chicago Board of Education in summer sessions.

Steinberg received awards from the Hyde Park Art Center, First Place, Crafts, 1975; Art Institute of Chicago, Chicago and Vicinity Shows, 1968, 1973; Municipal Art League Award, 1973; American Jewish Arts Club, 1970, 1974; Suburban Fine Arts Center Festival, Highland Park, Illinois, Award for Excellence, 1973; Burton Place Association, Chicago, Third Place, Sculpture, 1970; Randhurst Association,

Third Place, 1965.

JANE W. STEINER (Painter) was born in London, England, on November 8, 1906, and studied at the Art Institute of Chicago, American Academy of Art, Illinois Institute of Technology with Mish Kohn, Instituto Allende, and in San Miguel, Mexico from 1963–1974. She also studied with A. Raymond Katz, Rudolph Weisenborn and Ruth Van-Sickle Ford. She has traveled and painted in Asia, Africa, Europe, the Orient, Hawaii and Mexico. Her favorite media are oil, acrylic, watercolor and graphics.

She has held several one-woman shows at the Old Orchard Bank Gallery, the Commonwealth Plaza Art Gallery, and Mandel Brothers Gallery.

She has participated in group shows in Miguel, Mexico; Todros Geller Art Gallery; University Club of Chicago; Covenant Club; North Shore Art League; Rosenstone Art Gallery; Bernard Horwich Center; Mandel Brothers Gallery; Renaissance Society at the University of Chicago; Northwestern University and many others.

Her work is represented by the Art Rental and Sales Gallery of the Art Institute of Chicago.

During World War II, she taught painting and crafts at the Great Lakes Navy Hospital, a program sponsored by the Art Institute of Chicago. In 1973, Steiner with Janine Collier organized the Commonwealth Plaza Art Center, where classes in painting are conducted by prominent artist-teachers. It is a not-for--profit organization which sponsors talented students and through its scholarship fund assures their attendance at the School of the Art Institute.

Steiner has received a number of awards for her paintings and block-prints. Among these are the Temple Sholem Art Award, Second Prize and several Honorable Mentions for lino-cuts from the Chicago Society of Artists, and a Third Prize for an oil painting from the American Jewish Arts Club.

Steiner has been a member of the Chicago Society of Artists for twenty-two years and has contributed lino-cuts to the Society's annual calendar publication for as many years. She has also served on various committees facilitating the functioning of the organization.

FRANCES STRAIN (Painter) was born in Chicago on November 11, 1898. She studied at the Art Institute of Chicago. Her outstanding teachers were George Bellows, Randall Davey and John Sloan. She has traveled and painted in the United States, France and Italy.

Strain has had one-artist exhibitions in the Chicago Woman's Aid, the Romany Club of Chicago and in several other places.

Her work has been exhibited at the Art Institute of Chicago; the State Museum of New Mexico; the Newark Museum, New Jersey; Marshall Field and Company Galleries, Chicago; Increase Robinson's Studio Gallery of Chicago; the Little Gallery of Chicago; also in various other galleries throughout the East and Middle West.

For many years she has been the Director of the Renaissance Gallery of the University of Chicago, staging exhibitions of local, regional, national and international scope.

The work of Frances Strain has been written about in Chicago newspapers and magazines and in **The Arts**, by Samuel Putnam, Inez Cunnginham, Tom Vickerman and by J.Z. Jacobson in his book **Art of Today — Chicago — 1933,** L. M. Stein, publisher, Chicago, 1932.

Strain was a member of 10 Artists (Chicago), the Renaissance Society of the University of Chicago, and the Chicago Society of Artists.

Strain died in 1967.

BELLE SWEENEY (Painter) was born in Polo, Illinois, in 1891 and studied at the School of Design and Art Institute of Chicago. She studied privately with Rudolph Weisenhorn and Martyl. She was also a graduate nurse (1916) from the Presbyterian Hospital School of Nursing (P.H.N.S.) She traveled and painted throughout Europe in 1920, and in 1956 in Italy, Switzerand, Belgium and France. Her favorite media are oil and watercolor.

She has held several one-woman exhibitions in Oak Park and participated in juried shows in the Midwest, New York, Oak Park, North Shore and many in Chicago.

Her work was represented by the Art Rental and Sales Gallery from 1960-1969 and was included in private collections in California, Texas, Colorado, Illinois, Florida, Virginia, Michigan and Wisconsin.

One of her paintings was selected by the Art Institute of Chicago for a Traveling European Exhibition.

Sweeney received First and Second Awards from the Oak Park Art League, North Shore Art League and Oak Brook Art Fair.

She was a World War Nurse 1918–1919 in the Base Hospital #13 Limoges, France (ANC), and Head Nurse at Presbyterian Hospital, Men's Surgical, from 1920 to 1924. In 1926 she married Dr. William Sweeney and has lived in Oak Park, Illinois, for forty years.

She is a member of the Art League, Oak Park, North Shore Art League, Chicago Society of Artists and Life Member of the Art Institute of Chicago.

ELVIE TEN HOOR (Painter) was born in Watseka, Illinois, on October 23, 1900, and graduated from the Famous Artists, Westport, Connecticut School of Art and the Art Institute of Chicago. She also studied at the Gertz School of Art, Paris; Institute de Allende in Mexico and privately with Ann Roman, John Richardson, Atsushi Kikuchi and Ansei Uchima. She has traveled and painted in Mexico, England, France, Spain, Italy, Switzerland, Turkey, Greece, Netherlands, Germany, Portugal, and extensively in the United States and Canada. She works in oils, watercolors, collage and printmaking.

She has held one-woman exhibitions at the Esquire Little Gallery; Palmer House Gallery; Dunes Theatre Gallery, Michigan City, Indiana; Key Club; Charles Quint and Associates, Inc., Gallery; University Club of Chicago; Covenant Club, Chicago; Ligoa Duncan Gallery, New York; Town Gallery, Munster, Indiana; Hefner's Gallery, Grand Rapids, Michigan; Bibo Gallery, Peoria, Illinois; Station Gallery, Crown Point, Indiana; Rubino Gallery, Chicago, Illinois.

Her paintings and collages were included in juried group exhibitions at Ligoa Duncan Gallery, New York; Raymond Duncan Galleries 31, Rue deSeine, Paris, France, 1967; Art Institute 64th Annual Exhibition, Chicago and Vicinity; Roosevelt University; North Shore Art League; Union League Show, "New Horizons in Painting," North Shore Show; University Club; Hillel Foundation Gallery; The Chicago Sun-Times Gallery; John Michael Kohler Arts Center, 1972; Park Forest Art Center.

Gallery representation of her works includes the Sales and Rental Gallery, Art Institute of Chicago; Renaissance Society, University of Chicago; Arts Club of Chicago; Hefner Gallery, Grand Rapids, Michigan; Rubino Gallery, Chicago; Town Gallery, Munster, Indiana; Station Gallery, Crown Point, Indiana.

Her works are included in private collections in Illinois, California, Canada, Michigan, in other states and in Israel and Sweden, and in public collections of Faulkner High School, Art in Government State Office Building, Springfield, Illinois.

Ten Hoor's work has been reproduced in the following books by Dona Meilach: **The Artists Eye, Creating with Plaster, Creating Art from Anything, Creating Art from Fibers and Fabrics. Sculpture from Junk,** Henry Rassmusen, in **Work Bench** magazines, March issue, 1963; **Good Housekeeping,** July 1969; "How to Create Your Own Design," "Contemporary Leather," Pitman-Papercraft #62; and Pitman-Printmaking #54.

She has co-authored two books with Dona Meilach, **Collage and Found Art,** and **Collage and Assemblage.**

Ten Hoor has been awarded the outstanding award from Dunes Art Foundation, Michigan City, Indiana, 1959, 1961, 1962, 1963, 1964; Margaret Dingle Award, 1961, and the Union League Purchase Award.

Ten Hoor is listed in **Who's Who in Art and Antiques, Foremost Women in Communication, Who's Who of American Women with World Notables, Dictionary of International Biography** 1971, 1972, and **Personalities of West and Midwest,** 1972.

MORRIS TOPSCHEVSKY* (Painter) was born in Bialistok, Poland, (formerly Russia) on October 15, 1901, and studied at Hull House and the Art Institute of Chicago. His outstanding teachers were Miss Enella Benedict and Albert Krehbiel and he has learned much also from Aztec and Maya sculpture and the artists of Mexico.

He has traveled and painted in New York and Texas and has spent a great deal of his painting time in Mexico. His works were exhibited in the Pennsylvania Academy of Fine Arts, the Renaissance Society of the University of Chicago, the John Reed Club of Chicago, the Witte Museum of San Antonio, Texas and in a number of galleries in Mexico City. His work is in the permanent collections of

Dr. Moises Saenz, Hubert Herring, the Richmond Museum and the Mexican Ministry of Education.

His work has been written about in **Universal** and **Excelcior Magazines** of Mexico City, the **Chicago Evening Post,** the **Chicago Daily News** and **Survey Graphic,** by Eliodoro Valle, Ictioas, Margarite B. Williams, Robert D. Andrews, J. Z. Jacobson and Paul Kellog.

Topchevsky was awarded the Art Students League Goodman Prize in 1921.

He was a member of the John Reed Club and of the Chicago Society of Artists since 1928. For many years he taught art to children and adults at the Lincoln Center on the Southside of Chicago.

Topchevsky died at the age of 47 in 1948.

*Jacobson, J. Z., "Art of Today — Chicago 1933," L. M. Stein Pub., Chicago 1932, Pg. 152, 153.

ALEX TOPP (Painter, Printmaker) was born in Chicago, Illinois, on July 5, 1911. He received his early art training at Hull House in Chicago from Miss Benedict and Morris Topchevsky, his brother. Later he attended the School of the Art Institute of Chicago where he studied with Boris Anisfeld, John Groth and Clara MacGowan and received the M.F.A. degree. He also attended Loyola University and was awarded the Master of Education degree. He has traveled and painted in Mexico, Central America and Europe. His favorite media are oil, acrylic, etching, lithography, frescoe-mural painting and photography.

Topp held a one-man show at Northwestern University, Hillel Foundation, Evanston, Illinois.

His works have been exhibited in juried group shows at the Brooklyn Museum, New York; Art Institute of Chicago in the Etchers and Engravers Exhibition in 1939, Exhibition by Artists of Chicago and Vicinity, 1940, and the International Exhibition of Watercolors, 1942; Artists Equity Show in the Rubino Gallery, Chicago; Northwestern University Hillel Foundation in Evanston; Spertus Museum, Chicago; Covenant Club, Chicago; Todros Geller Art Gallery, Chicago; Meyer Kaplan Gallery, Skokie, Ill.; Rosenstone Gallery, Chicago, and many others.

His work is included in the private collection of the Mexican entertainer Chiara, in collections in Chicago, Mexico, Central America and Europe, and in the public collection of the Smithsonian Institute in Washington, D. C.

He was the Graphic Artist-Muralist and stage designer when he served in the Army during World War II. After the war he worked on the W.P.A. Project as easel painter and muralist for various government agencies and public institutions.

His early teaching career began at the Jewish Peoples Institute, but after he returned from service in World War II he began to teach in the Chicago Public Schools. For more than twenty years he taught at Wells High School and at Lane Technical High School in Chicago.

Topp received awards from the American Jewish Art Club and the Army's U. S. Graphic Award.

Topp is a member of the Artists Equity, American Jewish Art Club, and the Chicago Society of Artists.

LAURA VanPAPPELENDAM (Painter) was born in Donnelson, Iowa, and studied at the Art Institute of Chicago and the University of Chicago. Her outstanding teachers were Sorolla, Hawthorne, George Bellows, Nicholas Roerich and Diego Rivera. She has painted in Mexico and in various parts of the U. S., particularly in the West and Southwest.

One-woman exhibitions of her works have been held at the Art Institute of Chicago and the Chicago Galleries Association and in Madison and Milwaukee, Wisconsin, and in Keokuk, Iowa.

Group shows in which she participated were those held in Chicago; New York; Philadelphia; St. Louis; Minneapolis; Boston; Brooklyn; Omaha; Des Moines; Cedar Rapids; Columbus; Toronto; Memphis; Evansville, Indiana; Edinboro and Scranton, Pennsylvania; and Andover, Massachusetts.

Her work is represented in the permanent collections of the Chicago City Commission for the Encouragement of Local Art, the New Trier High School, Wilmette, Illinois, Curtis B. Camp, Walter Brewster and others. Her work has been written about in Chicago newspapers and in the book, **Art of Today, Chicago — 1933** by J. Z. Jacobson, L. M. Stein, Publisher.

She was Professor of Painting at the Art Institute of Chicago where she taught from 1909 until her retirement fifty years later.

Many prominent Chicago artists have studied with VanPappelendam and have achieved recognition and fame through their creative endeavors, inspired by her guidance and teaching.

VanPappelendam was awarded the William O. Goodman Prize of the Art Students League in Chicago; the William R. French Gold Medal in the American Artists Exhibition at the Art Institute of Chicago, in 1930; the Jules F. Bower Prize in 1932, the Frank G. Logan Prize in 1933; the Clyde M. Carr Prize in 1942, the last three prizes were awarded at the Artists of Chicago and Vicinity Exhibitions at the Art Institute of Chicago.

VanPappelendam was a member of the Chicago Society of Artists until 1962 when she resigned because of ill health. She was one of the earliest group of artists in the Society who contributed block prints to the first Chicago Society of Artists calendar published in 1937. She also belonged to the Arts Club of Chicago, the Renaissance Society of the University of Chicago, the Art Institute of Chicago Alumni Association and the South Side Art Association.

VanPappelendam died in 1974.

JAMES F. WALKER (Graphic Artist) was born in Kirksville, Missouri, on October 8, 1913, and studied at the University of Iowa, (B.F.A., M. A., M.F.A.): American Artists School, New York City and with Nahum Tschbasov, New York.

He has held one-man shows at Cliff Dwellers Club in Chicago, various universities, and Chicago and Vicinity Galleries.

He has exhibited in Show of 52 Chicago artists, Paris, France; Modern Chicago Artists, Germany; American Drawings, Museum of Modern Art, Paris; Thirteenth Artists West of the Mississippi, Invitational; 16th North Mississippi Valley Invitational; DePauw First Annual Invitational Drawing Exhibition; New Directions in Printmaking, U.S.A., Walker Art Center; the National Conference of Christians and Jews Brotherhood Show; Most Important Museums in U.S.A.; Drawings from 12 countries, Chicago Art Institute; Butler Art Institute, Youngstown, Ohio.

Walker's drawings are included in collections of the Chicago Art Institute, Kansas Friends of Art, State University of Iowa, Mrs. Marjorie Sawyer Goodman Graff, New York City, Mr. J. Patrick Lannan, Chicago, Margaret Day Blake, Chiang Er-Shik, New York City and in numerous other private collections.

He taught at the North East Missouri State Teachers College, Southwestern College, Chicago Art Institute 1954–1959, and High School District #214, 1960–1975.

Walker received prizes from the Iowa Art Salon; 12th Annual Art Salon; Kansas Friends of Art (Purchase Award); Terry Art Institute International Show, Florida; Drawings from 12 countries (Purchase Award); Pauline Palmer Prize for Drawing from Art Institute of Chicago; Pauline Palmer Prize for work in any media, A.I.C.; William III Tuthill Prize, A.I.C.; Alumni Association Prize; One Hundred Best New Talent List (Art in America Annual 1956 and 1959).

LIONEL WATHALL (Painter, Graphic Artist) was born in Chicago, Illinois, on October 11, 1914, and studied at the Art Students League of New York; Chicago Art Institute; Chicago Academy of Art; American Academy of Art; Summer School of Painting at Saugatuck, Michigan; Institute of Design of Illinois Institute of Technology; and privately from F. DeForrest Schook. His favorite media are watercolor, oil and gouache; he is also interested in photography, still and motion picture.

During World War II he served as staff artist for **Yank**, the Army magazine and did painting for Engineer Battalion war records, renderings of Engineer Battalion construction projects and sign painting. A continuing career in commercial art provided assignments for Rayette, Motorola, Zenith, Parker Pen, International Harvester, John Deere, Toni, Revlon, Maybelline and many others.

He has held one-man shows at Chess House Gallery, Chicago; twice at Esquire Theatre Little Gallery, Chicago, 1939, 1945. He held two-man shows at Deerpath Theatre, Lake Forest, 1960; Monroe Street Gallery, 1971; and a show sponsored by the Continental Can Company, 1971.

His works were included in juried group shows at the Union League Club of Chicago; the Illinois State Fair; Caller-Times of Dallas, Texas; Artists Guild of Chicago; Peninsula Arts Association Show, Hardy Museum, Door County, Wisconsin.

His works are included in numerous private collections and those of Robert McMillan, New York; Carl Frazier, Mr. & Mrs. D. Brown, Hans Teichert, Dr. and Mrs. Matthews.

Wathall received the "Most Popular" award from the Peninsula Arts Association, Door County, Wisconsin in 1940.

HELEN JOY WEINBERG (Painter) was born in New York City, and studied at the Art Institute of Chicago, Illinois Institute of Technology, Institute of Design, Summer School of Painting, Graphic Workshop (formerly in New York City), and privately with several well-known artists. She received her academic work at University of Chicago and Northwestern University. She has traveled in Great Britain, Ireland, Holland, Germany, Austria, Switzerland, France, Italy, Greece, Czechoslovakia, Israel, Canada, Cuba, most of the United States, Finland, Sweden, Norway and Denmark. Her favorite media are oils, acrylic, drawing and printmaking. She has lectured on modern art and Israeli art.

One-woman exhibitions of her paintings and prints were held at Riccardo's Studio Gallery, 1950; Newman Brown Gallery, 1953; Mandel Brothers Galleries, 1954; John M. Smyth & Company, 1954; Lake Forest Book Shop, 1956; Deerpath Theatre, 1957; American Institute of Architects, 1958, (Chicago Chapter); Northwestern University, Hillel Foundation, 1959; Monroe Gallery, 1959; Bresler Galleries, Milwaukee, 1961; Paul Theobald Gallery, 1962; Chicago Public Library (Main) 1954; and Rogers Park Branch, 1961, 1963 and 1970; Covenant Club, 1966; Rosenstone Gallery, 1970; Illinois Medical Center, University of Illinois, 1973, also several small group shows: 2-person, Sherman Hotel, 1952; Devlin Gallery, Janesville, Wisconsin, 1961; Bresler Galleries, Milwaukee, 1961, Ahda Artzt, New York, 1963; 3-person show in Gallery of the Board of Jewish Education, 1949; Meadows Club, 1961; 4-person show in the Robert North Gallery, 1955, 1956, 1957; Chicago Public Library, (Main), 1965.

Her work was included in juried group shows at the Art Institute Rental and Sales Gallery for a period of 15 years, 2nd Annual Sun-Times Chicago Area 1961; St. Paul's Episcopalian Church; Peoria Regional Religious Exhibit; Magnificent Mile, 1950; Pennsylvania Academy of Fine Arts, 1963, 1965; Boston Printmakers, 1963; Friends of American Art 6th Lake Michigan States, 1950.

Other shows in which she participated were held at Joslyn Museum (Omaha); Butler Institute of American Art; Museum of Modern Art, Haifa — 2 international shows; Decatur Illinois Museum; Renaissance Society of University of Chicago; Old Orchard Fair; Old Town Holiday Fair; Board of Jewish Education, invitational; Temple Judea; W. Suburban Temple; KAM Temple; Commercial Galleries: Fairweather-Hardin, Distelheim, Cromer and Quint, Robert North, Frank Ryan, McKerr, Avant Arts, Newman Brown, New Studio, Kasha Heman, Association of American Artists (NYC); Hazel Maryan (Madison); Collectors' Showroom (Chicago); Colleges and Universities: University of Chicago, Northwestern, Roosevelt, Rhode Island College of Education, Iowa State; Art Centers in Evanston, Kalamazoo, Janesville, Berkshire, and many others.

Her work has been exhibited in galleries in Chicago, New York, Milwaukee and elsewhere, including the Art Rental and Sale Gallery of the Art Institute of Chicago; Distelheim Galleries, Chicago; Bresler Gallery, Milwaukee; Adha Artzt, Gorline Galleries, New York; and is represented in numerous private collections throughout the United States, Vienna, Oslo, Jerusalem, Haifa and Ramat Gan, Israel.

Public collections in which her works are included are Art Institute of Chicago; Museum of Modern Art, New York; Brooklyn Museum; Israel Museum (Jerusalem); Haifa Museum of Modern Art; U. S. Information Agency; many prints in foreign embassies; Syracuse University; Board of Jewish Education; Bethany Theological Seminary, Oak Brook; Stauffer Chemical Co., (Dobbs Ferry, N. Y.).

She taught classes at Temples Emanuel and Sholom and privately in her studio for many years.

She received an Honorable Mention for a painting on a biblical subject, now in the collection of the Board of Jewish Education.

Weinberg has been active in Artists Equity Association, Chicago Society of Artists, American Jewish Art Club, serving on Boards of all three and holding offices in the Equity and the A.J.A.C.

EGON WEINER (Sculptor) was born

in Vienna, Austria, on July 24, 1906 and studied at the School Arts and Crafts and Academy of Fine Arts, Vienna, Austria.

One-man exhibitions of his works were held at the Art Institute of Chicago; Renaissance Society 1947; Illinois Institute of Technology 1949; University of Illinois 1951; Lawrence College 1951; Palmer House, Chicago 1955; Davenport Municipal Art Gallery 1958, 1963; Augustana College 1958; American Institute of Architects 1958; McKerr Observatory Gallery, Chicago 1961; University of Valparaiso, Indiana 1959; Concordia College, Chicago and Nevada 1960; Bloomington, Illinois 1961; Conrad Gallery, Chicago 1965.

He exhibited at the Art Institute of Chicago 1940–1964; Pennsylvania Academy of Fine Arts 1941, 1947, 1949–1951; Oakland Museum of Art 1942, 1945, 1946, 1948–1951; University of Chicago 1943, 1945, 1960; Syracuse Museum of Fine Arts 1948–1951, 1958; Portland, Oregon Art Museum 1948; City Art Museum 1949; Museum of Modern Art 1951; Arts Center, Chicago 1954; Religious Art exhibition, Minneapolis 1957; Denver Museum of Art 1958; Northwestern University 1961; American Embassy, Oslo 1960; International Religious Exhibition, Salzburg 1962; Seattle World's Fair 1962; New York World's Fair 1964–1965.

His work is included in Syracuse Museum of Fine Arts; Augsburg College, Minneapolis; Augustana College, Rock Island, Illinois; groups, reliefs, figures, Church of St. Augustine, Vienna; Salem Church, Chicago; windows (6), Standard Club, Chicago; figure Concordia College, Ft. Wayne, Indiana; Chicago Airport; Glencoe, Illinois; Amalgamated Meatcutters Union Building, Chicago; St. Paul Church, Mt. Prospect, Illinois; "Pillar of Fire," Fire Academy, Chicago, 1962; University of Wisconsin, 1963; bronze relief, Presbyterian Church, La Grange, Illinois, 1964; bronze figure for New Science Building, North Park College, Chicago; Gary, Indiana Public Library; American Church, Oslo; bronze, Marina City, Chicago; portrait busts, Sen. William Benton, for Encyclopedia Britannica, Chicago; Dr. Eric Oldberg, for Illinois Research Hospital, Chicago; sculpture in collection of the Vatican.

Other works are a design for marble cemetery monument to Mayor Baeck, Salzburg, 1960; figure for the American Embassy, Oslo.

He served as Educational Consultant for film on the Del Prado Museum, Madrid, Spain, 1969, and for International Film Bureau, Chicago. He participated in a Roundtable discussion at the 100th Anniversary Celebration of Frank Lloyd Wright in Oak Park, Illinois, in connection with the portrait bust of Mr. Wright which the artist completed in 1969.

He lectured in the United States and abroad and has held positions as Professor of Sculpture and Life Drawing, Art Institute of Chicago, 1945–1969, and Visiting Professor of Art, Augustana College, 1956–1969.

Weiner is a contributor to the **American-German Review**; **Frontiers**; **Figure** magazines.

Weiner received the following awards: the Grand Prix, Paris, 1925; Blumfield Award, Vienna, 1932–1934; Municipal Art League, Chicago, 1948; Gold Medal, 1969; Syracuse Museum of Fine Arts, 1949; American Institute of Architects, 1955; Citation 1962; Museum of Science and Industry, Chicago, 1955; Roosevelt University, Chicago, 1956; Medals: Art Institute of Chicago, 1949, Prize 1959; Oakland Art Museum, 1945, 1951. He is listed in the **Who's Who in American Art.**

He is a member and Fellow of International Institute of Arts and Letters; Municipal Art League of Chicago (Dir. 1961–1964); American Society for Church Architecture; Museum of Modern Art; Honorary Fellow of American-Scandinavian Foundation; National Institute of Arts and Letters (Advisory Council, 1968–1970). Weiner joined the Chicago Society of Artists in 1950.

LOUIS WEINER (Painter) was born in the Ukraine on May 28, 1892. He studied at the Chicago Academy of Fine Art and the Art Institute of Chicago. He has painted in various parts of the United States and Canada. His favorite media were oils, watercolor and linocuts. He enjoyed landscape painting primarily using the West and East of the United States as inspiration for his works. He was quite an authority on art supplies and introduced Permanent Pigment in Chicago.

Weiner's works have been exhibited at the Art Institute of Chicago; the Midland Club; the Palette and Chisel Club; the Covenant Club; the Cordon Club; the Todros Geller Art Gallery; Michigan

Square; McCormick Place Art Gallery; the Union League Club; — all of Chicago, and at the Pennsylvania Academy of Fine Arts in Pittsburgh and the Riverside Museum of New York City, New York.

Since 1937 he has contributed lino-cuts to the Chicago Society of Artists Annual Calendar.

His work has been written about in Chicago, Philadelphia newspapers and magazines by Irwin St. John Tucker, Eleanor Jewett, J. Z. Jacobson's book **Art of Today–Chicago– 1933,** L. M. Stein Publisher — 1932, and in **Liberty** magazine.

He was a member of the Palette and Chisel Club, the Little Gallery of Evanston, the Chicago Society of Artists, the All-Illinois Academy of Fine Arts, and the Art Institute of Chicago Alumni Association.

Weiner died on September 26, 1967.

BETTY J. WEISS (HURD) (Painter) was born in Chicago, Illinois, on September 3, 1925. She studied at the School of the Art Institute of Chicago, the Vogue School of Design, and with well-known Chicago Artists George Kokines, Elvie Ten Hoor and others. Weiss has a more than passing interest in dance, modern and ballet, which she also teaches. She has traveled extensively in the United States, in Europe and the Middle East. Her favorite media are collage and watercolor.

Her work has been represented by the Lower East Side Gallery, Aspen, Colorado, and included in private collections in Chicago and Aspen, Colorado.

Her work is also represented by the Art Rental and Sales Gallery of the Art Institute of Chicago.

LOUISE DUNN YOCHIM (Painter) was born in the Ukraine, Russia, on July 18, 1909 and studied in the European gymnasium and at the Art Institute of Chicago, University of Chicago (B.A.E., M.A.E.). She completed academic requirements toward a Doctorate at University of Chicago, 1962. She has traveled and painted in Ireland, England, Netherlands, Belgium, Germany, France, Turkey, Greece, Israel, Spain, Switzerland, Italy, Russia, Guatemala, Mexico, Canada and the United States.

One-woman exhibitions of her oils, watercolors, lacquer, gouache, casein, lithography, and prints were held at the Todros Geller Gallery, Chicago 1947, 1951, 1963; First Federal Gallery, Chicago, 1960; University of Chicago 1957; Northwestern University 1963; Covenant Club, 1964; Chicago Teachers College, North, 1964; Rosenstone Art Gallery, 1970; Northeastern Illinois State University 1972; University Club of Chicago, 1974; Chicago Public Library (main) 1974; 4 Arts Gallery, Evanston, Illinois, 1975; Triangle Art Gallery, 1977.

Juried group exhibitions in which her works were included are Art Institute of Chicago, 1935, 1936, 1942, 1944; Riverside Museum, New York, 1951; Associated Artists Gallery, Chicago, 1953; Illinois State Museum, Springfield, 1958, 1961; Butler Institute of American Art, Cleveland, Ohio, 1958; Des Moines Art Center, 1955; Renaissance Society of Art, University of Chicago, 1955–1958; Cleveland Museum of Art, 1958; Northwestern University, 1963; Chicago Teachers College, North 1964; Covenant Club, 1964; National Design Center, 1965; Union League Club of Chicago, 1965; University Club of Chicago, 1966, 1967, 1968, 1969, 1970, 1972, 1973, 1974, 1975, 1976, 1977; McCormick Place Art Gallery, Chicago, 1963; Contemporary Art Gallery, Chicago, 1962; Library of Congress, Washington, D. C. 1958; Associated Artists Gallery, Washington, D. C. 1958; Terry Museum of Art, Florida, 1961; A. Werbe Gallery, Detroit, 1961–1968; National Historic Shrines Foundation, New York, 1963; Spearfish Museum, North Dakota; Iowa Art Center, Des Moines; Kansas City Art Museum, Missouri; Omaha Museum of Art, Nebraska; Rapid City Art Gallery, Iowa; Museum of Art, Sioux City, Iowa; 4 Arts Gallery, Evanston, Illinois; McKerr Gallery, Chicago; Rosenstone Art Gallery, Chicago; Rosary College, Oak Park, 1973; Northeastern Illinois State University, Chicago, 1972; Circle Gallery, Chicago, 1975; Chicago Public Library, 1970, 1974; Invitational Art Exhibition, Lawrence, Kansas, 1974; Spertus Museum of Judaica, 1974, 1975, 1976; Spiesberg Gallery 1974, 1975; Monroe Gallery 1977.

Her works are included in many private collections in the United States and abroad and in public collections of the Hillside Theatre, Hillside, Illinois; Biro-Bidjan, Russia; and Eilat Museum, Eilat, Israel.

Galleries which represent her work are Anna Werbe Gallery, Detroit, Michigan;

4 Arts Gallery, Evanston, Illinois; Art Rental and Sales Gallery, Art Institute of Chicago.

Her teaching experience includes Longfellow School, Oak Park, Illinois, 1932; Junior School Art Institute of Chicago, 1930, 1931, 1932; Lake View Evening High School, 1934–1944; Chicago Public High Schools, 1930–1950; Chicago Academy of Fine Arts, 1952; Chicago Teachers College, 1952, 1953, 1960; Wright Junior College, Chicago, 1952, 1953.

Yochim was Supervisor of Art for the Chicago Public Schools 1950–1971; Art Consultant of Area C (235 elementary and high schools), 1971–1974.

She has also served as Art Consultant for Rand McNally and Company, 1967, and **Encyclopedia Britannica, 1968**, and collaborated on the motion picture, "Richard Hunt, Sculptor," **Encyclopedia Britannica Educational Corporation**.

Her work was reproduced and written about in publications — **Brush Points** magazine (1947); **Sentinel** magazine (1947); **Chicago Sun Times** (1954, 1972); **Chicago Daily News; Art Digest; Evanston Review** (1960). Her linocuts reproduced in the Chicago Society of Artists Annual Calendar (1950–1978).

Yochim has written a number of articles on art, artists, and art education. She has written the following books: **Building Human Relationships Through Art,** L. M. Stein, publisher, 1954; **Perceptual Growth in Creativity,** International Textbook Co., Pub. 1962; **Art in Action** Chicago Public Schools, 1969

Yochim received awards as follows: Woman's Aid Scholarship, Art Institute of Chicago, 1932; the Todros Geller Awards for painting, 1948, 1961; L. M. Stein Awards for painting, 1955; The Nathan Schwartz Award for painting, 1955; the Emily Bernstein Award for painting, 1958; the Susan Fried Award for painting, 1959; Old Orchard Festival, Honorable Mention, 1959; Chicago Society of Artists Award for mixed media painting, Honorable Mention 1970; Spertus College of Judaica, 1970, 1977.

Yochim is listed in **Who's Who in American Art; Who's Who of American Women; International Directory of Arts; Dictionary of International Biography; The Two-Thousand Women of Achievement; Contemporary Authors; International Directory of Scholars; Who's Who in the Arts;** and **Notable Americans of the Bicentennial Era.**

Yochim was elected Fellow of International Institute of Arts and Letters in Switzerland, 1960; Delta Kappa Gamma, 1964 (international honorary organization for women educators); and President of the Chicago Society of Artists, 1973–1979.

MAURICE YOCHIM (Painter, Sculptor) was born in the Ukraine, Russia, on April 17, 1908, and studied at Art Institute of Chicago, (B.A.E., M.A.E.); University of Chicago, DePaul and Institute of Design. He has traveled and painted in Ireland, England, Netherlands, Belgium, Switzerland, Germany, Italy, France, Spain, Greece, Turkey, Israel, Russia, Canada, Mexico, Guatemala and the United States. He works in oil, watercolor, guache, casein, wood sculpture, print processes-serigraphy, lithography and etching.

He has held one-man exhibitions at the Fisher Hall Gallery, 1946; University of Chicago, 1957; Northwestern University, 1960; Covenant Club Gallery of Chicago, 1967; 4 Arts Gallery, Evanston, 1967; Illinois Teachers College, Chicago, North, 1967; University Club of Chicago, 1975.

His paintings and sculpture were included in juried group shows at the Chicago Artists and Vicinity Exhibition, Art Institute of Chicago, 1936, 1942, 1943, 1945; Milwaukee Art Institute (Regional) 1944. He was represented in the Art Rental and Sales Gallery of the Art Institute of Chicago, 1960, 1961, 1962.

Other shows in which he participated are Mandel Brothers Gallery, 1953; Marshall Field Gallery, 1958, 1959; A.A.A. Gallery, Chicago, 1944; Fine Arts Gallery, Chicago, 1937, 1938; Cromer and Quint Galleries, 1952, 1953, 1954; No-Jury Show at Navy Pier, Chicago, 1957, 1958, 1959; Renaissance Society, 1960, 1961, 1962, 1963; Contemporary Art Workshop Gallery, 1960, 1962; McCormick Place Gallery, 1963; Marina Towers Gallery, 1967; Northwestern University, 1957, 1963; Des Moines Art Center, 1955, 1957; Sioux City Museum of Art, 1964; Detroit Institute of Art; Riverside Museum, New York, 1965; National Historic Shrines Foundation, New York, 1963; Butler Institute of American Art, Cleveland, Ohio, 1958; Associated Artists Gallery, Washington, D. C., 1962; Art Museum of Omaha, 1957; Sun-Times Plaza Gallery, 1960; Standard Club, 1944; McKerr Observatory Gallery, 1962; Rosary College, 1973; Spertus Museum of Judaica, 1974; Circle Gallery, Chicago, 1975; Spiesberg Gallery, Skokie, Illinois, 1975; Monroe Gallery, 1977.

His work is included in private collections in Flagler Beach, Florida; Augusta, Georgia; Des Moines, Iowa; Morton Grove, Illinois; Oak Park, Illinois; Wilmette, Illinois; Lawrence, Kansas; New York, N.Y.; Lincolnwood, Illinois; Skokie, Illinois; Chicago, Illinois; Glencoe, Illinois; Glenview, Illinois; Tel-Aviv, Israel, and in the public collection of Beth Lohamei Haghettaot, Israel.

Yochim's work is represented by the Werbe Gallery, Detroit, Michigan, and the 4 Arts Gallery in Evanston, Illinois.

He has co-authored a book **Arts and Crafts in the Jewish Schools,** published by Board of Jewish Education, 1952.

He has taught art for 43 years. He taught at Art Institute of Chicago Junior School, 1930–1932; Chicago Junior High School, 1930–1933; Chicago Public High School, 1938–1953; Chicago Evening High Schools, 1932 - 1942; Chicago Teachers College, 1952-1965; Illinois Teachers College, Chicago-North, 1965–1967; Northeastern Illinois State College, 1967–1970; Northeastern Illinois University, 1970–1973. Since 1973 he has been Professor Emeritus at Northeastern.

Yochim was Director of Children's Art Program, Horwich Community Center, 1963–1967; Supervisor of Art for Board of Jewish Education, 1949–1952; Director of Art for the Board of Jewish Education, 1953–1963; Director of Professional Art Exhibits at Northeastern Illinois University; Director of Fisher Hall, and Todros Geller Art Galleries, 1953–1963. He served on Speakers Bureau for the Chicago Board of Education for many years.

Yochim received the Memorial Scholarship, Art Institute of Chicago, 1930; Print of the Year Award A.J.A.C., 1946; Nathan Schwartz Award A.J.A.C., 1955; Morris DeWoskin Award 1958; Spertus Award A.J.A.C., 1961.

Yochim served as President and Vice-President of the Chicago Art Educators Association; President of the American Jewish Art Club; chairman of committees for Western and National Art Education Associations; member of Board of Directors for the Chicago Society of Artists 1948–1958.

JAN YOURIST (Printmaker) was born in Toledo, Ohio, on April 2, 1950, and studied at Lawrence Univeristy in Appleton, Wisconsin where she majored in art. She has traveled in England, Israel, France and Holland. She is particularly interested in lithography. She is also an amateur film maker and photographer.

She was editorial artist for Field Enterprises Educational Corporation for several years and art director for Clapper Publishing in Chicago. Currently she is a puppeteer and doing freelance artwork. She also teaches drawing at Jane Addams Center where she is assistant director of the art program.

She held a one-woman exhibition at the Midwest Foundation of Yoga, 1976.

Group shows in which she participated are the University Club of Chicago; Triangle Art Center Gallery; Rosary College in Oak Park, Illinois; Circle Gallery, Chicago; St. Lukes Presbyterian Hospital Gallery; 4 Arts Gallery, Evanston, Illinois; Caffe Pergolesi, Chicago.

Her works are included in private collections of David Simon; Linda Miller; Roseann Kacheris; Mark Nichols; Julie Andelin; Roy Reed.

Yourist was awarded Second Prize for her linocut submitted to the Chicago Society of Artists Annual Calendar publication in 1974. Her work is represented by the Art Rental and Sales Gallery, Art Institute of Chicago.

ALOISE AIGNER ZEHNER
(Painter) was born in Chicago, Illinois, on October 17, 1914, and studied at the Art Institute of Chicago, 1936–1939; the Chicago Academy of Fine Arts, 1932–1934; The Tree Studios, Chicago, for three years; and Ox-Bow, Saugatuck, Michigan. Before entering the art field she was a solo violinist and played in three orchestras. For five years, during the thirties, Aloise A. Zehner also served as social worker for the Northwestern Settlement House and Hull House in Chicago. She has traveled in England, Scotland, Switzerland, Germany, France, Spain, Portugal, Greece, Africa, Mexico, Canada, India, Nepal and Italy. Her favorite media are pen and ink, oils, watercolors and acrylics.

She held one-woman exhibitions at The Monroe Gallery, twice; Arlington Heights Memorial Library, a number of times; and in numerous schools, theatres, dining areas in the northwest suburbs; in the Vaccarino Gallery in Florence, Italy, for two years; and at

Lake Forest Academy.

Juried shows in which she participated include most annual Chicago Society of Artists Exhibitions since 1941; almost all of Countrysides Art Center exhibitions since 1962, ninety juried exhibitions in the Chicago area; group shows at the Findley Gallery; Mandel Brothers Gallery; University Club of Chicago; Monroe Gallery; Covenant Club; Old Town Triangle Art Center; Chicago Society of Artists Gallery; Countryside Gallery; Center for Continued Education, Womens Dorm, Mens Dorm; McKerr Gallery; Lake Forest Academy; Hyde Park Art Center; Rosary College; Vaccarino Gallery, Italy; Navy Pier — churches, fairs, libraries, Park District and Field houses, restaurants, schools and theatres.

Her work was represented by Countryside Art Center in Arlington Heights for many years, Chicago Society of Artists, and the Vaccarino Gallery in Florence for two years and is included in over sixty-one private collections in the United States, Italy, Spain, England, Canada and France. Public Collections in which her work are included are the Arlington Heights Memorial Library, and the Lake Forest Academy.

She is currently represented at the Art Rental & Sales Gallery of the Art Institute of Chicago.

She taught at Northwestern Settlement House and held private art classes for children and adults in her home in Chicago. Later she conducted the first children's creative art classes out of the Arlington Heights, Illinois Park District.

She lectured on art, art history and her travels, for the Volunteer Bureau Service for schools and for churches and other organizations in the northwest area of the Chicago district. She was appointed to the Cultural Commission of Arlington Heights for four years. She coordinated Picture Lady Groups for lower schools and catalogued slides for Mount Prospect Schools art department.

For her paintings Zehner was awarded Second Place, Best in Show, and two Honorable Mentions by the Countryside Art Center and a Purchase Award from the Union League Club, Chicago, 1972.

Zehner was one of the founders of Countryside Art Center in Arlington Heights, and president of the Chicago Society of Artists for four years.

M. GIEDRE ZUMBAKIS (Graphic Artist) was born in Lithuania on June 24, 1940, and studied at St. Xavier College (B. A. in Art), Northwestern University (M.F.A. in Graphics) and at Art Institute of Chicago with Vera Berdick. She has traveled and painted in Europe, Mexico, and Yucatan. Her favorite media are graphics and enameling-painting.

One-woman exhibitions of her works were held at St. Xavier College, Chicago, 1962, 1963, 1965; Lithuanian Cultural Center, New York, 1970; Curlionis Gallery, New York City, 1972; Cleveland, Ohio, 1976.

Juried shows in which she participated are Chicago Arts Festival, 1962; Union League Show, 1967; Hyde Park Art Association, Members Show, 1973–1976; New Horizons in Art, 1976; Mid-Continental Plaza North Shore Art League Members Print and Drawing Show, 1976; Celebration '76, National Graduate Student Print and Drawing Competition, De Kalb, Northern Illinois University, 1976.

Other shows in which Ms. Zumbakis's works were included are the Beverly Art Center — Lithuanian American Women Artists, Chicago, 1973; Northwestern University, 1974; Ballet College with Lithuanian American Women Artists, 1974; Gary Art League Lithuanian American Women Artists, 1975; "Twenty Living Lithuanian Artists," Bicentennial Traveling Exhibit, sponsored by Illinois Arts Council and Balzekas Museum; Chicago Public Library (Main); First National Bank, Uptown Federal Bank, Chicago Press Club, University Club of Chicago and Lithuanian Women Artists, 1976.

Her work is represented by the Art Rental and Sales Gallery of the Art Institute of Chicago and the Sales and Rental Gallery of the Springfield Art Association.

Five of her prints are included in the Standard Oil Company Arts Collection.

Zumbakis taught elementary schools in District #11, Mother Mc Alley High School in Illinois and held a Graduate Assistantship at Northwestern University, Evanston, Illinois.

She received an Honorable Mention at the North Shore Art League's Member Print and Drawing Show in 1976.

ROSEMARY ZWICK (Painter, Sculptor, Printmaker) was born in Chicago, Illinois, on July 13, 1925, and studied at State University of Iowa, where she majored in history, B.F.A.;

Art Institute of Chicago and De Paul University. She has traveled extensively and painted in Mexico, Canada, Europe and the United States. She taught art to children and adults in private classes. For a number of years she served as staff artist for **Jr. Arts and Activities**, a magazine for teachers of art.

She works in woodcuts, serigraphs, lithography, watercolor, oils, acrylics, ceramics and sculpture. She has worked as a freelance illustrator, studio potter and jewelry maker. Currently she devotes most of her time to painting, sculpting and printmaking in addition to serving as co-director of the 4 Arts Gallery in Evanston, Illinois,

She has held one-woman exhibitions at the Esquire Theatre, 1950; Contemporary Arts Gallery, Chicago, 1951; Ruth Dickens Gallery, Chicago, 1952; Public Library, Chicago, 1953; Indiana University (2 person), 1954; Mudelein College, Chicago, 1968; Northeastern Illinois University, 1969; Bloomington Art Association, 1969; National College of Education, Evanston, 1970; A. Hendler Association, Houston, Texas, 1970; First Federal Bank of Chicago, 1972.

Juried group shows in which she participated are Chicago Artists and Vicinity Exhibitions, 1947, 1948, 1949, 1950, 1951, 1952, 1953, 1954, 1956; Boston Society of Independent Artists, 1951–1961; Syracuse, N. Y. Ceramic Nationals, 1958–60–2; Wichita Ceramic National Exhibition, 1963, 1966, 1968; Smithsonian Institute Print Exhibits, 1950; Philadelphia Print Club; Art Rental and Sales, Art Institute of Chicago 1954–1976; Indianapolis Museum of Art, Art Rental and Sales; American Federation of Arts Traveling Shows; and Art in Embassy Program; Albany Art Museum; St. Louis Art Museum; San Francisco Art Museum; Rochester Print Club; Toledo Museum of Art; Houston Museum of Modern Art; Illinois State Museum; Library of Congress; Birmingham Art Museum; S. California Print Club and many others.

Local group exhibitions in which she participated are Old Orchard and Old Town Invitiational Art Fairs, Evanston Art Center, North Shore Art League, Art Rental and Sales Gallery of the Art Institute, the Renaissance Society of the University of Chicago.

She is included in many private collections including that of Mr. & Mrs. Maurice Yochim and in public collections of Standard Oil Company of Chicago; U. S. Post Office, San Franciso; Motorola Co., Chicago; Container Corporation, Chicago; Phoenix Arizona Public Schools; North Lake Public Schools, Reavis High School and many others.

Her work is represented by the Collectors Gallery, Chicago; Tom Thumb, Aspen, Colorado; Town Gallery, Muncie, Indiana; A. Hendler Association, Houston, Texas; Rental and Sales Gallery of the Art Institute of Chicago; and the 4 Arts Gallery in Evanston.

She was commissioned for two large ceramic sculptures for Wonderland Shopping Center, Detroit, and a ceramic panel for display room of Motorola Company, Chicago.

Examples of her ceramic sculpture were reproduced in John Kenny's book, **Ceramic Design**, and a lithograph was in AEA **Improvisations**. Her sculpture was included in Smithsonian Institute and American Federation of Arts traveling exhibitions.

Zwick received the Esquire Chicago Artists Exhibition Award, 1950; Oak Park Library Award, 1958; Water Tower Michigan Avenue Exhibition Award, 1954.

She is professsionally associated with the Renaissance Society of the University of Chicago, Artists Equity, American Craftsmen's Council, and the Chicago Society of Artists.

Presidents of the CSA, 1887–1979

1. Spread
2. Charles E. Boutwood
3. C. Lynn Coy
4. Emile J. Grumieaux
5. George Melville Smith
6. Increase Robinson
7. Ivan LeLorraine Albright
8. Clara MacGowan
9. Harold Schultz
10. Beatrice S. Levy
11. Todros Geller
12. Frances Badger
13. Donald Mundt
14. Hubert Ropp
15. George Josimovich
16. Kathleen Blackshear
17. Alice Mason
18. Gustaf Dalstrom
19. Harold Haydon
20. John Emerson
21. Robert Andersen
22. Orval Caldwell
23. Maurice Friedlander
24. Aloise Aigner Zehner
25. William Brincka
26. Catherine Cajandig
27. Louise Dunn Yochim

Membership Roster, 1887–1979

Abercrombie, Gertrude
Adams, Jean Crawford
Albright, Ivan LeLorraine
Albright, Malvin Marr (Zsissley)
Alexander, A. E.
Ames, Scribner
Anapol, Berte
Andersen, Robert W.
Anderson, C. W.
Anderson, Howard B.
Anderson, Mary
Anderson, Thomas R.
Angel, Rifka
Angell, Ann Kevorkian
Armin, Emil
Arnold, Ralph Moffett
Arquin, Florence
Atwood, Gerri
Aubin, Barbara
Aucello, Salvatore
Bacon, Peggy
Badger, Frances
Bahnc, Salcia
Bailey, Robert L.
Bannon, Laura
Baron, Dolores
Barton, Macena
Bath, Virginia
Becker, Bettie
Bekker, David
Beman, Margot
Beman, Roff
Beneduci, Antonio
Bennett, Eugene
Bennett, Rainey
Benson, Tressa Emerson
Bently, Claude
Berdich, Vera
Berg, Aileen
Berkman, Bernice
Beros, Georgia
Bianucci, Irene
Biesel, Charles
Biesel, Fred
Blackshear, Kathleen
Bockius, Mary L.
Bohrod, Aaron
Borde, Arlene
Bornath, Mary S.
Bornarth, Philip W.
Boutwood, Charles e.
Brace, Joan
Brams, Elaine Krimmer
Breinin, Raymond
Brincka, William
Britton, Edgar
Britton, Sylvester
Brockman, Anne
Brod, Fritzi
Brooks, A. F.
Brown, Ethel Crouch
Brozik, Jaroslav
Buck, Claude
Burg, Copeland
Burgess, Rachel
Burrows, Peggy Palmer
Butler, Gerri H.
Cajandig, Catherine
Caldwell, Orval
Cameron, Edgar Spier
Campagnoni, Blanche
Campbell, Hilda E.
Carter, Marjorie
Cassady, Edithe Jane
Chapin, Francis
Chassaing, Olga
Chassaing, Edouard
Cheskin, David
Cilfone, Gianni
Claussenius, Marie
Cliford, John H.
Collier, Janine
Colwell, Elizabeth
Colwell, Averil
Cooper, Charles E.
Coren, Lois
Corlette, Helen E.
Coy, C. Lynn
Dahlgreen, Charles W.
Dalstrom, Gustaf
De Diego, Julio
D'Onofrio, Salvatore
Dehn, Rudolph

Desai, Avinash N.
Diskor, Edward
Donaldson, Elise
Douthat, Milton
Doyle, Charlotte
Driscoll, Margaret
Drucker, Charlotte
Dunbar, Sally
Duvigneaud, Diane
Dyer, Briggs
Eddy, Elizabeth
Edwards, Nancy Bixby
Ekstein, Katherine
Emerson, Alyce Tossova
Emmerson, John W.
Engelhard, Elizabeth
Esarove, Judith
Evans, Katherine
Ewell, Hazel Crow
Fabion, John
Fagen, Barbara
Fahrenkrog, Darlene Crampton
Feldman, Sherri Z.
Ferry, Emma
Field, Jessie
Fink, Bruce
Fishbein, Lillian-Desow
Fleisher, Walter
Florsheim, Richard A.
Ford, Ruth Van Sickle
Fort, Evie
Foy, Frances M.
Frankovitz, Myrtle
Frano, Theodore
Friedlander, Maurice
Friedman, Charlotte
Fritzmann, Frank
Fritzmann, Mary Lou
Fry, Rowena
Gale, Mrs. Henry Gordon
Gallagher, William
Garland, Leon
Garland, Sadie Ellis
Garrison, Eve
Gasslander, Karl
Gehr, Mary
Gelick, Ethel
Geller, Todros
Gerard, Joseph
Gerard, Paula
Gessel, Margaret
Giesbert, Edmund
Giese, Clarence E.
Gilruth, May
Giuliano, Thomas
Glaman, Eugenie
Glass, Corrie-Lou Livingstoı
Glasser, Catherine
Goldfuss, Helen
Gordon, Bacia
Gordon, Diana
Greenburg, Samuel
Greene, Marie Zoe
Griffen, Davenport
Griffin, Nina K.
Griffith, Julia Sulzer
Grisbert, Edmund
Gross, Oskar
Grover, Jeanne
Grumieaux, Emile J.
Gullborg, Garnet
Hackett, Malcolm
Hall, Lillian E.
Hall, Marion
Hall, Thomas
Hallberg, Charles E.
Hancock, Betsy
Hannell, Hazel
Hannell, V. M. S.
Hansen, Oskar J. W.
Hantke, Henry R.
Hartmann, Marjorie
Harus, Tara
Hatch, Eleanor B.
Hauer, Christine
Havens, Leonard
Haydon, Harold
Heller, Richard E. (M. D.)
Hemingway, Grace Hall
Henricksen, Ralf
Henry, Natalie S.
Hester, Evelyn F.
Hetz, Ferdinand L.
Heuermann, Magda
Hoeckner, Carl
Hoelscher, May B.
Hohenberg, Marguerite
Hong, Anna Helga
Horwitz, Fern Gilbert
Hotz, Ferdinand
Howard, Alfred
Howlett, Carolyn S.
Huebner, Louis H.
Huston, Noyes
Ingerle, F. Rudolph
Jacobs, William
Jacobson, Emmanuel
Japha, Etta
Jerrems, Lee
Johnson, Edwin Boyd
Johnson, Willard
Jones, Elsie
Jones, Murray
Josimovich, George
Judson, Sylvia Shaw
Jurgens, Betty
Kaar, Virginia
Kaganove, Joshua
Kalan, William
Kapsalis, Thomas Harry
Karlsberg, Portia R.
Karzen, Michael
Katz, A. Raymond (Sandor)
Kauffman, Camille Andrene
Kavolis, Rita
Keane, Richard
Keeler, Lucile
Kenney, Anna
Kelly, Mary Lou Weiss
Kelpe, Thomas
Kempf, Thomas
Kempf, Tud
Kluczewski, Felix
Knop, Gene
Kravitt, Shirley Paperno
Krawiec, Harriet
Krawiec, Walter
Krullaars, William J.
Kutcosky, John
Lampher, Helen F.
Larsen, Mae
Laslo, Patricia
Lauffer, Alice
Leighton, Lucile
Lenzi, Alfred
Levy, Beatrice S.
Lewin, Marcella
Lewis, Barbara K.
Lewy, Evelyn
Linden, Carl
Loeb, Sidney
Lucioni, Luigi
Lund, Florence
Lusk, George
Lyons, Charlotte
MacDonald George
MacDougall, Janet
MacGowan, Clara (Cioban)
MacLeish, Norman
Macomber, Judith
Malcher, Lucretia A.
Mann, Helen
Mansfield, Shirley
Marks, Janina
Mason, Alice
Mason, Mike
Matis, Shelbee
McDonald, G. L.
McVey, Frances
Metrick Beatrice Roitman
Metz, Barbara Lazarus
Michalov, Anne
Miller, Edgar
Millman, Edward
Molloy, Lee
Morrison, Keith
Mullen, Verne

Mullen, Charles Edward
Mundt, Donald
Neal, Quintin
Neebe, Louis Alexander
Neebe, Minnie Harms
Neiman, LeRoy
Nelson-Adamek, Dolores
Nicholson, Thurman
Norton, John
Oatway, Margrette
O'Dell, Gino
Okner, Annette
Oppenheim, Elizabeth
Orloff, Gregory
Ostrowsky, Sam
Oswald, Fred
Ott, Peter Paul
Paine, Louise
Pearman, Katherine
Peiser, Jane Goslin
Perlmutter, Victor M.
Perri, Frank
Patacque, Jerry
Petacque, Judy M.
Pfeiffer, Judith
Phillips, Marjorie
Pierce, Louise F.
Pink, Harry
Plaut, Jean
Pleimling, Winnifred
Ponsen, Tunis
Porter, Fairfield
Pougialis, Constantine
Poull, Mary B.
Preo, Bruce
Prusheck, Gregory
Prussian, Clare E.
Pryor, Yvonne
Quick, Cheryl
Radice, Canio
Ransom, Louis
Rappaport, Fred
Rebbeck, Lester
Regoni, Gloria
Reibel, Bertram
Reichmann, Josephine L.
Reitman, Shane E.
Remahl, Frederick
Rice, Nan
Ritman, Maurice
Robinson, Increase
Robinson, Walter Paul
Rocke, Gilbert
Roeckner, H. Leon
Ropp, Hubert
Rosenberg, Ceil
Rosenthal, Bernard
Rosner, Charlotte
Ross, Louise
Ross, Torey
Roszak, Theordore, J.
Rothstein, Charlotte
Rubin, Hilda
Rupprecht, Edgar
Rupprecht, Elizabeth
Rush, Olive
Russman, Felix
Ruvolo, Felix
Sadok, Verna
Salwonchik, Marie
Samuels, Fern
SanFrateloo, Jasper
Saruk, Marvin
Saunders, Theordore
Schatz, Daniel
Schell, Alice
Schiff, Molly J.
Schiller, Beatrice B.
Schneider, George P.
Schofield, Flora
Schreiber, George
Schroetter, Mary M.
Schulse, Franz
Schultz, Harold A.
Schultz, Eve Watson
Schwartz, William S.
Segedin, Leopold
Selover, Zabeth
Seyffert, Leopold, Jr.
Shaar, June Coale
Shopen, Kenneth
Simon, Suzanne
Sinclair, Gerrit V.
Singer, William Earl
Siporin, Mitchell
Sister M. Charlotte, O. P.
Slaw, Lorre Ann
Sloan, Helen
Smart, Patricia
Smith, George Melville
Sodeika, Zita
Spaulding, Rita
Spears, Ethel
Spencer, Mary
Spitz, Barbara S.
Spitz, Robert D.
Spongberg, Grace
Spuehler, Florence
Spuehler, Lorri
Stafford, Dorothy
Starr, John
Steele, Ivy
Steinberg, Rubin
Steiner, Jane W.
Stellar, Hermine
Stenvall, John F.
Stephan, John
Stierlin, Margaret
Strain, Frances
Swan, James
Swawite, Augusta Anne
Sweeny, Belle C.
Szuba, Eugene
Tatakis, Margaret
Tatakis, Steve
Taylor, Elizabeth
Tengren, Gustaf
TenHoor, Elvie
Thecla, Julia
Thomas, Howard
Thompson, Marvin F.
Thompson, Nancy
Topchevsky, Morris
Topp, Alex
Torrey, Fred M.
Troy, Adrian
Umlauf, Charles
Unterman, Ruth
Vail, James
VanCourt, Franklin
VanHorn, Ida
VanPappelendam, Laura
VanRyn, Agnes Potter
VanYoung, Oscar
Vavak, Joseph
Vernon, William W.
Viviano, Emmanuel
Walker, James F.
Waltrip, Mildred
Warner, Helen
Wathall, Lionel
Weber, Hugo
Weinberg, Helen Joy
Weiner, A. S.
Weiner, Egon
Weigner, Joan Taxay
Weiss, Betty J. (Hurd)
Werner, Hans
Wexler, Marion Witt
Wilder, Alice
Wilimovsky, Charles A.
Wimmer, William
Witt, Marian
Woelffer, Emerson
Woodruff, Mrs. George
Wright, Norman
Yeoman, Patricia, M. D.
Yochim, Louise Dunn
Yochim, Maurice
Young, Ellsworth
Yourist, Jan
Zehner, Aloise Aigner
Ziroli, Nicola
Zumbakis, M. Giedre
Zwick, Rosemary

Index